RAIN
AND
DARKNESS

Rain and Darkness

Roy Arthur Swanson

Copyright © 2011 by Roy Arthur Swanson.

Library of Congress Control Number:		2011906612
ISBN:	Hardcover	978-1-4628-6149-1
	Softcover	978-1-4628-6148-4
	Ebook	978-1-4628-6150-7

All rights reserved. No part of this book may be reproduced or transmitted in any form or by any means, electronic or mechanical, including photocopying, recording, or by any information storage and retrieval system, without permission in writing from the copyright owner.

This book was printed in the United States of America.

To order additional copies of this book, contact:
Xlibris Corporation
1-888-795-4274
www.Xlibris.com
Orders@Xlibris.com
96582

*. . . there may be rain
and darkness too . . .*
-Roy Turk
as sung by Dick Haymes

Hence the fence.
-John M. Gran,
High-school teacher

A lady who wanted to be a poet was instructed in the way of nocturnal inspiration: Keep a pencil and note-pad on your nightstand; you may, while asleep, write down lines without knowing that you are doing so. The lady did this and one morning discovered that she had indeed written something during the night. She looked at her note-pad and read:
Down the gorge went George.

-Related by Robert E. Moore,
University professor

For Lynn, Dyack, and Dana

1

Blackie said that I was a loser because my need to be praised is always greater than my willingness to praise. I've come to understand what he meant and to admit that he is right. I'm not sure that Blackie was always willing to praise; but I know that he is a winner. He came to call me Ped, which is short for Pedant: he disliked my obsession with grammar, syntax, and pronunciation. I suppose that a real winner doesn't have to bother with the singularity of *kudos* or the plurality of *their*. Blackie has been an affluent businessman, an inflexible Republican, and a model of good grooming. I have been a schoolteacher with many debts, a knee-jerk Democrat, and needlessly careless about my appearance. We have very little in common, really, beyond our having been bonded friends since childhood.

My unevenness of tense (past, present, and present perfect) and the improbably functional clichés in my first paragraph are deliberate and, it is to be hoped, ultimately justifiable, not as literary art, but as a tentative move toward narrative anagoge.

Blackie and I were not like Neil Simon's odd couple. We are not like Abel and Cain; nor were we like Miguel de Unamuno's Abel Sanchez and Joaquin Monegro. Or Achilles and Hector, or Romulus and Remus. Nor were we like the Smothers Brothers. Our context is perhaps closest to that of Gilgamesh and Enkidu. When I had turned four and Blackie was almost six, we were playing, late one afternoon, in a wooden bin that was partially filled with fallen and raked October leaves. I slipped and fell into the pile. Blackie stomped on my chest and then on my face. I begged him to stop, and I was unable not to cry. He kept it up. I bled from my nose and mouth and began to breathe with difficulty amidst my sobs. Blackie kicked my stomach and jumped heavily upon my legs. I didn't know what to do about the pain, except to yield to it and accept it all. Blackie rubbed leaves into my left ear and across my face; then he piled leaves over me, as though burying me; and then he climbed out of the bin and was gone.

At dusk, I heard my mother call me, but I could only sob. My uncle, sent to look for me, heard my sobs and lifted me out of the bin. He carried me, bloodied and matted with leaves, into our flat. My mother cleaned me, tended my wounds, dressed me in my flannel pajamas, and hummed for me some songs of the time; I think one of them was *Bye-Bye, Blackbird*.

She and my uncle asked me who did it. They asked me many times. I would only whimper. Some force within what the first four years of my life had made of me prevented me from saying Blackie. My uncle walked to the police station, five blocks from our flat, and reported the beating. My uncle (my mother's younger brother) lived with us. He was unemployed, but he found occasional jobs, mostly bricklaying and cement work, fairly regularly. My father, a truck driver for a grocery chain, was not home that day. When he returned the following day, he patted my head, said something in German, and played a few games of Checkers with me.

RAIN and DARKNESS

During my eleventh summer, Blackie selected me first, as we chose up sides for one of our many softball games. There were eight of us, and we played in a vacant lot, where the rectangle of an old house-foundation jutted up as an impediment. Being the smallest and least skilled of the eight, I was almost always chosen last. Blackie was a first-rate pitcher and hitter. On this day, he chose me first; and, in a strange turn, no one seemed to take it as anything extraordinary.

Four years later, Blackie and I are walking home in the dark after sitting through a double feature twice. We had consumed a total of twelve candy bars and four large cups of popcorn. Arc-lights punctuate our route. Our shadows behind us grow short as we approach an arc-light, disappear under the arc-light, and then lengthen ahead of us as we move away from it. We have three miles to go. We can shorten the distance to one mile by using the Third Street Bridge instead of going on to the High Bridge and moving back to our street. Do we want to risk the River-cave Gang? We take the chance. I don't want to; but Blackie urges me on; and I'm imbued with my admiration for the gallantry of Errol Flynn in *The Dawn Patrol* and *They Died With Their Boots On*. We are in the middle of the boulevard, about twenty yards from the bridge, when three 'Cavers, in their black turtlenecks and black corduroys, appear as a mass darker than the nightblack from which they emerge. One is quite tall and can be only Jordy Klug, the river-king. He's probably initiating the other two.

Jordy comes at us with a .22 revolver and demands our wallets. Unwilling to give up my dollar bill and two quarters, I make a break around Jordy and past the cohorts behind him. When I get to the bridge, I hear Blackie running behind me and Jordy yelling obscenities. Blackie pushes me down as two shots sound out in the breezeless summer dark. There is another shot; Blackie groans in a short o-sound and comes down on top of me with a well checked fall.

Jordy is running toward us; but, as a car's headlights throw a yellowish ray up the boulevard, he and his 'Cavers veer off at the end of the bridge and disappear down the graveled embankment.

The car did not stop, its driver apparently not seeing Blackie, who had rolled off of me and waved his right arm from a sitting position. He called out—*Hey, stop* or *Hey, some help* or something like that—but he was short of breath and his voice was gutturally choked. Jordy was very likely to return with his 'Cavers, once the car was gone. My wrists burned from being scraped by the pavement; but I got up quickly and helped Blackie get to his feet. There was blood at the base of his neck, and blood was staining the shoulder of his light-colored shirt. *He'll be back: let's go*, he said. On the way to our street, Blackie stopped twice and leaned against me. We reached my flat in about half an hour. Blackie knew that his parents and sisters were not at home; so he came into the flat with me. All that had happened, I've since concluded, had amounted to my first lesson in responsibility.

2

There was a telephone in the flat now: I had to have one in conjunction with my paper route. My uncle called the police. My father was in bed. My mother did what she could for Blackie. When she removed his shirt, she saw that he had been shot at the base of his neck and in his back an inch or so below his shoulder blade. She bathed the wounds with some of my uncle's gin and had them neatly bandaged by the time the police ambulance arrived.

Blackie is in the County Hospital. There is a two-column-inch story of the shooting in the morning paper.

Under questioning he had said only *three guys*; he mentioned neither the 'Cavers nor Jordy Klug. I followed his lead. Three unidentified assailants. One of the .22 slugs had gone through the flesh of Blackie's neck just above his right shoulder. Another had flattened itself against his right scapula. He is recovering from surgery. The only care I needed for my raw scrapings was my mother's cleaning and disinfecting.

Blackie asks me why I ran instead of just handing over my wallet as he had been about to hand over his: *You don't disrespect a gun, Pete.* I really don't know. Later, I admitted to myself that I just did not want to lose my wallet and my dollar fifty and that running seemed to be a way of denying the reality of the situation. It is disappointing that Blackie does not tell me that I did well. Later, I berated myself for not having asked Blackie about his pain and his feelings. [Open the gates, George.] We find the plateau of our friendship and manage, by the time we are sharing Blackie's hospital dinner, to get into laughter.

Blackie's having taken a couple of bullets for me was an act that I took for granted. His lack of any expectation of my gratitude coincided with my failure even to think about extending him any. Maybe that is all in the nature of friendship, along with what I considered Blackie's betrayal of me when I was ten: we are walking home from the neighborhood store, where we had bought bubble gum that came with baseball cards. Blackie shoulders the arm of a woman hurrying past us in the opposite direction. As her stride is broken, she calls upon Blackie for an apology. He turns and abuses her verbally; and, as she walks away from us, I add to the verbal abuse. A few days later, I am called from my classroom to the principal's office. Miss Gallagher is a heavy, unattractive woman who wears thick glasses and whose grey-flecked wig is held in place by a hairnet. Blackie is in the office and confirms my guilt in the verbal abuse about which the woman, who must have known who Blackie was, had complained to the principal. Miss Gallagher scolds me, without asking any questions of me, and instructs Blackie to inform my parents so that they might suitably punish me. It appears that Blackie has denied any wrongdoing on his part, insisting that he was merely with me when I insulted the woman. After we have left the office, Blackie laughs and tells me not to worry because he won't say anything to my parents. The next day, Saturday, he knocks on the door of our flat and tells my mother that the school principal has scolded me for calling a woman some dirty names and has said that

I should be suitably punished. My mother gave me a very painful whipping with a thick but pliant willow switch.

I said nothing to anyone about Blackie's share of the guilt in this affair, nor did I call Blackie on his inconsistent behavior. Never have I either forgiven him for this betrayal or ceased to look upon him as my friend.

The hospital stay lasted four days. For another four days Blackie's left arm was in a sling, and it was another week before the bandage-changing and wound-checking were over. Then we resumed out summer. We continued going to movies; but, instead of making the usual walks downtown, we walked or biked to the outlying theatres. This meant seeing many movies for a second or third time. We mastered the cast lists, identified all the character actors, and memorized dialogue. In all three areas I was better than Blackie, and I appreciated his acknowledgment of my superiority, slight though both the acknowledgment and the superiority were.

In reading and movie-lore, and in most subjectivity, I was Gilgamesh to his Enkidu. But in science, mathematics, and graphics, I was the sensual Enkidu to his radiant Gilgamesh. It is good to be able to admit, and to recollect this now.

In September, the walks to and from high school, two miles from our neighborhood, began again. I would get up at four in the morning to deliver newspapers. Back at the flat by five forty-five, I would wash up, have my cereal, and dress for school. I'd call for Blackie at six-fifty. During most of any given walk to school, we'd do scenes of dialogue from the movies. By a kind of unstated consent, I always had all of Errol Flynn's lines. In this I credited Blackie with concession, but such was hardly the case: my friend was not a fan of Errol

Flynn, and he liked to identify himself with Flynn's screen antagonists, particularly Basil Rathbone.

With girls, though, he was always Errol Flynn to my Jean-Louis Heydt, one of the screen's perennial losers. Or I was Egil Skallagrimsson to his Thorolf. I had Heydt's bland, blond good looks and Egil's dark devotion to imagination. Blackie had Flynn's classic facial configuration and Thorolf's attractive and efficacious manner, with its firm aura of control. In coloring, however, I was the standard Teutonic Thorolf, and Blackie was the devilishly dark Egil. I daydreamed about girls and waited for one or another to make overtures to me. The girls flirted with Blackie; and none parried his cool advances. I did not have a girl-friend until I was a high-school sophomore: Blackie paired me with a friend of his girl-friend for an evening of bowling. There were other double-dates with the two girls; and I actually went to the movies twice on single dates with the friend of Blackie's friend.

Her name was Trixie (for Patricia, not Beatrice). When she turned me down for a third date in favor of one with Blackie, a pattern was fashioned. From Blackie I learned much about gaining ease with girls; but I had to resign myself to losing to Blackie any girl-friend of mine whom I introduced to him. There were times when such losses reduced me to hopelessly protracted adolescent pain. Never, however, or at least for most of my life, did I lose my capacity for therapeutic adolescent daydreams.

Strangely, it was in daydreams that I was initially inspired with an abhorrence of the generic masculine (e.g., Every human has his limitations.) and therewith to intensive opposition to all wrongly accepted aberrations from the grammatical (e.g., Every human has their limitations.). In daydreams of Ann Sheridan and Hedy Lamarr (and Trixie—and, in later years, of Maria Bello and Naomi Watts), I came to sanctify the inaccessible and grammatically inexcusably excluded female. Blackie considered this opposition to be a detestable quirk, but he put up with it. He didn't start to call me Ped until we were college students.

The Polar Conceit produces a constrictive predilection. Opposition to the split infinitive, identification of one's self with a particular athletic team, alignment with a political party, admiration of a particular celebrity or dislike of another, favorites of any kind or thing—these and their like are rooted, not in reason, but in weed-hedges around the Self. [Open the gates, George. Now and again I must resort to flaccid metaphor.] They become as unassailable as prejudice, and arguments against them are taken as insults to one's Self.

Daydream time was during my delivery of the morning newspapers. After the Trixie letdown, I led my imagination to the perfect girl, whose conjunction with me would produce what I was in adult life to call a dyad, a unit consisting of mutually dependent antitheses (plus and minus, male and female), differing from a dualism, or duality, in that separation of one antithesis from the other was destruction of both, as in the event of the smashed atom. In this union of two finite opposites was the heavenly force of infinity. My analogue was the infinitive, the heavenly force of which I recognized when, from Latin, my favorite high-school subject, I took *videre* and compared it to *sehen*, from my father's Muttersprache, and realized that *to see* was a dyadic unit and that the dyad was destroyed, in both efficacy and semantics, by tmesis. Vergil could write *septem subiecta trioni*, but he would never have written *subic septentrioni ere*, even if such splitting had been metrical.

My pedantry began, then, on two levels of subjectivity, the Polar Conceit and the Dreamgirl (later, the Dreamwoman) Vision. Infinity, as both a word and a reality, is a negative in its denial of limitation and a positive in its open-endedness. The infinitive denotes an action that is not acting. *To go* says, and forever says, *noli me frangere* (don't split me). *To boldly go* is a *caeli raptum*, because the positive antithesis of infinity is heaven, and heaven is Language. Changing the Dreamgirl idea to the concept of perfect marriage, I tried to explain this to Blackie in the words that I could muster at the age of fifteen-sixteen. *Bull fuckin' shit*, said he.

3

The generic masculine, I came to conclude, excluded half of the human race, most especially my Dreamgirl. The diminished plural (e.g., every human . . . their) was inauthentic because it vaporized individuality and disintegrated both the Dreamgirl and the dreamer. There were groans in Mrs. Bergstrom's English class whenever I brought up these matters of excluding the feminine, making the plural pronoun serve as singular, splitting the infinitive, and other of my pedantic abhorrences. She was sympathetic with me in my concerns but she argued that traditional grammar, as she called it, must undergo challenge and must yield to any practical and conventional usage. It pleased me that at least my preferences coincided with tradition. Mrs. Bergstrom pointed out vagaries in Shakespeare, like *of his bones are coral made*, as examples of the acceptably creative undermining of tradition.

My delight in reading Shakespeare was not affected by vagaries or inversions or by differences in spelling and meaning from those of our time. Blackie said that I was illogical in accepting Shakespeare's *coral are made* but finding fault with such solecisms when they were made by others.

Lacking any ability argumentatively to justify my inconsistency, I contented myself with an inner satisfaction in sensing the divine maternity of Language: Mother

Language; pedantry gave me the order that I needed, but great literature gave me an experience of holiness. Blackie was a half-year ahead of me in high school, but we were in the same English class, and in a few other classes as well. I helped him with Shakespeare, whose works he detested. He took a liking, however, to the character of Brutus, to whom I much preferred Marc Antony. We shared great pleasure, though, in the Prince of Morocco: he opens the golden box and finds, not Portia's portrait, but a rhymed reproach about gilded tombs. His reaction of disgust, *O hell!*, regaled us. His concluding words, moreover, gave to our laughter a diminuendo that was to intone our bond, *Thus losers part.*

In retrospect, I was, not Bassanio to Blackie's Antonio, but the Prince of Morocco to his Gratiano. Black to his white. Or, more likely, Feirefiz to his Parzival, a stage or two behind my being the young ungainly Parzival to his mature Parzival, discoverer of the Grail. The lapis lazuli that conferred self-regenerative power upon the Phoenix provided Blackie with a shadow for me to walk in, a shadow that diffused my vague translucence. In a corresponding irony, I was the young Jim Wade to his young Blackie Gallagher in *Manhattan Melodrama*, and the grown-up miscreant Blackie to his Governor Jim. [Permit me now to ponder, George, tollgates of onyx and chalcedony.]

He accepted my help in composition and general English, including a number of papers I'd written for him that I believed I'd been clever enough to disguise as idiomatic writing other than my own. Probably never will I know whether or not I actually fooled Mrs. Bergstrom. Blackie more than amply repaid me by doing my geometry homework. He also taught me, not the subject itself—no one could teach me geometry—but ways to make a test in the subject ensure my receipt of at least a D: here I was an apt enough pupil to receive an occasional C. With Blackie's help, I achieved a C- in Geometry. With my help, Blackie received a B in junior English.

Geometry is informed by a logic, the beauty of which has always been untenable by me. One has to complete a theorem to prove the equality of two vertical angles. I can understand proofs based upon what has already been proved, but I cannot understand why axioms, postulates, and corollaries are adduced as irrefutable evidence. At what point does self-evidence begin? Nowhere, I insisted to Blackie, because a point, being position without extension, does not actually exist. He explained that it does exist in theory.

It existed, I believed, only when conjoined to another point, with the two points constituting a line. *A theoretical line*, said he. It was my illogical conviction that a point was nothing and that the relation of two points or the conjunction of two points was something. Blackie allowed that, in theoretical physics, something could come from nothing, but not in geometry, the abstractions of which were applicable to matter but were never material.

Blackie was patient with me in his efforts to explain to me the nature of geometry. He clarified much of the terminology for me. My inability to master the logic was, he said, characteristic of a loser. When we talked about novels and poems and short stories, he settled for likes and dislikes and let me go on about matters of structure and theme and language. He claimed that, if there were such a thing as narrative logic, it could readily be formulated. *Like a theorem*, I asked. *More like algebra*, said he. Mrs. Bergstrom generously contributed many quarter-hours of her free morning time to discussing narrative structure with me. In my paper on *David Copperfield* I had complained that the first-person narrator could not possibly have remembered all of the direct discourse that he reports. I countered her observation that this was authorial license with my observation that this could be better presented as paraphrase or, at least, independent of quotation marks. She told me that in classical antiquity *verbatim* memorization of dialogues and statements was normal. In Plato's *Phaedrus*, for example, Socrates chides Phaedrus for having written down a dialogue that he should have memorized. First-person narration is illogical, she conceded, when the narrator recounts actions and dialogues external to his range of activity, as when the narrator is himself neither present at them nor in possession of a complete account of them. *Himself or herself*, said I. *Himself*, said she.

Blackie agreed with me that the movie equivalent of first-person narration, the voice-over of the narrator that subsumes many activities and dialogues pertinent to, but external to, the narrator's experience, was disconcerting; but movies are entertainment, and entertainment is not logical. He tentatively allowed that great literature was not merely entertainment.

4

My father gave me my name and my political bias. Genetically, he gave me his reticence, reclusiveness, and stubbornness, but not his gifts for music and mechanics. He was a master fiddle-player, without ever having taken a lesson—he played by ear, as the idiom has it. He was constantly in demand for square dances and other entertainments. His huge fingers deftly created the chords that brought Strauss's waltzes to appreciative family members and friends. And polkas, schottisches, marches, all the melody of his memory. He was a master mechanic by instinct, not by training. He could take an engine apart and reassemble it with the same effortless grace with which he made music. He could repair the twelve-speed transmissions of the overland trucks he drove for many years. I inherited none of these abilities. He spoke German, the language of his immigrant parents, and I absorbed enough of the language to be moderately and vulgarly conversant in it. My mother let him name me, his first-born. He gave me his first name, Peter. His own middle name was Schneit, for he had been born in wintertime. Asking my mother, on the evening I was born, what month it happened to be, he gave me the middle name Oktober. I began life, then, as Peter Oktober Blaustern. The family name denotes a wild hyacinth, the bluebell (*Endymion nonscriptus vel Scilla nonscripta*). When, many years after my early October birth, I asked him if he were going to vote for

Landon, whose icon was the Kansas sunflower, he huffed, *Denkst du, dass ich verrückt sei?* (It sounded like *Denkst ish ferreekt?*) I have been an uncompromising Democrat ever since that reply, even after he himself seared my sensibility by voting for Eisenhower.

My father's family was Lutheran; and I was reared as a Lutheran. My maternal grandfather was also German and Lutheran; his wife, however, was Irish and Roman Catholic; and so my mother was reared as a Roman Catholic. It must attest, I believe, to my father's implacability, and to the *Schutzmassregel* of his brothers and sisters, that I was not reared as a Roman Catholic. My mother was dark and very pretty, with a lyrical personality, always singing Irish or German songs as she cleaned our flat and cooked and sewed. When I was five or so, sitting at the kitchen table and looking at comic strips in a newspaper, she, pausing from her housework, gave me a long, warm hug and kissed my cheek. This was one of the few thoroughly happy moments of my life, and I have never forgotten it. Nor have I ever forgotten the haunting glide of her *Auf Wiedersehen*, the refrain of my favorite of the German songs she sang.

Her best friend, during her schooldays at St. Joseph's, was Hildy Jordan. Hildy had had to get married to Hermie Klug in her teens after he had impregnated her. Their first-born was Jordy; seven others followed. There would have been more, it is safe to assume, if Hermie had not been arrested and jailed for bootlegging. Hildy took in sewing and laundry, assisted by my mother until my mother married and moved to the flat in which she would bear five of her seven children and spend much of her life; then Hildy worked alone until Jordy supported the family by holdups, thievery, and burglaries. Recently, I came upon a moving line by Floyd Skloot about his mother: *she married a one-eyed chicken butcher and raged against the failure of her dreams.* It is strange that this well-written line should remind me of Hildy and of my mother, since neither of them had married an unattractive man, and neither of them raged or, to my knowledge, had dreams. The two of them, in fact, shared many pleasures—singing, dancing, drinking, gossip, *True Story* magazine, and listening to the radio.

The Konshaks were better off than both the Klugs and the Blausterns. They lived in a single house—rented, but with sufficient bedrooms. There were only three children—Blackie and his older and younger sisters. Blackie's father received government compensation for having been a victim of mustard gas in the war. He was entrepreneurial in sales and small investments. He, Karl K. Konshak, was also, like my father, a master mechanic and a musician; but his talents had been developed by formal training. He played the piano and composed songs, a few of which he had sold to local distributors. When Blackie and I were in high school, K.K. worked regularly for Riverview Chevrolet, supervising repairs and breaking in new models. Blackie's mother liked to cook, and she was well accomplished in cooking. She liked to read. None of her three children cared about reading; but she enjoyed my interest in it and encouraged my reading habits. Her name was Rebecca; she analyzed for me the vagaries [Open the gates, George] of Scott's Rebecca, Thackeray's Becky Sharp, Twain's Becky Thatcher, and eventually even du Maurier's Rebecca. She had a collection of *Rebecca of Sunnybrook Farm* books.

Every Rebecca, she explained, is both binder and bound, both captor and captive. Even Rebecca of Sunnybrook Farm. She named neither of her daughters Rebecca. Her children were Karla, Karl [Blackie], and Katherine. She must certainly have had dreams; she was much too gentle and self-sufficient for rage.

Her teachings stayed with me. In college, I wrote about the dyad of Enkidu-like Esau and Gilgamesh-like Jacob, born to Rebekah. Sitting in the sun, I read Robert Nathan's *Jezebel's Husband* and let his Rebecca, sent by her organization, take me back to Rebecca Konshak. The tentative irony here was Blackie's deep contempt for Nathan's sentimental fiction and verse. I did get him, however, to concede the cleverness of *The Weans*. Loser-like, I read and enjoyed most of Nathan's more than fifty publications.

Rebecca Konshak had a female Toy Police dog. She called the dog Clay. A month or so before I got my paper route, Clay had a litter of three males. Rebecca gave them all away, one of them to me. My mother was not pleased: the pup, whom I named Shoe, had to be kept in the flat with, including my uncle, eight of us. The flat had six small rooms and a bath. The kitchen was the gathering room; it was the only room that did no service as sleeping quarters—until Shoe took up a corner of it.

Shoe (not *Shoo!*, as most people thought) walked my paper route with me every day, morning and afternoon, in all seasons. When I was at school, or gone for any segment of time, my uncle took care of Shoe. The dog remained small, like his mother; he never wore a collar, never had a license, never received prophylactic shots: there were no such requirements at the time. During my junior year in high school, about the time I entered into my awkward quests for girl-friends, Shoe began to change. He would respond erratically, or not at all, to my commands. He began to bark and snarl at people on the paper route. I had to have my uncle keep him in the kitchen when I went to deliver the papers. Then Clay died. Two weeks later, Shoe disappeared. My mother, my uncle, my sister, one of my brothers, and I looked for him steadily for a few weeks. It surprised me that I did not miss Shoe, although for about a year I kept looking for him to show up. Not long after Shoe's disappearance, I gave up my paper route.

5

Blackie caught me one day at the end of my paper route, months before I had given it up, and asked for some help with the English on which we were to be tested during the following day. We went in the flat through the back door to work at the kitchen table. There, however, sat my mother and Jordy Klug. With a quick *Hi, Mom*, I led Blackie to the front room, where we sat on a sleeper sofa and used a chair as a table surface. Blackie listened impatiently as I explained the characteristics of the gerund, its governance by the possessive case, and the difference between substantive and verbal present participles. As usual, Latin was of considerable help to me in this. After I had given Blackie a review of the appropriate uses of *which* and *that* and of the difference between restrictive (no comma) and non-restrictive (use commas) clauses and checking his punctuation on a few sentences that I provided, he left by the front door. Returning to the kitchen, I joined my mother and Jordy at the table. Jordy ignored me and went on talking to my mother about some matters of imperative interest to his mother. His respect for my mother and his contempt for me melded curiously but well. After my mother and he laughed at some joke, he turned to me with a stiff but quick movement and asked if the flag-draper, his kenning for Blackie, had sneaked out the other door. I said that he had left by the front door.

Then Jordy, mocking my study of Latin (and my mediocre high-school instruction in the language), asked my mother for the use of the pencil held secure by her hair and her right ear and wrote on a white space in an ad in the newspaper that was on the table, *exstinxerunt nocte oculos femura aurea solis nunc hebetes radiis facta Lycoridis ei; illa puella in pulvinario cum considet unda ita salsa maris cretus amorque tumet.* That bit of paper, yellowed and brittle now, with its Latin, which was then almost entirely unintelligible to me, remains in my keeping. Jordy challenged me to translate it, smiling at my mother and then sneering at me. All that I could manage were disconnected renditions of the words I knew—*eyes, wave, so, love*—and a phrase (*thighs made golden by the rays of the sun*).

Jordy was as disgusted with my futile handling of Latin as I was stunned by his acquaintance with it. Jordy had gone straight to Vocational School from grade school. Most of the intellectually inadequate students did this. Jordy, as I gradually learned, was not intellectually inadequate. This splash of Latin was part of the proof of that. He did not translate the Latin for me. He left, shaking my mother's hand and giving me a hard stare above a downturned thumb. My mother, disappointed by my lack of facility with the Latin, encouraged me to work harder at it. She smiled, put her arm around my shoulders, and kissed my cheek. She could not dislike Jordy (nor, to my constant surprise, could I), even though he openly despised (and had shot at) her son.

Mr. Hanson, my Latin teacher, could not help much with the passage. He thought that my effort was commendable, despite its incompleteness; he reminded me that *nunc* was *now*, that *ei* was very likely an interjection or an expletive and not a pronoun, and that I should have remembered *illa puella* as *that girl*. He said that *considet unda . . . amorque tumet* was a well-wrought chiasmus, explaining chiasmus as an abba arrangement of words (in this case: verb noun . . . noun verb), and that perhaps this sequence could include *salsa maris cretus* (as abbcbba). Not until I was in college did I come up with what I considered a satisfactory translation of the passage.

Humbled, deflated at no longer being able to assume that I was at least Jordy's intellectual superior, I asked my mother how he had come by his knowledge of Latin. She believed that he must have got it from Hildy's father: Carlo Giordano had been a teacher, or professor, or something, in Italy, and, losing his position, had brought his wife and two daughters to this country. He couldn't get work in education and had settled down as a shoemaker and locksmith in the Italian community on the Levee. Hildy had often mentioned the books and manuscripts that he'd brought from the old country and his drilling his grandsons in the memorization of long passages of Latin. It pleased me when my mother suggested that Jordy probably didn't know the meaning of the Latin any more than I knew the meaning of some of the German songs that I had learned by rote. Gradually I had come to understand the songs, because my father continued to speak German; Jordy's grandfather, however, was fluent in English; and, although he frequently conversed with his daughters in Italian, did not converse with them or his grandchildren in classical Latin.

Jordy disliked me thoroughly, that is, both me and the things I did (or failed to do). His contempt for me, like the contempt of many persons for me, owed to my insufficiency of self-respect and self-assertion.

RAIN and DARKNESS

The respect that I needed was something that I looked to others to give; I could generate very little on my own. This default to inferiority corresponded to Blackie's estimate of me as one whose need for praise was greater than his [or her, I add] willingness to praise.

It was probably because my mother liked Jordy, both as the son of her best friend and as himself, and because he liked and respected my mother, that I refrained from disliking him. His arrogant contempt and his violence, especially his having shot at me and wounded Blackie, were abhorrent to me. Likewise, his insistent use of *try and*: after I had corrected him once, he punched me in the face, bloodying my nose, which was then swollen for almost four days. To try to do something is a single action. To try and do something are two actions. It is in the nature of violence to rend a thing, to render a single action as two actions. Blackie would scorn my attempts to correct his use of *try and*; but he would not punch me in the face; and over the years he, intentionally or not, made the transition from *try and* to *try to*.

When the American postmodernists infected higher education with their misinterpretations of Jacques Derrida's dyadic etymology, they confused deconstruction and destruction. Derrida, following Martin Heidegger's Way to Language, charted an independent and ultimately inconclusive trail that is still not unprofitable to follow, like the path away from Heidegger's authenticity cleared by Jean-Paul Sartre. Verbose though he was, Sartre, like Heidegger and Derrida, did no violence to Language. The postmodernists, as askew as their presumptuous name, were the Jordy Klugs of language. Disregarding the natural mathematics of languages, they accepted the equivalence of singular and plural, and they rejected the relative reverberations of denotation in favor of the contradictory resonances of connotation. Two of their favorite words were *resonate* and *valorize*, to which they resoundingly gave great value, along with the use of *privilege* as a verb. Denotation is the wave/particle function of speech. Connotation is, at best, indeterminate undulation. *Try and translate this*, Jordy had said. It would be many years before I was to entertain futility before the quasi- and would-be deconstructionists. Jordy Klug would not be among them in the academic world; but, with them, he would seek to destroy linearity and licitness.

Perhaps part of the strong bond between Blackie and me was Jordy Klug's inclination to destroy us both. He despised Blackie's *bürgerlich* rectitude and my weak dishonesty. The main standard against which he measured us, as far as I could, and can, tell, was the capacity for unqualified violence; Blackie and I could participate in violence under necessity or with hedonistic impunity, but never in answer to it as a vital imperative. We both sank into *Schadenfreude*, I much more readily than Blackie; but Jordy took no pleasure either in witnessing or in performing violence: for him it was the secular equivalent of *lebendigmachende Gnade*, a kind of vivifying grace.

6

Mousey and dull: that is Blackie's phrase for Trish Pine. He likes long-faced, blond-haired girls, taller than average, talkative and tensile. Trish is short, quiet, with dark, neatly set hair; her face is pale and infant-smooth in complexion. She sat two rows to my left and one seat ahead in the History class. I spent much of each class period staring at her from my good vantage. The sleeve of her light-colored blouse divided her arm halfway between her shoulder and elbow. Her skirt, always a dark one, defined the rondure of her thigh. She never looked in my direction. It was half a school year before I managed, after all my daydreams and silent rehearsals, to approach her after class and ask her a question, something about Jefferson's second term. She smiles and provides the information and does not walk away. With no ear for much of what she is saying, I attend only her soft voice, her smile, and her warm brown eyes. She tolerates my halting attempt at small talk and brings me into easiness with a question about a movie.

That night my thoughts of Trish brought me to sleep. At dawn, alone in silent satisfaction, I delivered my newspapers slowly so as to prolong my daydreaming about her. During the History class, again, I stared long and longingly at Trish, at her smooth-complexioned profile, her arm snugly touched by the line of her sleeve, the soft roll of neatly tailored dark blue skirt about her thigh.

She might look rightward to me, I think, but she does not. Not having the wherewithal of will to accost her after class, I remained at my desk until she and most of the other students had left. When I went out into the hall, she was waiting for me. We talk again, about movies and about Jefferson's abridgment of the Bible. Trish, a Roman Catholic, did not approve of Jefferson's deism.

After school that day, I did not walk home with Blackie; I walked with Trish. She lived only five blocks from the high school. At her gate, we talked until her older brother, Gene, and, shortly after, her younger brother, Tom, came along. Gene, who was now a senior, and I had worked together for a time on the school newspaper. Trish introduced me to Tom, who was a freshman. That day, and the following week-days as well, I was half an hour late with my afternoon newspaper delivery, a matter of displeasure to old, widowed Mrs. Gronke, whose daily routine was rigidly fixed. Blackie seemed displeased too, not so much for his walking home alone, or with Dick Shriven, who lived out our way, as, I think, for my having found a girl without his help.

My first date with Trish was a walking date to a movie *(The Under Pup*, I think). Thereafter, we would, once or twice a week, take early evening walks and have a soda or a malt at a drug store. After a time, we went roller-skating on a double date with Blackie and a long-faced, blond-haired girl named Liv (for Olivia). For the first time, as I skated around the floor with Trish, I held her hands. On a Friday soon after the roller-skating night, Trish and I walked to an uptown movie. Walking home in the warm, spring night, we stopped at the Lookout and sat on a bench. I put my arm around her, and she did not stiffen or object. Summoning up whatever it takes to make an advance, I placed my lips on hers. She did not pull away, but she returned no pressure. I followed through with no other amatory movements. It was my first kiss, and I was more than content with simply having accomplished it. We talked about the movie then, about its expressionistic chiaroscuro. I removed my arm and held her hand and had the great satisfaction of her giving my hand an affectionate bit of pressure. Then, as happy as I think it possible for me to be, holding her hand, I walk with her to her gate. There were other walking dates and movie dates, and another roller-skating date with Blackie and a long-faced, blond-haired girl named Dory (for Dorothy); Blackie had his father's car that night, and I was treated to some backseat necking with Trish, whose complacent unresponsiveness bothered me not at all.

Once, she firmly removed my hand, when I had laid it upon her thigh.

Gradually, there were fewer meetings after the History class, fewer opportunities to walk with her the five blocks to her gate, and fewer dates. One afternoon, when I phoned her for an early evening walk and she declined, I asked her why. She said that she was going out with Blackie that evening.

Trish repeatedly used two of the lapses from grammar that I abhor. One is the *can't seem* construction; the other is the placing of *only* at a variant distance from the word it modifies. A clause like *I can't seem to remember it* transfers the value of the infinitive to the semblance. To be able to seem to remember is not to be able to remember; the desideratum is *to be able to remember*, not *to seem to be able to remember*. I never corrected her. I never said that she should say *I seem unable to remember*, making the semblance of inability a statement of ordinarily actual ability.

When she would say something like *I only need to read thirty-four pages*, I would not insist that it were better to say *I need to read only thirty-four pages*. She would, I feared, have thrown me over, or, in a later equivalent expression, she would have dumped me. As it happened, she dumped me anyway.

To confuse semblance and actuality and to move the adverb, *only*, away from what it specifically modifies, with the result that it modifies something it is not intended to modify, are modes of illogical disconnection. In the song, *I Only Have Eyes For You*, the singer is saying that he or she will look at *you* but will not touch *you* or talk to *you* or walk with *you* or anything else. Eyes are all that he or she has for *you*, not arms or lips or whatever. To say correctly, and more endearingly in the context of love, *I have eyes only for you*, is to say that he or she will look (lovingly) at no one but *you*.

In my case, it was not even a semblance of inability: I was clearly unable to retain Trish's affection; she did not have eyes only for me. Although I greatly resented Blackie's having taken Trish from me, we never mentioned her while he was dating her. Late one afternoon, though, Trish called me on the telephone and asked me for a favor. Blackie seemed to be avoiding her. *I can't seem to get to him any more*, she said. She wanted me to find out if he still cared for her at all. I said that I was sure he did, that I couldn't imagine him, or anyone, not caring for her; and I promised that I would do what I could to find out if her fears were valid.

When I put the matter, rather bluntly, but without mentioning Trish's request, to Blackie, it was then that he said she was *mousey and dull*. That slur would never get to Trish from me. It was wrong of Blackie to put her down like that; it was wrong of me to solicit his opinion as I had; and it had been wrong of Trish to ask me to do it. Trish was not mousey and dull; her beauty and her presence excited me. After she had received no call from me for almost two weeks, she called me. It was good to hear her soft voice and to talk with her. Blackie liked her very much, I told her—really a lot; but he didn't want to get serious just yet; he was afraid that he would get serious if he kept on going out with her. We talked for about twenty-five minutes, and I was hoping that she might suggest a resumption of our walks. She did not. Some weeks after that call, I asked her brother Gene how she was getting along. *Fine. She's going steady with Rick Remo. He picks her up in a Buick convertible.* Rick's father owns Remo's Liquors.

7

While I am playing cribbage with my uncle, my mother hands me a note that she says Jordy Klug left for me. I still have it: *Asshole, put your feeble brain to this: Clara bonae tandem fecerunt carmina Musae quae possum domina deicere digna me digne tunc dominatur idem tibi non ego Visce nec tibi iam Kato iudice te vereor.* My initial efforts to translate the passage yielded very little, and I did not bother with showing it to Mr. Hanson.

Was it *good Muse's* or *good Muses* (*bonae Musae*)—genitive singular or nominative plural?

Did it refer to all of the Muses collectively, or to only one, with a kind of honorific? Perhaps then—perhaps much later—I decided that it must have denoted *kind Muses*, in the sense of the Muses as being kind or good to someone. There was no bringing the problem to Blackie, who ridiculed my desire to learn Latin, although I did tell him that Jordy had given me a couple of strange Latin writings. He was surprised at Jordy's having had anything to do with Latin but, beyond his surprise, not interested. He insisted that Latin was a dead language and was important only to deadheads and that that might account for Jordy's association with it, Jordy being close to brain-dead anyway. *That's being cynical, Blackie.* He denied that he was a cynic and claimed that he was a practical realist, that he knew the value as well as the price of everything, a cynic being, as he quoted Oscar Wilde, one who knows the price of everything and the value of nothing. That was not my idea of a cynic. Wilde was clever and witty and wrote English with commanding competence, but beneath his flash and finesse he was just a hollow smartass. *So, in your book, what's a cynic?* I had written a sophomore essay in comparison of cynicism and skepticism, and I had concluded that a cynic was one who believed that belief was foolish. This conclusion I offered to Blackie. He commended me on an effective use of self-reference (that is, if belief is foolish, then the cynic is foolish for believing it to be). In college we were to agree that Wilde's definition of a cynic was more in keeping with Matthew Arnold's account of the philistine than with Wilde's strained witticism about doggedness. Blackie's realistic and practical attitudes induced in him doubt as his first reaction to anything immaterial or subjective. He was a skeptic, I decided; and I was a romantic in need of a kind Muse.

Blackie wrote his Junior Essay on *New England: Pilgrims, Witches, Industries*. I helped him with it, eliminating clichés, revising his misconstructions and incorrect usages, and adding a little more than a page on Melville's *Tartarus of Maids*. He received one of the three prizes for that year. We had gone to see the film version of *Our Town* but had picked up no usable New England material from it. We enjoyed identifying Doro Merande, Arthur Allen, and Phillip Wood, and adding Ruth Toby and Douglas Gardiner to our catalogue of minor actors; but Blackie disliked the movie. I didn't like the liberties that had been taken with the original, particularly the change of the ending to a Hollywood happy one, but I liked its darkness, its play of lights and shadows, and the expert retention of the Stage Manager (played by Frank Craven).

Blackie liked Frank Craven in neither *Our Town* nor *City for Conquest*. The best part of the latter movie, in my opinion, was Craven as chorus to the action. After seeing *City for Conquest* with Blackie, I went twice again, and alone, to see the movie, just to study this role. In later releases and in television showings, the part was excised; and only fleeting glimpses of Craven were retained, even while his name remained in its cast listing above those, for example, of Arthur Kennedy, Anthony Quinn, and Elia Kazan.

Generic Hollywood, for all that my life has been given over, in large part, to movie-going, has let me down frequently and variously. Zanuck's *The Grapes of Wrath*, for example, fulfilled all the promise of *Our Town* and the earlier *Blind Alley* in expressionistic chiaroscuro and in the darkness that lies beneath American light, a darkness that *film noir* was to bring to inescapable view. Henry Fonda was perfectly cast as Steinbeck's Tom Joad, and his performance in that role was without peer for that year; but the Academy Award was given to James Stewart for a trivial role in the stratum of America's light. Blackie applauded the choice; I was viscerally disappointed by it. Orson Welles's *Citizen Kane* is perhaps the real beginning of *film noir*. Blackie shared in the weak and negative public reception of that film: he would not sit all the way through it; I had seen the movie during a newsboy trip to Chicago and then sat through the film again to the end, after Blackie had left, and went alone, again, two more times to see and study it. Its later elevation to a critical empyrean impressed Blackie not at all.

Darkness is primary, I said, *and light is the illusion that darkness is secondary.*

That may be, he said, *but, even if light is as evil as Lucifer, it is never right not to fight against darkness.* [I've corrected his *to not fight*.]

RAIN and DARKNESS

My predilection for the dark was consistent with my inability to dislike Jordy Klug; and, when he was caught with three of his River-cavers burglarizing a potato-chip factory, I listened eagerly to my mother's account of his hearings, which she attended with Hildy; and, pleased as I was that his three underlings were sent up to the mid-state reformatory for eighteen months, I was even more pleased that Hildy's lawyer, with his deep political connections, won a dismissal of all charges against Jordy, who had not to submit even to probation. Not once did his three fellow burglars waver in their loyalty to him: each signed a statement that Jordy Klug had no part in the breaking and entering and the theft. At that time, I could understand that my admiration for a guy who wanted to shoot me depended on my allegiance to darkness. Not very many years later I was to wonder if my feelings were similar to those of the Ka-tzetniks who developed, in the shadow of death, a filial devotion to their vicious commandants.

Romantics may be drawn inherently to the strangeness of darkness, or to the horrific primacy of what Nietzsche calls the Dionysian abyss.

The war in Europe, which was bringing its shadows to the phototropic U.S.A., brought steadier work to my father and my uncle. It also brought about Blackie's departure from our neighborhood. His father gained lucrative ascendence in automotive industrials [Open the gates, George], and the Konshaks moved upward, closer to the crested avenues. It was in their house, however, before they moved, that I was to be overwhelmed by my first radiance. Blackie's older sister, Karla, had already moved to her own apartment. She had gone up from typist to secretary to designer-consultant to head designer in a clothing-manufacture company that had gone up from local ownership to regional link in a national chain [their metaphor, George, not mine]. Blackie's younger sister, Katie, was composing a sophomore essay, and Blackie asked me to help her. This I was very willing to do. Katie had certainly been aware of my many lecherous glances at her. All women seem to be gifted with this awareness. Any one of them may be looking in quite a different direction, or may have her back turned to an ogling male, and she will be fully aware of the giveaway stare. There had been occasional instances, however, when I was certain that Katie was giving me the eye. She had dark brown eyes and deeply dark brown hair. *Did she ask for my help?*

She said I should ask you.

On a Friday afternoon I went straight from my paper route, which I would soon be turning over to my brother Paul, three years my junior, to the Konshaks. Katie greeted me at the door with a smile that made me tremble. She let me wash my newsprint-smeared hands in the kitchen sink. Karl Sr. was at work. Blackie and Rebecca had left to attend some furniture delivery and arrangement at the house to which they would soon be moving. Katie was wearing a silky white blouse, accented below its V-opening by a gold-plated cross on a gold-plated chain, a close-fitting red and grey small-checked skirt, nylons, and grey pumps (not her more customary bobby-socks and saddle-shoes).

We sat elbow to elbow at the kitchen table and turned to the draft of her essay on Louisa May Alcott. This was familiar material for me. My essay for nineteenth-century American literature had been on Stephen Crane's *The Red Badge of Courage*. The first seven words of Crane's novel had seemed uncouth to me: *The cold passed reluctantly from the earth* . . . Could cold effect a disinclination?

Passing slowly is a purely physical action; passing reluctantly is a willfully resistant action? Cold has no will (nor

RAIN AND DARKNESS

does wind, as in Longfellow's *a boy's will is the wind's will*). Cold could fluctuate, as in cold waves; but it could not be unwilling or averse. Having not yet heard of Ruskin's *pathetic fallacy*, I called this the feeling of the unfeeling. And why the earth instead of the hills on which an army was *stretched out?* From my reading of books by and about General Custer, I knew that probably a battalion, or at most a regiment, would be revealed on the hills by the retiring fogs, hardly an army. Why open the short first paragraph with dawn and close it with a description of the preceding night, with the *sorrowful blackness* of the stream and the gleam of *hostile campfires?* Blackness felt no sorrow, campfires no hostility, since neither had the sense of feeling, or any capacity for emotion. The term for such an expression, as I would later learn, was *transferred epithet* or *hypallage*. Worse yet was a sentence like *He had a wild hate for the relentless foe*. Mrs. Bergstrom had taken my negative essay to be as irritating as it was competent. Although I did not enjoy Alcott's novels, I considered all three of them to be markedly superior to Crane's novel about a war in which he had not fought. Katie had read only *Little Women* and half of *Little Men*. She had outlined Alcott's biography in pedestrian fashion, provided a tedious plot summary of *Little Women*, and concluded with mentions of *Little Men* and *Jo's Boys*. When I read her opening sentence, I forgot about my tentative plan cavalierly to end our session with my taking one of Katie's hands and kissing her on the cheek, a pass that might have led to the lips.

The sentence was this: *In terms of America's nineteenth-century literary classics, Louisa M. Alcott's* Little Women *is among the greatest*. While I liked the phrase *in terms of* in algebra—that is, solving equations in terms of x and y—I disliked its use in expository prose and would come to detest its serving lazy academics as a lolling pad. I advised Katie that what she meant was, plainly, that Louisa M. Alcott's *Little Women* is one of nineteenth-century America's popular works of literature. She agreed then to define a work of literature as written fiction, the specifics of which reflect undeniable but untenable truths, and to state that, as such, *Little Women* shows how a New England family and the American Civil War provide an experience of order both in opposition to chaos and as deriving from chaos. We worked out the autobiographical elements of Louisa M. Alcott in the character of Jo March and we related familial tensions to those of war (the family name being an echo of soldiering) and peace and life and death. We rewrote the entire essay, with Katie following my guidance at first and then bringing her own understanding of girls and women into an analysis of the tensions of female and male that went well beyond my thinking.

In a short time I was contributing no more than adherence to grammar, spelling, and usage. We completed a firm outline and a full draft.

As Katie collected and aligned her papers on the table top, one sheet drifted down to the floor. I bent over and down to retrieve it, but it had come to rest almost under her chair. Leaving my chair, I knelt on the floor. Katie turned on her chair, hiked her skirt up a bit, and parted her legs. She was wearing only a garter-belt under her skirt. I was offered a view of her thighs, white above the gartered nylons, and, farther, dark brown down over a small oval mound bisected by a roseate serrate crest, at which I stared, guiltily but steadily. I did not, or could not, move. My right hand held the fallen sheet of paper in the air. Katie took the sheet from my hand, laid the sheet on the table, and then guided my hand to the inside of her right thigh, where the stocking demarcated the skin. The sensual softness is indescribable. I move my hand up to what Gustave Courbet calls *The Origin of the World*, and she instructs my middle finger in its role of arousal. The warmth, the wetness, and the movements of vicarious embrace arouse me to a state of seeming to be laved by a thick bath of light. Katie relaxes in a continued fluidity and then directs me in my requisite partial unclothing. Her touch, her voluble grasp, and her teasingly tender stroking transform my bath of light into an explosion of almost palpable radiance. [Can't help it, George.] We clean each other with tissues from a box of Kleenex conveniently available on the table. We compose ourselves in silence. Katie leaves the kitchen for a time and then returns to make coffee, which she serves with coconut macaroons.

Leaving after 7:00, I wonder vaguely why Blackie and Rebecca have not yet returned and why Karl Sr. should be still away. It occurs to me that Katie and I had neither kissed nor embraced, that there had been no epilogue of sensual prolongation, that my depth of pleasure had not been a rush of endearment. The Konshaks moved eight days later. I helped with the loading and unloading, envying Blackie the location and spaciousness of his new home. Blackie and Katie would transfer to Garfield High in the fall. I would continue on at Randolph High. Blackie and I saw less of each other thereafter, but we went to movies together at least twice a week.

Subsequently, Katie never mentioned our intimate moment; and I knew somehow that I was never to mention it. There was to be no recurrence of any element of that moment. Katie would marry during the war and bear a daughter and a son. There was to be at any time no intimation on her part of that radiance, which, Jordy Klug notwithstanding, had been a large part of what has made my life worth living. Ultimately there developed in me a puzzling conclusion that the seemingly divine encounter in the kitchen had been a gift from the Konshaks to me.

8

An appropriate postlude to my elevation in the Konshak kitchen came about that same evening in the Blaustern kitchen. I had returned home in time for an evening meal prepared by my uncle, my father having got home about the time I had left Katie. It was a good meal: fried potatoes, hamburger, sweet peas, bread (still warm) that my mother had baked, coffee, milk, and Palmerhouse ice cream. Katie's macaroons had not blighted my teenage appetite. The whole family was there, including my three brothers and my sister (I was later to have another brother and another sister). After my mother and my uncle had cleared the table, my father brought his fiddle to the table and began to play. This happened rather rarely [and I doubt that even you, George, could effectively record the wave of pleasure that its every occurrence produced]. My father played five or six numbers in a display of his virtuosity, and then he played the German folk songs to which he had taught us to accompany him in singing. The last of these was always *Auf Wiedersehen*, invariably bringing us all to pleasant tears. But it was the second-to-last song that evening that had an exceptionally strange effect upon me, *Der treue Husar*. The effect resulted, I now think, from the shadow of war, the mystery of Jordy Klug's Latin passages, the imminent move of the Konshaks, and the radiant moment with Katie. Two lines kept singing themselves to me: *Ein ganzes Jahr und noch viel mehr, / Die*

Liebe nahm kein Ende mehr (A whole year and yet much more, / Love has no ending evermore).

I knew that my life would one day be invaded by the dark, ecstatic melancholy of their suggestion.

My father puts away his fiddle and stretches out on the couch, which also serves as sofa-bed. My mother, in our antique rocking-chair, makes sewing repairs to my sister Jane's Sunday dress. My brother Paul retires to the kitchen to get an early start on his homework for Monday. Jane shares the table with him, working at her water colors. My brothers Henry and Luther are sprawled out before the couch and rocking chair, listening to the radio with my mother and father. The program is *Gangbusters*, I think, or something like that. My uncle and I are playing cribbage on what has to be called our living-room table; to us the radio is only background noise. Ordinarily, Blackie and I would be out to a movie on a Friday night like this. I think about Katie and about what it might be like to go all the way with her. My thinking is subsequently limited to what she would let me do.

This Friday in May is a watershed day, of which I am to be reminded in every echo of a Mahleresque *Ewig*.

9

My parents are planning to move out of the flat, which has been the only home I've ever known. They're thinking of a buying a house on the other side of the river. They will do this two years from now. By then, Blackie and his parents and Katie will have moved again, this time to the Hilltop area. Right now we are about three miles from each other. Two years from now there will be eleven miles between our houses. Blackie and I still get together often; three miles is easy walking distance for us. Most of my movie-going, however, I do alone now. I'm alone, but not lonely. I like heading downtown with money in my pocket, buying a bag of candy bars, and sitting through a double feature. The movies are over at around eleven o'clock, and I walk home alone on the almost empty, quiet streets, which frequently glisten from the arc-lights after a light rain, preparing me for the pleasures of a nostalgia that *films noirs* will later bring about. The River-cavers have disbanded. The caves have been filled and sealed. Most of the gang has been sent off to the reformatory. Jordy Klug has become a legman for a political syndicate. I still walk home the long way, in remembrance of the night that Blackie took two of Jordy's bullets for me.

Blackie and I go to Cazzy's once or twice a month. Cazzy's is a bar-and-grill in the Rainey Street section of town. Some white people go there, but not very many. It is owing to Forsey Garman that Blackie and I became accepted habitués. Forsey has been our friend since we were in grade school. He was always part of our softball games. He once beat Jordy Klug into bitter submission on behalf of Blackie and me; and, like Blackie and me, he remains on Jordy's hit list. He went to a high school different from the one to which Blackie and I went; but we continued to get together. He took us to Cazzy's one evening for barbecued ribs. We couldn't be served beer or liquor, although we could have had either under the wood, had we wanted it. The food was superb, and inexpensive; and the music was probably the best in town. After a few more visits, Blackie and I came to be welcomed there, even without Forsey. After Blackie moved, I would go to Cazzy's by myself now and then. The band was into Boogie at this time; and, although my knowledge and appreciation of music has always been meager, I was enchanted by Boogie. Eight beats to the bar, and all that syncopation.

After seeing a single feature one evening (*The Goldwyn Follies*, I think), I went alone to Cazzy's, thinking that Forsey might be there. He wasn't. I had fried fish and beer-slaw and listened to Boogie that the old piano somehow managed to survive. That piano had been beat to riffs of sugar torment by guys like Romeo Nelson and Deryck Sampson. Entering Cazzy's, one saw the long mahogany bar on the left, a row of seven almost enclosed booths on the right, and, where the bar and booths ended, a big rectangle with a dozen open tables, each seating four, and, rising from the rectangle, the orchestra platform. The ladies' room was to the left of the rec and the men's room to the right. Seven of the tables were occupied. I was alone in one of the booths. Wiggy Tackman, Clang Gordon, and Corley Holcomb were heating up *Head Hop Rag*. I closed my eyes and rode my dream train to the Gulf of Earthly Glory.

RAIN AND DARKNESS

At the break, I returned from the Gulf, opened my eyes, and found myself staring at Jordy Klug.

A pan, or a lid, dropped noisily in the kitchen, which took up a narrow room behind the bar and was entered and exited through a swinging door between the bar and the *Ladies*. I expressed to Jordy my surprise at his being welcome in Cazzy's. He coughed out a surly scoff: *They're only open because we let 'em, Shit-head.* Mentally, I said, *open only because.* I asked Jordy if he followed me around at night. He said he always knew where I was at night. *Crumb-pot solo movie-goer walkin' the streets.* He opened out the left side of his black sports jacket, with its grey pin stripes, and showed me a holster holding the largest handgun I had ever seen. This was not a .22, he informed me; and, recalling his old attempt to bring me down with a .22 pistol, he insisted that this Army .45 would have gone right through the flag-draper and me and turned us both to cabbage. He suggested that it might some day put me, the flag-draper, and the *nigger*, by whom he meant Forsey, in mudland—Blackie, because he was a tight-assed *booshwa*, and Forsey, because he was a *high-assed animal*.

Why do you hate me, Jordy?

Hate! Shit, you ain't worth my hate. According to Jordy, I was just a wasted fuck; I had no character, no *integerty*, no talent; what I took to be the right way to talk and write was just old-fashioned habit-paste. I didn't stand up for anything, and I couldn't stand my ground on any challenge; I would never learn Latin because I had no blood-knowledge about history; my German was what his Pa called Platt deutsch; I was like a bedbug in a clean bedroom, and I had to be squished, and he would squish me, but only in one of my retreats from him.

He went over to the bar and brought back chilled gin for himself and a Rock 'n' Rye for me. As I sipped my drink, I took note of his good grooming and his well-cut, expensive clothes. The band crashed into another set, and we both listened. Jordy was tapping his fingers along with the piano beats, as I closed my eyes. After the set, Jordy said, *You seem to like nigger music.* Or maybe it was. *So you like nigger music.* It may be that I remember his saying it both ways in the gap caused by my inability to respond. He went on to say that I didn't have the brains to explain why I liked it, that the counterpoint went back to the arietta in Beethoven's Piano Sonata in C minor, that I had no ear for the ostinato bass or the broken-octave tremolos or the continuity of a riff, that I was just a waltz-and-melody *guap'*, a toe-tapping tin-ear.

I didn't understand him at all. The spelling in the foregoing sentence has been worked out many years after that night. For *guap'* I heard *Wop*; and I wondered why Jordy would call me a Wop, when neither of my parents were, like his, Italian. The Levee Italians were called Wops. For *ostinato* I heard *Austin auto*, which made no sense. Jordy smirked at my stupidity, which was evident in the tongue stilled in my half-opened mouth and the squint under my lined brow. *Arietta* brought only the picture of the exaggeratedly Italian Henry Armetta of many Hollywood comic roles. I wanted very much to learn about that Beethoven sonata. *Beethoven?*—that was all that I could say.

Jordy called out, *Francine!* The waitress, audibly chewing gum, came over to the booth. I had seen her frequently in Cazzy's, but I had never learned her name. Jordy was snowing me. He told Francine to get a sheet of ledger paper from the desk in the kitchen. *How 'bout this?* She held up a page from her order tablet. Jordy stared at her, his dark brown eyes steady and straight. She went off to the kitchen and returned with a ledger sheet and a pencil. Jordy had her take our glasses to the bar for refills and then wrote on the ledger sheet the following: *Contra mentem animose non dominae gerit artus sed penetrare aliter militis vis poterit et penes illam inibit labefactaque porta ostia se facient somnia perficient. In castra illius in nocte et non violenter et in amore levam caute et eam capiam.* He gave it to me and worked on his gin as Wiggy took the keys on a train ride to Mobile. I picked out the few words I knew; I could not connect them, something about love in a camp at night; *militis* is the genitive of *miles* (soldier). The piano banged to a stop. Jordy made his exit, leaving two ones and a fifty-cent piece beside his empty glass and the pencil. I finished my drink, called for and paid the check for my fish and slaw, and left, somehow confident that Jordy was through with me for that night. I walked home slowly, with Jordy's Latin in my shirt pocket. I thought about Trish and tried to relive the gift of the Konshaks with Trish in Katie's place.

It was one of those moments when things fall into a quadrate of sense. Once, waiting at the Seven Corners stop, I caught sight of the welcome yellow streetcar approaching from two blocks away. I stepped out from the sidewalk curb and moved to the boarding island alongside the tracks. The streetcar stopped with its door precisely where I stood. The door opened and I mounted the steps without having had to move either left or right. What I sensed was a particle of perfect universal order. Now I am walking home from Cazzy's with strains of Boogie reasserting themselves.

It comes to me that Jordy wants to control me by doing away with me, that Blackie wants to control me by preserving me, and that I am being carried by this undulant tension of universal order. Francine, who had never spoken to me, apart from asking for my order, before tonight, before I knew her name, had bade me, as I left the club, *'Night*.

10

Les Berg played clarinet for the school orchestra. He was also a pianist and a violinist. Blackie and I often ate lunch with him, usually to get academic information from him—he seemed to know everything—but chiefly to give him the company that he would otherwise not have. We both liked him, despite his being what a later generation would call a nerd (or a geek). He was unattractive, his head being disproportionately large for his tall, thin body. He was always well groomed, his black hair combed straight back without a part, his tie attuned in color and cut to his clean shirt, his pleated trousers sharply pressed, and his black shoes brightly shined. He liked to talk about his record collection and his electronic equipment. Neither Blackie nor I had any sound equipment except radios.

There were about twenty Bergs in the telephone directory, but it was easy enough to isolate Les's number. He was pleased to receive my call and began immediately to describe a set of speakers he had recently acquired. I asked him if he had a recording of the *Armetta* [*sic*] in Beethoven's Sonata in C Minor. *Opus one-eleven? The arietta? Oh, yes. Would you like to come and hear it? Sunday, about two?*

It was an easy bike-ride that Sunday. I lived two miles from school, and Les lived two miles therefrom in the other direction.

His mother served us coffee and cookies in a book-filled room. Then he took me to his huge music room: a grand piano, musical instruments, and an array of sound equipment. He brought a record, in its envelope, to the turntable and then talked enthusiastically about the final Beethoven piano sonata and its exceptional two movements (instead of the conventional three with conventional recapitulation). From maestoso to fugal variations, leaving C major for E-flat minor and C minor, and so forth. I had no understanding of what he was talking about, but sat through his learned lecture and nodded when he insisted that I hear the entire sonata. He handled the records deftly, holding the edges between his two hands so that the grooves were never touched. He placed the needle, at the end of its arm, skillfully onto the record. He pushed the little buttons and then sat back with his hands clasped behind his neck.

This was my introduction to an aesthesis. I lost my orientation as I was carried into what I look back upon as a cavern of fulfilling connection. I closed my eyes and saw what must have been Katie's breasts and then her heart expanding and contracting slightly with a magical rhythm in a prison cell which grew into a great church. Then twelve wingless angels, each one of whom was Trish, began to sing, six on one side of an altar, six on the other. What they sang were not words but lilting notes, the sounds of which soared upward, only to return and with a new host of notes to soar upward and return. These gave a kind of meaning to all of my desires to be more than I was and a serene consolation to me as I felt the futility of those desires. It must have been a minute or two after the music had stopped before I regained my orientation by Les's asking me how I liked it. The only response I could make was a nod, seeing which, and seeing the tears on my cheeks, of which I suddenly became aware, Les said, *Good! You'll have to hear the Ninth.*

Mrs. Berg, a tall and quite attractive woman with a constant smile, returned with hot chocolate and biscotti and then sat down with us. She asked me questions about myself that I found very easy to answer without embarrassment. When I addressed her as Mrs. Berg, she laughed and said I was to call her Rebecca. [I began, George, to see more connections.] When Les insisted that I come by next Sunday to listen to the Ninth, she seconded his insistence in such a way as to make me feel that I had become important to her. She was not boring at all, as Les seemed often to be. I asked about Mr. Berg and learned that he was a rabbi and in Cleveland for a month.

Les the Likable Bore and Rebecca the Gracious Lady welcomed me the following Sunday afternoon.

There was coffee and angel-food cake. Rebecca remained with us as Les played the Ninth. The light-hearted and the militant quests for happiness were followed by the epic striving of the strings toward an untenable heaven, with the repeated drumbeat of a return to the limitations of the physical. Here I had to wipe away a stream of tears. Rebecca's smile assured me that there was no need for shame. Then came the triumphant chorale and my satisfying surprise at being able to understand many of the words. During the coda, my arms were pressed tightly onto the arms of the easy chair and I was leaning forward and pressing my feet against the floor. When the symphony ended, I sank back into the chair and wanted only to relax and enjoy in silence the effect that the music had had upon me. Les, however, getting up to remove the records and put them back in their envelopes, began to talk about tonal conversions and orchestral conversation. Rebecca seemed to understand that Les was boring me; she got him to step out of the room with her for a short while, during which time I regained my dark pleasure and resolved to learn as much as I could about Beethoven.

Perhaps it was a short attention span that caused me often to be bored by other people. It was many years after my being bored by Les that I began to realize that I myself was, to many people, a boring person, that it is mainly those who themselves are bores who can find, and do find, others to be boring. I was too lazy and too impatient to let myself learn what Les Berg had to teach me. He had this low voice, with which he spoke slowly and monotonously; but he knew very much about very many things.

After the Beethoven music, popular music—Bing Crosby, the big bands—to which I had never been genuinely attracted, began to bore me, although I told myself that I liked Freddy Martin's popular rendition of Tchaikovsky's fifth piano concerto and although I thoroughly enjoyed Glenn Miller's music.

Biking home that Sunday afternoon, I recalled that it was Jordy Klug who had put me on to Beethoven. What he had meant about the counterpoint was now clear; but I was puzzled by his having provided this instructive information—puzzled, but, for some reason, not grateful. Had it occurred to me then to want to thank him, there would have been no way for me to have done so, apart from asking my mother to relay my gratitude to him.

The flat had the aroma of baked rye bread. My mother had baked about a dozen small loaves that Sunday. I ate two whole loaves. They were still warm. We smiled together.

11

My mother was spending a lot of time with Hildy Klug. Often, when my father was on the road, she would not get home until three or four in the morning. She was always home for the children, when they were ready for breakfast. She was always home for my father, when he came off the road. Her fidelity to him, however, was in her fashion, not in his. My father was not an exciting person, despite his talent for playing the fiddle and his exceptional ability as an automobile mechanic. He did not talk much or tell jokes. My uncle did both, and he spent more time with me than my father did. My uncle played cribbage with me, worked out crossword puzzles with me, and almost weekly tested me on the names and chronology of the United States presidents and on the capitals of all the states. He constantly and generously gave me the praise that he must have known I needed. My mother gave me love, although she never used the word, as later in the century it became a conventional duty to do. My father gave me security and a sense of pride in being German. My uncle gave me praise and my first lesson in the requirements of good teaching: never tell a student flatly that he or she is wrong: always correct a student indirectly but surely. *South Carolina?* Once I answered, *Raleigh. Right*, he said, *Raleigh, Carolina. South Carolina.* No, I'm wrong: Raleigh, North Carolina. This was enough for me to remember Columbia and to state it as though I were correcting him; and his laugh and firm pat on my shoulder made me feel as though I had done just that. He was equally considerate and helpful with my brothers and sisters. My father played Checkers with me and taught me German songs and rhymes, but his *Dummkopf!* and *Fleischkopf!* were more frequent than his *ausgezeichnet!*

With some interest, but without much pleasure, I was comparing the versification of Walt Whitman and Carl Sandburg, when my father sat down at the kitchen table with me and told me that my mother and he were going to be separated. He looked beat, as he added that she was going to live with Hilda Klug and that I would have to help Joe—that was my uncle—with the kids. It was surprising that my uncle would not leave with his sister, but my mother had actually asked him to stay.

The separation did not take place, however. My parents decided to wait until I had graduated from high school. Within that year, my mother gave birth to my second sister, Leanna. After I had graduated and was enrolled at the university, we moved to the house on the other side of the river. My mother and father appeared to have reconciled; I was of draft age, though, and they may have decided not to separate if and while I was off to war.

Separation and divorce result from the failure properly to consider the familiar allicin that opens up the relational ion channel [Bear with me, George.]. The pain of habit and responsibility and obligation is eliminated when it should be enhanced. Instead of jalapeño, garlic, or wasabi, the bland cooling draught of infidelity is taken to be spice. We take away the apostrophe + s from the possessive of singular nouns that end in s, like *Sophocles'* for *Sophocles's* because the obligatory inflection seems tedious or cacophonously elongated in pronunciation. We remove the comma from the second-to-last member of a series (She nurtured roses, hydrangeas and hyacinths) because it seems unnecessary and because the potential ambiguity seems negligible. We break the marital vow because the obligation seems tedious and the responsibility seems unnecessary. The avowal, however, is a commitment to the language of maturity. One's word, one's vow, is ultimately one's Self; this I learned from the English language, as it directed me toward Language. Catholic Christian doctrine, born in a decadent dialect of the classical Greek language, is closer to Language than elastic doctrines that descend to limpness and desiccation, although many of its adherents follow the doctrine as doctrine and not as direction. Mrs. Grote nurtured roses, hydrangeas, and hyacinths. The Latin language was to teach me that divorce is a *turning away*, a losing of the way, a digression, a diversion. When Blackie and I discussed this after the war, in the coffee-house off campus, he said that divorce was the way of the quitter, not the way of the loser. The person who is dumped by the divorcer is the loser; the divorcer is the quitter. We could not solve, however, the problems of beaten wives, molested children, and incorrigibly promiscuous spouses.

TAPINOSIS: at the end of the Decade of Greed, in the movie, *Total Recall*, Doug Quaid will fatally shoot his wife Lori and say, *Consider that a divorce.*

Divorce always entails loss, which, in its turn, is psychological entropy, a matter of necessity. Change, even for the better, is divorce: a turning away. Graduation from high school turned me away from a pleasant and relatively unchallenged passivity. Blackie, whose move had divorced us from our walks to and from school, had graduated a semester before I did. Walking with Dick Shriven went well, because he looked up to me as his superior. Walking with

Trish was now a nostalgic daydream. The senior year offered some satisfactions: Mrs. Bergstrom gave me the lead role in the senior class play; Mr. Conrad appointed me, despite the better qualifications of four other candidates, editor of the school paper. The appointment was my second lesson in good teaching, a lesson that would later be consolidated by Professor Landis in graduate school: belief in a student's competence germinates that competence in a student. Of whatever joys and memories the senior prom was to have provided I was not to have a share. Each of the three girls I asked to be my date had turned me down, and I had turned down the one girl who had asked me. Blackie's attempts to teach me to dance were not particularly successful, despite the patience of the female partners with whom he paired me. On the night of the prom, I went to a movie and then to Cazzy's.

After graduation, there was a void, a bleakness for which I had not been prepared. Blackie had enlisted. With my paper-route savings I enrolled in the university, abetted by letters of recommendation from Mrs. Bergstrom and Mr. Conrad. Upon advice from a counselor, I elected Beginning French and Anthropology; Freshman English was required. The university was on the quarter system at that time, and 3-credit classes met five times a week. The music department had listening booths, in which I was free to listen to recordings of Beethoven.

Freshman English was a surprise and an awakening. We wrote themes on green paper, the size of stenographer's notebook pages, and we read and interpreted novels, the first of which was W. Somerset Maugham's *Of Human Bondage*. Beginning French increased my deepening interest in the nature of language; and it included a reading of abridged and annotated chapters of Victor Hugo's *Les Misérables*. Anthropology was taught in a large lecture hall to about a hundred and fifty students, and I was unable to take any real interest in it, apart from its insistence that there were only three races.

The day broke gray and dull: this set the tone for the early life of Maugham's Philip Carey, said the instructor, turning my attention away from my preference of *grey* to *gray*. In Javert, whose name tied him mystically to Jan Valjean, his prey, I caught serial intimations of Jordy Klug.

The worst of the bleakness, the great emptiness, came over me during a streetcar ride home from campus one autumn afternoon. I sat in the worn, wickerwoven seat and stared out the window at the sun-grey street and the dusty sidewalks of the passing afternoon. There was nothing to look forward to, no one to do anything with. The study assignments meant nothing. The prospect of a movie was dark and hollow. The sanctuary of high school, along with my daydreams within its routine, had been eliminated. Later I would learn, reading Kierkegaard, Sartre, and Heidegger, that this feeling of illimitable loss was the horror of nothing. Between existence and me there was nothing. *Angst*, dread. At a moment like this, fully aware that there is only existence and nothing, I was most alive; but, when one is most alive, one wants least to live. Without the strength to determine one's direction within this moment, one flails about for distractions to wall off the meaninglessness of amorphous existence. Prone to passivity and impelled to no activity—repelled, in fact, by any thought of activity—I made my transfer to another streetcar, got off at my stop, walked home, sought out my bed, and listened on the radio to *Maria Elena, Dolores,* the Freddy Martin arrangement of Tchaikovsky's *Piano Concerto in C, The Woodpecker Song,* and swam with the current of what must have been despair into a sleep without dreams. There were to be at least three more times in life during which I was to suffer this great emptiness (Sharny; Anne; the suggilate night; yes—and two other times as well).

In the house into which we had moved, I had more privacy: a small room all to myself. My uncle, working regularly now at a factory with a Defense contract, had taken an apartment close to his work and to a beer joint, which he increasingly frequented. Gradually, the university routine walled off dread: I developed acquaintance with two male classmates and one female classmate; the last was not attractive but was very friendly and we enjoyed each other's company—well, I know that I enjoyed her company. There was an exceptionally pretty woman in my French class; she was courteous and was pleasantly responsive to my approaches; but she turned me down when, at length, I asked her to go to a movie with me. Blackie's letters came regularly. I wish that I had saved them so that I could now include some of them in this narrative. I saved only my Freshman English themes and pictures of Ingrid Bergman and Olivia DeHavilland, and movie ticket stubs; all of these, though, I eventually threw away.

Jordy Klug got a draft deferment. He wore large rings and a grey fedora, and he drove a huge Packard. He gained public notice upon being arrested in connection with the murder of a Negro, who was an alleged kingpin drug pusher. After the jury selection, his defense attorney won a dismissal of the case on two crucial technicalities. My thoughts turned to that big .45 that Jordy had carried in Cazzy's.

RAIN and DARKNESS

My thoughts turned also to the s that belonged with the apostrophe in possessives of singular nouns ending in s. I saw myself as the metaphoric state of that s, removed from that afterturning to which I felt that I belonged. And I came to despise, as a Polar Conceit, every instance of the excluded s. I grew to despise divorce—on grammatical and psychological, not on moral, grounds.

12

Winter, with heavy snow and extended periods of below-zero temperatures, makes the streetcar rides to the university grim and numbing. It is dark as I walk three blocks, carrying books and notebooks, to the streetcar stop for the 5:55 a.m. car. My feet get cold during the walk and do not get warm during the long ride. Over the bridge and into the downtown area. Transfer to the always crowded car that goes to the university in the neighboring city. Standing and maintaining my balance until a seat becomes available after stops near the Midway factories. Sitting is then a pleasure, although my feet continue to be cold. Finally, I get off at the second of the university stops and walk two long blocks to the Administration building. Inside, blissful in the burst of warmth that blankets me, I walk past the heavy doors and down the long, dimly lit corridor, then into the rest room, where I take over a toilet stall, place my books and notebooks on the floor, remove my coat, and sit for about twenty minutes, until I am quite relaxed and my feet are thoroughly warm. This is a time and a place that are all my own.

Now I walk over to Randall Hall, up the stairs to the third floor, and into the classroom where my 8:00 a.m. Freshman English class meets. I am, as usual, ten to fifteen minutes early. At about 7:49, Peggy Strandberg comes in, greets me, takes her seat across the room from me, and reads. By 7:56,

RAIN and DARKNESS

the other seventeen students have all come in and are seated. Promptly at 8:00, the instructor, Miss McMahon, a gaunt young woman, who is a teaching assistant, begins the day's instruction. One of the students uses the word *ostentatious*, and I am impressed. I never ask questions or volunteer information, and I speak only when directly called upon. We are addressed, not by our first names, as in high school, but as *Miss Strandberg, Mr. Blaustern*, and so on.

In mid-afternoon, after classes, some library work, and reading program notes as I listen to Beethoven in a music booth, I reverse the streetcar ride and travel home, my feet not bothered now by cold, to the large meal my mother sets before me and to my study assignments, which require much more time than high-school homework had ever done.

In January, I secure part-time work, two and one half hours per day, except on Friday, at a U-town store, which serves meals in the basement and on the third floor and sells men's clothing on the first floor and women's clothing on the second. My job is custodial work for ninety minutes and operating the elevator for an hour. Once I have helped to clean up after the lunch crowd, I am allowed to use one of the booths on the third floor for study. This is very pleasant: padded seat, smooth table surface, and a small, sufficiently bright wall light. I am also entitled to provide a meal for myself from what is available in the kitchen. The ride home is now much later in the day. There is a comfortable acquaintanceship with another part-time working student, whose hours precede and briefly overlap mine, with Alec, the elderly regular elevator operator, who has taught me a Scottish bit (*'Tis a braw bricht moonlicht nicht tonicht; if ye con say that, ye're all richt, I* [pronounced ee] *ken*), and with Bob, the full-time custodian. The days become less depressing and less dull.

On a Friday in early spring I sit through a sappy movie, *Mrs. Miniver*, starring Greer Garson, who will marry Richard Ney, the guy who plays her son in the movie. Garson will not prove her movieness until she stars opposite Ronald Colman in *Random Harvest*.

On another Friday I enjoy the successful silliness of Robert Montgomery and James Gleason in *Here Comes Mr. Jordan*. The diminutive Claude Rains, whose perfectly modulated voice, challenging the smooth perfection of the voices of Ronald Colman and, later, Frank Overton, plays God. After seeing one of these movies—I think it was the latter, because I felt good after leaving the theatre—I went to Cazzy's. Forsey was there that night. He was in uniform and was to be entrained for a camp or fort on Monday for basic training in the infantry.

Cazzy's was noisily crowded; but most of the customers were white, which change from the proportions of clientèles of the past made me feel rather less than more at home. I asked Forsey if he knew anything about the murder charge against Jordy Klug. Forsey put his hand on my wrist, bent across the booth table to me and told me in a voice that was almost a whisper that Jordy Klug had stuck a .45 in the mouth of Angel Jake Angelito, the big Puerto Rican supplier who was skimming the take due the local syndicate, and blew his head off. The traffic in reefers and angel dust was handled under the wood by Cazzy's manager, but the business income, recorded by the bookkeeper, had to be reviewed by a CPA, and the bookkeeper refused to make the relatively easy turn of queering the books for Angel Jake. *So how did Jordy get off?*, I asked. Forsey said that the Organization, or Foundation, whose connections extended to Washington, D.C., Havana,

Bogota, Le Havre, Istanbul, Cairo, and Shanghai, liquidated the .45 and put Jordy in Shakopee with three witnesses at the time of the murder. *Angel Jake was a badass pusher, Pete, but that Jordy Klug has a heart of iron forged in Hell.*

There was no Boogie that night. My impulse to request *Grand Slam* and *Bouncing at the Beacon* was checked by the lengthy conversation that Forsey and I were having. That Francine no longer worked there was part of all the change and passing away that I disliked. It was a relief to learn that Forsey had not actually witnessed the murder of Angel Jake. I wanted to ask him why he hadn't told the police all that he knew; but I had heard, chiefly from my mother, what the Organization did to informers and to the families and friends of informers. Forsey asked about Blackie. I told him that Blackie was training with the Field Artillery in Arizona. We talked for a long time, reminiscing and speculating upon the length and consequences of the war; we ordered chips, beer (under the wood), and roast-beef sandwiches. We left about a half hour before Cazzy's closing time. Standing outside, where the red and blue neon was reflected on the wet sidewalk, we shook hands. *So long, Forsey.—See you, Pete.*

During the second quarter of my first school year, taking advantage, for the first time, of an instructor's office hours, I visit my second Freshman English instructor, Mr. Nedayan. I ask him why he uses *due to* as an adverbial phrase and why, quite often, he begins a sentence with the adversative *However*. He seems pleased and not offended and thanks me for calling these lapses to his attention, allowing that it is all too easy to run slipshod on the field of bad usage [His metaphor, George, for which he quickly apologized].

Mr. Nedayan did not agree with me about the phrase, *more perfect union*, in the *Constitution*. Against my insistence that it was a qualification of the absolute, he said that *perfect* was clearly modified by an understood *nearly*. He nodded tentatively, with a frown and with his right middle finger pressed against his temple, when I asked if every such qualification—like *more complete, deader than a doornail, rather unique,* and *living to the fullest*—were to benefit from an understood *nearly*. The analogue, he said, was the *to* that was always understood with infinitives governed by potential or modal auxiliaries, as in *One can go* or *One should go*. He could not, however, provide authoritative statements about the understood *nearly*. Touching the tips of his extended fingers together and moving them toward and away from his chin, he moved slightly backward and forward in his swivel chair and offered a friendly lecture on idiomatic expression and the lack of infallible and unbreakable rules in English. Seething inwardly, I nodded and reserved my adherence to the Polar Conceit. Sentence fragments, as stylistic expressions, are *understood* because they carry consistent meaning; aberrations from correct usage are not to be *understood* as correct usage.

Over coffee, I talked about this with Tom, the other part-time working student at the U-Town store. His bothersome stutter concealed an intellect that I admired and envied: *Luh luh language is flew flew flew fluid, P Pete*. In his opinion, it could not be dammed or forever frozen.

The loneliness of my late homeward streetcar rides I managed to lessen by reading as I rode. Tom had recommended the short stories and novels of Ernest Hemingway. Mr. Nedayan had recommended William Saroyan's *My Name Is Aram* and *The Human Comedy*. The recommendations provided a good balance: Hemingway was oriented toward death and nothing; Saroyan was oriented toward being and life. Later, when I came to read Greek literature, I realized that Hemingway was a Hippolytus, lusting not to be touched as he disguised his inherent chastity with machismo, an unwitting devotee of Artemis pretending to be a Heracles.

I was offended by his would-be tough-guy story, *The Killers*, because, while he has one character refer to another character as *the nigger*, which reference is acceptable as characterization, he goes on to have his omniscient third-person narrator make the same reference, as though the derogatory epithet were innocuous and acceptable—like Dickens's derogatory use of *the Jew* in *Oliver Twist*. Thinking of Forsey, I resented the elevation of this racist term to standard parlance. *A Farewell to Arms* captured my complete interest, however: reading the last fifteen pages, I went two miles beyond my streetcar stop. Having then to catch another streetcar going in the opposite direction, I resented paying the additional fare.

Hemingway's studied simplicity was much less to my liking than Saroyan's spontaneous simplicity. A sentence like this seemed to be awkward and elliptical: *I meant tactically speaking in a war where there was some movement a succession of mountains were nothing to hold as a line because it was too easy to turn them.* The antecedent of *them* has to be *mountains!* And [*The guns*] *smelled cleanly of oil and grease* is not grammatical. Ford Madox Ford's weak defense of the adverb, in his introduction to the Modern Library edition that I was reading, made me laugh.

Seated in the streetcar as the daylight turns grey, I appreciate Hemingway's *I felt lonely and empty* and, in the next sentence, *I was feeling lonely and hollow*. In another dusk, I turn from the book to stare out the window of the streetcar at grey sidewalks and old houses as a hollow simile fails to work: *She had wonderfully beautiful hair and I would lie sometimes and watch her twisting it up in the light that came in the open door and it shone even in the night as water shines sometimes just before it is really daylight.* I can see the *twisting* but not the *wonderfully beautiful*, and I try to think of light coming in a door, instead of *in through* a doorway, and of the kind and location of the shining water (tap water? river water? Mediterranean Sea water? dog piss on the base of a tree?); and is it the hair or the light that *shone even in the night?* Hemingway is a good storyteller, but the emotional surface of his narrative is equivocal. His artistry lies in the depth of his preoccupation with nada.

Saroyan seems to dance on the surface of his narrative, leaving death and nothingness behind him. Turning from his short novels to his short stories, I come upon this: ... *a dream, carrying him to something new, a newer loveliness, a little girl named Maxine, in the third grade. In the dream he went to her and she saw his love and she loved him.*

I cannot see *wonderfully beautiful*, but I can experience the *newer loveliness* of Maxine in Saroyan's dream—especially when he goes on: *She sat two seats in front of him, across the aisle, and all day he sat staring at her soft brown hair, still living in the dream.* Saroyan returns me to the Trish of my daydreams, and I almost decide to try to seek out the Trish of the waking world, the Trish with whom I once had walking dates and with whom I would have been utterly content to be able to spend the rest of my life. But it is a cold spring now; and, when I get off the streetcar at my stop, I have to walk through dark slush.

When I wrote to Blackie about my comparison of Saroyan and Hemingway, I excluded mention of Trish. He did not like Hemingway, had not read Saroyan, and recommended Henry Adams's *History of the United States.*

During the final quarter of that school year, I was enrolled in the ROTC program. The drilling and saluting and care of the uniform went well, but the classroom work was dreary and uninteresting: cartography, Mercator projections; logistics of supply; defense tactics; and I made no progress. The instructor, an Infantry first lieutenant, was a kind man and let me off with a grade of D-.

Spring brought days that eventually grew warm and green. The school year ended. I checked Henry Adams's *History* out of the public library and had reached chapter VII and a paragraph about the Cardinal de Retz when my draft notice came in the mail.

My mother's eyes glazed with curious sadness. My father expressed his unhappiness that I might have to stand in battle against Germans. My fourth brother was born. The army base was just a streetcar ride away. Les Berg and I went through the physical examination together. Les didn't pass. He couldn't lift both arms straight up. His left arm quivered at shoulder height and fell. Within a week, I was in uniform and quartered at the Fort. Close-order drill: right face, left face, about face, forward march, to the rear march, cadence count. My uncle gave me a khaki shirt that had never been worn. It had pleated pockets, like an officer's shirt: this was not standard government issue for draftees. The First Sergeant, a huge, soft-voiced Cherokee Indian, insisted that I had secured it illegally and politely refused to accept my denial. He did not make me surrender the shirt to him; but I was to dispose of it. Disciplined, I spent a day digging small trenches in the rich peat soil. I returned the shirt to my uncle. There were batteries of tests.

The most confusing and frustrating of these was a kind of discernment exercise in identifying electronic dots and dashes. After a time, I based my responses on purely subjective reactions that were neither mere guesses nor auditory logic. (Subsequently I learned, to my astonishment, that I had received a high grade for the exercise.)

After five weeks of orientation, tests, drill, and calisthenics, sixty of us were driven in trucks down the streetcar route to the train depot. In groups of twelve, we boarded the train. An MP was in charge of each group. Whether we carried our duffel bags or even had duffel bags at that time, I can't recall. I do recall de-training for a couple of hours in Kansas City and then boarding an MKT (Missouri-Kansas-Texas) train. Our destination was an Infantry division in Texas.

13

Army life was not my can of beer. I went through it with the attitude of a disinterested observer. Failure found me at every bend; but luck led me not infrequently along. We lined up in squads, tallest to shortest: I was third from the short end; the tallest was appointed squad leader and given a chevroned armband. I was among the first to do KP duty. I reported at 5:00 a.m. (0500 hours). By 3:00 p.m. (1500 hours) the Mess Sergeant was telling two or three of the workers to take off. Other workers began to report for duty. It was 10:00 p.m. (2100), and I am the only one of the morning group still scrubbing pans and pots. I ask the Mess Sergeant if I may be relieved, since I have been here since oh five hundred. He says Oh sure, he hadn't noticed me. This same Mess Sergeant was later disciplined for buying gaudily decorated pillows in town and selling them to basic trainees for three times their cost. [Months later, in a different Infantry division, but still in Texas, I was assigned to Sunday KP duty. I slept through the morning and did not report for duty. Two weeks afterward, I was called before the Captain and asked to explain my failure to report for KP duty: was it for religious reasons? *No excuse, Sir.* Had I been ill? *No excuse, Sir.* I was close to enjoying the moment. *Put this man on regimental detail: three weeks.* The punishment entailed scrubbing barracks floors in full uniform and field pack for three hours every night. Easily secured empty *Quaker* oatmeal boxes were substituted for the cylindrical blanket rolls within the shelter-half (one half of a pup-tent) wrapping; I was given this advice by others who had done regimental duty. The risk was a surprise full-field inspection by an officer; but everyone took the risk. We did scrub floors; but, for most of the three hours, we played Poker or shot Craps with the sergeant in charge of our detail, who also provided beer and peanuts. Not until this writing have I put these two KP incidents together in anagogic balance. (Word of honor, George!)]

Back from the bracketed flash-forward to basic training between the two KP events. My score on the weird sound-perception test had been, as I mentioned earlier, very high—nothing but luck in that—and so I was assigned to the Headquarters Company communications platoon. Laying telephone wires; carrying heavy pack-radios; Able Baker Charlie Dog; Roger, Over and out. Four or five of the platoon members talked constantly about radio theory; it was not luck that got them into the platoon—they *knew* radio. Looking at one of their books on theory, with all of its squiggles and symbols, I marveled at its incomprehensibility. During the Division's extended Maneuvers, the simulation of combat activities, I carried wire and helped to set up field telephone connections. Never good at reading maps, I strung a reel of wire one night down two miles of a ravine that was a half-mile south of the ravine designated in the orders. Mission not accomplished: a chewing out, but no punishment detail.

More luck: my intelligence-test score was high enough for me to be transferred with a small contingent to an ASTP (Army Specialized Training Program) unit in Paris, Texas. The specialist duties for which we would be trained pointed toward non-combat activity. My hope for foreign-language training and translation duty was not met. This was a curriculum of Engineering. The classroom work and the relaxed discipline were very welcome after the dusty drain of basic training. I studied persistently, sought and received help from the others, and made some progress in essential Physics; but the solid geometry and the trigonometry were well beyond my competence. The slide rule was a particular convenience for capable students.

 I could do little more with it than swing it about like a baton in its neat leather case.

 Examinations were imminent; and I recalled my futile ROTC efforts. Confessing my shortcomings, I requested a transfer. The Captain advised me to take three days to think it over. The guys in the barracks who had been trying to help me out of my difficulties tried sternly to dissuade me: *For Christ's sake, man, this is your LIFE!* But I knew that, even if I moved on, with the gift of a low passing grade, it would mean work for which I was not qualified. My concern was not for the people whom I would inevitably let down but for the impossibility of my mastering praiseworthy tasks, of not really knowing what I was doing. I explained my situation in a letter to Blackie. By the time his answer reached me, I was in another Infantry division. Blackie said that I was making the wrong decision and that I should hold on. The Captain—I can't remember his name—at the ASTP unit, for whatever strange reason, sent me a letter in care of my new company commander. This was about a month after my transfer. He informed me that, two weeks after I had left, the entire unit was disbanded and all of the enlisted personnel had been sent to San Luis Obispo en route to the South Pacific. He suggested that I may have been lucky [luck? again?]; and he wished me good fortune. It occurred to me that my father would have preferred my being sent to that theatre of war. At that time, my father's preference was still a possibility.

Twilight again. The barracks buildings were sided with tar-paper. The autumn wind raised dust along the streets. The 6-by-6 truck stopped at a yellow-lit headquarters building. *Blaustern!* The usual pronunciation: blaw-sturn; first syllable slightly accented; not my father's BLAoo-stairn. I hauled my duffel bag out of the truck and into the yellow-lit Headquarters Company office. The First Sergeant and a T Corporal (with a bulb-nose, of which I was later to be reminded by Karl Malden's nose) were working on some mimeographed papers. After a few minutes, the T Corporal looked up at me and said, *Yeah?* I held out my envelope. The First Sergeant took it, opened it, and told the T Corporal to take me to I and R. The walk up the dim, dusty street was uncomfortably long. The dreary barracks was empty: chow time. I tossed my duffel onto the designated upper bunk and followed my bored guide to the mess hall, where a meal was nearing its end. A tray of stew, beets, and some kind of pudding was ladled out for me, along with bread rolls and coffee.

I and R was the Intelligence and Reconnaissance section, six or seven scouts and observers headed by a Staff Sergeant and accountable to a First Lieutenant, the company's Intelligence Officer.

Next morning, the company fell out for a full-field-pack twenty-mile hike. I hadn't been issued my field equipment yet, so I made the hike unburdened by that weight.

Weapons instruction included firing-range qualification with the .45-caliber pistol, the .30-caliber carbine, and the M1 rifle; also, familiarity with the .30- and .50-caliber machine guns; the mortar; the Bangalore torpedo; the Bazooka; and the hand grenade. I made Expert with the .45, the only weapon, along with the hand grenade, that I liked. While handling it and firing it, I thought, almost fondly, of Jordy Klug. The weapon I most disliked was the M1; I could tear it down, clean it, oil it, and re-assemble it in the requisite few minutes; but I was inept at target-shooting with it. Five shots at 100 yards would get me an average of four red flags (Maggie's Drawers, signaling a complete miss of the target) and one disc at the end of a pole (locating a hit) at the lower outside edge of the target. The TO (Table of Organization) weapon for the Anti-Tank platoon was the .45. For the I and R section it was the M1. My request for transfer to the AT platoon was denied. Qualification (Marksman) with the TO weapon was mandatory. Each Sunday morning following each of my failures to qualify, Corporal Rewalski drove me in a Jeep out to the rifle range, only to return with another failing score. On the fourth Sunday, he falsified my score (two points above failure); and no question was asked.

14

Three-hour passes were available for leisure time to be spent in the town near the camp; I can't recall its name: Gatesville, maybe; although that may have been the town near my first training camp—let's say Gainesville then.

Overnight and lengthier passes, to Dallas and Denton, were available. I went to Dallas only once, after I had been in the camp for about three months. To Denton I went many times. In the town, the USO (United Service Organization) would locate a room for me in a house with a hospitable family. The North Texas State Teachers College for Women sponsored dances that servicemen could attend. My awkward attempts at dancing were tolerated with smiles and encouragement by the students. Eventually one enjoyed my company enough to spend time off-campus with me. This was Shannon Estrella (Irish mother, Hispanic father), who, with her dark hair, dark eyes, soft unblemished complexion, and modestly winning smile, reminded me of Trish.

Shannon may, rightly, have sensed safe company in my shyness. We had long conversations in the park, in a restaurant, and taking walks during my limited days and nights in Denton. We attended two unenjoyable movies, *The Sullivans* (about five brothers in the Navy all killed on the same ship) and *Days of Glory* (Gregory Peck's first picture). She was a movie-goer, like me; and we talked very much about movies. She came to show her pleasure in our concurrences on movies and scenes by taking my hand. This led to hand-holding, which graduated to kissing and amorous embraces, but never to breaches of clothing or anything like the Gift of the Konshaks. I followed her lead, as I had in dancing, and that was it. She played the guitar and sang Spanish songs.

Repeatedly I ask her for *La Golondrina*. The somber waltz has the melodic melancholy of Beethoven's adagio. Her dark brown eyes take on the blackness of her hair as she sings the sadness of the exiled swallow. She taught me one line and made me sing it with her whenever she came to it: *buscando abrigo y no lo encontrará*. Despite my tone deafness and inability to carry a tune, she got me to master the melody, with which she harmonized. We dwell on the *no*, on the only final *o* in the line that is not elided. In that moment of harmony we understand all that we need to know about each other. We are not in love; we do not need to be.

We exchange letters between my almost weekly visits to Denton. She sends me, at my bothersome insistence, her translation of the song and her apology for imperfections that I cannot possibly recognize. The translation is here before me as I write. Her writing is faded, and the folds of the paper have worn into inch-long holes. Many of the words are no longer legible; but I have made written, and typed, and word-processed copies; and I have memorized it beyond forgetfulness:

> *Where will the swift and weary / swallow that leaves here go, / or what if it will get lost in the wind / seeking a shelter it does not find? // Close to my bed / it will find that nest / where it can spend a time of rest // Likewise am I / lost in the world / -O heavenly sky!- / and unable to fly. //*

Likewise I left my beloved land, / the house that looked upon my birth. / I live today in anguished wandering, / and I cannot go home again. // Dear, cherished pilgrim bird, / my heart will come to yours. / I shall hear your mournful song, my swallow; / I shall remember my land and weep, // shall remember my land and weep.

Buscand' abrig' y no l' encontrará. Seeking shelter and not finding it. After the passes to Denton came to an end, as too many things do in the army, there was one last exchange of letters. Hers ended, not with the usual *Devotedly, Shan*, but with *¡Adiós mi Perico!*

15

A Private is routinely promoted to Private First Class after a specified amount of time served. My promotion came about three weeks late because the company clerk (Malden-nose, as I think of him now) was lax in checking my record. It was to be the highest rank I attained in the Army. My two-week furlough was similarly delayed; my parents were genuinely happy to see me, but they seemed to grow awkward in my presence; my brothers and sisters were not impressed by my uniform with its single chevron; Les Berg gave me a true welcome, and we spent hours together listening to Beethoven; the train-ride back, during which I read the Modern Library edition of Col. G.F. Young's *The Medici*, was delayed for two days by a flood, for which delay I had not been obliged to give an accounting, as I would be a short time later for the already mentioned dereliction of KP duty.

Orders were cut for every Private and Pfc. in the Division to be shipped out and overseas as replacement riflemen. Here luck came about again. I am standing on the roadside with all of the Battalion's repple-depple (replacement depot) assignees, waiting, with my packed duffel bag, for the 6-by-6's, when the Battalion clerk comes running and takes me back to the barracks, where the I and R section will now consist of the Staff Sergeant, another Pfc., and me:

my record, again dilatorily noted, listed the need for partial dental plates, and I was not to be shipped out until I had undergone this dentistry.

Those who had been shipped out to repple-depples were replaced by a contingent of more ASTP candidates, along with Air Force trainees, whose hopes to avoid foot-soldier status had been, like mine, defeated. The seven who were added to the I and R section, making it over-strength, were Brady Malanothes, Irving Black, Schuyler Crispin, Michel Guinotte, Theron Kermon, Matthew Craymer, and John Ballew. Malanothes was a tall, oval-faced, inceptively exophthalmic mathematics enthusiast who despised me. Black was a short (about my height), stocky, dark complexioned, mechanically inclined individual who despised me. Crispin was a sturdy, pale-faced intellectual, who, despite his civility, did not bother to conceal his contempt for me. I was satisfied that, with my intellectual pretensions, I deserved their scorn. As something of a veteran in the Section, I must also have projected an assumption of seniority, forgetting, I suppose, that I had felt culturally superior to those in the Section whom I had initially joined. When Staff Sergeant Jeffrey Dermott left the Section for a week of special training for non-coms (non-commissioned officers), First Lieutenant Conway Clark, who, for whatever reason—maybe because he had been impressed by my offhand references to Beethoven and the Medici—had taken a liking to me, put me in charge of the Section, not for his positive attitude toward me but because, as a holdover, I now had the status of cadre.

My leadership was ludicrous. Guinotte, Kermon, Craymer, and Ballew dutifully but unenthusiastically kept to my cadence; Malanothes, Black, and Crispin openly ridiculed me, Crispin merely by sneering, Malanothes and Black by insubordinate activity and name-calling. I called the seven to attention, for example, to march them to a morning detail, and Black, lax and sneering, shouted out, *When they called for shit, you came sliding in on a shingle.*

Guinotte was the first of the true gentlemen I have met in this life of mine. Actually, I can recall perhaps only two others. He may not have liked me, but he consistently accorded me respect, never insulting me or joining others in verbal abuse.

He was dark, very good-looking, and gifted with movement of easy grace. His parents had moved to New England from Montreal and had become U.S. citizens before his birth. He was fluent in French and a graduate of an eastern prep school. He helped me with my rudimentary French, complimented me on my English usage, and agreed with me that *more perfect* was an imperfect comparative. It was good to be treated as an equal. Guinotte, Lt. Clark (CC, as we called him), and Theron Kermon were about the only persons in the Army to offer me any praise.

Crispin and Malanothes sucked up to Guinotte and secured themselves to him as the only ones capable of being his peers. Crispin had this capability. Malanothes, I was convinced, did not have it. I mispronounced *primer* (a beginning textbook), using the *i* of *prime coat* instead of the *i* of *prim*; Crispin condescendingly corrected me. Guinotte said that he himself had initially mispronounced it as I had and that the variation in *prime* and *primer* was not entirely logical. Once, when Malanothes and I were on the bus to town, Malanothes spoke of someone's having made *accostic* [maybe *acaustic*] *remarks*. I said that the word should be *caustic*. Malanothes summoned his scorn and said that he would accept correction from Guinotte but not from a *low-class prick like* me. I let this go, with the wan grin of one who knows that he is right, and smirked inwardly at the fury that reddened his oval face.

Malanothes was very proud of his membership in DeMolay and insisted repeatedly that I could never qualify for inclusion in that international order *comprised of* exceptionally intelligent, high-class young men. I didn't bother to correct his *comprised of* to *comprising*. He boasted that his father had connections that would get him out of *this stupid infantry*. The boast was made good: his father prevailed upon a senator to get the son out of a line outfit (a division in line to be sent into combat) and into Annapolis. Crispin had similar connections; but his senator worked more slowly: Crispin was a combat veteran of a month before his senator had him transferred to West Point. At bayonet practice, Guinotte, lunging with balletic grace, would intone *Thus smite I thee with ensate steel* and plunge the M1-mounted blade into the straw-filled uniform. He showed me some of his poetry. There was a line about a lady *reading Ovid in the tub*. Guinotte, Crispin, and I are drinking beer at the PX (Post Exchange). Guinotte quotes Pope: *True ease in writing comes from Art, not chance, / As those move easiest who have learned to dance.*

The couplet musically defines the never exceeded limits of my dancing and my writing. Crispin puts in his thoughts about *Great Wits* who *snatch a grace beyond the reach of Art*. Guinotte puts down Longfellow, Whittier, and Dreiser as writers of *such lays as neither ebb nor flow, / correctly cold and regularly low*. Crispin looks to me for my contribution and sees, smugly, only my swig of beer. Thinking back to my work at the U-town store, I vaguely recall a theme that Tom, the other part-time custodian, had let me read. His quoting Pope's couplet about *words* being *like leaves* had impressed me. I cannot, however, recall more than those words and something about little sense abounding; so, with my head turned away from the conversation, I keep thinking that the two quotations chosen by Guinotte sum up my movements and my writing.

Crispin wonders why *guerilla*, the diminutive of *war*, should denote the agent instead of the action. *It's like NURSE*, Guinotte explains: *nourishment becomes the nourisher, fighting becomes the fighter, action becomes the actor; how do you tell the dancer from the dance?* Crispin recognized the reference to a line from Yeats; I did not. Guinotte thinks it more curious that *gorilla* is traceable to the nineteenth-century *Gorillai*, a traveler's word for a tribe of hairy women. I drink more beer.

There is another increment of buck privates, necessitating reassignments in HQ Company. Black and Guinotte are transferred to the AT platoon. Malanothes is transferred to the Communications platoon, but will soon be off to Annapolis. I wish that Crispin instead of Guinotte had been transferred, and I am puzzled that, with my request to be transferred to AT on record, I remain in the I and R section. Later, trailing off from his singing of *Mairzy Doats*, during a night exercise, CC confides to me that, called upon to do so, he had made the recommendations for the transfers from the I and R.

A few days after the night exercise (patrolling to locate machine-gun emplacements), the PX sound system played Sammy Kaye's *Mairzy Doats*, and the title was clarified as *Mares eat oats*. Other numbers were constants: *I'll Be Seeing You; How Sweet You Are; Sunday, Monday, and Always; Long Ago and Far Away*: Bing Crosby, Dick Haymes, Frank Sinatra. There was Glenn Miller with *Elmer's Tune* and *American Patrol*, the Andrews Sisters with *Ferryboat Serenade* and *Boogie Woogie Bugle Boy of Company B*. Sinatra was something new because of the bobby-soxer-swoon staging that caught on successfully. He was better in phrasing, legato, and expression than the other crooners of the time, but not so mellow as Crosby. Crispin had called Sinatra *vocal smoke*.

Guinotte had nodded and said that Crosby and Sinatra amounted to *vocal ease and vocal ooze*. For *Mairzy Doats* I came up with a phrase that I had planned to try out on Guinotte: *hideous homophony*. Before the opportunity to do so came about, I had realized that *hideous* was wrong, being applicable to sight or morality (like Stevenson's *Mr. Hyde*) and not to sound; and, in silence, with beer, I seconded Crispin's *debauched conundrum*, which Guinotte, for whatever reason, bothered not to top.

What I learned from Guinotte I have retained along with my inability to put the lessons entirely into practice. Don't laugh at another person's mistakes. Don't openly or directly correct another person's syntax, pronunciation, or usage. Always assume that another person is at least your peer. Study Latin so that you can think in Latin [I should not have neglected it during my first year in college.]. Do not consider yourself educated if you have not achieved competence in mathematics and classical Greek. Every woman is a Dantean Beatrice, a guide toward what is perfect; no woman is an object or a project. The appreciation of true literature is a spiritual experience. You can lose faith; but, while you have faith, you can't lose anything else. Heroism is the refusal to yield to the futility of a necessary fight. Living is a necessary fight.

Crispin regularly invited me to join him when he went to the AT platoon to pick up Guinotte for a walk to the PX and beer. I owe him that.

16

The Division moved out. A troop train carried it from Texas through Louisiana, Mississippi, Alabama, Georgia, the Carolinas, and up to Camp Shanks in New York. I remember our stopping in Jackson, Mississippi, where we got out of the train and performed calisthenics. I remember passing through, or by, Washington, D.C.

I remember Camp Shanks as hills of forests, with leaves just beginning to turn yellow and bright red, a camp as different from the camps in Texas as the first I and R guys with whom I trained, and their preoccupation with *machismo* and *cunt*, were from the current ones, whose preoccupation was with class and academe.

Training was given over to orientation in the realities of combat and to writing our first letters to be censored by officers. I wrote a letter to my mother; I told her that I was now training in a different camp and that, when and if I should be sent overseas, my only worry was about the competence of the officers in this outfit: would they be good enough to ensure our effectiveness and safety in combat? I knew that whatever officer read the letter would pass it around to the others. It was my way of making, with impunity, a unilateral statement to the officers, not to CC, although I knew that he would get to see it and I regretted his having to do so, but to the fledgling shavetails fresh [emphatic redundancy] from OCS (Officer Candidates School). The letter was returned to me as improperly informative; only a few lines had not been excised. I wrote a letter to Blackie and used our *Dawn Patrol* format: Donny catches up to Scotty, meaning that shortly I would get to the ETO (European Theatre of Operations), where he was. I figured that a letter addressed to a First Lieutenant would impress the censor; and I later learned from Blackie that not a word had been cut out.

There were lectures, calisthenics, and KP; but there was also much free time with extended opportunities to spend it in New York City. Those of us in the HQ platoon generally paired off to head for the city. Terry Kermon and I made the trip many times—a short train ride and ferryboat ride. Terry's parents had connections in New York. His mother had relatives in show business; his father provided him with phone numbers of companionable women. Terry, a suave, smooth-voiced aesthete, had never been to New York; but he was impressed by neither its fame nor its size. I was very eager to see Times Square. Many movies had establishing shots of Times Square, with the glittering Planters Peanuts sign on the *Times* building. When we stepped off the ferry after our first crossing, Terry yielded to my insistence that we go straight up 42nd Street to Broadway to see Times Square. *So?*, he droned, when we got there. I was disappointed: the glittering sign was advertising something other than Planters Peanuts—some beer, I think. We went to the Stage Door Canteen. It was small, not very crowded that late afternoon, and without the presence of any celebrities. Terry called a recommended contact, and we went to Brooklyn to be entertained by her and her friend, both of whom must have been as old as Terry's father.

RAIN AND DARKNESS

Currie, my friend for the evening, was thin; and she giggled a lot. I was deflated and embarrassed as she undressed: her undergarments were loose and unattractive; her breasts were small and sagging; her black pubic hair spread to her thighs and almost to her navel. Skillfully, she gave me my first blowjob. My pleasure was attenuated by what was being done to my vision of womanly glory. Three disappointments in the big city.

Another disappointment marked a trivial turning point. Terry had Sunday KP. The barracks were empty, except for two day-sleepers. Feeling uneasy in the empty daylight and not wanting merely to remain, either on the edge of my bunk or in the day-room with a book, I took the train to the city. Without Terry's resources, I was limited to walking about, looking in shop windows, sitting for awhile in the lobby of the Hotel Astor, and, finally, going to a movie just off Times Square. The picture was *Frenchman's Creek*, based on the novel by Daphne du Maurier. Mitchell Leisen's direction of the costume drama centered, it seemed, on the costumes and not on the drama. Joan Fontaine and Arturo de Cordova, condescending to Talbot Jennings's script, sank into vapidity. After forty minutes, I walked out of the theatre into the off-white afternoon. Up to this time, I had never walked out on a movie, no matter how dull it might be. It would have been the equivalent of not finishing a book I had begun to read or of leaving untouched any served portion of food or drink. It was a type of incompleteness that I associated with the invalid sentence fragment.

I walked out of the theatre, however, without compunction. It surprised me a bit that I felt good about doing so. It was a statement. Not one that could be heard. A statement, though, is no less a statement for not being heard. One always hears one's self, in any case. At that moment, I revised my concept of sentence fragments: they may be stylistically good or bad; but, as a key to a whole, they are generally valid. I began to understand Mr. Nedayan's indifference to sources for subjective judgments. Later, I would leave unsatisfying books unfinished (beginning with Lloyd C. Douglas's *The Robe*), taking my cue from aleatory segments of a text with negative literary odds.

Blackie alone was to understand the import of this exit. He answered the letter in which I explained it to him and, although showing friendly contempt for my sentence-fragment analogue, commended me on this spurt of independence.

17

We are carrying our duffel bags into the grey vaulted steel of the troopship at dusk. Jokes, profanity, and laughs are harshly echoed from the hard metal that fills the hollowness. We reach our bunks, which rise in cramped tiers of four. Mine is a bottom bunk, only a few inches above the steel. I am not claustrophobic, but I am not comfortable.

The first two days on the Atlantic Ocean are calm with sunshine. It is pleasant to sit on the deck, to look out over the sea with its warm salt smell, and to watch our naval escort. On an upper deck, Catholic GI's kneel in confession, one at a time, before their chaplain; they receive communion.

On the third day, the sky is dark grey and the sea is rough. I become seasick and vomit continuously; when there is nothing left to vomit, the heaving continues: the dry heaves. I lose my orientation and, in dizziness, know neither left from right nor up from down. Nausea: the Greek word for the condition of being on a ship. On the fifth day, the Captain, informed of my state by a Sergeant, gets me into a shower, which, despite its thin spiky stream, feels very good, and takes me into a mess kitchen for toast and water, which I manage not to regurgitate.

The sea is calm as we pass through the Straits of Gibraltar. It is dusk, but there is enough light for us to see both the Rock and the African coast.

Marseilles, and the solidity of land: I feel a new surge of life. There is a long march, through the narrow streets of the city, where old men and women hand us bottles and cups of wine, and out into the countryside and darkness and, after many hours, to a high, barren site, where we buddy up, combine our shelter halves, and pitch our pup-tents. My buddy, here, is the battalion bugler. The ground, muddy from recent rain, is riddled with jagged stones. The mud will not stabilize the tent pegs that I try futilely to pound into it.

Others, with more dexterity and control, are getting their tents up and into use. I flounder and curse, and lose my breath, irritated that Jack, the bugler, offers no help and, lying back on his equipment, simply says, *Man, you're beat.* Not long before Jack goes off to the newly set up flag mast to sound *Taps*, the pegs at last accept the bracing of stones that I have put to use. Jack returns to crawl into the tent and under the blankets that I have laid out. Before the hours of sleep have fully restored my energy, Jack wakes me by crawling out of the tent to sound *Reveille*. Getting up with the bugler gets me to the head of the line at mess; for this, my resentment of his reserving the right not to help with the tent fades a bit—and, later, after a few days, it disappears as he talks to me about his gigs, his cornet solos, his having done a turn with the Glenn Miller Orchestra in Chicago, and his theory about Boogie-woogie (counterpoint as the disciplining of crowded desires).

Rides into Marseilles were frequently available. Sometimes there were details, like loading sacks of potatoes and canned food supplies onto 6x6's from cargo ships; sometimes, after leaving our names with the First Sergeant, there were unsupervised rides into the old and tired city. Ballew, Guinotte, and I spent an afternoon and early evening—the last 6x6 would leave Marseilles at 1830 hours—walking about streets of the port and frequenting the brasseries. We were seated at a small round marble-topped table in one, when two gendarmes entered. *La loi*, Guinotte called out and invited them to join us. They smiled but demurred. Guinotte went over to them at the counter and engaged them in small talk. They told him, he said, that we could get our canteens filled with wine here. We did this before leaving; and I spoke my first French to a resident of France, *C'est plein d'eau* (*It's full of water*—meaning my canteen), mispronouncing *plein*, I think; but the serveuse nodded, repeated my pronunciation of the clause, and took my canteen. *Rouge ou blanc?* I answered, *Rouge*. She emptied the canteen and returned it filled with dry red wine. I thought that my French might have impressed the laconic Ballew, but he, deceptively listless as always, was vaguely occupied in staring at the tightly aproned breasts of the serveuse, who, without need of words, filled his canteen with red wine.

Guard detail at the staging area was the worst of the duties. Walking around the Company's perimeter for two hours was almost achingly boring. I pulled two of these watches, both of them after midnight on moonless nights. Thinking through memorized songs and poems, contriving sentences in French, daydreaming about naked women, I tried unsuccessfully to neutralize the static passage of time.

The chill in the air was defeated by my constant movement and my shifting of the M1 from one shoulder to the other, but the dark stretch, aggravated by the elongated quarter-hours, knew no defeat and even followed me through the brevity of my resumed sleep.

Jack returned from sounding *Reveille* one morning and told me, almost expressionlessly, that during the night the high and massive telephone pole at the other end of the camp had fallen diagonally through a line of tents. A number of sleeping GI's were injured, and two, who had taken the full weight of the pole across their bodies, were killed. After morning mess, a few of us went to look at our battalion's first casualties, the bodies were still under the canvas; the pole was still transecting them.

At my suggestion to Jack that it could have been us who took the weight of the pole, he insisted, somewhat at variance with his usual easy cool, that it could not have been. *That's not our music, Pete.* Thinking of Beethoven, I said that maybe my music was the third movement of the Ninth. He smiled and said that what he meant was the music that existence orchestrates for each of us. Then he nodded and said that I must catch the third movement of Mahler's Fourth, which begins in the heaven to which Beethoven's strings aspire and then drops with disconsolate humor to earth. Then he described Mahler's *Das Lied von der Erde*, and I was enthralled, and I realized that the pole could not have fallen on us. Softly Jack sang the haunting *Ewig . . . . ewig.*

Limiting this review of a loser's life to those recollections that most vividly assert themselves, I have to mention the broken-yoked water wagon standing in a ditch of the road at the east end of the camp. In one of his letters, Blackie said that winners survey broad plains of memory, while losers look to distant peaks of things recalled. He said that I could understand the nature of losing by bringing many peak events into a lonely landscape of recollection. *Just the peaks, Pete.* Zane Grey comes up with better metaphors than that; but I got his point; and that water wagon is a peak I don't know why. The long metal cylinder I now see as orange with black lettering; but it must have been sand-colored in its wooden frame. The tires on the wheels were flat, one shredded by shot. There was no sign of the horses; either they survived or their carcasses had been somehow disposed of. The yoke was snapped, probably by the wagon's having been pushed by a tank or wrecker into the ditch. The black letters spelled out TRINKWASSER.

Matt Craymer and I were on the road and walking toward it, when a sergeant from Communications, whose name I can't recall, pointed to it as he came toward us from the opposite direction and said, *That's a German water wagon.* He pointed to the black letters and said, *That means Drinking Water.* Matt and I looked at each other and agreed in silence that we probably could have figured that out.

18

The rumble of the 6x6's was constant after *Reveille* one day. By dawn they were stretched out in a long olive-drab line on the narrow road. In the cold morning mist, I pulled out the stakes, removed the ropes, separated the shelter halves, and rolled a field pack into each. Jack, sitting on a large, round stone, took his and nodded. It was now gratifying, instead of irritating, to do Jack's work along with mine. We let the packs lie, went to the mess tent for what would be our last hot meal for a while, and then returned to sit on the packs and wait.

Shortly after 0830 hours, Jack went off with a lieutenant to a G Company jeep. I and R climbed into one of the trucks that were carrying F Company. I sat with Matt. We both looked back at the ditched water wagon as our truck rolled past it. Matt is, I suppose, volatile. He's bitter about military hierarchy, hates non-coms and officers when they give orders or pull rank. Back in Texas he had refused to sew on his Pfc. chevrons until the First Sergeant threw a needle and thread on his bunk and slapped him on the head. He loses his temper easily. But he's often in an amused state of mind and ready with his Confucius Say or his wisdom of the *Mighty Mandarin Ho Shih Lit*. Like: *Confucius say, Officer who often stand with finger up his ass ought not to pick his nose.* Or: *Mighty Mandarin Ho Shih Lit curses silly, slothful farmer,*

RAIN AND DARKNESS

May the zizzyvas expose your wife's unholy hole by consuming her cotton underpants!

Around 1400 hours, the long, spread-out column of trucks comes to a halt, and we are ordered by arm-waving non-coms to dismount and disperse. Two fighter planes are heading directly for the column at what is clearly an altitude for strafing. Trying to imagine the range of the spray, I run far out onto the roadside field and curl up behind a small tree. The planes are American. Back in the truck, Matt quotes the Mighty Mandarin Ho Shih Lit: *Great gullible green American infantry division annihilated on way to front.* He gives his r's an Oriental liquid distortion.

The ride up the Rhone valley is long and wearying. During night stops, we dig holes and sleep, usually two men to a hole, in shelter halves and blankets. We reach the Vosges Mountains and stop some fifteen kilometers behind the front line. Matt and I share a hillside dugout spotted with traces of its German diggers, including usable wafer candles, by the light of which we write letters. Early in the morning, variously littering with K-ration boxes and cans the deep green swards of the rising hills, the battalion lines up in columns on the road-shoulders and moves forward. At the high point of a long uphill trudge, Headquarters Company falls out; the rifle companies continue on, downhill now, toward the sound of mortar shells and rifle shots. Moving slowly, tiredly, and gratefully along the road back toward the echelons behind us are platoons of the division we are relieving. A rectangular sign reads *Col du Haut Jacques.* Crispin, whose French is almost as good as Guinotte's, tells us that this is Jack's Height. My awkward reading of it had been *James High Pass.*

The area is heavily wooded beyond the clearing in which we stop. A road runs west, or at least left, from our direction of approach, and disappears into the pines. Battalion officers are quartered in the single house on the east, or right, side of our approach road. The I and R settle into the garage, or shed extension, of this house. We surrender our blankets and shelter halves and are issued sleeping bags, cumbersome but lightweight. That night, sheltered from light falling snow, warm in the new sleeping bags, we sleep well.

The morning sky is grey with clouds. Matt, Terry, and I have latrine duty. We remove from the outhouse at the rear of our quarters a huge, tin, hemispheric container, running over with shit and piss, from its enclosed pit to a newly dug waste pit across the clearing, at the edge of the pine woods.

There we pause to stare at a dead German soldier. He is supine, his tunic ripped open, his boots, helmet, and rifle gone, his skin stone white around the blue hollows of his half-closed eyes. Next day, at dawn, Matt, Crispin, and JB (Jack Ballew) take the road down the valley to man an OP (observation post). Dermy (Sergeant Dermott) returns after taking them to the OP, which is an attic in a house overlooking a long valley of receding hills. CC sends Terry and me on various errands for the officers. The E Company captain is now among the officers. He had chickened out and could not take up E Company's CP (command post) in yesterday's attack. A platoon lieutenant had two riflemen bring him back to HQ Company and assumed the captain's duties. The captain was thereafter assigned the duty of Awards and Decorations Officer. His first award, by order of the Battalion Commander, was a Bronze Star to the lieutenant who had relieved him and who, within a week, was promoted to Captain, taking over

RAIN and DARKNESS

E Company. During the weeks to come, we were always glad to be where the ADO was, because it meant that we were not very near the enemy. Between duties, as we were lunching on K-rations, Terry and I heard, and felt, the vibrations of an explosion. We looked to the small field to the left of our shed-quarters to see a jeep turned on its side, shrouded in smoke lined with red flames, and a GI on his knees with his blackened arms raised as he tried to move. The small field was bordered by the junction-angle of the two roads; the area was going to be used as a pool for three jeeps and a command car. The first of the jeeps had set off a mine. A couple of medics were immediately at the site to place the inert driver upon a stretcher and to attend to the kneeling GI. A second mine, timed to explode within five minutes of the first, then blew up right under the medics. Now there came black smoke, orange flames, black faces streaked with blood, and flailing arms. One of the medics died; two medics and the passenger were severely wounded and evacuated within the hour; the driver, a Tech Sergeant, died, his lower extremities having been blown off. Tmetically and sympathetically, Terry said, *Tough fuckin' shit*. [What's it all about, George?] The dead—the medic and the Tech Sergeant—were laid out on a wooden walk in back of the house, or, as we learned, the inn, in which we were quartered. They lay, covered with canvas, only a few yards from the latrine. The canvas did not quite cover the Tech Sergeant's hair and forehead. The forehead was white in the icy air, which, in its counterclockwise movement, stirred strands of the light brown hair.

My turn for the OP watch came. The observation post was, as I've said, a roadside house overlooking a long winter-green valley bounded by the hills of the Vosges mountains.

Four of us took turns sitting in the loft, from which enough roof tiles had been removed to provide a lookout. Each turn was for two hours. After half an hour, my imagination was bringing shells directly into that aperture. I pictured myself shell-shredded and annihilated. The sounds of shells and rifle-fire along the hills aggravated my uneasiness. I went downstairs. *Get your ass back up there*, Crispin ordered. Returning to the stairs, I picked a book at random from the few that remained on a dust-covered shelf at the base of the stairs. There was a choral order: *Don't be reading up there!*

The spot by the opening in the tiles was comfortable. There were blankets to cover myself with, and a down comforter and a heavy wooden crate to lean back against. I scanned the valley with the binoculars: columns of shell smoke, but no vehicles or men. The book was a leatherette-covered, pocket-sized copy of Thomas Hardy's *Jude the Obscure*. Surprised at the book's being an English novel instead of some text in French, I began to read in the early afternoon light: *The schoolmaster was leaving the village, and everybody seemed sorry*. It was to take me some six weeks to finish this novel, by daylight and candlelight, during moments of inactivity. It was to become my unchallenged favorite novel, to fashion my resolve to get back to Latin, which I was now very sorry not to have continued during my college year, and to learn Greek as well, to direct me toward school-teaching for a livelihood, and eventually to identify Jude Fawley as my existentialist exemplar. Blackie would come to comment on the appropriateness of my identifying myself with a loser. *Here a little book of tales which Jude had tucked up under his arm, ... to read on his way ... before it grew dark ...* I would pick up the binoculars at irregular intervals; but Hardy's story was now in command of my imagination. When the war is over, I told myself, I shall read everything that Hardy has written. I had already read *The Return of the Native* during study-hall periods in high school, but I would read it again. *Somebody might have come along that way . . . . But nobody did come, because nobody does.* I was still reading when Matt came to relieve me. He smiled, said nothing, and picked up the binoculars.

19

The Battalion successfully carried out its first combat mission, to take and secure *Hill 6*. The Section moved out from Col du Haut Jacques and from its OP to quarters in a luxurious, but now much neglected house farther along the narrow road. Here we took it easy for one night and two days, writing letters and, in my case, reading *Jude*, and playing Monopoly with the Protestant chaplain and his assistant. The chaplain was proud of his Monopoly board, which he kept in good condition. He reserved the role of Dealer to himself. He regularly palmed $500 bills, and he regularly won. Once, when I saw him move his little automobile piece illegally, I glanced at his assistant, whose resigned grin meant that he was used to this.

Mail call. Les Berg wrote about music and expressed his pleasure at my having tented with Jack. My mother wrote about my father's new steady job on road construction and about his buying a new fiddle, about my brothers and sisters at school, and about Jordy Klug's making a lot of money at a munitions plant.

At dusk, after our second day in the comfortable quarters, we crowded into 6x6's for an hour's ride to another sector. Then, attached to F Company, we marched, with lengthy halts, for about two hours to a village, where barns and small houses served as quarters for two nights and days. On the

RAIN and DARKNESS

second day, Crispin departed, on his way back to the States and West Point.

A daytime march, after a welcome hot meal, took us down a cold, winding road, on the shoulders of which lay a number of dead German soldiers in various postures of retreat. We broke ranks twice to take off-road cover from mortar shellings. Then we turned off the paved road onto a wagon-rut road, where we moved silently around and past quite a few dead GI's. I stared curiously at one who had been propped up against a tree, his head bent toward his left shoulder, his hands folded in his lap, his helmet on the ground. A buddy or, more likely, a chaplain may have attended him as he died.

The Company turned off into a woods, formed echelons, dropped frequently under increasing mortar whistles and bursts, and moved forward to the trees' edge at the end of an open field, at the other side of which lay a village—a few houses along a dirt road, a small church and churchyard, trees, and, well covered and dug in, German riflemen, a machine-gun emplacement, and two mortar emplacements, the components of which rear guard we were only later to learn. Our 75's and mortars screamed and whistled overhead, crashing in red blasts along the village front. F Company moved out in flanking arcs. Halfway across the field, they began to fall. I could see Lieutenant Antonelli running forward, then back to check one of his fallen men, then forward, yelling and waving his .45. He and a flanking squad were the first to reach the village; they took out the machine-gun emplacement with a volley of grenades. As the other flankers got to the village, one platoon and the I and R, led by CC, moved across the center of the field; but by now the defenders were throwing down their rifles and helmets. *Kameraden!*

The Germans who had surrendered were searched for potato-masher grenades—but chiefly for watches and Lugers; they were marched back to Regiment. Medics carried wounded GI's on stretchers back toward an aid station. I watched in admiration as Lieutenant Antonelli, his canteen pierced by enemy fire, checked out his platoon. He was still flushed from the heat of the advance. He swore and called out, *They got Stoney. They got Mack.* Stoney was a tall, angular Blackfoot Indian, who had done Regimental Detail with me and whose antipathy to discipline I had much admired. His buddy, Mack, was a fair-haired, tight-assed, spit-and-polish athletic guy from Fargo. They had been drafted together. Good friends. Good soldiers. First across the field, Stoney had been cut down by machine-gun fire. Mack had run over to him and fell from the same fire. Stonehand (I never knew his first name); and Martin (Mack) Bluestein.

Short, almost obese Father Murphy, who had moved out with the left flankers, moved now among the dead and performed last rites. Scratching the back of my neck, I wondered how he could have run all the way across that field, some three hundred meters, without getting thoroughly winded and without getting hit.

With the platoon with which we had moved across the field, now led by CC and Lieutenant Szymanski, and with Barney Corson of the Communications Platoon, carrying his huge back-pack radio, we advanced eight kilometers up the road to a small town. We spread out, picked up four German soldiers (three stragglers caring for one with a leg wound), commandeered seven or eight houses for quarters, and began liberating food and valuables.

RAIN AND DARKNESS

Barney radioed the *All clear*. By nightfall, F Company and Headquarters Company had settled in.

Around 2300 hours, the 6x6's were rolling through the town. By morning, we were Regimental Reserve.

20

As dead as a fern-leaf in a lump of coal... Hardy's Sue Bridehead says this of mediaevalism; but it turns my thoughts to Stoney and Mack and the guys who went down before we moved out over the field. The GRO (Graves Registration Office) team, surgically masked, will come for them in a few days. I shall eventually conclude that Hardy's Sue is wrong: mediaevalism, as the stern convictions of a cabbage-patch world, will carry its divine darkness into the twenty-first century and, doubtless, beyond, unless or until human shortsightedness yields to the bleak glare of reality.

A hot meal had been served: steak, creamed peas, fried potatoes, buttered buns, and apple pie (all piled onto insufficiently large mess kits), along with hot coffee (in the mess cups into which our canteens are otherwise fitted). The four compliant Wehrmacht *Soldaten*, whom, by twos, we take turns guarding, had gratefully been served the same meal and are even more gratefully enjoying the optional cigarettes. One of them, during my watch with Terry, had asked the old woman of the house, as she was about to go out across the *cour* to feed a cow and a horse, *Ist dies dein Haus?* She had nodded, spearing her pointed Alsatian chin sharply down. Dermy, the I and R Staff Sergeant, is napping on the bed, the only one in the house, which he had used his rank to appropriate exclusively for himself. I am sitting on a wooden chair, its brown paint chipped, exposing a dark green layer. I am reading more of *Jude the Obscure*. I like the third-person narration. A number of colloquialisms bother me somewhat.

Later, when I ask Guinotte about them, he explains them all and agrees with me that Hardy's use of *he only wore spectacles when reading at night* and *to hastily tidy* and other aberrations, like *the future lay ahead*, does not confer correctness upon them. Guinotte explains that the instances of faulty prose do not despoil the intensity of the novel: they constitute *shelf language*, usages too readily available to be avoided in favor of condign precision. I dislike the metaphor, but I accept the explanation (the excuse).

The depth of the cow's lowing is broken by its palatal sounds. The horse snorts. Snow is falling. Weariness overtakes my growing loneliness for Trish. Shadows spread over the fallen snow. During the night, the old lady kept a fire going for us. In the morning, MP's came for the PW's. It was after I sought out Guinotte and while we had our hot lunch together that I talked with him about *Jude the Obscure*. He didn't care much about Hardy, whom he saw as one who whined too lengthily about societal constraints. I took *Jude* to be an opposition to the constraints that individuals impose upon themselves by nullifying their ability to get what they want by willingly settling abortively for something less. Jude Fawley, I said, never settled for less than learning the Latin and Greek that, in fact, he would never get to master. Guinotte recommended Henry James, James Joyce, and Virginia Woolf. I would read *The Waves* and *The Years* in Armed Services editions after VE Day and other of Woolf's novels after I returned to the university on the GI Bill of Rights—and Henry James and James Joyce and Thomas

Mann and Marcel Proust, and more and more—but after *Jude*, my liberated leatherette-bound copy of which I kept in my field-jacket pocket long after I had finished it, I read Thomas Wolfe's *Look Homeward, Angel* and *Of Time and the River*, which Matt had received from home, long before VE Day, and had let me read, and then, again after VE Day, Robert Graves's *I, Claudius* and *Claudius the God*, which, like the Woolf novels, became available in Armed Services editions and which furthered my determination to get back to the study of Latin as soon as possible.

My mother, in response to my asking her to send me a couple of books to read, but without, unfortunately, my having specified any titles, sent *The Pony Rider Boys on the Alkali*—as a pre-teenager, I had read many of the *Pony Rider Boys* books—and *Dave Dashaway on Guadalcanal*. I was about to throw them into a little fire that Joe Radosta had built beside his jeep, while he worked on the engine. Joe asked if he might have them. He was to read them both and pass them to others.

Thereafter I saw various readers of one or the other of the books, including, to my disappointment in surprise, the Headquarters Company CO, Captain Ashley. He was reading *Dave Dashaway*.

21

A unit that had been on line in an attack would subsequently be moved into reserve. Companies would revert to battalion reserve, battalions to regimental reserve, regiments to divisional reserve. Divisional reserve provided hot meals, showers, and, occasionally, entertainment—such as, in our turn, Marlene Dietrich and, at another time, Bob Hope with Jerry Colonna—but also chickenshit details: guard duty, KP (kitchen police, police meaning clean up, as though the etymology were Latin *polire* [polish, refine] instead of Greek *polis* [city, state]), shortorder drill, and other forms of idleness-prevention. Within this well-ordered system, our battalion was on line in attack maybe twenty percent of the time. About thirty-five percent of the time, we were dug in on line in defensive positions. Our regimental section of the European Theatre of Operation was Alsace-Lorraine, through the Maginot and Siegfried Lines into Germany, from Landau to Worms, across the Rhine and northeast to Hanau and Fulda, then southwest to Aschaffenburg, then generally southeast to Wertheim, Waiblingen, Urach, and Landsberg, into the Alps to Garmisch-Partenkirchen, and finally to Austria: Telfs, Zirl, and Innsbruck, with our Company (HQ) stopping some nine kilometers from Innsbruck on the Inn River at Wattens, our location as the war ended in Europe.

In combat, I lived with the helpful but unfriendly earth in disorienting darkness and ominous daylight, sleeping in a warm bag upon hard ground, living in dugouts, observing (as scout) from hillside holes roofed over with logs, prone under shellings of mortars, eighty-eights, and screaming meemies (the *Nebelwerfer*).

If I'm still alive on my next birthday, I'll make it, I told myself; and so, as a matter of history, it came to be. Once, digging in along a roadside, I noticed the Protestant chaplain's assistant digging for the chaplain a hole that went almost seven feet into the black earth. On a hill one night, behind a tree, and flat to the earth, I trembled and perhaps wept under an eighty-eight shelling that crashed into and shattered trees and caused the earth to undulate in wracked upheaval, so that my unbuckled helmet left my head and rolled audibly down the hill and out of retrieval and the partial bridge that had saved me from repple-deppledom flew out of my mouth, never to be found. Nor was my helmet recovered; it lay, somewhere in the darkness, as we left the area after the shelling. It was not until we went into regimental reserve, about a week later, that I secured a helmet replacement; I had, meantime, pulled up and worn over my head the button-on hood of my field jacket.

The names of villages, towns, and cities drift about in recollection, as I now look over my erratically composed diary-notes: Colroy la Grande, Ville (Weiler), Neuve Église, Séléstat (Schlettstadt), Diefenthal, Schalkendorf, Gunstett, Soultz, Wissembourg, Rechtenbach, Guenviller, Mattstall, Lembach, Pfaffenhoffen, Obersoultzbach, Klingenmünster. Over the years, I somehow, in recollection, conflated Klingenmünster and Salmünster; the former was the terminus of our Battalion's all-night task force, as it broke through the German line; the latter was the scene of a pleasant interlude, during which the I and R Section shared the home of twelve-year-old Karl-Heinz and his mother and sister. I had come to think that Karl-Heinz's home was in Klingenmünster.

Are the names right? Is *Aschaffenburg* perhaps *Aschaffenberg?* Is the route right? It's hard to say; and I'm too lazy to get my huge National Geographic atlas and check the maps, map-reading having always been a tedious exercise for me. Nor have I ever had any directional sense: I can read the morning and evening sun, the evening and morning star, and the North Star with its constancy; but, as a scout with a compass, I would shoot an azimuth on a cloud and get lost.

Schalkendorf to Bitschoffen to Mietesheim to Mertzweiler to Morsbronn to Gunstett, where we jumped off as front line; through Kutzenhausen, Surbourg, Soultz, Oberhoffen, and on to a hill near Rechtenbach, where resistance stopped our advance. The hill, part of a heavily wooded mountain range (Harz? Hardt? Hart?), looked across a deep valley, at the bottom of which flowed a little stream, the Otterbach, I think. The hill on the other side of the valley was fortified by pillboxes.

Here, over five days and nights, from our base in a dugout, the Section manned the Battalion OP, carried rations to Companies F and G, which were dug in on Pillbox Hill, as we called it, carried messages to the same rifle companies, carried pole charges to Company G; riflemen had to thrust the explosive-laden pole charges through the pillbox embrasures and set them off. We guided artillery wire-men, carried new radios to replace radios damaged by shells and rifle fire, and took PW's to the Battalion CP (Command Post) in Rechtenbach.

The valley floor was green, although it was December, and the little stream made pleasant trickling sounds. Each detail took us down our valley side, across the stream by a short jump, up the pillbox valley side, then back down the pillbox valley side, across the stream, and up our valley side. On the third day, Terry and I joined four G Company riflemen on a patrol to determine the incidence of machine-gun emplacements behind the line of pillboxes. Splitting up into pairs, we did not have to go far before spotting the giveaway nettings at about forty-meter intervals. Terry and I were to report this to Battalion CP. As we moved back past the line of pillboxes, one of the riflemen, a tall guy, was shot in the back of the neck, just under the helmet rim. Patrols were not usually fired upon; but it appeared that our patrol was to be taught a lesson. We managed to carry the rifleman back to the G Company CP. He was dead when we reached it.

Terry and I crossed the stream and rested in a hollow that bordered it. The hollow was about five feet deep and without grass, its brown-soil walls extending for about twenty meters in either direction. After about ten minutes, Terry moved up and out; and when he was about ten meters away, I followed. We were caught almost immediately in a mortar barrage. These came routinely into the valley twice a day—never at the same times. We hit the earth. *Terry, let's get back to the ditch.* I was already crawling backwards toward it. *I'm hit,* Terry called back. I wanted only to get back to the relative safety of the hollow. The shells were still whistling in and bursting on the valley floor. I ran forward in a crouch and dropped down beside Terry. He had taken shrapnel in his right shoulder. The barrage lifted after about a dozen rounds had come in. I offered to treat the wound with a sulfa-drug packet; but Terry said, *Let's get out of this shithouse.* I took his M1 and helped him up the hill. The pain made him angry, and his anger gave him the energy needed to get all the way up to the Company CP. He was taken to the Battalion aid station. He would soon write us from Baccaleurs, where he was sent for surgery and recuperation. Within a few weeks, he rejoined the Section. Terry earned a Purple Heart.

His account of the incident led CC successfully to put me up for a Bronze Star. Each medal was valued at five points in the point system devised for sending GI's back to the States after VJ Day.

There were many casualties on both sides of that green valley, but no massed attack from or upon Pill Hill. The 45th Division relieved us. We marched from Rechtenbach to Wissembourg and we were then transported by 6x6's some 129 kilometers northwest to Diefenbach, a shell-shattered town. After a night there, we rode another nineteen kilometers to Guenviller. It was now Christmas Eve.

22

Our next move was to Merlenbach and then to Mattstall, out from which the Section maintained two OP's on the Maginot Line, overlooking Lembach and Wingen. Mattstall was shelled daily, always at different times. Then, one night, at 2200 hours, we saddled up and hit the road for a 33-kilometer strategic withdrawal, the euphemism for retreat. We marched in single file on either side of the road. Between the lines, jeeps and trucks and weapons-carriers kept moving. The cold and the roadside snow were bothersome only when there was a halt to let the vehicles pass. Field packs, however, M1's, and other impedimenta constituted weight that sleeplessness aggravated. Around 0400 hours, sounds of great weariness and despair increased. GI's actually fell asleep while walking and fell on the road in the dark. A few actually moved off to the side of the road to sleep and willingly to await the status of prisoners of war. Their officers could not get them to resume the march, not even by telling them that they would simply be shot by the advancing *Krauts*. Although I was very tired and found myself nodding at times and almost falling, I could not understand the willingness of these riflemen simply to give up; but I had not been a recent victim of dysentery or jaundice or exhaustion.

During the last few days, I had slept well in the Company CP in Mattstall and not in an open hole outside the town.

RAIN AND DARKNESS

Twenty-mile hikes in fair weather in the States, with rations, full canteens, and ten-minute breaks, were not equivalent to this thirty-three-kilometer forced march in cold midwinter darkness. A long rippling of resentment and potential revolt ran through the columns.

No light, beyond the dead grey snow along the sides of the road. The trees beyond the road were black. Village houses along the road were almost black. I remembered walking home from movies in the city's darkness; but there were arc-lights. I remembered Jordy's shooting at Blackie and me on the dark boulevard; but there were, again, arc-lights, and the headlights of a car. It would be good to slow our pace, to take a break; but we were prodded into non-stop jogging. A few more men dropped off to the sides of the road. The officers disregarded them now. We had to move faster. Entrenching tools, then sleeping bags, then field packs were tossed aside, but no M1's or BAR's (Browning automatic rifles). Faster. Darker. I seemed not to get at all accustomed to the darkness. Shellfire to our rear increased in proximity and volume.

After 0200 hours there were no more vehicles to hinder our stride. Eventually, a wave of weariness wore our movement down to a normal slog. Pick 'em up and put 'em down. Dawn did nothing for our spirits. I learned that one's spirits are a form of energy that, with enervation, can only wither. The overcast sky was a ghastly grey, almost too heavy to stare at. Under this sky, the familiar hill of Pfaffenhoffen rose off to our left. Our retreat was here defined. We were back in Pfaffenhoffen. I thought of Father Murphy: was this a *place of hope* for him? Not for me, too tired to lift my eyes to the lead-grey sky. I bent forward under the bleakness of a morning grey that was broken now only by the red, yellow, and white flashes of the big guns behind us; and

I was shaken with a fear I hadn't known before. *If ever,* I thought, *I come to think of war as anything but dreariness and death, I'll call to mind this moment.* At about 0800 hours, we moved into Schalkendorf, which once had been Division reserve. Quartered in a small house in two small rooms, we sank to the floor and slept until noon. What is now strange is that, long after the end of the war, I came to recall this moment of movement past Pfaffenhoffen in that grey January morning as the most beautiful of all the moments I had known in war.

23

About two months later, the Klingenmünster dawn, following a successful all-night task-force advance, was bright and welcome. We had broken through the Siegfried Line defenses and moved into Birkenhördt. From here we followed tanks and TD's (tank destroyers) toward Silz. We were cut off from behind and had to spread out from the road and into wooded areas to flush out German infantrymen. I found myself in darkness, cold with fear, not really knowing what to do, and certain that a rifle shot from somewhere would bring me down. My hope was that I would be only wounded and not killed. Irv Black, now with the Antitank Platoon, had borrowed an M1, from a GI wounded earlier in an artillery barrage that had hit our staging area, and was making angry noises. Listening to his curses and invectives—*Fuckin' Krauts!*—I felt encouraged. Then the order from the road: *Mount up—All clear*. The Third Battalion and the 14th Armored had broken through behind us. The 36th Division, covering our old sector, had taken Pillbox Hill without a fight. On trucks and weapons-carriers, we rode down the night road to Silz and into Klingenmünster with the dawn. PW's coming out of the woods and the roadside houses were lining up on the road. A number of us began singing the line, *What a difference a day makes*, changing it to *What a difference THE day makes*. We were now in Germany. Our campaign in Alsace-Lorraine was over. Field equipment, truckloads of

GI's, and weapons-carriers were rolling through the town. By morning's end, PW's were clearing rubble and policing the area. Within seven hours from our arrival, Klingenmünster had become Corps reserve.

After three days in Klingenmünster, we rolled out in trucks for a five-hour ride. I remember Maudach and Mundenheim. Our next quartering was in Ludwigshafen, where we looked across the Rhine to Mannheim. Spring came. On April 1, we watched Marlene Dietrich and her USO show in a park just outside of Ludwigshafen. Seated on the stage near her was the new General of our Division, Anthony C. *Nuts* McAuliffe.

We crossed the Rhine at Worms. The truck rides were long. The war was moving away from us. The General wanted to catch up to it. As we drove through Hanau, our Company clerk played waltzes on an accordion that he had picked up along the way. About twelve days after leaving Klingenmünster, we came to Salmünster. Yet my memory wants to place our Section's walking up the stairs of the house in which Karl-Heinz lived, not in Salmünster, but, at the terminus of our advance by the nightlong task force, in Klingenmünster. It is only by checking the remnants of my crude and puerile diary notes that I can counter the vagaries of my recollection. Blackie, without written notes of any kind, can accurately retrace his outfit's rolling advance to the outskirts of Berlin.

Karl-Heinz was about twelve years old, a very handsome boy, with dark hair and a smooth complexion. He, with his mother and sister, occupied the lower part of the house—a living room, kitchen, and two small bedrooms with a bath between them. Upstairs we crowded into two bedrooms, a bath, and a small kitchen. We never got to see the sister. Karl-Heinz said that she hated Americans, because American soldiers had killed her fiancé. She had moved back to this home after Hanau, where she worked and lived in an apartment, had been bombed out. Karl-Heinz called her Liesl. She never left the room she shared with her mother while any one of us was in the house. Karl-Heinz's mother was in a state close to mourning because she had been informed that her husband had been taken prisoner by the Russians. Karl-Heinz was certain that his father would be returned to them.

Despite the rules against fraternization, we were pleased to have Karl-Heinz and his mother spend many hours upstairs with us. The mother baked bread and cookies and made coffee for us. We provided her with flour, butter, sugar, and coffee that we hustled from the mess. They expressed contempt for our Battalion commander, Major Drasin, who they insisted was Jewish. It was impossible to dislodge Karl-Heinz and his mother from their anti-Semitism; but it was otherwise enjoyable to spend much time talking with them. Karl-Heinz reminded me of my brother Paul. They often expressed puzzlement or amusement at my halting and faulty German.

We would sing together the song about the Lorelei. We played guessing games: *Antworten Sie: Ja oder Nein!* It pleased me when Karl-Heinz and his mother made it clear how much better than the others in the Section they liked me. It may have been my German background; but Jack Ballew spoke better German than I and brought many smiles to the face of Karl-Heinz's mother. Jack was deep, though; and his easy charm covered a dark wisdom that, unfathomed, elicited reserve in those who knew that they were being charmed. My shallowness brought me more readily into this little household. Karl-Heinz and I established a sincere fraternity, for which, I came to understand, his mother was very grateful.

Matt came up with many *Ho Shih Lit* sayings, mostly about the unseen Liesl, like, *Girl who mourns for fallen Schatz joins the squad of tightwad twats*. Dermott, without regular detail assignments for the Section, spent most of his time playing Poker with four or five other Company non-coms. Guinotte had been sent back to Aid with, as it was called, *yellow jaundice* (I resented the redundancy); I was sorry not to be able to seek out his company. Ken Frank, who was added to the Section in Obersoultzbach, where we enjoyed a period of Division reserve between the retreat to Pfaffenhoffen and the advance to Klingenmünster, had been sent back with a case of clap. Terry spent his nights at the edge of town shacking up with a *Strohwitwe*.

27. Bn Hq Sect.
G. 6 scouts, observers, intelligence, who operate at bn. observation post(s) or accompany front line units, patrols, raiding parties, or reconnaissance and security detachments as intelligence scouts.

The Staff Sergeant in charge of us made seven. At this time we were: S/Sgt. Jeffrey Dermott, Cpl. Joe Cameron, one of the original members of the Section and second in command (or third, by counting 1st Lieut. Conway Clark, the officer to whom we were immediately responsible), Pfc. Theron Kennon, Pfc. Matthew Craymer, Pfc. John Ballew, Pfc. Kenneth Frank, Pfc. Peter Blaustern, and Pfc. Lauer Bertrand. Larry *Hellbent* Bertrand had been moved to the Section from A & P (the Ammunition and Pioneer

Platoon) when Frank went back to get his clap treated. *Ol' Hellbent* was a huge person who did nothing in small ways. *Burn the earth!* He liked to roar, as he killed, butchered, and cooked calves and lambs, or looted houses, or stripped PW's of their watches. He gained possession of two Leica cameras and three Lugers. He kept the Lugers well cleaned and oiled and managed to maintain a good supply of 9mm. ammunition.

The Section was almost always at full strength, frequently overstrength, as replacements were regularly available from both AT and A&P.

Karl-Heinz and I sincerely enjoyed each other's company. I respected him and considered him my peer, not *ein Junges*, as the others, particularly Ballew, considered him. His mother trusted only me to be alone with him, as when he led me out to a little warren behind the house one afternoon to look at his three rabbits. He also showed me his small box of treasures: a fountain pen, a framed photograph of his father in uniform, four gemstones, a supple leatherbound volume of lyrics by Heinrich Heine that he had won as a prize for elocution, a Kummerly+Frey map of Suddeutschland, and other items, the significance and value of each of which he enthusiastically explained to me. There was also a necktie-pin topped by a miniature ivory reindeer skull with five-point antlers; it was enclosed in a beige paper box with a light-green suede cover. The box measured an inch and a half by four inches. When he asked me if I would like any one of these treasures as a souvenir, I immediately selected the tie-pin. This he said he could not part with, because it was a gift from his father. I then chose the map, which he gave me with a smile. When, later, I asked his mother if I should keep the gift, she nodded, smiled, and kissed me on the cheek. That's the most any map has ever brought to me.

The headline in *The Stars and Stripes* was ROOSEVELT DEAD. For most of us this was a shock and gave us an undulance of regret. The Protestant chaplain held a special service, attended by about thirty of us. *Ol' Hellbent* did not attend; he was not moved by the death of FDR, whose person and policies he despised: *fuckin' ol' fagholder and spoon-in-the-mouth bleedin'-heart prick*. Karl-Heinz and his mother seemed also actually to be pleased by the news, as I read it to them. They insisted that Roosevelt was Jewish. When I laughed at this, Karl-Heinz began to cry softly. I put my arm around him and said nothing. His mother stroked his head. After a long silence, his mother began to sing whisperingly, *Ich weiss nicht was soll es bedeuten* . . . I followed along at the second verse. Karl-Heinz soon joined in. *Traurig.* My thoughts about Truman were not sanguine.

Karl-Heinz was keeping up with his schoolwork. I helped him as much as I could and got caught up in our attempts to translate some Latin poetry into German: *Hic gelidi fontes, hic mollia prata, Lycori; hic nemus; hic ipso tecum consumerer aevo* . . . I enjoyed working with Karl-Heinz's octavo Latin dictionary, and I resolved again to take Latin when I returned to college. The name *Lycori* reminded me of the Latin with which Jordy Klug had challenged me.

At this time, the war in Europe was coming to its end. Our combat-prone General clearly wanted more action. For the next month, which was the last month of the war, we would be, in effect, moving to catch up to the front, riding in trucks and ducks (amphibious vehicles) south through Germany.

First, there came our final day in Salmünster. The trucks (6x6's) are lined up on the road. We are getting our gear together and preparing to saddle up. The Section leaves the house. I hold back so as to say goodbye to Karl-Heinz and his mother. I shake hands with his mother. She gives me a maternal hug. I shake hands with Karl-Heinz. We say, each to the other, *Comrade, Brother, Auf Wiedersehen*. The mother has gone into another room, and Karl-Heinz and I are alone at the door. As I turn to leave, Karl-Heinz tugs at my sleeve and hugs me around the waist as I turn to him one last time, places something in my hand, and then is gone. He has placed in my hand the small paper box with the green-suede cover, inside of which is the deer-antler necktie-pin.

24

About the time that we pulled out of Salmünster, we learned of Ernie Pyle's death from sniper fire in the Pacific Theatre: the GIs' great war-correspondent was, like thousands of GI's, killed in action. And, in either Schlüchtern (Schlichtern?) or Jelingen, sprawled out on the floor of a large room in a large house, we heard on the radio, *Der Führer ist tot*. We caught up to the front after a 468-kilometer ride in ducks. Our battalion was then committed to get through to the second of the regiments in our division, which had been cut off. We marched for a few hours on the Reichsautobahn and pushed through a town named, I think, Owen.

It was reeking with the smell of burning houses and dead horses. The Germans were out of gas. They were moving in horse-drawn wagons. Our section, attached to F Company as a reserve support squad, moved into Brücken. We spent a night and a day here. In a bedroom of one of the houses we found an old lady in her bed; she had been shot in the face. In another bedroom, two small boys, each in his own bed, lay with their heads chopped in by an axe. In the loft of the house, the Gauleiter and his wife, who had killed the old lady and the two boys, possibly fearing the worst from the advancing enemy forces, had hanged themselves. The Gauleiter's glasses were still on his face; he wore knickers and a striped shirt; his shoes were untied and hanging half off. His wife was in her stockinged feet; there was a ragged circle of dried blood under her body. Their tongues were purple and dangled out from their deeper purple lips.

We rode in 6x6's up to Hulben past the bullet- and shell-mutilated bodies of many Germans along the road. Urech. Geislingen. Langenau. On AT trucks we crossed the Danube. It was not a beautiful blue but a forbidding brownish green. Through Bavaria to Altenstadt, where we slept. In the morning, we marched to Schöngau, where the retreating Germans had blown the bridge. Engineers were building a Bailey and floating a pontoon bridge. We walked over on the debris. Passing us from the opposite direction were three elderly men carrying on a door the body of a woman. The corpse had long black hair, wore a black jacket, a white blouse, a black skirt, and black boots. Her face and hands and legs were white and bloated. I stared at her as I had stared at the corpses on Col du Haut Jacques. Later that day, some of us stood in silence for a moment and stared at the corpse of a dead German soldier laid out supine in the doorway of a loading dock. He was without helmet, belt, weapon, and jackboots; but he had about his neck a red scarf.

The next day, at 1800 hours, we loaded onto trucks and rode in twilight and then in darkness up into the Alps.

25.1 (THE *INN*)

We didn't know it, but, as we moved into Austria, our Battalion had seen the last of front-line combat. There were still patrols and the moving of PW's and guard duty. Staring back at the road from trucks moving generally south, our Section and a squad or two of riflemen would see emaciated men, still wearing the black-and-white striped pajama-like garments—rags, really—of the death camp from which they had been released, limping, or walking haltingly along the roadsides. One called out to us, *Why came you so late? Why came you not two years ago?* (Those are the words as I remember them.) I could not summon what I knew should be the right reaction (*richtiges Aufassen*), some kind of apology for the failure and insufficiency of humankind. Others in the truck issued various snorts and grunts. It surprised me to see a tear on *Ol' Hellbent's* cheek. Matt called out, *Go to hell*.

Eventually we rolled through Innsbruck and then a few kilometers more to Wattens, a tidy roadside town between a rise of green and wooded hills and the Inn river. Here we enjoyed pleasant quarters, learned that the war in Europe had come to an end, went off skiing in the Alps above Innsbruck, visited mediaeval castles, applauded a performance of *Wiener Blut* in the Innsbruck opera house, and speculated upon our being shipped off to the Pacific Theatre. When? With maybe an intervening furlough? Guinotte, always evincing the good grace to take my answers seriously, asked me for my thoughts on the possibility of heading out to the Pacific. Translating my wishful thinking into unreasoned opinion, I said, *I think the war in the Pacific will come to a sudden end.* Guinotte expressed pleasure at hearing that; and events would somehow come about to validate that opinion.

The war in Europe was over. The war with Japan was just a few summer months away from ending. We relaxed and enjoyed the sunshine. There were Company details and a D-Day parade in Schwaz. Matt and Ken taught the others of us in the Section how to play chess; and we had a few informal tournaments. A copy of Thomas Wolfe's *Look Homeward, Angel* was passed around. I read five Shakespeare plays and memorized some passages. Movies were shown in a vacated restaurant: Spencer Tracy convincing as Dr. Jekyll but laughable as Mr. Hyde; Dennis Morgan and Barbara Stanwyck in the drippy *Christmas in Connecticut*; Ella Raines and John Wayne in a kind of western murder mystery, *Tall in the Saddle*; Cornel Wilde as Chopin in *A Song to Remember*—after ten minutes of Paul Muni's grotesque overacting, I walked out into the afternoon sunshine.

With the passage of a few weeks, the sunlight became dull, almost harsh. Uncertainty about transit to the Pacific, the boredom of stability, unenjoyable trips to tarns and resorts, and the high enclosing hills induced in me a sense of depression. There was Hedwig; but even the thrill of Hedwig was fading toward weariness.

On a pass to Nancy earlier in the year, I had had my first taste of sexual congress. At a table in a brasserie, two women were sitting with a GI who had passed out. My duty was to take care of the GI, as other GI's and local patrons were ignoring him; but I shirked my duty in favor of walking the two women, one older with dyed red hair, and one younger, somewhat plump and with straw-blonde hair, to their apartment, where they invited me to spend the night. At their urging, I left to buy a couple of bottles of vin rouge and returned to an orgiastic education. I spent two more nights with the women, buying food and wine for them and taking the younger one to see the movie, *The Duke of West Point* (in English with French subtitles). This experience had prepared me for Hedwig, when she invited me to her bed.

It was on a stroll along the rushing river that I met Hedwig. She was not shy: *Soll'n wir spazierengehen?* She invited me to her small house and introduced me to her mother, a slight and weary, blonde and blue-eyed *Frau*, who showed no immediate resemblance to her taller, brown-eyed, almost black-haired daughter. Frau Nette was civil toward me, polite, even considerate, but never outgoing, and in no way affectionate. She appeared to be indifferent to her daughter's having sex with me. The first night of Liebenmachen was an experience I've never been able to describe. Hedwig did everything; I responded from a blissful passivity. During the third week of our consorting, the pleasure had become, no less intense, but something I had begun to take for granted.

Hedwig giggled often, and sometimes laughed at my German, which she would correct. Her English was better than my German, but not always correct: *I can a little more*, and similar idiotisms. At such expressions, I would feel a ripple of superiority, but no inclination to correct her. Instead, I would reflect upon my German, and my need to improve it, and upon my also striving diligently to speak correct English. I was to discover that Hedwig was also fluent in Italian.

That discovery took place on an evening that I have come to call spectral. The incident was real; but it does not fit well into my recollections of my army time. That is, the recollection of that evening is different in mode and continuity from all the recollections I have selected for inclusion here.

Frau Nette let me in that evening and led me to the rectangular oak table, at which Hedwig was seated with a dark-complexioned man, whose hair was thick and grey and whose face was clean-shaven. *This is Mischiato, Peter*, Hedwig said. As the man rose to shake my hand, I could see that he was quite short. He said, *Enchanté*; so I thought he was French; but he spoke Italian thereafter, offering only occasional French phrases. I managed a formal but somewhat choppy *Es ist mir eine Freude, Sie kennen zu lernen.* He looked at me steadily, after we had sat down, with the pleasant expression of a friend, as though he knew me or knew about me. His black and grey clothing was styled for hiking, I thought, or maybe mountain-climbing. Frau Nette set wine glasses, small plates, and napkins on the table, served dark bread, cheese, and red wine, and then left.

Mischiato talked very rapidly and lengthily. Hedwig translated his statements, mostly into German, but frequently into English. Whatever the language, I had little idea of what he was talking about. I got the strange impression, however, that he had come to Hedwig's expressly to see me; and this made me uneasy. *Ottaviano ... Properzio ... Gallo ... Marcantonio ... Virgilio.* At one point, after dipping a tear-off piece of bread into his wine, he removed his wristwatch to show me a tattoo: black letters spelling out ROVINA NERO. Hedwig translated, *Black ruin*. Thereafter, he mentioned a number of times, *Giorgio Scaltro*. He called Hedwig *Signorina Nette*, a formality that I took to be a concession to me, seeing that he repeatedly reached out to hold her hand and caress her fingers with his thumb. When he said, *o fondamento o sostegno*, Hedwig wrote down on the tablet she was using only *fondamento oder sostegno*. After she corrected my pronunciation of the Italian words, I could gather only *fundament or sustain*.

From Hedwig's translations and from what she wrote on her tablet I put together something about Mischiato's belonging to a Black Ruin movement that had begun in ancient times, when some Roman officials worked secretly against Octavian, who became the first Roman emperor. Some poets lined up for and some against the ascendance of Octavian. Those opposing him were systematically liquidated.

The opposition movement, in later days to be called Black Ruin, was part of a much older and larger movement that had expanded westward during the time of Alexander the Great. Black Ruin was dedicated to anarchy and chaos. Mischiato looked to me to be too neatly dressed and groomed to be an advocate of chaos; but I have come to learn that his concepts have much in common with current notions of Chaos Theory. The larger movement, which included the darkness of Zoroastrianism, had some polysyllabic (and multivocalic) name that Hedwig could neither translate nor transcribe. Mischiato wrote it down on a separate tablet page, showed it to me, and then crumbled it and put it in his pocket. Then he wanted me to deliver a cigarette case, chrome– and gold-plated and soldered shut, to an address in New York. He gave the case to Hedwig, who handed it to me. I seemed to be standing outside of a scene that I could see only dimly and in part. Hedwig stroked my wrist and said softly, *Liebchen, Liebchen*. Then there was a long silence.

The silence was broken by Mischiato. Ah, he said, and then, taking a new tablet sheet, he wrote, *et modo formose quam multa Lycoride Gallus mortuus inferna uulnera lauit aqua.* He stared at me and smiled, as though this would make everything clear. I turned to Hedwig and shrugged. This further reminded me of the Latin with which Jordy Klug had challenged me. I even recalled the Lycoride or something like it. Here again I determined to get into the study of Latin, once I got back to college. Hedwig's Latin was much better than the little that I had learned from Mr. Hanson. Together we produced the following: *and O how many wounds, from beautiful Lycoris, dead Gallus now washes with infernal water!* Hedwig had worked out a German version that I couldn't follow but wished later that I had saved. She spoke to Mischiato in Italian briefly. Then she told me that this was an elegiac distich by Propertius. *Properzio. Properz.*

That night I did not stay with Hedwig. Mischiato was still seated at the table when I called goodnight to Frau Nette, received a kiss from Hedwig at the door, and left with the cigarette case and some of the tablet writings, among which was a New York address. I heard the rush of the river and looked at the stars in the clear black sky. Dead Gallus?

25.2 (THE *LECH*)

Our Division returned to Germany. Our Company took quarters in Landsberg. Our Section had the ample space of an entire second storey of what I think had been a business establishment. There were tables, chairs, beds, and two sofas. Guinotte, who was now spending most of his time with us, joined us for an evening of Schnapps, Poker, and chess. We griped about just moving from place to place and doing nothing, about how slowly things were going. Matt was ready with the wisdom of Ho Shih Lit: *To be slow is to live long; consider Adwaita, the Aldabran tortoise, who is 190 years old*. Matt, whose passion was biology, had to spell out for us the two strange words.

Guinotte showed me a two-volume edition of *Ulysses* that he had found in the building in which AT was quartered. He told me about his first reading the novel in college *mainly for the pornography*. Now he was going over its eighteen episodes to study its narrative shifts and stream-of-consciousness passages. He persuaded me to read at least the first episode. I spent a good part of four days with the text. I could picture the crenelated parapet, the crumbling gun mount, and the slovenly Stephen. The Latin was easy enough to work out—much of it, that is—but I had to ask Guinotte about *Chrysostom* and *Sassenach* and many passages that he explicated in such a way as to make me feel complimented for my questions. When next I wrote my mother, I asked her to buy and keep for me a copy of James Joyce's *Ulysses*, along with a copy of Thomas Wolfe's *Of Time and the River*.

Outside and just beyond the city's swimming-pool area, Guinotte noticed me as I struggled to swim across the Lech River from the prison side. He came to the river-bank, where he offered encouragement as I flailed against a current that I had not expected to be as swift and strong as it was. He assumed no posture of readiness for rescue, and he assured me merely by his languid presence and his mien (to use a word he liked) that I would succeed. I found the will properly to stroke with the current, but sideward, and to reach the bank without being carried more than fifty meters downstream. Blackie would probably have shouted *Go back!*; and Jordy Klug would most likely have sneered in silence or mocked me with profanity.

Heaving, catching my breath, I walked up to Guinotte, who did not ask me why I had attempted to swim across the river. (It was an impulse. The river was narrow and looked cleanly unchallenging. I remembered chickening out at a youthful impulse to swim across the much wider Mississippi.) We talked about *Ulysses* as we strolled to the swimming pool, where I changed back into my uniform.

It was to that swimming pool that I once made the mistake of bringing my billfold and leaving it in a pants pocket of my uniform while I swam. The theft of it dispirited me: it had been a gift mailed to me by Paul, and it contained a snapshot of Blackie and me (and one of Trish, with which I had wanted never to part). I was not much concerned about the money, the equivalent of ninety dollars in German currency. I thought of Iago's *Who steals my purse steals trash*; but Iago was a dissembler. The Duke of Venice was weightier with

The robbed that smiles steals something from the thief but that managed not to lighten my loss. How would the thief be aware of my smile?

The prison near the river was the one in which Hitler had been held and in which he had dictated *Mein Kampf* to Rudolf Hess. Matt, Terry, and I visited the place and spent some time looking at the small, neat room that Hitler had occupied as a prisoner. Terry wondered if that was the actual bed that *the bastard slept in*. Walking to the window, I imagined Hitler staring through it at the daylight. Matt had Ho Shih Lit say, *He who write book in penal stir mistake pencil for penis*. I laughed politely. Terry asked Matt if he meant that writing a *mee-moir* was a form of *jackin' off*.

26

Near the end of July, our Company, and, I think, most of the Regiment, if not most of the Division, was transferred to another Division.

The Section was broken up, and I was sent to a staging area in Aichach and then to an AT platoon in a little place called Kuhbach. The Pacific war ended in August, after the Atomic Bomb annihilation of Hiroshima and Nagasaki; but V-J Day was not proclaimed until September 2nd. It would be seven months before I would be home and honorably discharged. During that period, I would go on a week-long pass to the Riviera, and, before being quartered in Laufen and then Schliersee and being transferred to still another division, spend two months studying English Composition, French, and Philosophy at the Biarritz American University, one of two universities set up in Europe for the benefit of GI's awaiting shipment back to the States. The other was in England.

Biarritz lay in the southwest corner of France, on the Gulf of Gascogne in Basque country. Not far to the south was St. Jean de Luz, near the Spanish border and the Pyrenees. Biarritz retained its resort character even through November and December, although the last two weeks of December brought rain and dark days. The luxury hotels, looking out upon the Atlantic, were grandiose; the interiors were would-be classical and one was unattractively embellished by false marble columns. My home from late October through December was the Maison Carée, in which I shared a room with Nat Moughton and Ted Mahler; we three Pfc.'s enjoyed the company of a chambermaid named Marie. My classes in English Composition and French were held in the Villa Square Edouard VII, and in Philosophy in the Villa Sanchomata. The library, with its ample supply of small, rectangular, paperback Armed Services editions, was set up on the second floor of the Bon Marché, a clothing or department store in peacetime. Here it was that I read Robert Graves's *I, Claudius* and *Claudius, the God* and reaffirmed my determination to study Latin, a course that was not available at BAU.

Nat Moughton was a tall guy, whose brilliance and gentility reminded me of Guinotte. Like Guinotte, he inculcated in me a sense of my having worth. His interests were History, Philosophy, and Law. He became, in the years after the war, a judge. Ted Mahler was a smooth, easy-going, charming guy, who conquered Marie immediately and many other women in Biarritz, including the prettier of the two WAC's who were enrolled there.

Ted and I went regularly to the movies that were shown at the Lutetia and the Colisée. None of them was much good—*Tales of Manhattan, The Male Animal, The Corn is Green, Captain from Castile* (Samuel Shellabarger's novel had been even more boring than the movie), and others of the same mediocre quality.

None was as enduring as *Laura*, which I had seen in Aichach, courtesy of the USO. Nat joined us a few times; but he did not care for movies.

Nat and I were reading in easy chairs in the Bon Marché library late one afternoon. We looked out over the Atlantic and saw the deep yellow sky turning, just above the horizon, to a deep, almost purplish, blue; a mist, combining and spreading those colors, seemed to be moving toward the shore. Nat thought it was beautiful in its strangeness. I thought the yellow was sickly, the blue oppressive, and the mist ghastly; I felt that it was ugly in its eeriness.

During those two months in Biarritz, Guthrie McClintock and Richard Whorf directed two stage plays with GI student actors, Shakespeare's *Richard III* and Maxwell Anderson's *Winterset*. I cannot remember who directed which, although I believe that McClintock directed *Winterset*. I was pleased to see Whorf in person, because I remembered him as Jigger in *Blues in the Night*. I liked Anderson's character, Mio, and I added to my ambitions my intent to play Mio on stage. That ambition was never to be realized

In mid-December, after an all-BAU lunch in the Carlton Hotel, Marlene Dietrich served cake to us. We lined up; she cut the cake into generous portions, and handed each of us a piece as we filed into her presence. As she placed my piece on my dish, I marveled at her perfectly smooth complexion; but I was disappointed in the stiff, straw-like texture of her obviously dyed yellow hair.

Looking out over the Atlantic, beyond the Bay of Biscayne, from one of the huge hotel windows, or from the Grande Plage, or from the promontory called the Rocher de la Vierge, I think that this is much, much better than being in the Inn valley, where one sometimes sees the new day's sun not until late morning. Here the sun appears early and shines on the water and goes down, except on that one garish yellow-blue day of menacing mist, in a promising red circle. Here began my permanent preference of the seacoast to mountains.

27

The train, on its way to Germany, stopped at a station on the outskirts of Paris. A number of GI's got off the train to spend time there. I envied them; but I had not the enterprise to make my way back to my unit on my own, as they would have little trouble doing. Ted tried without success to persuade Nat and me to jump. Nat was too laconic and I was too insecure. Our train riding ended in Munich, where Ted and I said goodbye to Nat and were transported in a 6x6 to Rosenheim. There, each of us being assigned to a different truck, we said goodbye to each other. I rejoined my platoon in Laufen.

The Salzach River flows between Laufen, Germany, and Oberndorf, Austria. A thick, soft fall of snow one evening found four of us crossing the bridge to the church in the little Austrian town, where Pastor Joseph Mohr and his organist, Franz Gruber, are said to have written the carol, *Silent Night.* The church was candle-lit. An elderly woman, who was practicing on the organ, played the carol for us at my awkward request. We gave her K-ration chocolate bars, cigarettes, and *Kaugummi* (chewing gum).

In early February, our unit moved to Schliersee, a picturesque resort town. Here I met some refugees from Yugoslavia., Četniks, who, loyal to King Peter II and Draja (General Dragoljub) Mihailovič, had been displaced by the followers of Marshal Tito, who had won the support of the Allies by aiding in the fight against the Nazis. One of the women, Kača, took me on as her *Balkan Boy*. She was in her late twenties, blue-eyed, blond-haired, and very attractive. She wore, most often, a powder-blue turtleneck sweater, a close-fitting black wool skirt, and leather boots. Her attempts to teach me Yugoslavian and to enlist me as an officer in the Četnik cause bore no fruit. What she taught me in bed, however, I did learn; and, if there was any bearing of fruit, it owed to my having impetuously taken advantage of her as she slept, with neither of us having taken proper precautions. She was angry, but forgiving. Our affair lasted seventeen days. I left Schliersee on the beginning of my journey home. Thinking often about the town, imagining myself as a Četnik lieutenant and the father of a child, I fashioned a refrain: *I must go back to Schliersee, if I am ever to have been there.*

The journey began with a truck ride to Rosenheim and a layover there. Nat was there, also in transit; and he had a nice, pleasant room, complete with his own dog-robber, who, for chocolate and cigarettes, kept Nat's shoes shined, uniform pressed, and room cleaned. He had lost his right arm at the elbow, but worked as efficiently as anyone without a handicap. I took him to be about forty; but I realize now that he could not have been beyond his early thirties, if that. We both enjoyed his company, despite his rudimentary English, my faulty German, and Nat's *schlectes deutsch*. He deferred to us, addressing us as Herr Moughton and Herr Blaustern. We didn't learn his name; we each addressed him only as *mein Freund*.

During the second of my three days in Rosenheim, the three of us spent an afternoon that I file in memory as my *kosen* time. It is one of the four episodes of my army life that is set apart from the olive drabness of that life. The first was the grey morning of Pfaffenhofen; the second was the word-gaming with Karl-Heinz and his mother; the third was the spectral evening with black-clad Mischiato. I dislike the words *cozy* and *snug*, but I'm much given over to the concept of coziness. Lexicography links *cozy* to the Norwegian *koselig* (from *kose sig*, to make oneself comfortable). This may have meant, originally, to be at ease in speaking with others and, subsequently, to be physically at ease in one's surroundings. *Kosen* actually means *to caress*, or to engage in love talk, even *to make love*. *Cosig*, however, a variant of some sort, could be understood as *cosy* or *cozy*. That was an afternoon of talk and euphoric comfort. Not love-talk, and yet, in a way, not unlike the camaraderie in Plato's *Symposium*.

Nat had secured a black-covered copy of Thomas Wolfe's *Of Time and the River*. Coached by *unser Freund*, we were trying to pronounce (and to memorize) the novel's epigraph, which was Goethe's lyric, beginning *Kennst du das Land wo die Zitrönen blühn*. The apostrophe, *O mein Geliebter*, reminded me of my father's intonations; and *Kennst du das Haus* seemed to be an echo of *Ist dies dein Haus?* Our friend was more approving of Nat's pronunciation than he was of mine, inhibited as mine was by a habitual lack of polish. At about four o'clock that afternoon, Nat and I recited, word-perfectly and pronunciation-passably, the entire lyric and were rewarded with our friend's applause.

The walls of the room were grey, but I think of it as the Black Room. There was a black leather sofa and the two black leather chairs in which Nat and I sat. The single bed was covered by a black flannel blanket, folded back under the wide margin of a white sheet, topped by a white-cased pillow.

RAIN AND DARKNESS

There was a black night-stand, with a brass basin and a white pitcher atop it. Against the wall stood a black chest of drawers and, against the opposite wall, a black wardrobe, both accented with thin white border-stripes.

Our friend preferred not to answer my question about his lost forearm. Nat asked him if he'd been in the army. Yes, he had been a *Gefreiter* in the *Wehrmacht*. Once again: three Pfc.'s in a room. Nat asked him if he was happy. Das Glück he said, was just a momentary emotion (Ruhrung). He had gained *Zufriedenheit* (contentment): his job as *Hüter* (custodian) was enough to provide him with *Zimmer, Essen, Kleidung, und Weib* (a room, food, clothes, and a woman). We would learn, he suggested, that this was one's *Grund* (base), that everything else was secondary. Nat nodded. I felt relaxed. Just being in this room, with Nat and our friend, insulated by the afternoon, was, I sensed, what happiness amounted to. Going to Orangeblossomland with Trish would be bliss, perhaps; but thinking about it here in this room was happiness. What, or who, would be dwelling in the hollow—the brood of a dragon, or the brood of a shrewish Eliza Gant? *In Hohlen wohnt der Drachen alte Brut.*

From Rosenheim I rode to Dillingen. Here I was quartered with a Field Artillery battalion. I thought of Blackie, a Field Artillery officer, already back in the States. The last two letters I had received, which reached me in Schliersee, were from Blackie and my mother. I would have liked to write to Blackie to tell him that I was now in a Field Artillery unit. I would also have liked to write to my mother to ask her about her strange question: *Did Misheeyato see you?* In transit, though, I wrote no letters. Mischiato had appeared to know about me, but he had made no mention of my mother. Blackie had enrolled for the winter quarter at the University.

Quarters in Dillingen were a dormitory set up over what had been a store or a business establishment of some sort. My cot was next to Ed Hillman's. I spent most of my time with Ed. We saw a movie, *Where Do We Go From Here?* (Fred MacMurray, Joan Leslie, June Haver), about which I remember nothing except the prominence of June Haver's breasts. Ed was exceptionally egotistical and self-aggrandizing, differing from me only in that he was ingenuously overt about his high opinion of himself, while I tried to dissemble with regard to my self-centeredness. His capacity for self-praise quite displaced any need for praise from others. Ed was popular. I was tolerated by the other GI's only because Ed tended to keep me at his side.

I found it odd that the others would take so easily to his boasting about his championship trumpet-playing, masterly musical composition, first-rate tennis game, multiple track victories, even his skill at chess. I would win two out of three chess games with him; but his win would always be followed by *Hey, that's the nature of mathematical strategy*. I began to understand his popularity when I realized that I actually liked him.

Then, reshuffled into various groups, we boarded freight cars, eighteen to a car, and were carried across southern Germany and up through northern France to Le Havre and, in that area, borne by cattle trucks to Camp Philip Morris, where our quarters were cots in huge musty tents. In later years, I would recall the mists and drizzles and slippery mud in the camp as I read Jean-Paul Sartre's *La Nausée*, in which he called Le Havre by the name of Bouville (Mudville). There was no available water in the tent, where, in the absence of GI regulations, we bothered not to make our beds (that is, straighten out the blankets on our green cots) or police the

RAIN AND DARKNESS

litter of candy-bar wrappers, cigarette butts, dented cans, and muddied boots. At night, the tent was illuminated by yellow candle-flames and heated by two metal stoves.

Novy (first name not remembered, if ever known), an affable, heavyweight blond-haired Pole, taught me some Polish expressions and the correct pronunciation of Lwøw (something like *wush*). Chuck La Rue, small and dark, with a thick black moustache under a thin, protruding nose, was fluent in French (his *langue maternelle* oder *Muttersprache*) and he let me practice conversational French with him. I regularly defeated him at chess, but I was regularly beaten at the game by the scholarly, softly speaking, bespectacled Harold Debus.

Deferred for a couple of years because of eye problems—astigmatic myopia and more—Debus had finally been drafted. He sought no limited service, not even, as a seminarian taken from his studies, the job of chaplain's assistant. He became the BAR (Browning Automatic Rifle) man in a rifle company and, despite his devotion and commitment to Christian doctrine, took a marksman's delight in killing, when it was his duty to kill. He fascinated four or five of us, Novy included, with his explanations of aiming his mounted weapon properly at standing, crouching, or crawling *Krauts*. His audience dwindled to Novy and me when he turned to his seminary work and subjects like the Complutensian Polyglot and the *hina vs. hoti* contest relative to the *Parable of the Sower*.

He won my envy and awe as he eased into his erudition. The presentation of the *Old Testament* in three languages seemed to me not to be a problem. He said that the problem was twofold: two of the texts would be secondary documents and all three of the texts would ultimately be parabolic translations. Whether Jesus spoke in parables to prevent listeners from understanding or to ensure that they understood: this was a problem that I could recognize; but Debus said that, actually, there was no problem here: the *so that not* (*hina . . . nē*) and the *so that* (*hoti*) constituted the initial nature of literature; the essential nature of literature was the compounding of the *so that not* and the *so that* with parabolic translation, the latter being the problem of critical interpretation, which is stimulating and edifying in great literature but divisive in Holy Writ. *This,* Debus said, *is the problem of life itself.* Novy, bound by his Catholic orthodoxy, said *human* life. Debus complimented him, saying that, yes, human life means consciousness, which, doctrinally, is the soul, but that problems do not necessarily entail consciousness of problems: the sower *threw forth* the seeds and the seeds were the unconscious things thrown forth. A problem is a throwing forth and applies to what is thrown, even if the agency of the throwing is not human. The problem of life applies to the lilies of the field and to Blake's tiger in the forests *of the night* and to the Arctic tundra. Novy nodded, but at this point I didn't know what Debus was talking about.

Movies were plentiful in Camp Philip Morris—junk like *That Night With You, Thrill of a Lifetime,* and *Pardon My Past*. Novy and I enjoyed *State Fair*, with the very pretty Jeanne Crain singing *It Might As Well Be Spring*, after which some GI behind us in the dark called out, *Hold my seat, Joe: I've got to go change my socks.*

Armed Services editions were in great supply. I picked up fifteen, some of which I still have, but I did not read much, except while waiting in lines for typhoid, typhus, and flu shots and for what would be my last short-arms inspection.

28

The Victory Ship that we boarded for the trip back to the states was named *Hood*. That was also the name of the camp in Texas where I had gone through my basic training. North Camp Hood, an adjunct to Fort Hood, bore the name of the Confederate General John Bell Hood, who had been a singular loser. I assumed that the ship bore his name as well. The troopship, *Monticello*, had carried our entire division to Marseilles. The *Hood* carried only 1500 GI's, about the number in a battalion. This much smaller and lighter ship would be tossed on the north Atlantic for eleven days in early March. Atlantic: compare Atlanta, where Sherman decisively defeated Hood, who, subsequently defeated by Thomas at Nashville, retreated to Tupelo, Mississippi, and resigned his command in January, 1865.

As soon as the *Hood* left the breakwater and was into the English Channel, my seasickness, despite the prophylactic pills I had taken, began. During the two days that I could eat, I would vomit into my canteen cup. Novy would take it away and clean it up for me. Soon Novy was taking my meal ticket and was going through the chow line twice. He would bring me fruit and water, until even this bit of sustenance would come up immediately. By the fourth day, I could not get out of my bunk, and the dry heaves began. Novy arranged for me to get into sick bay; and he and a nearby bunkmate, whom we called Amigo, carried me up the steel stairs to check me in.

Four very cheerful medics cleaned me up and put me between crisp, white sheets. They gave me a hypo and set up an I-V to feed me glucose. I felt my strength returning. The nausea finally vanished. After a couple of days, they gave me small amounts of grapefruit juice, than which I can remember few things ever tasting better or providing more satisfaction. The medics talked constantly, and I enjoyed listening to them. One kept polishing a .45, which he had had chrome-plated. Another played with and petted a small brown and white dog that he had named Calvedos. Novy came to visit me every day. On the eighth day, I began to eat solid food. On the ninth day, Novy and Amigo took me out on deck. I enjoyed the fresh air, but I had come to dislike the salt smell.

The dizziness, disorientation, and nausea were gone. I had again appreciated the fact that the word *nausea* meant *ship condition* or *seasickness*. (When one has nausea, one is nauseated, not nauseous; it is the ship, in conjunction with the rolling sea, that, in causing nausea, is nauseous.)

Although I was well enough to return to my green cot in the stifling hold, the medics let me stay in the sick-bay bed, in which I had been luxuriously coddled for a week. I knew the names of none of them; but I knew the name of the dog. Amigo asked me about the propriety of keeping a dog in sick bay. I shrugged my shoulders; Calvedos seemed as much a part of the place as the I-V hookup.

After the *Hood* had passed the Ambrose lightship, Novy and Amigo came to return me to my area. I tried to thank the medics for all that they done for me; but they just patted me on the back and smiled their goodbyes. I patted Calvedos for the last time.

We were all on deck to see the Statue of Liberty, green in the grey day. The *Monticello* had departed at night; there

RAIN AND DARKNESS

had been no chance then to see the statue, as we filed, in the dark, into the vaulted steel of the troopship. From the *Hood*, however, we stared in silent entry, perhaps not proudly, but with a sort of personal satisfaction.

After disembarking, we loaded onto a train for the ride to Camp Kilmer, New Jersey. There were orientation sessions and hours of leisure. I ran into Debus, whom I had not seen on the *Hood*, and we spent some hours with chess in the day-room. In the group departures for various destinations, Novy was among the first. He was headed for his home in Pennsylvania. As he stood by his duffel, waiting to entrain, I tried to thank him for his friendship. He waved my gratitude aside and reminisced about Camp Philip Morris. Then, as he was about to board the train, he put his hand on my shoulder and said, *Powodzenia i zwycięstwa* (*Good luck, and win*).

A day and a half later, I was on a train to Camp McCoy, Wisconsin. During the three days here, there were more orientation sessions, inspections, checking of duffels and contents, clothing issues, and counsels. On the basis of my T.O. assignment as a Scout and Observer, one counselor advised that I become a forest ranger. I listened to the well-intentioned advice, knowing that, as a former paper carrier and as an ex-infantryman, I would never want any kind of outdoors employment. I had decided that I would become a librarian. Oversleeping each of two mornings, with no one coming to roust me out, I missed all of one breakfast and most of another, and I was late for two important morning appointments. Waking, I would think about things like the phrases *back and forth* and *now and then*: don't we go forward before we go back?

Shouldn't then come before now? The second evening, after chow, we filled the movie house, not to see any films, but to listen to details of honorable discharge and civilian life. I was one of seven GI's called up to the stage to be decorated: I had my general-order citation read and received my Bronze Star.

When I learned the train schedule, I called my mother. She made a high-pitched sound of happiness and asked a number of questions. She promised to look up the Konshaks' telephone number and get word to Blackie. I packed my duffel for the last time. I was now a civilian.

On the train, in which military uniforms were now in the minority among the passengers, I looked out the window at the mid-western terrain. Spots of snow were visible below the ridges of some hills and in the shade of lines of pine trees. I thought about the war that I was leaving behind me. I had served for two years, seven months, and 20 days. In my combat division, 847 GI's had been killed; that was a little more than half a battalion. Other divisions greatly exceeded that number of fatalities. I thought about two photographs that I had seen in magazines: the perfect composition of Joe Rosenthal's picture of marines raising the flag on Mount Suribachi; the cheap impulsiveness of a sailor bending a nurse backward with a kiss, in Times Square on the occasion of the war's official end, in Alfred Eisenstaedt's photograph. Both photographs were to become classics; the Rosenthal picture, however, would eventually be disclosed as staged; the sailor's action would retain its iconic propriety, even through times when such acts would be recognized as sexual harassment. I thought of Pillbox Hill, of the wandering concentration-camp survivor who called out to us, and of Calvedos wagging his tail in sick bay.

The train pulled into the station. I carried my duffel up the iron steps that I had descended some 950 days before. At the top of the steps, Blackie met me.

29

Dinitia Smith writes that Janna Malamud Smith has written: *Human dignity is based on shielding and protecting the deepest parts of the self from scrutiny. Moreover, the most important of human relationships are formed within the carapace of privacy.* These words appeared within the time that Adwaitya, about whom Matt's Ho Shih Lit had spoken, sank beneath its carapace and died in its third century of life. The words by Janna Malamud Smith, as reported by Dinitia Smith, are words to which I can subscribe, although I would say *emotionally within the carapace of privacy*. My task, in these memoirs, is to find the deepest parts of my self while simultaneously shielding and protecting them from scrutiny. I must also avoid what Mary-Liz Shaw calls *a bunch of embellishments to make a loser's life seem less loser-like.* I take Shaw's clause to be superior to the statement by Dinitia Smith, or by Janna Malamud Smith, because it does not include a metaphor (in the rhetorical sense); metaphors and similes are embellishments of narrative. I put these writers' words together, though, to serve as cautionary guides.

 The deceptiveness inherent in memoirs, whether it is that of mendacity or of art, is indicated by the fact that the word *memoir* and its plural, *memoirs*, can function as synonyms. The difference between *writing one's memoir* and *writing one's memoirs* is merely apparent. I had accepted Thomas Babington Macauley's equation of Bertrand de

Barères's memoirs, and, by implication, all memoirs, with lying. I qualified this acceptance when I read St. Augustine's *Confessions*. It occurred to me, thereafter, that one should seek the deepest parts of one's self within the careful study of one's daydreams. When, much later, I had at last read Marcel Proust's multi-volume novel, I decided that the truth of an event lies, not in its actual occurrence, but in one's memory of it, to the extent that one can understand that memory. The objective historicity of an event lives in its consequences, not in the event itself. The remembering of an event, an experience of its subjectivity, lives by its presence in the deepest parts of one's self. These recollections of mine have been teaching me about the depth of my passivity; the fictions within them are consequences of, not embellishments upon, what has happened to me.

My attempts to thank the sick-bay medics and Novy had been patted aside. I had not asserted myself. I had only patted Calvedos. I was moved by Novy's gesture and words as we left each other's life.

I did not understand the words. I could pronounce them, in mimicry of his pronunciation; and I remembered the pronunciation. It was some five decades later, when, remembering them, I pronounced them for a professor of Slavic Studies, and he wrote them down and translated them for me. Only then did I apprehend the truth of that event in the irony of the word for *victory*.

Recalling now the stance of Blackie atop those iron steps, I gain from that event the truth that Blackie was always to be there for me, but up ahead of me, whether on a flight of steps or in natural enterprise. The event, then, can be seen as a metaphor for the truth disclosed by a recollection of it.

RAIN and DARKNESS

I went through my segment of the war less as an intent participant than as an obtuse observer, needing and sometimes getting the praise that I did almost nothing to merit, getting often the crude denunciations that memory shows I needed, fearing the subjectivity of participation almost as much as the nearness of death. Memory tells me now that I have never overcome that obtuseness, that I could not and cannot make William Butler Yeats's choice between perfection of the life and perfection of the work. Losers lack acuity of perception or intellect; their intelligence is blunted, their sensitivity is shallow. *Bluster, where the hell were yuh, yuh wasted fuck?* My answer was, not the fight that, even lost, betokens the winner, but the shallow silence of the listless loser—passive non-resistance. So much, I should like to say, for *embellishments* that might make me seem *less loser-like*.

Novels and movies omit more information than they include; but what they have omitted never was, any more than what they have included ever is. What they say, however, is discerned in intellectual echo. Memoirs and history omit masses of information about what actually happened; what they say, however, is similarly discerned beyond the information selected for inclusion. I know how faulty my memory is; and, in concession to that faultiness, I have denied myself the use of quotation marks. I also know that the truth of my deepest self is to be experienced in the act of memory—not in what is remembered, but in what remembers me. [Open the gates, George.]

Blackie was wearing highly polished black shoes, sharply creased black pants, a grey, single-breasted jacket, a light blue shirt, a flat (as opposed to shiny) black necktie, and a lightweight raincoat (tan? beige?). I was in my OD (olive-drab) uniform, pants tucked into combat boots, Eisenhower jacket with a Pfc. stripe, five ribbons (including the Bronze Star ribbon), blue Combat Infantryman badge, shoulder patches of the combat and occupation Divisions in which I had served (the former on the left shoulder, the latter on the right shoulder), and the overseas cap with blue piping.

 I held the strap of the stuffed duffel slung over my right shoulder. Although curious about Blackie's officer's uniform, I was relieved that he had not worn it. My uniform would have been in embarrassingly inferior contrast to it; and, officially, I may have been obliged to salute, even though we were both civilians now.
 Blackie was driving a black second-hand Olds that was clean and in good condition: the gas-ration stamp was still affixed to the windshield. We went to Gallagher's and ordered Scotch. I was still under the legal drinking age, but the bartender asked no questions. I asked Blackie about Cazzy's, where age was lost in eight beats to the bar. Cazzy's had been closed down and was now boarded up. *Forsey?* I looked up at Blackie. *K.I.A. Salerno*, he said. He advised me to pick up the weekly unemployment check available to GI's; I should do this until June and then get back to the University. We ordered another Scotch and went to a booth to have a sandwich. There was much to talk about and even to laugh about.
 It was close to three when Blackie dropped me off at home. I hugged my mother, who cried a bit. My father was at work as a mechanic at a trucking company. Paul was in the Navy. My sisters and brothers stared at me and smiled. There was a small room upstairs all ready for me: a single bed, a chest of drawers, a night-stand with a lamp and an alarm-clock, a

mismatched table and chair, and a closet. On the table, by a green-shade lamp, lay the Modern Library edition of *Ulysses* and a copy of Wolfe's *Of Time and the River*. I unpacked my duffel, and, amidst the clothing and material souvenirs, I came upon the cigarette case that Mischiato had given me. I laid it on the table, next to the books.

When my father came home, he shook my hand, smiled, and patted me on the shoulder as Novy had done. After an evening meal of Italian sausage, brown beans, and fried potatoes, my father brought out his newly acquired ornate Hardanger fiddle and played *So lang der alte Peter* and *Der treue Husar*.

A few days passed before I asked my mother about her mention of Mischiato. I had bought enough new clothing to fill my small closet, had packed my uniform away in one of my mother's trunks, and had enrolled in the 52-20 club (weekly twenty-dollar unemployment checks for a year).

She said that Jordy Klug had asked her if I had written anything about a guy named Mischiato. (I spelled the name for her.) Had he come to meet me in Austria? A couple of days later, before Jordy left for New York, he had given her a note for me in a sealed envelope. She couldn't remember where she had put it. When I was putting socks and underwear in the chest of drawers, I found it in the second drawer, P.O.B. printed on the envelope; the letter: *Mischiato should have gotten to you in the Innsbruck area. The R.N. goes back to a Roman praetor and doesn't fail. You should have a sealed cigarette case and a New York address. If you haven't delivered it yet, send it by registered mail to the address. If G. Scaltro got to you in the Heidelberg area, he will have given you a locked wooden box. Break it open. It's yours—as pay. Valuable Latin stuff, which one day you may be able to translate. If you decide to sell it, have it appraised by experts (professional classicists). It's worth a hell of a lot. Don't fall in a shit-hole. J.K.*

Shaking the cigarette case, as I had done many times, I heard once again no shuffling or noise of any kind. I remembered the name *Scaltro*, which Hedwig had spelled out for me; but I assumed that the wooden-box business was just some of Jordy's bullshit. I had been in Ludwigshafen, which was not very far from Heidelberg; and, if the R.N. didn't fail, Scaltro would have got to me as surely as Mischiato did. No matter: I did not want to cross ol' spooky Jordy. I got one of the brown-paper grocery bags piled up in the anteroom to the kitchen, cut it to size, and wrapped the cigarette case very securely, with three layers of paper. I printed the New York address as neatly as I could and decided against printing out a return address. The registration ought to take care of that. I was certain that Jordy was involving me in some sort of illegal activity. Two days later, I took the package to the downtown post office, where a helpful, smiling, somewhat elderly clerk, with a huge gold band on his left pinky, made short the task of sending the package by registered mail.

Relieved, I walked over to Gallagher's for a Scotch; but, in civvies, and without Blackie, I was asked for my driver's license or some valid identification. I had no driver's license, or even my dog-tags, for which I automatically reached; and my Social Security card carried no birth date.

Leaving Gallagher's, I walked to the Public Library and sat down with T.S. Eliot's *Collected Poems 1909-1935*, which some wise-ass GI in Biarritz had recommended to Nat and me as an antidote to our enthusiasm for Thomas Wolfe.

Boarding a streetcar in the welcome traffic noise of the city's afternoon, I thought of Eliot's *sound of horns and motors.*

RAIN AND DARKNESS

The horn of Blackie's Olds sounded, a long and three shorts: Morse Code for B, or, as I was to learn, a first paeon. I would come to prefer the fourth paeon, three shorts and a long (Morse Code for V; also, the opening of Beethoven's Fifth Symphony, and the V [for Victory] of the war). I went out into the early evening of April's final Friday. The air was warm and fresh and touched with the scent of leaves that had been washed by a rain-shower. I greeted Blackie and was introduced to Vera Kirk, a tall, long-faced, blond-haired young woman, who was talking and laughing. I got into the back of the car and sat beside a very attractive dark-haired young woman. I stared, as I should not have done, at the contours of her breasts defined by her white blouse under a beige, open jacket, and then at her nylon-stockinged knees and legs, beyond the hem of her dark brown skirt. Vera introduced me to her. This was her good friend, Kristina Skoczny-Nadobny (SKOTE'-snee na-DOBE'-nee). My date for the evening seemed unconcerned about my lecherous staring. She smiled, took my left hand in both of hers and brought it to rest securely in her lap. From a gold chain around her small neck hung a gold cross. She was slight, but not petite. I thought of her eyes as burning brown. Except for the sexual desire that she aroused in me, she put me very much at ease, asking me about the Infantry and about my interests and plans. She was from Hamtramck, Michigan—not far from Detroit. She had worked in Detroit as a managerial secretary in a hotel chain and was transferred to this city, where her duties carried more responsibility and higher pay. She pressed my hand down onto her mons veneris.

We parked in the underground garage of the hotel where Kris, as she asked me to call her, worked, took the elevator up to the dining room, and enjoyed Martinis (served illegally, but unquestioningly, to Kris, Vera, and me), a lobster dinner, white Italian wine, and coffee, for all of which Kris signed a tab.

Blackie, Vera, and Kris politely disregarded my awkward reactions to the elegance of the table settings and the meal, during which I, in turn, did nothing to correct their lapses from grammar and usage. Kris, for example, had a problem with adverbs. She used *like* as a modifier of verbs and *due to* as an adverbial phrase; she also liked overloaded adverbs, such as *thusly* and *firstly*. Vera pronounced *err* as *air* and liked to say *just between the four of us*. Blackie used *infer* when he should have used *imply, less* when meant *fewer*, and *the reason is because*.

Leaving the uptown hotel, we went downtown to the Riviera to see *Gilda*. I liked the movie's depiction of the dark side of the three principal characters. I grew impatient only with the conventionally good Uncle Pio (played by the irritating Steven Geray). Kris held my hand, sometimes pressing it against her stomach and sometimes moving it along her left thigh. About the time that Glenn Ford's Johnny Farrell began to betray George Macready's Ballin Mundsen, she guided my hand around her shoulders to her right breast. We looked at each other under the stream of light issuing from the projection booth; she smiled; and I began to understand my own inherent darkness.

After the movie, we walked two blocks to Capoletti's. Blackie and I ordered Coney Islands; Vera had an Italian salad; Kris had fried cod and cole slaw. We talked about the movie. Blackie insisted that Rita Hayworth had not done her own singing. Vera liked the photography and Joseph Calleia. Kris thought that Gilda had no strength (she said *strenth*) of character and that Farrell's disloyalty to Mundsen gave him only a *mushbag female* as his reward. I applauded and seconded her remarks; and, again, she smiled.

RAIN AND DARKNESS

We drove to the Lookout and parked. Blackie and Vera went into a clinch in the front seat. Kris and I did the same in the back. When she kissed me, I trembled. She guided my hand about her body. I wanted very much to slide my hand under her skirt; but that was not be.

At the end of our night, Blackie went first to Kris's apartment building. I walked with her to the door. We kissed *good-night*. She said, *Pete, we're right*, and then she went in. Blackie then drove Vera home. This surprised me; I thought he would drop me off first. Finally, parked outside my family's house, we sat and talked for a while. I asked him if the four of us would go out together again. *Not likely*, he said; Kristina was just doing a favor for Vera.

She has about six guys after her. Hotel guys, with hotel money. *You had a good time, though?* I said that I had never had a better time. Somehow I felt too good to be disappointed, that is, crushingly disappointed. It may have been because of the pint of Scotch that we were sharing as we talked. Upstairs in my room, I took out my box of letters, notes, photographs, and souvenirs; and, in a notebook that served as, perhaps, a diary, I wrote, *April 26—Kris*. I went to bed and let daydreams take me down to sleep. In my daydreams, I went all the way with Kris; before I slept, Kris had become Trish.

30

Long walks to and through the neighborhoods I had known before the war offered only the freshness of the springtime air. The trees and grass were growing green, but the houses that had been mine, Blackie's, and Trish's stood grey and almost strange. I located Les Berg, and we spent a pleasant Sunday afternoon listening to music. His mother, again, was warmly solicitous. Les, however, seemed a bit preoccupied; and I had the feeling that he may have been waiting for me to leave. He brightened when I told him about the *Stille Nacht* performance in Obendorf. He asked about the organ, mentioning flue pipes, diapasons, semichorus reeds, trackers, manual divisions, and other essentials about which, he finally understood, I was totally uninformed. I could tell him only that the organ had long, wooden pedals. Les was studying aeronautical engineering. I knew something about the airplanes of the first World War-like the 150 horse-power Hispano-Suiza engine of the SE-5a, and the hump of the Sopwith Camel—but Les's mathematical and theoretical divagations about jets and rockets and supersonic speeds intimidated me and could have amounted to taunting if I had not known that Les would never taunt anyone.

The Public Library became a haven. I had renewed my card, and, having finished reading my copy of Wolfe's *Of Time and the River*, drew out and carried home *The Web and the Rock* and *You Can't go Home Again*, along with T.S. Eliot's *Collected Poems*. I was still struggling with Joyce's *Ulysses*, taking the gigantesque S, M, and P of the Modern Library edition to represent, maybe, Stephen, Mensch, Penelope. What caught me about the deliberately devious and difficult narrative style was its inevitability. This is what prose had to become, just as physics had to incorporate quantum mechanics. I was as confused and frustrated by the foreignisms and macaronics of Eliot as I was by those of Joyce; and, here, with regard to poetry, I detected the same inevitability.

I had been writing, and would continue to write, pedestrian lines like *Curt Leeding came into a rusty world / a world of twisted wire and a tree*. Eliot's sophisticated fragments and melancholy music were beyond my discernment and, frequently, my comprehension. I didn't like his anti-Semitism, but I liked his honest expression of it, like Matt's calling down the concentration-camp survivor. Joyce's Jewish Ulysses was a successful overture to non-Christian society but a less successful disguise of his own patronizing of the same. The celebration of the unorthodox worked well for Stephen's Christianity but not for Bloom's Judaism. To Joyce's ecumenicism I preferred Eliot's nostalgia for Christian orthodoxy: *Because I do not hope to turn*, I preferred Eliot's Mrs. Porter and Mrs. Turner to Wolfe's Mrs. Jack; but I turned to Wolfe for his easy and enjoyable prose. I knew that his *Ces arbres* and his epigraph from Plato were pretentious, but the knowing was satisfying. Unsettling, but painfully rewarding, was, for example, Eliot's use of *Oed' und leer das Meer*. Tristan, Isolde, Kris, Trish, Blaustern.

My mother was trying to get used to the conversion of the neighborhood grocery store to a superette, as the age of the supermarket was beginning. I accompanied her twice a week. Every other Saturday, my father would drive us to a veritable new supermarket, about three miles away, for what would be for me an hour of excessive boredom. My attempts to record this boredom in imitations of Eliot's *The Waste Land* found their crumpled way into the waste basket after Blackie said they were a waste of effort. Blackie liked the poetry of Robert Service. He liked to talk about the phenomenon of the supermarket and about business cycles and blue-chip investments. He managed to make this kind of talk interesting to me, as Les Berg had failed to make his engineering jargon either interesting or comprehensible to me; and, if Blackie were condescending in any way, I was not aware of it.

He and Vera set up more blind dates for me, but none of them won me over as Kris had done. He confided in me that he and Vera were engaged, although she was not wearing a diamond ring

In midsummer, I bought an old Model A Ford roadster, complete with rumble seat, from one of my father's friends. The price was $215; and my father kept it tuned up and running for me. Near summer's end, I drove to the University, where Blackie guided me through the registration and enrollment processes. Giving up my unemployment benefits, I claimed the benefits to which I was entitled under the GI Bill of Rights; these included a monthly subsistence, full tuition, and the costs of books and supplies. On the following day, I completed a battery of General Education Development tests and earned enough credit to take me through two quarters of sophomore rank. On the third day, I sought advice about the Library School curriculum. My counselor was a mild, soft-spoken, grey-haired lady, who wore thick-lens glasses and a round wrist watch with a grey leather band. She spoke less about the curriculum than about the three male librarians with whom she worked and about the growing recognition of Library Science as a career for men. She gave me, finally, a printed list of courses required for the B.S. in Library Science. Leaving the library, I looked across the mall at the new Journalism building. I enrolled in Beginning Latin, Intermediate French, English Literature, and Introduction to Journalism. Classes were to begin in about a week.

Returning home after my third trip to the University, I pulled my Model A up next to the garage in the back yard. The garage itself was for my father's Chevrolet and his tools. I picked up the mail and was surprised to find an envelope addressed to me with a return address for K. S.-N.

Dear Pete, Have you noticed that The Killers *is at the Orpheum? Why don't we go see it on Friday? Just you and me. I hear you've got a car now. I'll wait for you outside the hotel between 5:00 and 5:30. If you don't show up, well, maybe some other movie some other time. Love, Kris.*

The postmark was Monday. Today was Wednesday. I went into the kitchen and gave my mother a long hug.

31

There were always fewer taxicabs at the uptown hotels, like the one in which Kris worked, than at the downtown hotels. Now, as I drove up to the uptown *Commodore*, one taxicab was pulling away, and none was taking its place; and Kris was alone on the hotel's steps leading down to the sidewalk. My breath caught as I saw her close-fitting black skirt, her light-blue blouse, and her opened leather beige jacket. She ran lightly to the curb as I pulled up, and I stared at her legs, in nylon stockings, and her beige high-heeled shoes, perfectly matching the purse she carried. She opened the passenger door before I could get out of the car; and she sat down close to me, as she leaned slightly around the gear-shift and emergency-brake rods. She appeared to be delighted with the car; and I was relieved and pleased that she was not disappointed in its age and worn exterior. She gave me a quick kiss on the cheek and said, *Let's go*.

I hadn't been interested in the movie because I hadn't liked Hemingway's short story. In particular, I disliked, as I've said, Hemingway's having the counter-man George call Sam, the cook, *nigger*, and then having the third-person narrator do likewise twice. Use of the epithet by George is acceptable as characterization; but its use by the omniscient third-person narrator is wrong. The movie, however, pleased me very much. To begin with, the cook (played by Bill Walker) was called only by his name, and, in his dignity, reminded me of Forsey. In an early scene, the two killers (played by William Conrad and Charles McGraw) walk through the darkness on a path of light. Movies like *Gilda* and *The Killers*, destined to be called *films noirs*, reversed the villainous black and heroic white of Hollywood stereotypes. Darkness became a refuge and light an evil. The killers in this movie walked in light. The Swede (played by Burt Lancaster) died in the light from muzzle blasts of the killers' guns. After the Swede, in flashback, is injured in a fight that he wins, so that he must give up prizefighting, he signals his entry into crime by walking away from the arena and into a white-out of light.

Heroes are shown to be susceptible to winning advantages through dishonesty and deception. Like Johnny Farrell, the Swede yields to a base desire for a beautiful but evil-enveloped woman, the *femme fatale*. To paraphrase, or to adapt, Curtis Wilkie (as he is quoted in the fourth edition of *The American Heritage College Dictionary*), *Accompanying the light, an evil envelops the woman*. Or, change *Accompanying* to *Informing*.

Kris and I held hands during the movie. Kris encouraged no sensuality beyond that; and I made no effort to further it, much as I should have liked to have done. Despite my interest in the movie, I could not help staring at Kris's knees, repeatedly, even though I could see her smile to herself as I did so.

After the movie, we walked three blocks to Alexei's Broiler and ordered a sea-food dinner. I was pleased to be able to afford paying for the movie and the dinner and pleased that Kris was allowing me to do so, after initially insisting that it was her idea and should be her expense. Alexei's was crowded; but Kris knew the *maitre d'*, who provided us with a secluded, candle-lit booth.

We talked easily and companionably about the movie, comparing it to a number of movies that we had seen before we knew each other—*Phantom Lady, Double Indemnity, Christmas Holiday, The Woman in the Window*, and others. I pointed out its having been patterned after *Citizen Kane*, which I had seen in Chicago before the war, when I had gone there on a bus holiday for newspaper carriers, and, later, with Blackie. Kris had not seen it. She listened politely as I compared similarities in complex chronology, low key-lighting, essential immorality of Kane and the Swede, non-linear quest by the Kane reporter and by the insurance agent in *The Killers* for the meanings of, respectively, *Rosebud* and *something wrong*; and I suggested that there was perhaps a calculated resemblance of Vince Barnett's Charleston in *The Killers* to Orson Welles's middle-aged Charles Foster Kane.

It was between 9:30 and 10:00 p.m. when we left Alexei's and walked in the somewhat humid air to the Model A. Kris said *No* to the Lookout and asked me if I would like coffee in her apartment.

She lived on the second floor of a four-storey brown-brick apartment building, *The Manitoba*. Her single-bedroom unit was impeccably clean and orderly, sparsely but neatly furnished, with a large wooden cross centrally aligned above a long sofa that was protected by a light blue slip-cover. A small fan, placed under the two juxtaposed front windows provided sufficient coolness, although nothing like the artesian-cooled air of the Orpheum.

The aroma of the coffee induced in me something akin to euphoria. Kris poured it from a pewter service into very delicate china cups. She also placed on her walnut coffee-table a platter of sugar-wafers that she had baked. We talked for a long time about various mundane topics—movies, her job, my plans for school, her friend Vera, my friend Blackie. She made it clear to me in a number of straightforward words and gestures that there was to be no sensual, much less sexual, activity that night. My mild resentment was overcome by my great satisfaction and sense of intimate security at being in her presence in this perfectly arranged apartment. I sensed from her lengthening silences when it was time for me to leave.

At the door, I asked her if by *We're right* she meant that we were right about *Gilda* or right for each other. She was a little surprised that I did not know what she had meant. After a disconcerting pause, she said, *Both, Pete*. She allowed me a long good-night kiss. She said, *Thanks for tonight: I really had a good time*. I offered my thanks in return, and left, hearing her door close only after I was out of sight of it on the staircase.

As I drove home, I was sorry that I had not asked her for another date; but then I realized that, had she wanted me to do so, she would have orchestrated my doing so. My daydreams before sleep were tempered by Kris's restraint. I thought much about her letter's close, *Love, Kris*. It occurred to me in the morning that in those briefer daydreams Kris had not become Trish.

32

Blackie and I are back in classes at the University. We are both third-quarter sophomores.

The next three years will be, for me, the most enjoyable years of our friendship. We have lunch together every school day either at the Union or in U-town. We talk about academic matters, national and international events, movies, women, and television programs. We argue about politics: Blackie thinks Truman is an asshole; I insist that Dewey is a prick. We laugh at jokes and share reminiscences about Forsey and Jordy. We are free from military call, although Korean war shadows gather, and we are unencumbered by debts or serious troubles. Our acquaintances on campus call us Damon and Pythias. I take myself to be Pythias, whose name is not used in Friedrich Schiller's *Die Burgschaft*, in which Damon is sentenced to death. I could have been either one, however, in the classical version that I had learned from Guinotte, in which Pythias is sentenced to death and Damon is *der treue Freund*. The campus cliché, though, probably centered on an inseparability of friends instead of the legendary depth of friendship.

When I told Blackie about my recent date with Kris, he had been quite surprised. He let me know that Vera had told him that, shortly after the four of us had gone out together, Kris had turned down a proposal by telephone from a Detroit hotel guy and that back in June she had said *no* to one of the hotel guys with whom she worked. He praised me for my initiative in asking Kris out; and, when I told him that she had done the asking, surprise sent his eyebrows up and his jaw down. Then he put his hand on my shoulder, as Novy had done. His quizzical but warmly approving smile was, figuratively, at least, worth paying *am Kreuz mit der Leben*.

One of Blackie's jokes: Admiral Yamamoto is addressing a group of highly honored fighter pilots. *Emperor has new pranes for you. Very smarr, very fast, roaded with exprosives. You fry over big American ship. You dive straight down onto ship. Prane brow up. Boom! Boom! Ship sink. Sairors arr die. You die for grory of Emperor. Prane carred Divine Wind (Kamikaze). Any questions?* Way in the back, a little pilot raises his hand, and Admiral Yamamoto tells him to ask his question. The little pilot says, *Honorabre Admirar Yamamoto, you outa you fuckin' moind?*

Although I could have enrolled in Intermediate Latin, I chose to start all over. It was the right choice. Mr. Hanson's instruction, adequate enough, now betrayed various deficiencies. He had been a bit misleading, for example, on the sequence of tenses and inconsistent on the use of reflexive pronouns. He had not got to the subjunctive until the last few weeks of the second year. We had read, except for a number of aphoristic statements and short periods, only made-up Latin. Now, within the first quarter, we were reading whole chapters of Caesar's *Commentaries*.

It was enjoyable to measure Roman warfare against the warfare I had known. When we read about Caesar's putting some infantrymen of the Tenth Legion on horses and the joking (*non irridicule*) comment that Caesar had elevated them to the equestrian class (*ad equum rescribere*), I remembered Guinotte's exclamation when we passed a GRO crew loading some dead German soldiers onto donkeys, *Comrades, der Führer has rescribed you to the jackass class*, and I now experienced the pleasure of appreciation.

My French instructor, who translated *Va au diable!* as *Go to the Hell* and, in explaining the redundant *ne*, pronounced *redundant* as *REHd'n-dahn*, complimented me on my uvular r but despaired of my tonic phrasing.

A sophisticated Virginian with body-movements suggestive of homosexuality, who had taken his doctorate at Yale, taught *English LIT-tra-tyoor* with theatrical flourish and articulation, and with a vocabulary that sent me daily to the dictionary. The class was large—more than sixty students—and we were seated alphabetically. During every MTWThF class meeting, from my front-row seat, I thought, *This is it.*

The Journalism class was diverting but almost fully a waste of time, as far as my real interests were concerned. Had it not been for my GI-Bill-paid tuition, I would have dropped the course in mid-quarter. The instructor's differentiation of editorialism from objectivity carried good compositional advice, however; and there was benefit in considering the importance of simplicity and clarity. *Avoid similes* was his refrain. He allowed that creative-writing classes appropriately emphasized the basic importance of effective similes, *but even the most objective reporting is already a simile of what it reports, and no one really likes what reality is like, unless* he or she likes (he said *they like*) *to avoid what reality is.*

[George, I'm reading Peter Plagens's review of a book about Thomas Eakins. Plagens cites these examples of *awful writing*: Eakins wielded *his brush with a hand as steady as the one Dr. Gross used to guide his scalpel*; and *Like a dam breaking, a deluge of unabashedly laudatory praise followed*. In the first sentence, the second *his* is actually ambiguous. In the second sentence, a dam is equated with a deluge, and the redundancy of *laudatory praise* is offensive. What is wrong with both sentences, apart from the facts that each is badly written and each is infected with a bad simile, is the use itself of simile.

Eakins wielded his brush with a perfectly steady hand.... An effusion of praise followed.]

33

My mother baked a white cake with chocolate frosting for my birthday. We had a little party. After an evening meal of meatloaf and creamed corn, I blew out the candles on the cake and listened to the singing of *Happy Birthday to You* (a ritual I have always dreaded). I cut the cake and served it. My mother placed scoops of chocolate ice cream on each dish. My brothers and sisters had pooled enough money to buy me a genuine leather billfold. My parents gave me a light-blue shirt and a navy-blue tie. My father took up his fiddle and played some of my favorite old tunes. After the celebration, with the table cleared, the dishes washed and dried and put away, and the routine of evening settling in, the phone rang. My mother answered it and handed it to me with a smile.

I thought it must be Blackie, although he had given me Vera's and his birthday greetings earlier in the day. *Happy birthday, Pete.* It was Kris. She said she knew Monday was a bad night to go out, but could I drive up to see her for just a few minutes: she had a *little present* for me. It was almost 8:00; I said I'd be there in less than an hour. I washed, shaved, put on a clean light-blue shirt (not the new gift shirt: my mother would wash and iron that first) and my new navy-blue tie, tossed on a windbreaker, and went out.

The streetlights spread their softened glow through a light fog that did not impair visibility. Twice I pulled up

RAIN AND DARKNESS

to a curb and parked for a few minutes so as to contend with nervousness. When I parked outside the apartment, I sat for a few more minutes, until I was breathing less with nervousness than with pleasant anticipation.

She opened the door, and I did nothing to check my lecherous up-and-down stare. She is wearing brown terrycloth slippers, nylons, a close-fitting dark-brown skirt, a lighter-brown short-sleeved blouse, against which her gold cross gleams. Her burning-brown eyes complement her smile. The subtle waves of her dark-brown hair draw my hand upward. Before I can touch her or utter a word, she has closed the door and, placing her arms around my neck, has begun what will be a prolonged kiss.

The spotlessly neat apartment is warm with lamplight. Light from floor-lamps on each side of the sofa reach and edge with a subtle border the wooden cross on the wall. In a small walnut holder a tapered blue candle burns on the walnut coffee table. There is in the center of the coffee table a small rectangular package wrapped in light-blue paper and tied with a dark-blue ribbon.

Kris asks me why I remove the paper and the ribbon so carefully; and, when I say that I want to save both, she smiles and strokes my cheek. I open the hard-paper box and remove a black suede-covered box, which I snap open to disclose a silvery shining flex-band wristwatch. It is a Gruen, rectangular frame, light-grey face, gilt numbers 12, 3, 6, and 9, with gilt lines for the other digits. I set the time: 9:08. I remove my old watch, purchased long ago in Texas at a PX. Its black leather band is worn, torn, and faded, its plastic window cracked and scratched, its black face and green illuminated numbers neutered with age, and its minute-hand slowed. I slip on my patently expensive Gruen and move toward a wastebasket next to a table-desk. Kris stops me, takes the old watch, and says she will keep it.

My thanks are awkward and haltingly conventional; but Kris's smile renders them acceptable and, as it occurred to me then, effectively ennobles them.

Now, Pete, I'm going to ask you to give ME a present.

I stammered something that was emphatically affirmative, but not as resoundingly and heartily affirmative as I had wanted my response to be. She went into her bedroom and returned with a diamond ring. She explained that it had belonged to her sister, whose fiancé had been killed in the war. *I want you to give this to me. As an engagement ring. I want you to promise to marry me.* She handed the ring to me. Looking at the full-karat diamond ring in its gold setting, I raised her left hand and slid the ring onto the third finger.

We stood by the coffee table and embraced, closely, then loosely, then closely again. When I trembled, she held me tightly until I relaxed. Then we sat together on the sofa. From the drawer of the coffee table she drew out two blue-metal, cork-bottomed coasters and placed them neatly before us. She went to the kitchen and returned with two cordials filled with Grand Marnier. She placed them on the coasters, went to her table-desk and turned on the radio, and, as the music began, returned to pick up one of the cordials. I rose and picked up the other. We clicked them. I said *Recti sumus*, showing off my Latin; *Whatever that means*, she said; and we sipped the liqueur to toast our engagement. We put down the cordials and embraced. She did not resist my touching her breasts and buttocks, which I did as gently as I could, knowing from a tentative rigidity in her stance that I was to go no further. From the radio came Dick Haymes's rendition

RAIN and DARKNESS

of *I'll Get By*; and that became *our song*. We parted with one last long kiss and close embrace. Again, her door did not close until I was well down the staircase.

The fog had increased, but there was no visibility problem.

It should have been *recta et rectus sumus*; no, to avoid elision or hiatus, *rectus et recta sumus*, or *recta rectusque sumus*. Latin, too, favored the male. Actually, English was more concise and free of prejudice here: *We're right*.

The house was dark, except for the dim glow in the kitchen of the staircase night-light.

My mother had also left the back-porch light on. Inside the kitchen, I turned it off.

In bed, I retained the vision of Kris in the perfect brown ensemble that set off her burning-brown eyes; and silently I was singing *There may be rain / and darkness too* . . .

34

In U-town's small Japanese place, Blackie and I were sipping sweet gin-laced tea. He had finished his bowl of shrimp and rice. I had finished my favorite sandwich, fried egg with raw onions and yellow mustard on untoasted white bread. Calling Blackie's attention to my new watch, I told him it was a gift, not from my parents, but from Kris, and that Kris and I were engaged. Again, his eyebrows went up and his jaw went down: *Huh! . . . No shit? . . . How . . . ? When . . . ?* I told him about the diamond ring. He recalled Kris's telling Vera and him about her sister's loss of her fiancé during the war and the subsequent postulancy. He asked me if I were definitely sure about this. I tried to describe the depth of my need for her; I allowed that I couldn't be sure that he wouldn't take her away from me. He laughed—loudly enough to cause other customers to turn their heads. No, I need never worry about that: Kris was very pretty and very desirable; but, apart from his complete commitment to Vera, he could not take to Kris. I asked him why, and his answer surprised me: *She's too much like me.* When I asked him to explain, he would say only that she had a steel-trap mind for order.

After a pause, he said, *You goin' to turn Catholic for her?*

I hadn't thought of that, but I supposed that I wouldn't. Despite my reverent regard and admiration for Father Murphy, I could not be sincere about becoming a Catholic. Blackie thought about this for what seemed a long while.

RAIN AND DARKNESS

Then he refilled our cups with tea and said that Kris was not the kind of person to insist on anyone's changing his [*or her*, I added silently] religious commitment but that her kids would sure as Hell be brought up Catholic. That did not bother me at all.

He and Vera had decided on a June wedding. Maybe we could have a double wedding. The suggestion didn't quite please me; but I promised to offer it to Kris. (When I did, she was emphatic: *NO!*)

We left the Japanese place and walked back to campus. As we were about to separate to head for our respective classes, Blackie gave me a Novy hand-on-the-shoulder and said he was glad to have been wrong about the four of us not getting together again.

Carrie Coreghian, who sits next to me in the English Literature class, joins Blackie and me at the Bridge for coffee. It's a little after 4:00. None of us has any more classes for the day. Carrie is tall; she has long, straight black hair, very dark brown eyes, a prominent nose, and a projecting chin.

She wears a red sweater and a black skirt most of the time; and she is doing so today. Like Kris, she wears a gold cross on a chain about her neck. She sits sideways on the booth bench so that her long legs, in nylons and black loafers, can rest, crossed, outside the booth. *Why*, she asks, *do people think Joe Christmas has a greatly enlarged prostate?* With riddles I'm inept, even with easy ones like this. *Who's Joe Christmas?*, Blackie wants to know. Carrie gives him a three-minute synopsis of Faulkner's *Light in August*. Blackie answers, rather cleverly, I think, *Because he can't put out a Yule log by pissing on it*. Carrie chuckles politely and says, *Nope. Because Christmas only comes once a year*. Blackie laughs. I say, Because *Christmas comes only once a year*, transposing *only* and *comes*. Blackie says that from now on my name is *Ped* for *pedagogue*. I assure him that the real pedagogues are on his side in this matter; but the assurance is of no matter to him. [Open the gates, George.] I tend to think that Blackie meant *pedant*.

Carrie thinks that Faulkner's play for similarity, *Bunch* and *Burch*, is too obvious. The repetition of *b*'s, *u*'s, liquids, and plosives in *Lucas Burch* and *Byron Bunch* seems, I put in, to create an undertone of identity and is consistent, I add, with his play on *Joe Brown* and *Joe Christmas*. Carrie demands to know, *What does THAT do?* I offer, *Overtones of a brown Christmas in August*. Carrie and Blackie both moan; Carrie also clutches her throat and sticks her tongue out and to the side.

Blackie argued with Carrie and me for a short time, challenging our liberal political views. Then Carrie and I picked up our favorite argument: she upheld the superiority of Byron to Wordsworth. She went on again about Ezra Pound's references to *dippy Wordsworth* and *ole sheepy Wordsworth*. I conceded Wordsworth's low points with Harry Gill's weak swelling ankles and the like; I claimed that Byron nowhere matched the heights of Wordsworth's transcendent simplicity in, for example, the concluding lines of . . . *Brougham Castle*. Carrie called that *so much sheep-shit* and recited Byron's *Prometheus*, which Blackie admiringly approved. I reminded Carrie that Pound called Byron *rotten*.

More coffee. More arguments. Carrie and Blackie trying to outdo each other with dirty jokes. We left the Bridge as the dinner customers began to crowd in. Carrie waved us off, *So long, Blacko; see you, Pete*. She had rejected Blackie's *Ped*. Blackie went off to his Olds, I to my Model A.

RAIN AND DARKNESS

Driving home, I intoned, *The silence that is in the starry sky, / The sleep that is among the lonely hills.* I thought of Joe Radosta, frost-proofing his Jeep with shelter-halves one winter night and saying, as he stared up at a dominant star, *Che bella stella, si finisc' la guerra* (rhyming *stella* and *guerra*, so that the latter became *wella*): What a beautiful star, if the war were over. I thought about Pill Hill, cold Alpine nights, and the hills rising above Wattens. Wordsworth had walked among the Alps. There were summer nights when Hedwig and I sat by the river and she would sing *In der Nacht ist der Mensch nicht gern' alleine.* There was a current of sadness in her voice; there was also the intimation of a satisfying smile. She had taught me the lyrics; and I would join her briefly at *Habe ich da ein Prinzip, / Und ein ganz bestimmtes, festes Ideal.*

As my Model A, nearing home, rolled across the bridge (on which no one was selling flowers to even imaginary lovers), I thought of Kris. It would be good to look up at the stars with her. The fan-blade rattled again. I would tighten it or replace it, as my father had taught me to do. He had secured half a dozen replacement blades from a guy he knew at Ford. Four were left.

Hey soldier! My uncle greeted me on the porch. I was very pleasantly surprised. He had gone to California to work for Lockheed during the war. The pay was very good; and he sent checks regularly to my mother. He had taken up with a *Rosie-the-Riveter* woman with whom he worked. Her husband had left her; and her two sons, a year apart in age, were in the Service, the elder in the Marines, the younger in the Army. He said that she would be coming up to join him in a month or so. I showed him my watch and told him about my engagement. *All grown up*, he said, with a broad smile, and *Congratulations!*, as he shook my hand. My mother set out a big meal. My father got out his fiddle. There was singing; I asked my father if he knew *In der Nacht ist der Mensch nicht gern' alleine?* He nodded; but he said it was silly (*albern!*) and he wouldn't play it. There were reminiscences, and my uncle and I indulged in respective recountals of assembly-line work at Lockheed and wartime travels in Europe. My room was the one my uncle had used before he left. I said he should take it back, but he refused. My mother made up the sleeper-couch in the living room for him.

35

When I told Kris about my uncle's return, she said, *Well, you can move in here with me.* After a twinge of delight, I told her that my uncle would be finding a place for himself and his woman from California. *How soon?* I said that it was a matter of only a few days. Then, as we sat together on her sofa, she took my hand and said that she had arranged to be off from December 26th through the 31st; we could be married on Monday the 26th (She smiled: *Good day: right?*), spend five nights and four and a half days in Chicago on a honeymoon, be back home for New Year's Eve. She would work Christmas Eve, Christmas Day, and New Year's Day. The Chicago hotel was part of the chain to which the hotel she worked at belonged, and she would get almost forty per cent off the normal rate. I nodded and reached out to her. She danced away and put on a recording of *our song* that she had bought. Then she returned to embrace me and to dance. I was not a good dancer. I could waltz and I could do the Stomp to Glenn Miller's music. I tried waltzing. She checked me and led me in a two-step (I think that's what it was).

My uncle's woman from California never showed up; and the two letters he sent her were not answered. I began spending the nights with Kris. I would sleep on her sofa. Our intimacy did not go beyond my hooking up her brassiere and zipping up her dresses. Often we slept for hours, fully dressed, in each other's arms. The Model A I kept parked in the hotel lot. We went to movies. We went out a few times with Blackie and Vera. Kris went every Sunday to an early Mass. She never asked me to join her, or to walk with her to church, or to meet her after the service. One Sunday, after a blizzard the night before, I walked with her to church, waited in the narthex during the service, and walked back with her. *That was sweet, Darling*, she said; *thank you very much*. Then she made breakfast: fried eggs, toast, jam, orange juice, and coffee.

Kris joined me for Thanksgiving dinner with my family. I was somewhat nervous about our proletarian setting, but I need not have been. Kris had never looked down on my old Model A; and she showed a respect for my mother, father, uncle, and brothers and sisters that was entirely sincere.

She insisted on helping my mother clean up the table and kitchen and on doing the dishes with her. She was delighted by my father's fiddle-playing. Before we left, she sang *I'll Get By* and asked my father if he could play it. He did, with his usual ease and his play-it-by-ear competence. He played it a second time, and she sang in accompaniment.

The wedding went flawlessly, exactly as Kris had planned it. It took place in Polish Hall, which Kris's parents had rented, in accordance with Kris's plans. The ceremony was performed by the minister from the Lutheran church that my parents attended and in which I had been confirmed. Vera was Maid of Honor and Blackie was my Best Man. Kris's parents and sister, the latter in postulant dress, were present. Eight hotel people, who were able to get away for the morning, and three of Kris's managerial superiors were in attendance. Les Berg and his parents and a few of my high-school friends came as invited, among them Cpl.

Dick Shriven, who had re-enlisted and was on furlough for Christmas. Blackie's parents and sisters were there. Katie, my erotic homework ward, came with her fiancé. My mother, father, uncle, and brothers and sisters were dressed in their best. I had sent invitations to my I-and-R buddies and to CC; they sent gifts and regrets; CC included a long letter and an account of his hospitalization for lung cancer. Les Berg played Beethoven's *Adagio* from the Ninth Symphony on the Polish Hall's small but well-maintained organ. A lady from the church sang a selection from the *Lutheran Hymnal* and, at my request, *La Golondrina* and, at Kris's request, *I'll Get By*. Kris had arranged for a reception at her work-place hotel. The wedding gifts were on display there. Les Berg, at the piano, and four of his musician friends played dance music, concluding with a rendition of *I'll Get By* that brought tears of pleasure to Kris's eyes. There was a small banquet and an elaborate four-tiered wedding cake. After Kris and I returned from having changed into traveling clothes, Blackie and Vera drove us to the depot, where we boarded the *Hiawatha* for Chicago.

36

The many-colored holiday lights shone appealingly through the blustery snow. Kris and I sat tightly together in the cab, holding hands and kissing. *We did it, Pete*, she said. Nodding, I said, *We're right*, wondering, as usual, if I would ever really know what that meant.

The clock showed *twenty after nine* when we reached the hotel desk. A thin grey-haired clerk checked our reservation and then asked for our identification. At Camp McCoy, a billfold-sized photo-reduction of my Honorable Discharge had been laminated in plastic for me. My attempts to use this as identification were never successful, and I would regularly then produce my regularly accepted driver's license. Before I had got past my coat to my pants pocket, intending once again to present the Honorable Discharge card, Kris had said to the hotel clerk, *Would you ask Gus to come out? Tell him it's Tina.* Gus Mireaux, a stocky guy with thinning light-brown hair and a receding chin, came out smiling: *Tina! Tina! Is this your groom?* Kris said, *Hi, Gus. Yes this is him.* I managed both not to show my displeasure at the *him* and, more important, not to interject *he*. Gus asked what refreshments he could send up, compliments of the house. Kris ordered crab salad, Melba toast, a Martini mixer, ice, and pitted olives.

In the well-appointed but not lavish suite, we closeted our coats, unpacked our few bags, removed our shoes, washed hands and faces together, and were about to sit down when Room Service delivered the order.

As we sipped our Martinis, we talked about *Gone With the Wind*, which we had each seen separately before the war. Kris liked the depth that Olivia DeHavilland gave to a too-good-to-be-true character. I liked the Max Steiner score. We agreed that Thomas Mitchell was his usual pursed-lip hammy self. We disagreed on Hattie McDaniel and Butterfly McQueen. Kris insisted that they were convincing and true to the time. I argued that they were extensions of the Willie Best / Stepin Fetchit / Aunt Jemima context. I disliked the caricature as I disliked animated cartoons, by which I was never entertained or amused, except, perhaps, for Disney's *Snow White and the Seven Dwarfs* and Max Fleischer's *Gulliver's Travels* (mainly because of the songs in each). (The Civil Rights movement and Juano Hernandez's performance in *Intruder in the Dust* were only a few years away. Eartha Kitt, Sidney Poitier, Morgan Freeman, and Denzel Washington would follow, along with the Democrats' loss of the Solid South following Lyndon B. Johnson's enactment of Civil Rights legislation.) Also, I insisted that Hattie McDaniel's Academy Award was tokenism, a constant determinant in the award selections, along with tardy compensation for merits overlooked. I ceased to take the Academy Awards seriously, or to give them any kind of credence, after an award was denied to Henry Fonda for *The Grapes of Wrath*. (His award for the maudlin *On Golden Pond* would be an insulting compensation, like Paul Newman's for *The Color of Money*.) Kris agreed that *The Grapes of Wrath* was superior to the previous year's *Gone With the Wind* and that Henry Fonda should have been the best-actor winner for his role of Tom Joad; and, turning from our admiration for Gregg Toland's photography back to our discussion of *Gone With the Wind*, we were in accord in our admiration for Barbara O'Neil and Evelyn Keyes. I don't recall our having said anything about Vivien Leigh or Clark Gable.

We pushed the tray, with its depleted spread, over to a space near the door. Kris went into the bathroom, and I drew back the bed-clothes and began to remove my clothing. Kris came out of the bathroom after switching off its light. She stood in the mellow lamplight of the room, wearing a beige flannel robe, which extended to her knees and which she held closed about her, its sash hanging down the sides. Then she drew the robe open, removed it, laid it over a chair, and stood before me in what I still think of as golden beauty. She stood, without self-consciousness, her left leg slightly bent against the other, her right arm bent at the elbow and the forearm resting across her taut abdomen. Wide-eyed and open-mouthed, I stared. She smiled and, after a moment, turned full circle. Then, holding out her arms, she came up to me, placed her arms around my neck, and pressed my head between her breasts. Finally, she helped me complete my undressing and guided me back onto the bed. I had placed a condom on the nearer pillow. She chuckled, took the prophylactic into the bathroom, and flushed it down the toilet. Returning, she said, *None of that: we're on the rhythm method.*

My performance was immature and inept. In Europe, the women had carried out all the sensual maneuvers. Here, Kris, abandoning her usual initiatory stance, assumed passivity; and, in the active role, I had no staying power. Kris laughed and said, *Is that all there is?* I was humiliated by my inadequacy and hurt by Kris's question.

At the same time, I was very proud and indescribably pleased to be in bed with, and holding in my arms, this beautiful woman, who was my wife. Kris was my wife! We were alone, beyond the cutting snow of winter, in our exclusively golden world. Kris caressed me and embraced me, not, I realized, to soothe my offended vanity, but to assert her possessiveness, an assertion that, at that moment, in that soft and warm bed, I welcomed and cherished. We held each other, front to front; her breath sent me the scent of mint. I fell asleep.

The room was dark, except for a line of light from the partially open bathroom door. There was a bath towel on the bed-sheet. Kris had put it there to cover our slight spots of blood and semen. I slid out of the bed, walked over to the light, and opened the door. Kris, seated before her portable mirror, was putting her hair up in curlers. She was in her robe; the sash was tied. As she turned and smiled, the effect of her dark hair rolled tightly to her head was almost unpleasantly surprising. The burning brown eyes and the smooth oval face retained their deep attraction but seemed strangely isolated without the framing mass of her undulant dark brown hair. She placed something like a shower cap over her curler-covered head. We returned to the bed and to our close embrace, on one side of the bed, away from the towel. When next I woke, there was grey daylight in the room. Kris was in the bathroom again. Her hair was free. She was dressed and applying her make-up.

We saw only a few dim stars during our honeymoon week. There were no brightly moonlit nights and only one period of sunshine during one mid-morning. We took advantage of that sunshine by walking all the way to the lake and the Art Institute of Chicago; the art museum was massive and greyingly indifferent to the winter-morning's sun. Inside, the great hollow spaces carried currents of echoes. We stared for perhaps ten minutes at Grant Wood's *American Gothic*;

and I recounted to Kris, as though the observations were my own, what Guinotte had told me about the diabolic trident motif, the actual identity of the models, and the connotations of the word *Gothic*. Kris was neither impressed nor much interested. She had seen many prints of the work and was a bit disappointed that the original was hardly more compelling to her than the prints had been.

One evening we had dinner at a French restaurant: breast of guinea hen and wild rice. That meal remains in my memory as the finest I have ever had. Kris taught me how to react to the service of formally dressed waiters, how to linger over the food and draw out the best that it offered, and how to approve of the proffered wine before it was poured. She placed her hand on mine as she explained the quality of the décor and the aesthetic correctness of the ambience, checking me before I could follow my impulses to look up, around, and all about.

I was very proud of my sophisticated wife, my *bonne ménagère*.

The movies took much of our time. Each day, we went to at least one. Matinees included *Undercurrent, Crack-Up*, and *To Each His Own*. *Crack-Up* had a superb early scene, in which evil light, in the form of an onrushing locomotive's headlight, overwhelmed the mind of the character played by Pat O'Brien. Kris and I were taken with Robert de Grasse's mood-consistent expressionistic photography and let down by the drivel with which the movie ended. *Undercurrent* and *To Each His Own* were pretentious soap-operas; Kris praised them; I conceded that they were entertaining. I praised *San Antonio*; even in decline, Errol Flynn exhibited the magnetic star quality, the cinematic charisma to which physical attractiveness and the easy charm of voice and movement were prerequisite but of which they were not in every film star a guarantee. I thought of Blackie and our nights of dialogue memorization, even as my arm went over Kris's shoulders and my hand caressed her breast. Kris conceded that the movie was very entertaining, despite its cornball plot. S. Z. Sakall, shaking his sagging jowls, belonged to the cartoon world that I detested. In our hotel room, we sang *Some Sunday Morning* together. That is, Kris sang it in her faultless soprano voice, and I followed along to the tone-deaf best of my ability.

The Razor's Edge had some strikingly good scenes, like the coal-mine scene and the bistro scene. The song *Mam'selle* (sung in French) worked the Romantic melancholy neatly into the tragedy of Ann Baxter's Sophie. Herbert Marshall was ideally cast as W. Somerset Maugham, whose homosexuality was shunted off onto the tedious Clifton Webb. Tyrone Power, second in star quality only to Errol Flynn, brought Maugham's Larry Darrell convincingly to the screen. I had read an Armed Services edition of the novel in an area of Germany much like the one in which Darrell indifferently enjoyed the lovemaking of a German woman. Kris and I were both enthusiastic about the mystically terrestrial Elsa Lanchester and at least uncomplaining in our tolerance of the popular-magazine gloss of Gene Tierney and John Payne.

We sat through *The Locket* twice, surprised and pleased by the telescoping flashbacks within flashbacks, caught up by Laraine Day's innocent-faced femme fatale and the incomparable taedium vitae of Robert Mitchum, whose drooping eyelids kept him always at a distance from self-disclosure.

Over a breakfast in a small, solidly furnished restaurant, with tablecloths and table candles—a short, bitterly cold walk from the hotel (into a caressingly warm interior)—I asked Kris about her sister. She said that Karrie (for Karolina) and her fiancé had been devoted to each other. They were saving money for their wedding and for taking over his widowed aunt's farm and mill in Michigan's Upper Peninsula. The aunt would live with them and help with the housekeeping and bookkeeping. Bob (the fiancé) was drafted fairly early and was killed on Omaha Beach. Karrie, two years older than Kris, resolved then never to marry. She gave her ring to Kris and decided, about a year ago, to become a School Sister. She was near the end of her postulancy and hoped to begin her novitiate in February. She had been granted a dispensation to attend our wedding. I recalled my impression of Karrie: taller than Kris, attractive but not so pretty as Kris, a constant smile, brown (but not burning brown) eyes that misted sadly in the pallor of a face devoid of make-up.

As the week sped on, my staying power improved, but only slightly. I would never be to Kris what George S. Kaufmann was to Mary Astor. Kris initiated no sexual eroticism, but she accepted all of mine; and she managed not to laugh at me again.

On our last night in Chicago, we went to a night club, where there was a stage show and dancing. We both had to show identification. Our table was close to the flapping doors of the kitchen; but we could hear the comedian and the singer very well; and we enjoyed the space and freedom of the dance floor. I tended to turn all of our dances into the Stomp; finally, Kris took the lead and tried to teach me the intimacies and minor intricacies of conventional dancing. I sent a note to the orchestra, requesting *I'll Get By*; but the request was not honored. I had tipped the waitress who carried the note but had neglected to send along a tip for the orchestra leader.

In bed that night, Kris put her arms around me and said. *Thank you, Pete.* I almost said, *You're welcome*; but I wasn't sure why Kris was thanking me, and I reminded myself that she had paid almost all of the expenses for this honeymoon and had made all of the arrangements. Looking at her, seeing her face in the dark, to which my eyes had become accustomed but which obscured the cap-and-curler mass, I said, *You're beautiful, my Kris.* She kissed me and held me very firmly.

37

Karrie, Vera, and Blackie had delivered the wedding presents to the apartment and had set them on and around the table-desk. We turned the thermostat up and unpacked our luggage. It was early evening. New Year's Eve. We showered separately. Kris's period had started on the train, a half-day earlier than she had expected. There were canned goods, but no fresh vegetables or fruit; there was no bread. Kris had laid in a good supply of liquor and snacks for our New Year's Eve celebration, but we needed some sort of evening meal. I called my mother and gave her and the family our New Year's greetings. Then we went out to a nearby drug store, in which there was a dining counter and booths. We carried a tray of salads, sandwiches, and coffee to a booth. The jukebox was playing *One O'Clock Jump*. Kris asked me why I was smiling. I told her that Matt, one of my army buddies, used to sing some coarse words to that instrumental. She didn't ask me what they were. I put a nickel in the jukebox and selected *I'll Get By*, recalling, as I did so, Matt's lyrics: Spread your legs / You're breakin' my glasses / How 'm I gonna see down here?

After we listened to our song, I suggested that Kris go to school with me. *Hardly!* Her right hand came down hard on the booth's table-surface. We needed her income for rent and food and all the other necessities. She was right. My allotment wouldn't pay the utility bills. *But wouldn't you like to do it?*

RAIN AND DARKNESS

She said, *Yes, I'd like to study music.* I said that maybe, after a few years, she would be able to do that. She nodded; but she had other plans, as I was to learn. Our song was followed by *Sleepy Lagoon* and *Stomping at the Savoy*. We bought some magazines—*Life, Look, Harper's,* and *Ladies' Home Journal*. It was snowing as we walked back to the apartment.

We turned on the radio for the New Year's festivities, looked over our wedding gifts—small appliances, dishes, kitchenware, linens, a maroon decanter with six matching wine glasses, and checks amounting to $525. We would wait a few days to put it all away. We paged through our magazines and turned to our pretzel sticks, potato chips, smoked oysters, and Martinis; there was Guy Lombardo's music on the radio.

On the radio came the music and bells and cheers and *Auld Lang Syne* at midnight; whistles, bells, and sirens sounded outside. We held each other tightly and kissed lingeringly. We went to bed and fell deeply asleep in a close embrace.

Kris, dressed and smiling in the morning lamplight, urged me out of bed at 5:30 and served a breakfast of canned beans, potato chips, and coffee. I was to join her at the hotel for lunch and dinner. For the following day, which she would have off, we planned to go out for breakfast and then shop for a large supply of groceries. After Kris left for work, I spent the morning with Latin and French paradigms and literary criticism.

38

The New Criticism provided specific directions for the study of poetry. It seemed to be inapplicable to the study of prose. Trends of criticism tend to be successively exclusive; each aims to supersede all previous methods of analysis and commentary. Robert Perm Warren, in his soft Southern voice, would insist that an Arnoldian reading of Archibald MacLeish's *Ars Poetica* didn't *butter any parsnips*. Disregard of poets' biographies was mandatory. I asked if there were to be no exceptions: Wordsworth had to BE at Tintern Abbey, hadn't he? Why disregard biography in an autobiographical poem? Because, says the New Critic, the poem is what *it* says, not what the poet *did*. I learned to play the game and I let my reservations sink into the silence of conformity. I much preferred reading novels under the tutelage of Joseph Warren Beach. His course on the American Novel was greatly in demand—deservedly, I thought. He clarified the experience of reading a novel and required no single approach to the study of literature.

My critique of *God's Little Acre* won from Professor Beach a high grade, marginal compliments, and concluding praise. I had connected Ty Ty's sacrosanct but variable plot of ground with his wisdom: *When you try to take a woman or a man and hold him off all for yourself there ain't going to be nothing but trouble and sorrow the rest of your days*. Reserve something of yourself for God and something of yourself for only yourself; but don't think that, Godlike, you can gain possession of the something of another's self reserved by that other self for only her or his self. Driving home, I envisaged Kris reading and admiring the paper and adding her enthusiastic compliments. This was not to be. She turned over each of the seven pages, reading, perhaps, only parts of each page and then pronouncing aloud the final grade and saying, *Well, good*.

I would drive to the university early enough each morning to secure a parking place behind the Pharmacy building. I would have lunch with either Blackie or Carrie, or, more frequently now, with both. My classes were over by 3:00 p.m. I would leave the university around 3:30 p.m. and be back at the hotel parking lot around 4:00 p.m. In the apartment, I usually studied until Kris came home at 5:45 p.m. She would shower, dress comfortably in a housecoat, and make our evening meal. She was an accomplished cook. We did the dishes together and, while she attended to various household chores, I studied at the table-desk, which had become my territory. During good weather, she would occasionally change into slacks and we would go for a walk to the Lookout.

Our entertainment during week nights was limited to records and the radio. Our record collection included our song and some Glenn Miller and Frank Sinatra selections, along with Beethoven's Ninth, Wagner's overture to *Parsifal*, and Tchaikovsky's *Capriccio Italien*. We subscribed to the morning, afternoon, and Sunday newspapers. Our small bookshelf was filling up with my textbooks, classics (most of them in Modern Library format), and some recent novels. Kris had secured for me a Royal typewriter that had been replaced at the hotel by a newer model.

We would go to bed about 10:00 p.m. There was sensual play and indulgence; but intercourse was limited to the safe nights of the rhythm cycle.

Friday nights were given over to the movies. Weekends were times for getting together with friends from our now diminishing circle, among whom our best and most loyal were Vera and Blackie.

In my latest French class, the poems of the Parnassians, Imagists, and Decadents were not subjected to the New Criticism.

I brought Eliot and Pound into a class discussion; but the professor was a white-haired, tired man, whose lectures were, with vestiges of erudition, close to rote recitations and note-reading and whose receptivity to new critical trends had long been blunted by the attention he had to divert to his bodily ailments.

Vergil's *Aeneid* contained many passages that I found to be relatively easy to enclose within the limits of irony and paradox, two of the New Criticism's favorite configurations. But the Classics instructor was cogent in her argument that we could not cease to contemplate the history and legends of Rome and the Augustan patronage under which Vergil flourished, without which biographical information we could not fully understand or appreciate the *Aeneid*.

Before the winter quarter was over, I had given up in my attempts to interest Kris in my literary and linguistic studies. She showed very little interest in my grades and academic progress. She enjoyed seeing and talking about movies and listening to and talking about music, not, however, at Les Berg's level—not that I could reach that level. Nor was I sufficiently appreciative of Kris's successes at her work. She had received a three-hundred-dollar bonus

RAIN AND DARKNESS

for devising a new and economical elevator schedule. Two of the four elevator operators had to be terminated under this strictly-business arrangement. Kris had two elevators converted to self-service at minimal cost; she retained one full-service (stop-at-every-floor) elevator with uniformed operator and one, with uniformed operator, that rose directly to the eighth floor and then to each of the seven (six, actually, there being no floor numbered thirteen) top floors. She smiled, and giggled a bit, as she told me about it. I nodded and offered only a perfunctory compliment.

Mercury says, *Varium et mutabile semper femina* (a woman is something forever inconstant and fickle); where Kris was concerned, I read the line as *a woman is something forever complex and versatile*. She was more of an Anna to Karrie's Dido than a Dido herself, just as I was perhaps something of an Achates to Blackie's Aeneas. But I concluded that it is the male who is inconstant and fickle, always intent, in what he takes to be his love, upon the *formosa fastigia feminae* (the beautiful superficies of a woman), while the woman implants [Open the gates, George] her love within the true little acre of a man's self, the reality lying well beneath the variable performance that he takes to be his life. As newlyweds, and as wife and man, Kris and I professed love only conventionally. We sensed that, in using the word *love* we were reading a given script. Our devotion was inherent in our pet names, *BlissKris* and *SweePete*.

Mercurially, I would often read the Sunday paper while Kris would walk alone to church.

In one indelible way the New Criticism was applicable patently and solely to poetry. *Word* is what it says: it is a word. *Tree* is also a word, but it is not what it says; it represents an object, or calls an object to mind. *Click* and other onomatopoetic words are what they say, to the extent that they denote the sounds they make. Metrical terms, like *iamb* and *spondee*, are what they say, to the extent that they exemplify the quantities or stresses that they denote. In general, words are not what they say, and they must be interpreted within a context. To the New Critic, a poem, as a poem, is what it says; and it is not subject to interpretation. Kris, using words and intonations, as she talked to others, was subject to interpretation (and misunderstanding). Kris, making the Sign of the Cross, was Kris and Kris alone, a lucid poem.

39

The quarters multiply, and Blackie appears less often at the Bridge for lunch. He and his new lunch companion, one of his Business-course classmates, go to the more commodious, and more expensive, Northern Light. Carrie Coreghian has succeeded him as my regular lunch-mate. I feel more comfortable, I think, with her than with anyone I know, than with, in some ways, even Kris. Carrie, to me, seems more like a guy than like the woman she is, in rapport, if not in appearance. She has a fund of very funny dirty jokes; and she shares my proletarian lack of style and grace. Whenever we meet, she has a ready and sincere compliment for me: I look handsome; some article of clothing I'm wearing suits me just right; whatever idea or bit of writing I submit to her is given careful and admiring attention.

If this is flattery or fawning, it is at least evidence of her taking the trouble to please me; and Carrie seems never to expect any kind of requital. Kris, with body language, facial movements, and vocal intonations, keeps me up to her expectations at the table, in dress, and in attentiveness to her. This is entirely fair, given all that she does for me: cooking and serving healthful and pleasing meals; washing and ironing my clothes; doing all of the housework for the apartment, except for what little I occasionally volunteer to do; and taking care of most of our bills and expenses. She manages, also, always to be clean, neat, and attractive enough to be, in my estimation, beautiful. She works full-time, and she supports us. I enjoy life as a student. I am a bit troubled when she says that I am not really a student, that, in fact, I am playing the role of a student; and, further, when she says that, in almost all that I do, I am more of a role-player than an authentic agent. She doesn't complain about my inauthenticity or urge me to change my ways; no, she says that, as an accomplished role-player, I am good at what I do; and I am satisfied when, upon saying to her, *Well, YOU are the real thing, Kris*, she smiles and gives me a warmly sensual embrace.

Kris's potentially successful drive to possess that little acre of my real being disclosed to me the possibility that my passivity harbors the force of activity and is connected, in the current of Language's reality, to the Latin deponent verb. To this segment of Latin grammar I wedded my thought for weeks, months. Even now, encouraged by my reading of Martin Heidegger, I consider, in something akin to amazement, the precision with which this utterance of Language speaks me. A deponent verb is one that is passive in form and active in meaning. The explanation is that the verb has laid or put aside (*de* [from] + *ponens* [putting]) its active form. It doesn't do this completely, however; it retains some active forms with active meanings (future infinitive, present and future participles, gerund, and supine), and it has a passive meaning in the gerundive and, sometimes, in the perfect passive participle. My Classics instructor, insisting that the passive form with active meaning was merely a matter of usage, would not entertain my suggestion that this was Language saying something about Itself and about the dyadism of being human. She did not like my use of the term *dyadism*. She knew about chemical and linguistic divalences; with regard to the latter, she said that deponent verbs were not different from standard verbs in the various valencies. I defined a dyad as a unit consisting of two incompatible but interdependent factors, like an atom with a proton and an electron, like a verb form that is both active and passive. To the amusement of the others in class, she stifled me with an effective argument based on the Aristotelian categories (about which I knew nothing) of action and passivity and the synonymity of *dyad* and *duality*.

Checking up on the Aristotelian categories, I decided that I had to learn Greek. Bringing up the subject in class again, I proposed that a duality was two integral units, the separation of which need not result in the destruction of both, like the body's living after the mind had died (in a brain-dead person), and a dyad was one unit consisting of two incompatible factors, the separation of which necessarily resulted in the destruction of both, as in the atomic bomb. *Look*, she said, *a and b are units; right?* I nodded. *And they are factors of the unit ab; right?* I nodded, or maybe said *Yes*. She said then that, if we separate them, neither one is destroyed. I claimed that, assuming they were incompatible, they were indeed destroyed as factors, since, separated, neither was a factor of anything, except, possibly, itself.

It was when I used a male-female analogy that she permanently ended the discussion. I said that, in lovemaking, the female was passive, as recipient, and active, as donative determinant. Her irritation, impatience, and anger were evident in her refusal to respond and in her turning exclusively to the text before us, which, ironically, presented Queen Dido preparing to commit suicide because Aeneas, by whom she had been, presumably, laid, was deserting her. Vergil was at his best here; in *pius Aeneas* he exposed the ultimate inferiority of the active-heroic male to the passive-active female: Aeneas's running away from the Didonian passivity, which was betrayed by its incompatible factor, Dido's donative determinance (determining Aeneas's pleasure by the degree to which she gave of herself), resulted in the destruction of both the determining and the giving, namely, Dido's suicide. These specious thoughts devolved into remembrances of Jordy Klug and Austrian echoes of Dead Gallus.

The Latin deponent verb became important to me. By now, I was aware of myself as a passive person. I needed to ennoble that passivity of mine by identifying my active factor, which I had assumed must move upon that little acre of my real being. It occurred to me that Kris's ready acceptance of me must have been due to her having intuited it. I talked to her about it, about, that is, the Latin deponent verb, activity and passivity, and my real being. She reacted with what I detected as a surprising strain of contempt. She said that I ought to be learning Business, like Blackie, instead of wasting all my time on words and fiction.

Blackie was almost equally unsympathetic to my self-directed divagations upon the Latin deponent verb. I say *almost* because there was in his reaction, instead of contempt, a sincere concern. According to him, I was romanticizing, giving words and syntax a life they didn't and couldn't have. Few things repelled him more than grown men devoting their lives to the study of poetry and the relationships of words. *Get away from it, Ped.* If I couldn't handle Business, I should get into Math and Physics or one of the other real sciences (as opposed to literary criticism, Sociology, and similar pseudo-doodles). All I could do with Literature was teach it to others and proliferate unprofitable pretentiousness—and delude myself by indulging in its delusiveness.

Carrie, however, was receptive to my ideas on the subject and sincerely interested in following them out. She hadn't studied Latin but decided, after listening to my explanation of the Latin deponent verb, that she would. She said that prostitutes represented the basic truth, the very ground, of the active-passive dyad. We got hung up, to be sure, on the facts of male prostitutes, homosexuality, and forms of rigidity; and we tried, without real success, to resolve these as aberrations. We did better, at least to our satisfaction, when we posited a universal female force that was not limited to human females.

In a few years I would come upon Jung's *anima* and *animus*. And I would get to Aeschylus's *thelykrates* (the power that moves women); and I would connect these concepts with the universal dyad that Carrie and I worked out: the female force (consciousness: Eve, Pandora, Athena) and the male force (energy: Adam, Chaos).

Largior, miror, patior, sequor, vereor: I give, I admire, I put up with, I follow, I fear. The male comes to expect all this from the female, who meets the expectation with donative determinance, as the women in Ibsen's plays decide, to their misfortune, not to do. *Utor, fruor, fungor, potior, vescor*: I use, I enjoy, I perform, I take possession of, I feed upon. Manifest masculine activity in passive form. Then, as the action subordinates the passive, the semi-deponent prevails: *audeo, fido, gaudeo, soleo*: I dare, I trust, I rejoice, I am in the habit of. When I study Greek and get to the middle voice, I shall applaud the practical and revelatory economy of male-oriented Latin.

I theorized: the female force, if it is dominant in a male, subordinates energy to consciousness; the male force, if it is dominant in a female, does the reverse; the former is deponent; the latter is semi-deponent.

Carrie and I agreed that, as an analogy, this was all nonsense, but that, as the speech of Language, it pointed the way to the reality of Being.

40

Vera and Blackie were married the last week of June. Kris and I expected to be asked to be matron of honor and best man. Vera did ask Kris so to serve. Blackie asked his Business-class friend to be his best man. I think that I have never got over my heavy disappointment at this choice. Kris understood and sought to ease my pain. She told Vera that she felt it would be better to remain at my side as part of the general wedding party than to remain separated with the bridal group. Vera was very understanding.

It was a lavish wedding, with an orchestral reception at a downtown hotel. Blackie was a fine host; he paid considerable attention to me and introduced me to all whom we met as his *best friend*, to which his best man showed no reaction other than a cordial smile. He and Vera thanked Kris and me often and, it seemed, sincerely for our wedding gift, which Kris had picked out and which I cannot remember. Well, no; I do remember. It was a setting of silverware, along with the pattern's soup ladle and serving spoon. Kris knew the pattern that Vera had been collecting as part of her hope chest. The gift was expensive. It took the whole of my month's allotment and three times that much from Kris's savings—our savings, now.

Blackie's best man gave the newlyweds, for their honeymoon, a week at his cabin on Lake Superior. From the photographs they later showed us, the cabin looked more like a resort mansion than like what I had been accustomed to think of as a cabin; there was a tennis court, beach, dock, and boathouse. When they returned, Kris and I helped them move into their new apartment. Blackie skipped the first summer session at the university. I had enrolled for both sessions. Carrie did not attend summer sessions; she was an assistant director at a summer camp for handicapped children. During the first session, I gave up having lunch at the Bridge alone. I did not take the initiative in forming an acquaintance with someone with whom to have lunch; instead, I waited to be approached. No one in the two classes I was taking approached me. I asked Kris to make me a daily lunch. She was very pleased to do this. I would carry the lunch—two satisfying sandwiches (usually lunch meat, tomato, lettuce, and Mayonnaise), with fruit and a Mars candy bar—in a brown paper bag, along with black coffee in a thermos jug, and enjoy it either in my Model A or under a tree on the river bank.

Pride in my German lineage had been growing, as I learned about *Das Nibelungenlied,* von Eschenbach's *Parzival,* Goethe, Schiller, Thomas Mann, and other great writers, and listened more and more to Beethoven, Mozart, Wagner, the Strausses, and Mahler; but no satisfaction quite equaled, for me, that which I had developed for French literature and culture. My enthusiastic preoccupation with Latin literature and with the Latin language and its mysteriously engaging deponent-verb system, would not come about until I moved into my study of the Roman elegists.

My first-session courses were given over to Victor Hugo and Hermann Hesse, the latter in translation, although I took the trouble to locate and read some of the originals. During the second session, when my lunches with Blackie resumed, his Business-classmate/best-man friend spending the summer in New York, I took courses in Herman Melville and in the English Romantic Poets.

Kris and I went on a few picnics with Vera and Blackie. We invited them to dinner once; and I was proud of Kris in her preparation of the meal. Vera and Blackie returned the invitation. Vera's dinner was more sumptuous than Kris's, with esoteric hors d'oeuvres and special vintage wines; but the service did not include the silverware to which we had contributed a setting.

Vera and Blackie were dressed quite casually, Vera in a middy blouse and culottes, Blackie in a Hawaiian-print sport shirt and khaki slacks. At first, I had dressed casually in jeans and a terrycloth pullover. When Kris, dressed in a new, pale green summer suit, saw me, as I had dressed, she said, in a moderately loud and firmly insistent voice, *You are NOT wearing THAT!* Her burning-brown eyes were bright with the anger with which she spoke.

[George, what's a moderate but stronger cliché than *I was taken aback?*] This was the first time that I had seen the anger of which Kris was capable. In my complete surprise, I felt somewhat betrayed. I had not been in any way aware of this side of my Kris. Meekly, I said, *No*, and went to the bedroom to change into my brown lightweight Shantung suit. Returning home from the Konshaks' dinner, I said, *Hey, BlissKris, they were dressed kind of casual, weren't they?* She said she wasn't concerned with how THEY were dressed. What mattered, she added, was our respect for each other and our never letting that fade away. I interpreted this to mean that hereafter I should first check to see how she was dressed, or was going to dress, and then dress accordingly. I was right, to that extent; but I was to learn that it went a lot further than that (to where *we* were right).

41

The next academic year was going fairly well. Blackie and I lunched together more frequently. His best man had graduated and was at work for a prestigious advertising firm. Carrie joined us on Thursdays, during which regularly extended lunches we shared volumes of jokes. The English professor who considered me an A+ student had become my advisor. My Latin classes were sparsely enrolled and all the more pleasant for being so. The courses given by Professor Landis, the chairman of the Classics department, were exceptionally instructive; and he, too, singled me out as a promising student. He listened sympathetically to my ideas about the deponent verb. He showed interest but could not accept my notions as linguistically valid. Nonetheless, he encouraged me to pursue them.

The Model A was having more breakdowns, and my father was less readily available to attend to them.

I could replace the fan when it broke and choke out the carburetor and do a few other things to keep it going; but trouble was developing with the connecting rod, for which my father diagnosed an imminent irreparability and about which he cautioned me. Kris and I decided to get a different car at the end of summer. I drove the Model A sparingly and used the streetcar more often.

Winter was severe. On Mondays, Wednesdays, and Fridays, when he had no early morning classes, Blackie would go out of his way to pick me up and take me with him to the university. On Tuesdays and Thursdays, I would take the streetcar. Kris and I would use the Model A on weekends. Blackie dismissively rejected my offer, following Kris's concerted insistence, that I help pay for his gas, while I was his passenger.

Spring was surprisingly sudden in its appearance; and the early verdure led my advisor to quote Keats, *The poetry of earth is never dead*. I said, *Professor Seward, yours is the grasshopper's song, mine the cricket's*. He answered, *Possibly, but you know how profitably to be in drowsiness half lost*.

After my early-morning French class, I would go to the library for two hours of study. This one morning is so gloriously fresh that I stop outside the library and sit on the sun-warmed wooden bench. The easy, lenient sun lets the pines and budding oaks on the mall send long and soothing shadows over the rain-green grass. I sink into a gentle peace that is fanned by a breeze that seems to carry memories of days of happiness that I had really never known, and, then, memories of no memories, wherein a vow sustains a soul: *renounce the Devil and all his works and all his ways*.

Someone had joined me on the bench. *Hi, Shit-head*.

Jordy wanted to know if I had opened the box. I told him that it had never been delivered to me. He said that he was not surprised, that I had the luck of a nightcrawler stranded on sidewalk dew. I asked him what the sealed cigarette case had contained. *A jeweled Habsburg key*, he said, *for the coffers of il fondamento*. Was *il fondamento*, I asked, the Mafia. He laughed and said the Mafia was only a late Viking contrivance set up among a few ass-licking Sicilian families, a kind of afterthought of the turd-brained Norskies who had set up Black Mail in Scotland. I asked him what the undelivered box had contained. *Some Latin stuff by Gallo,* he said; *it would have made you rich.* Gallo, he explained, had established *il fondamento* [*fundamentum femineum*] in Egypt. It became the basis of the underground Roman empire [*orbis terrarum imperium infernum*].

Empty-headed hordes from the frozen-ass North slowed it down, but Carlomagno got it going again in the ninth century. Giovanni di Piano Carpini carried it all the way to Karakorum; but Marco Polo carried it on to Yangzhou and Hangzshou. It's been global ever since. Franco knew how to ride it; but Mussolini, and then Hitler, tried to isolate and control it. Jordy became strangely pensive, but then recovered his scorn. *Fascismo* constricts and debilitates its pattern or mode: it's got to be global, not national.

None of this grinningly expressed arcana made sense to me; but I asked him if he were part of the movement. *Doesn't matter*, he said; *we'll all be part of it in time. The box could have made you rich, a famous Latinist. Instead, you'll sit around and never even learn how to fully wipe your ass*. I resented the split infinitive and being put down for a delivery that someone had failed to make to me; but, to Jordy, the failure was mine because my *passività* kept me out of life's currents.

So. You married a Polack cunt and the flag-draper has taken on a skinny Swedish putanna. I figured that *putanna* was the equivalent of French *putain* (whore). This is where convention called upon me to smash Jordy in his smirking face and then fight as well as I could while he beat me into a bloodied and broken-boned mess. I didn't move. Jordy, dressed all in black, was now at least six feet tall, with broad shoulders and a leathery, dark complexion. *Come on, Jordy*, I pleaded, *you have no call to talk like that.* He smiled and held up the middle finger of his left hand: *Don't I now?* He said the flag-draper was making good business connections but that they were not going to be deep enough to get *with base*. I thought he meant *on base*. He didn't; he meant *with base*.

When I asked him how he had found me here, and where he'd got his information about Blackie and me, he said that, on his return from New York and Detroit, he'd paid his usual visits to my mother, a *truly fine lady*, who deserved a better *primogenito* than I, and that she had filled in whatever blank spaces there were.

He rose from the bench, frowning as he stared at me, his right thumb hooked inside his black belt, and said, *Try to do something with that Latin; see you around*, then turned, and walked smartly away. Over lunch, I told Blackie about my meeting with Jordy. He nodded and seemed not surprised. *One way or another*, he said, *Jordy will always be shooting at us*. He seemed, also, to be familiar with *il fondamento*, as I tried to recount Jordy's comments. He had heard something like this in a class taught by a professor from India, who had outlined it as both mystical, in its character of collective acquisitive impulse, and practical, in its disposition of monetary fascism, the root of monopolies, cartels, and war as a means of stabilizing, by protracted increase, the wealth of its highest echelons.

He added the professor's claim that the secret institutional order began with Kubla Khan and some *telesmatic golden gerege*, which looked like a fraternity paddle without a handle. Blackie had never heard of Gallo, however; and, when I told him about the undelivered box, he laughed. Thinking about Coleridge's unfinished poem, I asked Blackie if there really was a Kubla Khan. He assured me that Kublai, the Great Khan, was a Mongolian conqueror and a contemporary of Marco Polo, that, in fact, he had provided Marco Polo's brothers, Niccolò and Matteo, with a gerege to ensure that they would be safe and receive help on their journeys, or so the professor from India had said.

That night, I sat at the table-desk and looked at the Latin writings that Jordy had given me while I was in high school. I had less difficulty now working them out, but they were still challenging enough to me to elude my making full sense of them. Kris, seated on the sofa, was in her beige pajamas, with the green-stemmed red rose embroidered over the heart-area. Her hair was up in curlers. She had laid aside her blue-beaded rosary and was reading the current issue of *Redbook*. After a while, I put the Latin writings off to the side of the table-desk and went to kneel by her. I unbuttoned her pajama top, opened it out, and fondled and kissed her breasts. She pulled my head closer to her and rested her cheek on it. Later, we sipped some wine and then went to bed and thoroughly enjoyed the sanction of the rhythm method.

42

Over the next few days, I typed out all of the passages that I had received from Jordy and translated them—satisfactorily, I thought. I showed it all to Professor Landis, the Classics chairman, during one of his office hours. He took an interest in my compilation and read it all very carefully. *Where in the world did you get this, Peter?* I explained that the lines had been given to me piecemeal over a period of time by an acquaintance, who had challenged me to translate them. *Was this acquaintance a classicist or a Latin teacher?* I said that he was neither one but that he had some European connections. Professor Landis said that four of the lines appeared to be a demotic laudatory inscription and that, as elegiacs, they could have been addressed to Caesar Augustus by Cornelius Gallus during Gallus's Egyptian prefecture. *Dead Gallus,* I mumbled almost involuntarily. *Yes!* He looked up approvingly, *As in Propertius's second book.* He asked me what I knew about Gallus. I said that he was identified in one of my anthologies as a Roman elegist, along with Catullus, Tibullus, Propertius, and Ovid, but that, so far, I'd read only a few poems by Catullus and the other elegists. He provided me with information about Gallus and gave me four references to check out.

Gaius Cornelius Gallus (Gallo, in modern Italian) was born in 69 B.C., a year after Vergil was born. He was of equestrian rank; that is, he was a knight (or, businessman).

He enjoyed the erotic favors of a freedwoman actor, Volumnia Cytheris, who had been the mistress of Marc Antony. She teased and tormented him with her sporadic resistance and infidelities; and he composed poems in elegiac distichs about her, calling her *Lycoris* and referring to her as his *domina* (dominating mistress). Other elegists who joined in the trend of celebrating pseudonymous domineering mistresses were Catullus (84-54), Propertius (about 50-2), Tibullus (about 49-19), and Ovid (43 B.C.-A.D. 18). He was admired by these poets, as well as by Vergil (died 19 B.C.). Reportedly, he wrote four books of elegiac verse, none of which has survived. A few lines in the *Anthologia Latina* are attributed to him, perhaps spuriously. During the confiscation of properties after the assassination of Julius Caesar, Gallus, as one of Octavian's officials, made it possible for Vergil to retain his family's land-holdings; and Vergil, in his bucolic poems, sang his praise of Gallus. After Octavian defeated Antony at the battle of Actium (30 B.C.), Gallus participated in Octavian's Egyptian campaign and was appointed as the first prefect of Egypt. He put down an insurgency in the Thebes area, established the Ethiopian kingdom as a Roman protectorate, and placed a nominal ruler over a region that served as a barrier to hostile forces.

He recorded these accomplishments on a stone inscription at Philae (29 B.C.) and ordered statues of himself raised in Egypt. He was recalled to Rome and censured by the Senate, ostensibly for his self-aggrandizement. He was denied access to Caesar Augustus (Octavian) and forbidden residence in any of the Roman provinces. In 26 B.C., he either committed suicide or was murdered.

Responding to my question, Professor Landis agreed that Gallus's secret establishment of an international power base would have been a more likely *causa exili* than political pretentiousness and would account more for his being murdered than for his being, more honorably, ordered to commit suicide but could, nonetheless, hardly be more than speculation. From his file cabinet he withdrew two folders and from one of the folders a page displaying the papyrus text. He pointed out a number of errors in my translations by suggesting that I might want to change this or that phrase or word to, perhaps, a phrase or word that he supplied. He asked me to copy out five lines from the papyrus reading, to be added to the four from papyrus text that I had received, in the form of a prose passage, from Jordy, and translate them. *These passages do scan, you know. Can you set them up as elegiac distichs?* I said that I would try.

One of the five additional lines contained the word *Lycori*; the other four amounted to fulsome praise of *Caesar* (referring, probably, to Augustus). At that time, I was far from adept at metrical scansion, which entails syllable quantity: a long syllable is one with a long vowel, or with a short vowel followed by two consonants. There were some helpful rules for differentiating short and long vowels; but I had frequent recourse to the shortcut of checking words in Charlton T. Lewis's *An Elementary Latin Dictionary*, in which a macron is placed over each long vowel. There is also, as in modern Italian, the resolution of hiatus by the elision of vowels at the end of a word followed by vowels at the beginning of the next word.

Much to Kris's displeasure, I stayed up late, after she had gone to bed, for three nights, working on the project. On the fourth night, receiving the flaming-brown-eyed anger of her frowning stare as she stood beside my chair, I followed her to bed.

After a little more than a week, I brought my effort to Professor Landis during one of his office hours. He was enthusiastically complimentary, even as he made corrections to every line except the five that he had given me himself. The project, in his hands, took finally the following form:

>Extinxerunt nocte oculos femura aurea solis
>>nunc hebetes radiis facta Lycoridis. Ei!
>
>Illa puella in pulvinario cum considet
>>unda ita salsa maris cretus amorque tumet
>
>Contra mentem animose non dominae gerit artus
>>sed penetrare aliter militis vis poterit
>
>et penes illam inibit labefactaque parta
>>ostia se faciens somnia perficient
>
>in castra illius in nocte et non violenter
>>et in amore levam caute et eam capiam
>
>tristia nequit[ia . . . .] a Lycori tua.
>
>Fata mihi, Caesar, tum erunt mea dulcia, quom tu
>>maxima Romanae pars eri<s> historiae
>
>postque tuum reditum multorum templa deorum
>>fixa legam spolieis deivitiora tueis.
>
>Clara bonae] tandem fecerunt c[ar]mina Musae
>>quae possem domina deicere digna mea.
>
>Digne tunc domin]atur idem tibi, non ego, Visce,
>>nec tibi iam, Kato, iudice te vereor.

The square and pointed brackets enclose editorial additions and emendations. That the arrangement ended with *vereor*, a deponent verb (meaning *I am afraid*) gave me a feeling of propriety. Professor Landis said that the ascription of any, or all, of this to Gallus depended on the mentions of Lycoris, the use of *domina* and the postulated *dominatur*, and the actual attributions to Gallus in citations. He thought that it was all rather shoddy stuff and that it did not adequately reflect Gallus's high reputation among his contemporaries. Revising almost the whole of my translation, he produced what he called *our translation:*

> Now the thighs of Lycoris, made golden by the sun's rays,
> > have blinded my night-dulled eyes.
>
> While that sweetheart of mine cuddles on a cushion,
> > my love swells like a sea's salt wave grown huge.
>
> Against the mind of his mistress the force of a soldier
> > does not bring spirited limbs, but penetrates in other ways
> and in her presence will make entrance as the door gives way:
> > openings will fashion themselves, dreams will bring them about.
> Into her camp at night, and not with violence, I
> > shall loosen her in love and carefully take her.
>
> sad deeds {ADD *facta*] brought about, Lycoris, by your sins
>
> Caesar, my fate will be fine when you become
> > the greatest part of Rome's history,
> when I read, upon your return, of temples of many gods
> > enriched by the show of your spoils.

> The kind Muses have finally made bright poems
> which, worthy of my mistress, I could let fall.
> She is worthily dominant, then, while, Viscus, and Kato too, I
> fear neither of you as judge.

Professor Landis asked again about the person who had given me the material that I had brought to him. When I gave him the name of Giordano Klug and said that he had got them, probably, from an academic granduncle in Italy or Germany, Professor Landis asked me if I could arrange a meeting with Mr. Klug. I said that I would try to do so and added that Mr. Klug had indicated that there might be a box, containing more of this material, somewhere around Heidelberg. He told me that I ought to make serious efforts to secure that box. I nodded, wishing that I had not mentioned the box, which I was sure that Jordy had contrived as a taunt.

Professor Landis frowned a bit, rubbing the side of his nose with his forefinger and pursing his lips. He thought the scansion was scratchy, even rough; the first four lines lacked elegiac proportion; there were, however, some niceties in the next six lines (syllabic epanodos:-*iter . . . -erit*; polyptoton: *faciens . . . perficient*; and hemistich rhyme: *levam . . . capiam, nequitia . . . tua, Romanae . . . historiae, spolieis . . . tueis,* and *domina . . . mea*); but, all in all, it didn't square up, and he'd like to know how it came into Mr. Klug's possession.

I had no phone number for Jordy. That evening I called my mother and asked her to ask Jordy if he would be willing to talk to one of my professors about the Latin passages he'd given me. She promised to do so: *But you know Jordy*. That I did. That I did.

Sunday morning. Kris had gone to church. I answered the phone. Jordy greeted me with his usual obscene epithets and told me to get my head out of my asshole and wash the shit out of my eyes. He might talk to a mathematician or physicist, but never to any fart in the liberal arts. Couldn't I learn Latin on my own? Courses in literature and in any of the languages were pure bullshit and steamy cowpiss. *Tell your prickhead professor to get himself a real job.* I asked Jordy if there really were a Heidelberg box. *Not any more. Not as far as you're concerned. Say Hi to your Polack; she IS nice to look at. But she's a complainer.* I asked him if he had met her. *Switch to Business, if you want your marriage to work out. See you around.* He hung up. I turned back to the Sunday paper, wondering why I could not entirely dislike Jordy.

Professor Landis was disappointed when I told him that Mr. Klug was inexplicably averse to any meeting with university faculty members. He did not pursue the matter, but he urged me to make efforts to secure more of this material and to find out what I could about the box that I had mentioned.

43

Hearing my description of Jordy—tall, dressed in black (like a Hollywood villain), black wavy hair, aquiline face [*What's aquiline*, she asked; *Eagle-like*, I said: *craggy face, hooked nose*], *long thin fingers*)—Kris said that she had never met him but that she often sees people like that in the hotel lobby. *Does he wear a big black hat?* I said that I had not seen him in one. We played our new Ink Spots recording of *I'll Get By:* . . . *there may be rain* came on as . . . *though there be rain*. It was a much better version than the one by Dick Haymes, to which version, however, we remained sentimentally loyal. We learned that the Ink Spots had recorded their version three years before Dick Haymes had recorded his.

Blackie was convinced that Jordy's predisposition to business had to do with his illegal activities. All business is robbery of one kind or another, he concluded. The trick is to keep your dealings above the line of the law; but the biggest profits are almost always below that line. The Liberal Arts can do no more than add a little smart-ass talk to Business and Law. All you can do with the Liberal Arts alone is to teach; and *Teaching is bullshit. Well, so is business promotion, but Business can be profitable.* Jordy doesn't work; but the cost of one of his black silk shirts amounts to a month's salary for a teacher. I asked Blackie about Science. He allowed that Science was different: you really needed to know something and your knowledge could bring in big money; but, in the end, *Science is an unrelenting acquisition of knowledge about the world, which the full acquisition of that knowledge will destroy.* He smiled when I jotted down what he had said. Seven years later, I would compare this observation with Arthur C. Clarke's short story, *The Nine Billion Names of God*, in which a computing machine brings the world to an end by bringing up all of the names for God.

Vera, Blackie, Kris, and I went to a crime movie one Friday night. It was *Out of the Past*, a cinematic improvement upon Geoffrey Homes's (Daniel Mainwaring's) novel, *Build My Gallows High*. We talked about it, over coffee and doughnuts, in one of the cushioned booths in *Nick Lyon's Den*. Blackie identified the minor actors: Harry Hayden, Mary Field, Frank Wilcox, Adda Gleason, Wallace Scott—*and how about Ken Niles!* He didn't like the movie's contrivances, like Dickie Moore's casting a fish-line some thirty or forty feet up to a cliff ledge, hooking Paul Valentine, and pulling him down to his death on the stones of the stream.

Vera noted the smooth and facile evil of Joe Stefanos, the character played by Valentine. I liked Nicholas Musuraca's light-and-shadow photography and the complex structure, with flashbacks like those in *Citizen Kane* and *The Killers*. I was proud of Kris; she pointed out the relation of the innocent-faced Kathie Moffat (played by Jane Greer) to light: she walks in out of the sunlight at La Mar Azul; she walks in out of the moonlight at Pablo's; she kills Fisher (played by Steve Brodie) in firelight—and, as Robert Mitchum's Jeff Markham here sees for the first time what she really is, a cold killer, the music (*The First Time I Saw You*) defines the theme—she kills Kirk Douglas's Sterling by firelight; and she kills Jeff in their getaway car after they have made their last plans by the same firelight. Kris wondered what the fish references meant: the name *Fisher*; the fish-nets on the beach, where Kathie *catches* Jeff (and he says, *Baby, I don't care*); Dickie Moore's fish-line and hook; the name of Ken Niles's character, *Eels*. Vera complimented Kris, saying that she had, in fact, by listing the references, already explained them: fishing for easy advantage and getting hooked. Kris nodded; but she said she wasn't sure that that was it.

Vera thought that stolid Jim (played by Richard Webb) gave himself away pathetically in lamenting his loss of Ann (played by blond-haired Virginia Huston) to Jeff: Jim said that he once *fixed her roller skates*. He should have said *carried her schoolbooks*; fixing her roller skates must have given him the opportunity to look up her skirt. Blackie laughed. Kris tuned her head to stare out over the tables. She suggested that Jim could have meant repairing the roller skates instead of fastening them to Ann's feet. I imagined what looking up that skirt might disclose.

Vera complimented Kris on her beige nylon blouse and brown pullover sweater, and on the exquisite new spun-gold chain for her cross. Kris complimented Vera on her hair-do and on her long silk-like blond curls' being set off *perfectly* by her magenta blouse. Blackie sat back in candle-lit splendor as Vera listed, with pride and pleasure, his academic accomplishments and the good fortune of his having his work toward the M.B.A. subsidized by the Company that he would eventually be associated with full-time. I went on for a bit about Kris's successes at the hotel, including her recent advancement. I hoped that she would mention my high grades and my election to an honor society; but she placed her hand upon mine and was silent. I began then to talk about Professor Landis's interest in the Latin passages that Jordy had given me and about the mystery that Jordy refused to resolve.

Impatiently, Blackie changed the subject, predicting calamities consequent upon the Democrats' ill-advised push for Civil Rights. He said that there would be a Republican presidential victory and the Democrats' loss of the Solid South. We argued, seriously, but without rancor. Vera and Kris went to the Ladies' Room.

In bed that night, Kris lay on her back, with her legs parted; I lay on my side, with my right hand cupping her pudenda. She turned her head and kissed me. She said that, if Kirk Douglas, in the movie, were a bit thinner and had black hair and wore all black, he would fit the description of Jordy that I had given her. I envisaged the changes and agreed, with the reservation that Douglas's nose was less pointed. She said that maybe the fish-allusions had something to do with human evolution: what is evil in human beings is the survival instinct, which we carry from our birth in the sea, through our amphibious stage, and amplify by our developed consciousness. (I'm polishing her phraseology.) *Doesn't that go against Catholic doctrine, Bliss?* I was pleased with her answer: *It goes against Catholic ignorance but not against Catholic truth.*

During one of our lunches the following week, Blackie and I had one of our earnest talks. I wish that I could reproduce it verbatim, as so many first-person novelists do; but I must resort to faulty recollection, inventive reconstruction, and paraphrase. I employ *italics* for words, phrases, and clauses that I am certain I recall exactly; but I cannot claim infallibility even amidst my certainty.

We were into coffee refills when Blackie asked me if Kris complained a lot. Remembering Jordy Klug's *she's a complainer*, and wondering again how Jordy had reached that conclusion, I told Blackie that she did complain about my choice of clothes to wear, some of my personal habits, my spending too much of my time reading and studying, and my not talking to her enough. I added, though, that she was generally right and that she deserved more from me, given that she was working while I went to school, that she did all the cooking, laundry, housecleaning, and bill-paying, without complaint. Blackie sipped his coffee, nodded, and asked if she paid me many compliments. I said *No*, but I added that I was hardly lavish, either, with compliments for her. *She doesn't need them*, he said; *you do*.

Then he asked me if she ever aimed those dark brown eyes of hers straight at my Aryan blues and said *I love you*. I told Blackie that we didn't get into that I-love-you routine, but that we had pet names for each other, and that, physically, our endearments went far . . . He interrupted: *I guess that's not my damned business, Ped*.

I insisted that, between us, nothing was *verboten* or off limits.

He nodded and went on to say that, although Kris and I were a striking and complementary couple, we generated odd sparks of distance. *You really should have married Carrie Coreghian: she is not much to look at, but looks can't carry a marriage, and two people never looked more at ease and psychologically satisfied in each other's company. The kind of devotion she has for you and the deep pleasure her presence brings to you are marriage itself.* I said that, yes, I did like her company and never tired of it, but that I was not aware of devotion on her part. *She loves you, Ped. You need much more praise than the average male ego requires*—and Carrie would more than meet that need, not to mention the sack. Blackie's preterition jolted me: I had never thought of Carrie as a sexual partner; I was surprised now to find that the thought was not unpleasant. I insisted, more as a question than as a statement, that, whatever the advantages and prospects of happiness, I would not—and could not possibly—exchange my marriage with Kris for one with Carrie. I wondered, *Why?*

It's the rain-dark forest, Blackie said. *The what?* He explained: *Health and happiness live in a strange and rain-dark forest; we find them only when we are lost in it.* That is what his mother, the strange and wise Rebecca, had told him.

Carrie was walking down the mall on her way to the Union. Catching up with her, I suggested that we have some coffee. After she bought a text at the Union bookstore, we had coffee on the Terrace, overlooking the river. Being, as always, fully at ease and comfortable with her, I told her, almost jokingly, what Blackie had said about our compatibility and her devotion to me (love, praise, sack, and all). *Well,* she sighed, *he's right, Pete.*

The river channel was narrow out below the Union, the current swift enough to effect elongated breakers. I looked rightward to the west, where the channel widened in a spacious bend and the current slowed in the spread as the river eased its way out of sight under a series of bridges and through the city toward the suburbs and then southward.

Carrie graduated *summa cum laude* and moved to New York. Blackie received his M.B.A. and entered the world of business. Coping on campus with emptiness, loneliness, bleak sunshine, dark rain, and funeral snow, I sank more seriously into the study of literature.

44

Kris and I had dinner with Vera and Blackie in their new house. We played seven games of *Hearts*, Kris winning two and Blackie five. Then we relaxed and listened to the election returns. Kris and I said goodnight to our hosts around eleven-thirty, when the unexpectedly close race seemed to be favoring Dewey. Blackie was grinning and confident. Back in the apartment, I turned the radio on and listened to the returns for another forty minutes. There was still no decision or concession when I joined Kris in bed.

Except for the early washouts of Wallace and Thurmond, there was still no decision or concession midway through my first morning class, at which the instructor had plugged in a small radio. My second morning class lasted only twenty minutes: the California returns were coming in. The instructor said we should all go to the Union and listen to the results. It was over by noon. Truman carried California, and Dewey conceded. Truman had belied the polls and had overcome two Democratic splinters, the southern Democrats under Strom Thurmond's States' Rights Party and Wallace with his Progressive Party. On campus, I had no one with whom to celebrate or to discuss the great upset. Carrie was now doing graduate work in English at Columbia University. Blackie was at work, for the company that had subsidized his M.B.A. work. Alone, with coffee and a chicken sandwich at the Bridge, I enjoyed the excitement of others and thought of Blackie and of how disappointed he must be.

I recalled the party that Rebecca arranged for Blackie when he received his M.B.A. She had invited Kris and me, and Kris's mother, who had come for a visit, and my mother and father. The other guests were Blackie's sisters and their husbands, his best man, and five or six of his growing host of business associates, two of whom were accompanied by their wives. Rebecca played the piano. My father played his Hardanger fiddle. Vera and Kris sang *Fascination* and *I'll Get By*. The two married business associates looked away from their wives now and again to stare furtively and lecherously at Kris.

Rebecca brought me a Scotch. I asked her about her metaphor. Shouldn't it be *love and happiness* instead of *health and happiness?* She said that love was an act of giving but that both health and happiness were passive states of being, the one physical, the other mental. Finding them is experiencing them in the realization that the seemingly active appearance of either is actually a passive state. We pursue both health and happiness; but it's only when the pursuit becomes confused and self-defeating that we actually predispose ourselves to their reception. *But proper diet and regular exercise . . .*

They're good for the body, Pete; but they're not health, which, like happiness, is an abstraction. What's the Latin for the word health?

Salus or valetudo.

What's the Latin for sickness?

Aegritudo or valetudo.

That's the nature of health, Pete: it's a positive that is a negative. We pursue only the positive. Like hap: it's both good and bad, good hap and mishap; we pursue only the good. She said that love is different from both: it's not a passive state of being; its categories are action and relation: the relation of the relation of the physical world to the individual human being, and the relation of one human being to another. Wordsworth expresses the first: *Love had he found in huts where poor men lie; / His daily teachers had been woods and rills, / The silence that is in the starry sky, / The sleep that is among the lonely hills.* The true love of one human being for another is unilateral, with no expectation of requital, even though there may be requital. Think of Dante's unrequited love of Beatrice, like Don Quixote's unrequited love of Dulcinea. In its relativity, love can be learned and love can BE; it can't, except in folly, be pursued.

My love for you IS.

She kissed my cheek and went across the room to talk to my mother.

At that moment, I yearned to be held in Rebecca's arms, not as my mother had held me when I was a child, but as Kris would hold me when there was rain and darkness.

Dewey had defeated Truman; T.S. Eliot received the Nobel Prize for Literature; and my time to graduate finally came: I received my B.A. *cum laude*, with a major in English. At the urging and encouragement of Professor Landis, I began to work toward a master's degree in Latin.

I had also undertaken the study of Greek, for which beginning course I received no graduate credit. Greek took much more time and concentration than any of my graduate courses. Its verb-system is very complex, including, for example a tense and a voice that French and Latin, not to mention English, do not have: the aorist tense denotes past action as action without duration; the middle voice is passive in form but intones reflexive action, that is, action with reference to the self; deponent verbs are drawn from the middle voice and elude what I still take to be the mysterious dyadic potential of the Latin deponent verb.

Professor Landis says that Greek is triadic: it tends to have three words for everything; it posits two extremes and a mean between them as the basis of conduct and morality (Always seek the mean; do nothing to excess.); it culminates in the logic of the syllogism, two premises and a conclusion drawn from them; Plato and Aristotle conceive of a tripartite soul—the rational element, the irrational appetite, and the energetic element (likened to a charioteer, a dark horse, and a white horse; the charioteer [reason] must control the white horse [energy] so that the two together can control the dark horse [sensuality]). Greek says, *Neither this nor that,* but *something in between.* Latin tends to be dyadic (Professor Landis at first said *dualistic,* but then agreed with me that *dyadic* was the better term.), eschewing the mean and either choosing between or combining extremes. *Sacer* means both *blessed* and *cursed. Sancio* means both *I approve* and *I forbid.* Latin says, *Either this or that,* and *sometimes both.*

We looked at Catullus's poem, *Odi et amo* (I hate while I love). When I related what Rebecca Konshak had said about love, Professor Landis nodded and said that Catullus's problem was his possessiveness, his assumption that love was a taking and not a giving. Catullus could not resolve giving and taking by caring unilaterally; he was unwilling to cope with, much less accept, non-requital. No, Latin offers no dyadic word that can mean both *love* and *hate,* perhaps because the language insists that hate is an aberrant emotion and love is an absolute; and an absolute is not subject to qualification. *Odi* (I hate) not only intimates aberrancy but it also does so defectively: the verb has no present tense; it expresses the present by means of the past tense. Triadic Greek has three words for *love* and three words for *hate*. It also has at least three words for *health*, but none carries the positive/negative quality of *valetudo*. In my increasing preoccupation with the category of relation, I tried to find a dyadic relationship in the categories of action and passivity.

45

For two years, Kris's rhythm method had been infallible. When she put her arms around my neck and told me that she was pregnant, I knew that it had to be by her design. I thought back to a very dark night when she had initiated our lovemaking with a heightened and fully irresistible sensuality. My Kris. Changes would have to be made; we would have to replace the undependable Model A; we would have to move out of the apartment; we would have to adjust to the loss of Kris's salary; I would have to get some kind of work. Kris was ready for it all. I was not. I was proud of Kris and delighted with the reality of her carrying our child. At the same time, there was a resentment that I did my best to conceal from her.

During Kris's pregnancy, I tried not to upset her. I wore the clothes she wanted me to wear, took her out to dinner when she did not want to prepare dinner, helped her with all of the housecleaning, and refrained from correcting her lapses from grammar and usage. My good intentions occasionally were defeated by my habitual predisposition to pedagogy. My objections to back formations were almost instinctive. *Don't say ENTHUSE, Kris*, or *Kris, don't say SCULPT*. Her lips would tighten and her eyelids would lower over her flashing, burning-brown eyes, *This is not a schoolroom!* She would always follow my instructions, but her abhorrence of them would smolder. [Open the gates, George.] I made an effort to talk about subjects of interest to her: food, styles, furnishings, color coördination, popular singers, and her work at the hotel. Our conversation flourished only on the topics of movies. *So what?* was her dismissal of my mention that Joe Louis had retired from the boxing ring. Her *Big ding-dong deal!* put down my enthusiastic notice of *Lucky Lady II* a B-50 bomber that flew non-stop around the world in ninety-four hours and one minute, with four in-air re-fuelings. She was right in her observation that the flight had less to do with an advance in technology than with the capability of dropping atomic bombs.

 March's lambent sunshine increased in brightness and turned the snow covering to sidewalk streams. The remaining snow was washed away by a heavy March rain during the night that my son was born. Kris named him after her father and her maternal uncle, Anton Nicholas Blaustern. My preference had been Thomas Mann Blaustern or William March Blaustern. Kris had smiled these suggestions away and had said that I could name the baby if it was a girl, but that she would name it if it was [*were*, I said to myself] a boy. My choice of name for a daughter had been Lucy Rebecca, at which Kris had smiled but to which she had not objected, except to say that *Lucy* was a nickname for *Lucille*, not a full name. I tried to imagine Wordsworth's having written *Lucille*, instead of *Lucy*, poems.

 Our home, to which we brought our baby, was a small two-bedroom house on a tree-bordered street, within sight of a high streetcar-overpass. We had purchased it with a gift of $3000 from Kris's parents, $2000 of our savings, and a six-percent GI bill mortgage. We had also turned the Model A in on a five-year-old Dodge. To my Greek and graduate courses I had added a post-B.A. program in

Education, which provided me with a B.S. in Education and teaching certification. Except for Practice Teaching, the Education curriculum was pretentious nonsense; but, with the certificate, I secured a position at a county elementary school just outside the city.

Kris's parents, Marya and Anton, arrived after the birth of their grandson and occupied the empty second bedroom, for which they had purchased a double bed. They were godmother and godfather at the baptism and christening in the Catholic church. I had wanted Blackie and Vera to be the godparents, but that was not to be. Anton returned to Hamtramck after the baptism. Marya stayed with Kris for two weeks and was very helpful. Kris was happy in motherhood; she breast-fed the baby; she glowed with a contentment that I could not help sharing.

As eighth-grade teacher at my school, I taught all of the subjects to the one class—all, including music, at which I was incompetent. Vera gave me some rudimentary piano lessons. Les Berg, surprisingly, was pleased to instruct me in notation and phrasing. Three girls in class, who had fine voices and were musically very talented, chose not to expose my bluffing and, as exceptional assistants, became, indirectly, the real music teachers of the class.

I compensated by offering those three girls and four of the gifted boys lunch-hour and after-school lessons in chess and Latin, which they appreciated and for which their parents commended me. My salary was only slightly less than what Kris's hotel-work salary had been.

I gained the respect of my students. I looked forward to driving home to Kris and my infant son. Kris and I met our expenses and had no insurmountable debt. Mail was delivered to our own mailbox, not to one of an apartment's twenty-two locked slots. The morning, evening, and Sunday papers were delivered to our own doorstep.

My M.A. work had been interrupted by the turn to the Education program. I resumed it now with late-afternoon and early-evening classes. Professor Landis had left the university for a more prestigious permanent Chair at a university in a neighboring state. One of my most enjoyable classes was a course tracing Vulgar Latin words through regular sound changes to Old French. It met on Thursday afternoons from 4:15 to 6:15. There were two others in the class with me, Charlie Raney and Doug Durand, both of whom were majoring in French. The erudite and unassuming professor called the Rhaeto-Romance language a *mountain flower*. He shared with us a sonnet, written in classical Latin and coinciding in spelling and perfect correctness with modern Italian. His devotion to words and Language was something of an inspiration to me. It was frequently difficult to drive through, for example, heavy snow or ice storms from my elementary school to the university, a distance of twenty-three miles; but I managed never to miss a class meeting. By the time Andy was two, I had only one course, along with my written and oral examinations to complete for an M.A. I had also successfully applied for a teaching position in the city high-school system.

Kris called me to the phone. It was Professor Landis. He offered me a position teaching Latin at his university's high school, together with work toward a doctorate in Classics. He waited while I explained his offer to Kris. She lowered her head; her shoulders fell. She looked up, her eyes moist; she smiled, nodded, and said, *We're on our way*.

We entrusted the sale of our house to the real-estate agent who had arranged our purchase of it. During the summer,

RAIN AND DARKNESS

I completed a course in Latin Epigraphy, studied for and passed my written and oral Master's exams, and moved the furniture we wanted to keep, especially the table-desk, to my parents' house for storage.

My father tuned up the Dodge and sold it for me. With that bit of money and with the money from our house equity, Kris, Andy, and I moved to the neighboring state and into a temporary housing unit in a village set up by the university for veterans and their families. The unit was a trailer house, with a small bedroom at either end, a toilet and shower adjacent to one bedroom, and a kitchen and living area in the middle. The nominal rental fee was very low. This would be our home for three years. I had taken Kris and Andy from a reasonably secure existence—a house and a high-school teacher's steady income—to a life defined by my candidacy for a degree of which I did not believe myself capable. Professor Landis believed I was capable of it. His belief determined our situation. The unit included an icebox and a coal-burning stove, but no washing machine. We bought a washing machine (with a wringer) from Sears and a refrigerator from an appliance store. We also bought a Westinghouse roaster and, much later, a Columbia 360 record-player. Every Sunday evening we listened to Tallulah Bankhead's variety show on the same small radio on which we had first heard *I'll Get By*.

Wheeling Andy in a cloth-and-metal stroller, we walk through the area of fraternity houses and admire the elaborate homecoming displays, for which prizes will be awarded. The autumn evening is mild but cool. The apple cider sold in gallon jugs is rich and satisfying. Later, in December, we shall enjoy the best egg nog in the entire country.

James Jones's *From Here To Eternity* tells a better story than Norman Mailer's *The Naked and the Dead*: the narrative is steadier; Mailer's flashbacks need not be labeled *Time Machine*, Jones has decidedly the better title; but Mailer is the better writer. J.D. Salinger's *The Catcher in the Rye* touches directly upon an ennui that I have been experiencing, a feeling of colorlessness in my isolated environment of petty shopping and unexciting study, while GI's have been dying in Korea. I turn from easy reading to my work with Greek and Latin lyric poets and, in English studies, with Geraldus Cambrensis, John of Salisbury, and Geoffrey of Monmouth.

Kris and I wheel Andy to Eisner's, about a mile and half away, load the stroller with two bags of groceries, while each of us carries one more, and make our rather tiring way back to the unit. My Latin class at the University High School goes very well. My performance is better than adequate. The boys enjoy my jokes; the girls appreciate my wit. I learn more Latin by teaching it than I have managed to by solitary study. I am—what?—nine or ten years older than my students.

There are many nights, when, with Kris asleep at my side and Andy asleep in his bed at the other end of the unit, I stare up into the dark and fight a pain of unrelenting emptiness. Occasionally we plug the radio in near the bed and listen to Freddy Fredickson's *Night Owl* music. I called in a request once. Some sweet-voiced woman took my call. After twenty minutes, Freddy mentioned my name and my request: the instrumental I had requested was not available; so, in substitution, Freddy played some sugary instrumental by Mantovani. Kris had fallen asleep. I turned the radio off.

Kris was still, despite some added weight and a few stretch marks, very attractive. She satisfied me in bed, kept our unit meticulously clean, and was a very fine mother to

Andy. Our son was lively, healthy, and well-behaved; his thick hair was dark brown; his eyes were dark burning brown. Kris complained about many minor things, but never about having to live in a cramped housing unit while I attended university classes. She was not satisfied with the furnishings of the unit, or with our utensils or linens or clothing supply. Emotionally, however, she was serene. Every Sunday morning she wheeled Andy to a Catholic church five blocks away. She was satisfied with our life, if not with its meager accoutrements. She was spiritually secure. I found no dissatisfaction with our material goods, except when something, like our Presto iron, failed to work and there would be the expense of repair or a new iron. My emotional state was bleak. I disliked the colorless sunlight on bare sidewalks. Life was not enough for me, because I was not enough for myself. I had not the confidence and well-being of the self-sufficient. Professor Landis's belief in me kept me at my studies; but I had no substantial belief in myself.

One of my colleagues at the University High School, the one I most admired, was Max Beberman. Max was a good family man and a brilliant mathematician. He was to become famous as one of the founders of the New Math. He had a heart ailment and was permitted to teach all of his classes on the first floor, so as not to have to climb stairs. I sought him out as much as I could, despite my detection of his contempt for my intellectual inferiority. In this he reminded me somewhat of Crispin, but without Crispin's unjustified egotism; in gentility, however, he was very much like Guinotte.

Bill Rellinger, an English teacher, Erwin Goessling, the German teacher, Max, and I were at lunch one day in the school cafeteria. Bill had a large black moustache; and the talk turned to moustaches.

Erwin said that he had never been able to grow one beyond a stubble. Max said that a moustache would be too much of a bother for him. Erwin asked me if I intended ever to grow a moustache. *Yes*, I said slowly, as I thought about it, *when I'm a success*. At that, Max tuned to me and smiled very slightly: *So, when I see you with a moustache, I'm to take it that you're a success?* I nodded. Although I was not sure whether Max was putting me down, I knew that he was not ridiculing me, as would have been the case with Crispin. My hope was born then that I would one day rightly grow a moustache for Max.

Railroad tracks bordered the university-housing village at one end. Adlai Stevenson gave a short whistle-stop campaign speech there. As an enthusiastic Stevenson supporter, I was disappointed that the crowd was not large. I was disappointed also by Stevenson's formulaic speech. Apart from some opening levity and some remarks about the town and the university, he merely recapitulated his radio addresses and his signature theme of talking *sense to the American people*. As the train's shackle noises signaled its departure, he became bouncy and enjoyed that euphoric rush of extended generosity that characterizes the ending of an entertainer's act or the fulfillment of a speaker's duty: *Oh, I wish I could stay for an hour and just talk with you*, he called out as he blew kisses with both hands. The dark-clad, serious aides, standing in a semicircle behind him, were all taller than this bald candidate in his dark brown suit. The disappointment of that afternoon had faded by the time I heard, on our radio, vice-presidential candidate Nixon's mawkish and grossly insincere defense of his receipt of campaign gifts, with his references to Pat's cloth coat and the dog named Checkers. I listened to the radio broadcast of the election returns, expecting to be as pleasantly excited as I was by the returns

RAIN AND DARKNESS

of the Truman-Dewey contest; but Eisenhower's landslide victory was evident within the first two hours. *Blackie will be happy*, I said to Kris, as we turned to our snack of saltines, blue cheese, and full-bodied Port wine.

46

The winters were mild; but the coal fire had to be kept going. There was one coal bin for every three units, and it was kept well supplied. I learned how to bank the coal fire and how to remove ashes without raising dust. Blackie and I corresponded regularly. He was amused by, but not contemptuous of, this Spartan life. He and Vera had purchased a large three-bedroom house. They had no children yet. They hosted numerous parties and wished that Kris and I could be there to enjoy them. On any of our visits to the city, we were invited to be their guest: they had plenty of room.

On winter Sundays, I would carry Andy to the church. After a time, I attended the services with Kris and Andy. I didn't do any of the genuflecting in the aisle or make the Sign of the Cross; but I sat, knelt, and stood in the pews along with the congregation. A mass was not so long or so trying as the Lutheran-church service. Communicants did not drink the wine. I followed the Latin liturgy, noting the difference in pronunciation from the classical Latin that I was learning and teaching. Kris always thanked me for attending the mass with her and Andy. She never urged me to do so, and she never complained if I did not stay. The priest was tall, slender, and deep-voiced—quite different from the chubby, heroic Father Murphy, for whom I would always say a prayer during the appropriate moments. One snowy Sunday, as, snug and warm in our unit, we enjoyed Kris's meal of baked ham and scalloped potatoes, I started to tell Kris about Father Murphy. She turned to Andy, as she always did in expressing her lack of interest in what I was saying, and straightened his collar, arranged his napkin, and helped him with his food.

After his nap, I took Andy outside and built a snowman with him. This pleased Kris. That evening we snacked on crackers, cheese, and wine as we listened to Tatullah Bankhead's *Show of Shows* (I think that's what it was called). The cast and guests concluded, as usual, with singing Meredith Wilson's *May the good Lord bless and keep you*. I took out the Greek *New Testament* and began to explain to Kris some of the mystery concealed in its figurations and sequences; but she joined Andy in playing with his small collection of toy cars.

The difference between the actual Koinê Greek and the King James translation of it had astonished me, even more than the ready comprehensibility of Plato's Attic Greek as opposed to the cloudy simplicity of the Jowett translation, with its insufficient accounting for the intonations and denotations of the Greek particles.

These are not dead languages, Peter, Professor Landis insisted. No language that has produced as rich, variable, and perennially readable a literature as Greek and Latin have each produced can be rightly adjudged dead. Translations into modern spoken languages are secondary documents, clues to the originals, but not fully reliable substitutes for them. In retrospect, I nod to his words, as I now read a review (fortunately negative) of Ann Goldstein's translation of Alessandro Baricco's translation of the *Iliad* (reduced to one third of the Greek epic's length) into Italian as adapted from Maria Grazia Ciani's Italian translation. Professor Landis liked to talk about the importance of unearthing the plays of Menander and the elegies of Gallus. *What we've found of Menander has been disappointing.* One has to wonder about his considerable influence upon Greek comedy. It may be that Gallus's elegies are actually as mediocre as those passages we scanned. If that box I mentioned should contain a papyrus roll or a codex of Gallus's elegies, as influential upon Latin lyric as they have been historically designated, it would be a paramount contribution to classical studies. Again I promised to do what I could to pursue the matter, in which Professor Landis's growing interest had begun to disquiet me.

Once again, I wrote to my mother. Once again, she wrote to say that Jordy only laughed at my request and said that I should think of other things and not of opportunities that existed now only in dreams that died in the darkness of the war. She said that this time, though, he wrote something down on some white space in the newspaper that lay open on the kitchen table and had said to her, *Here, send him this.* She had cut it out of the newspaper and enclosed it with her letter. It read: *caelo in sidereo quae aeterna silentia noctu somnus qui solos est et apud tumulos.* I scanned and translated this with ease and anger. It was clear that Jordy was playing a game with me, but a gifted game, one that involved not only his competence in Latin but also his having had some sort of contact with Rebecca Konshak, the one and only person with whom I had shared an overt appreciation of Wordsworth's *The silence that is in the starry sky, / The sleep that is among the lonely hills.* Shared, back in the city, that is, at Blackie's M.B.A. party.

RAIN and DARKNESS

Reluctantly, apologetically, I handed Jordy's jotting to Professor Landis. He laughed wistfully: *Your source is joking with you? Translating two lines of Wordsworth's iambic pentameter into a Latin elegiac distich?* I shrugged my shoulders slightly. *It works,* he said, *but imperfectly and mechanically. The SILENTIA NOCTU is, I must say, rather good.* He also liked the extra-contextual but fitting *aeterna* (never-ending). Gallus might have composed a couplet like this, under the influence of Vergil; but it is not in keeping with Latin elegy. He talked at length about Gallus, about his political deviousness and military activity, about his celebrated affair with Lycoris (the actor Cytheris, presumably), an affair consistent with the elegiac staple of the independent and uncoöperative mistress, and about his Egyptian prefecture, his failed military campaigns, and his loss to the Nubian queen Candace Amanirenas. I took notes, as I usually did when he shared information with me. My regret is that I had no mastery of shorthand. I should like to have recorded and to report his words verbatim; but I cannot. Even my paraphrases are affected by my involuntary invention.

(Dexter Filkins, writing an enthusiastic review of a book by Laurence Wright, says, *Wright has drawn up verbatim reconstructions of entire conversations, some of which took place more than a decade ago. Many of these conversations are riveting. Still, in some cases, it's hard to believe that memories are that good.* To say *some cases* is to understate. Wright is recording history; that has to be less venial than the device of infallible memory in the writing of first-person fiction, like Pip's verbatim reproduction of a forbiddingly long speech by Abel Magwitch [a.k.a. Provis] in Dickens's *Great Expectations*. This device has long been my black beast in the matter of first-person fiction. Greek and Roman historians admitted that the long speeches they recorded were contrived—consistent with occasions and propriety, but contrived. This cluttered my reception of the speeches: I shall always prefer Lincoln's Gettysburg Address to Thucydides's rendition of the Funeral Oration by Pericles. It is worse in first-person fiction, which, to begin with, is contrivance. [I'm sorry, George; I do not countenance compound contrivance in narrative.])

Professor Landis asked if I'd mind reviewing for him the history of my receipt of the Latin passages I'd shown him. I said I wouldn't mind but that it was rather a long story. He had a meeting to attend in ten minutes; we agreed to get together following my afternoon Uni High class on Friday.

There were heavy clouds and intermittent rain that Friday. Professor Landis's desk lamp provided a small area of light in his darkened office. On a narrow table by the window he had a coffee service—an electric percolator, sugar boat, creamer, and two china cups—and some chocolate, vanilla, and ginger-snap cookies.

He used cream and sugar. I took my coffee black. He took no notice of my unmannerly dunking of vanilla wafers in my coffee.

I began with my study of Latin in high school, Jordy Klug's initial challenge, and Mr. Hanson's recognition of its chiasmus. My European chapter began with Hedwig and the strange visit of Mischiato. When I mentioned the name, Giorgio Scaltro, Professor Landis, taking a sip of coffee, said, *Scaltro is the equivalent of Klug, you know.* I admitted that I hadn't known that. I could see that he was incredulous about the cigarette case and the Habsburg key. He listened, nonetheless, with polite, although, I'm sure, skeptical, interest to all that I had to say. After I had concluded with Jordy's provision of the Wordsworthian distich, he said, *That's quite a story, Peter. Remarkable.* Professor Landis allowed that numerous secret societies had their origins in antiquity. A root of Freemasonry, for example, may have spread within the easternmost conquests of Alexander the Great, the sort of legend that Rudyard Kipling picks up in *The Man Who Would Be King.* He said that *fondamento* meant no more than *base.* Gallus may have used the term to indicate organized machinations in his quest for power; in which event, his *suicide* may actually have been an assassination, and the spread of his Base may have survived him, sprouting in various forms during the Middle Ages, including possibly the Mafia. He thought it would have been greatly to my advantage, in what he recognized as a perverse game that Jordy Klug was playing with me, if I had broken open the cigarette case; but he applauded my *pietas* in not having done so. He lit his pipe and, looking over the rims of his Benjamin Franklin glasses and the brief flame of the match, he projected the glory of finding the poems of Gallus in that box, in the actual existence of which he was too rigorous a scholar to place any credence. He had been thinking that I should write my dissertation on Gallus; but preferred now to discourage me from the undertaking: *It is probably what Mr. Klug wants you to do; and I would judge from what you have said that Mr. Klug is a dangerous person.* I can hear those words even now. I had not mentioned Jordy's shooting at Blackie and me or Blackie's conviction that Jordy wanted somehow to shoot us both down. As we rose in the still dark office, shook hands, and smiled, I understood that my decision to give up the security of high-school teaching in the city and come here to work with Professor Landis had been the right one to make.

The overcast sky had grown darker. I walked quickly and reached our unit about ten minutes before a short but heavy fall of rain.

47

This is a time of dullness. All of the units in this veterans' village are painted a uniform grey. Morning Glory vines cling to the eastern ends of many of the units, including the one in which Kris, Andy, and I live. They become top-heavy, as the leaves and blooms move upward, deserting the straggling vine-strings. The grass around the units and bordered by the wide asphalt walks is well-kept but uninviting, except beneath the scattered trees. The threat of the Korean War no longer bothers us. Wintry darkness is succeeded by summery bleakness. There is a need for color. Music is the dull flow of big bands and crooners. Television programs are still, in all their smallness, black and white. Kris, Andy, and I sometimes go to the Union to watch a variety show on one of the television units set up in the lounges. Movies, competing with television, try to offer more with larger screens (Cinemascope), 3-D, and garish modes of tint. Every *Limelight* is countered by a *Demetrius and the Gladiators*. I carry Andy, as Kris and I walk to one of the three theaters in the area once or twice a week. Innocently, he would watch with us even such a film as *One Summer of Happiness*, with its display of Ulla Jacobsson's bare breasts. There is a good Italian film version of Gounod's *Faust*. There is the varied music and humor of *New Faces*. Only movies like *Limelight* and *High Noon*, of those that are distributed in this area, approach the kind of movie that Kris and I like to see and talk about.

Although I have yet to detect it, there is a projectile of color being readied to break up this dullness.

Its adumbrations are the breasts of Jacobsson, the institution of Hugh Hefner's *Playboy*, and the anti-Constitutionalism of the House Un-American Activities Committee, the Loyalty Oath that academics now have to sign, and Senator Joseph McCarthy's misdirected and fallacious anti-Communism.

The dullness is mildly offset by the pleasure I take in my University High School teaching. This gives me the daily opportunity to indulge in my penchant for performing; and it makes me realize that I can learn a subject by teaching it. There are moments now during which I think in Latin (but only in disconnected phrases or clauses).

The senior members of the Department of Classical Philology do not share Professor Landis's belief in my competence. Among the three of us who are doctoral candidates in Classics, there is no friendship, only competition.

There is, among the faculty, a young Assistant Professor of German who judges my work in German Romanticism to be *ausgezeichnet* (excellent). There is a very old Professor of English, who treats me as an equal as we examine Ailred of Rievaulx, the bull-roaring Margery Kempe, and Dame Julian of Norwich. It is only Professor Landis, however, who commends my Latin and encourages me in my efforts to master Greek.

Professor Kristofer Zloty nods to me in the corridor and has complimented me on my uvular r, when, for example, I translate Xenophon into French. In his class we must do oral translation from the Greek or Latin into any language but English. He corrected my German too often; so I switched to French, with which he found less fault. Hetty May Boom uses her native Dutch, which I manage to understand. Gordy Black uses Czechoslovakian, which I do not understand at all. Professor Zloty is fluent in eighteen languages. During almost every class meeting, he will point out errors in the Liddell & Scott Greek Lexicon, frequently standing in indignation, pointing to the open lexicon and saying, with his Polish accent, *Mees-preent!*. He is distant; but, with his Old World gentility, he is approachable and kind. At the two social gatherings that Kris attended with me, while neighbors took care of Andy, he was winningly gracious to her.

More distant is the soporific Professor Ferris V. O'Neill, an international authority on the Greek Romance and the Ancient Novel. He sits, like the Master in *The Browning Version*, without looking at the text, as we translate Aeschylus. He appears to have in memory the whole of extant Greek tragedy. With lowered head and closed eyes, he will interrupt his snorting to correct a mispronunciation of the Greek or a mistranslation of the text.

He comes to every class meeting precisely six minutes late, with an effluence of Irish Whisky on his breath. Most distant is the anagrammatically named Professor Daniel Delian Denial (the last name pronounced DEN-yal). I no longer attempt to greet him when I see him outside of class: he has never acknowledged my verbal or my gestural greeting. In class he lingers over his praise of Benito Mussolini or his vituperative condemnation of Franklin Delano Roosevelt. Like Professor O'Neill, he never uses notes; unlike him, he is always precisely on time for the beginning of class; he begins to lecture as soon as he sits down. Once, when the three of us, who constituted his class, had been delayed by a special orientation session and had come almost ten minutes late to class, we found him lecturing to an empty room. I have taken three of his courses, each involving research projects; and he has given me a grade of B– each time. He is a bee-keeper and makes a profit from his apiary's production of honey (*DDD's Delight*). He has a stable of horses. On Thursdays he rides *Thursday*, a black horse, to school and tethers it at a bicycle rack; he leaves the horse's droppings for the campus grounds-keepers. His peers call him *D.D.* Our student soubriquet for him is *Tweedle*. Professor O'Neill we call *Kneel*. Professor Zloty we call *Goldy*. Tweedle, Kneel, and Goldy. Professor Landis is, simply, *Landis*.

Hetty May is finishing her dissertation and will defend it next month. Gordy has failed his advance Latin-translation examination and will re-take it, for the second and last time, within three months. I had no trouble with my advanced Latin-translation examination; but, anticipating failure in my advanced Greek-translation examination, I am considering applying for a high-school teaching position. The placement bureau of the College of Education at my home university, in answer to my request, has sent me one, and only one, notice of opening: it is for a senior high school in Lusk, Wyoming. I dismissed the thought of re-applying for the high-school position in my home city. Even Kris feels that it would be a demeaning move backward, if, indeed, I should even be given a second chance. She shudders, however, at the prospect of moving westward to Wyoming. *Cheyenne, maybe, or Laramie. But where, or what, is Lusk? It sounds like a deep dip in a dark mountain.* I tell her that it's southwest of the Black Hills, near the Nebraska border; I think that it's on a plain.

The late summer morning was cool. I used up the maximum allowed time to complete my *Ad Greek trans*. I was confident that I had resolved the intonations of the particles and had properly rendered aorist and perfect verbs, but I could not achieve any idiomatic flow with the cramped syntactic, as opposed to a smooth paratactic, passage.

RAIN AND DARKNESS

It had been a fair test. As I walked over the flickers of shade on the sidewalks, I listened to the soughing leaves. Kris was ironing when I came into our unit. She brought the iron to rest on its back edge on the ironing board, looked at me, and said, *Lusk?* I nodded.

Later that day, about three in the afternoon, I am working on a letter of application. Andy is napping. Kris is having coffee with one of her friends in a nearby unit. There is a knock on the door. It is Professor Landis. He smiles at my pale surprise. I invite him in, and we sit at the table. *I didn't want you to have to wait until tomorrow*, he said. *You passed.* He smiled again, this time at my quizzical expression. *Oh, it was a bit rougher than it should be*, but, he added, I had caught every particle and had managed the main drift of the text. I thanked him for his kindness and rose to make coffee; he rose, shook my hand, Novy-shouldered me, and said, *Well, I must be off, then.*

After he left, I checked on Andy, took my Cambridge Wordsworth from the shelf, sat on the cushioned built-in sofa, the back of which could be opened to permit storage, stared at the unopened Wordsworth on my lap, and tried to deduce the meaning of Professor Landis's unorthodox visit. He must have prevailed upon his colleagues, Tweedle and Kneel (Goldy was in Europe, tracking manuscripts of Sophocles), to accept an ordinarily unacceptable effort. He must then have hurried to reassure me, so as to forestall my yielding to motives occasioned by depression.

I opened the book and read: *Rise as he may, his grandeur scorns the test / Of outward symbol, nor will deign to rest / On aught by which another is deprest.* The words *test* and *deprest* are fortuitous; but the context is wrong. I think of Eliot's *Prufrock* and adaptively intone, *I am not Trajan, nor was meant to be.*

When Kris returned, I relayed the good news. She put her arms around my neck and kissed me. *That's wonderful, SweePete*, she said. The late afternoon was hot now, and bleak. And dull. Ahead were prelims, dissertation, and finals.

During the previous year's presidential campaigns for nominations, Senators Taft and Kefauver both spoke on campus, prior to Governor Stevenson's whistle-stop speech. Kefauver was slow-spoken and uninteresting. Taft spoke in a high voice, waved his arms, and appealed to the largely conservative students. Like Tweedle, most of the students had scorned Truman, who, among other failings, had fired the *majestic* General Douglas MacArthur. Still, the General's much quoted *Old soldiers never die; they just fade away* had given way to the campus joke, *Old salts never die; they just peter out.*

This campus is situated on an extended plain. The late summer sun defeats the leaves of elm trees, although adherent leaves may still rustle in the morning; it defeats the upward striving of the Morning Glories on the grey ends of various village units. It will eventually retreat before insistent autumn rains. It will eventually permit the early darkness, the fall of leaves that summon brisk, cold air, and football cheers that sound their way back to a new school year—eventually, but not beyond this dullness.

48

Hetty May Boom was Tweedle's protégée. Tweedle let it be known that her dissertation on the rhetorical gradients in Demosthenes's *Philippics* was brilliant and that her defense of it would have impressed an Oxford Don. We were all invited to her celebration party, even Gordy Black, who had failed his second *Ad Latin trans* and was no longer a doctoral candidate. Kris stayed home with Andy; but she insisted that I attend. She did not like Hetty May, who had once made a pass at her. Hettie May was about five-foot-six, stoop-shouldered, and severely myopic. She wore her light brown hair straight back to a bun. She was almost always dressed in a color-coördinated silk blouse and cotton cardigan, a long black skirt, and black loafers. I admired and respected Hetty May because she was a proven professional and superior to me in every area of Classical Philology; I nursed a biting dislike of her for the same reasons. She had told me at least twice that neither Gordy nor I were competent graduate students: we were intellectually mediocre and lacked the qualifications for sustained research.

She added that I, with my *good looks*, could be an effective high-school teacher, as I had already proved to be at Uni High, and should aim no higher, but that Gordy, simian in appearance, with thick black hair down almost to his eyebrows, constant black-cheek stubble, dull squinting eyes, and furry arms, should go into military service or work in a steel mill.

Gordy had told me, over coffee and doughnuts in the Newman Hall cafeteria, that Hetty May and her room-mate, both of whom were bisexual, had paid him for sexual favors (cunnilingus and vaginal and anal penetration) at least six times over a year and a half. I was skeptical but not incredulous, and I enjoyed the graphic details that he provided. The celebration party was held in the recreation room of the dorm in which Hetty May and her room-mate now lived. There was no wine or liquor, just cider, along with shaved ham, cubed sausage, various kinds of cheese, saltines, baguettes for slicing, and fruit salad. Greek bouzouki music played at 33 1/3 rpm.

We took turns reciting Greek or Latin passages from memory. Tweedle led with a long section from the first *Philippic*; Hetty May picked it up where he stopped and completed a shorter section. Gordy grunted out about six selections from the *Priapea*. I did about fifteen lines from Propertius and then swung into all of my *Gallus* material and noticed with pleasure Tweedle's sudden puzzled interest. There were sonorous renditions of lines from Homer and Vergil. Two of Hetty May's undergraduate wards went to the piano and entertained with parts of Orff's *Carmina Burana*. The party lasted from eight to a little after eleven.

Kris was waiting up for me. We drank some wine as we listened to Mahler's fourth symphony. Then we went to bed.

September brings three new graduate students into our doctoral program. One of them, a woman from the University of Alberta, replaces Gordy, who has gone to St. Louis to manage a fast-food restaurant, a Steak 'n' Shake.

Jean-Pierre Lanier from Tulane, funded by his wealthy parents, brings his Gallic charm and fluent French into our midst. Edward Gardengrade, from England, replaces me at Uni High, as I settle into my dissertation work, supported now by a University Fellowship that Professor Landis has secured for me.

Singling out a dissertation topic, Professor Landis and I hesitantly renewed our combined interest in Gallus. When I convinced Professor Landis that too much of my material depended upon the vagaries of the dishonest and devious Giordano Klug—the source of the fragments he gave me, the mythical Heidelberg box, Jordy's ridiculing my requests for information—he agreed that we should do something outside of Latin lyric poetry.

Some of Jordy's offerings coincided with legitimate and already edited lines, but they provided no grounds for arguing the authenticity of the other offerings. Elegiac distichs written on note-paper or in the white space of newspapers would produce no scholarly gravity. We decided finally upon my nebulous topic of anagoge. Professor Landis liked my application of anagoge in the *New Testament* to various Greek and Roman writers, from whom, we could argue, the Koinê literary artists had themselves appropriated it. Professor Denial lent his approval to the topic and suggested that I read Heidegger to bolster my inquiry into the mystic character of Language. He had supposed that I might rather have wanted *to pursue those whelps of Gallus to their lair*. I had given him a full copy of my Gallus material, and he was giving serious attention to it. Professor O'Neill liked the combination of Greek and Latin that the examination of anagoge would entail. Professor Zloty was non-committal but offered no objection.

Through the winter and into the spring, I spent full days in the library, working from a carrel, and evenings at my typewriter and index files. Kris complained about my lack of attention to Andy and to her. I would bring my discouragements to Professor Landis, and he would always praise, advise, and assure me that my work was progressing well.

Carter P. Rittenhouse, professor and chairman of Classics at a neighboring-state university, and fellow graduate with Professor Landis from a prestigious eastern university, came to campus to lecture on Senecan Drama. Professor Landis invited *Ritt* and me to lunch. Two weeks later, I drove a rented car from one state to the next to be interviewed for a position in Professor Rittenhouse's department. I made two informal presentations, one on anagoge and one on Gallus. Both were well received. My having followed Professor Landis's advice, not to bluff when I could not answer a question, worked to my advantage. Within a week, I was offered a position—a lectureship, if my dissertation remained to be completed; an instructorship, if I joined the faculty as a Ph.D.

Anagoge is the literary provision of a spiritual experience. A literary passage, composed with proper artistry, will make a statement and will, by means of the placement of its words and letters, along with its use of figures of speech and syntax, comment transcendently upon the statement it is making. The writer has succeeded in getting Language to comment upon the use speech has made of it.

In the *New Testament*, the opening of *The Lord's Prayer* (*Matthew* 6:9-10) is a statement by Jesus to his disciples: he tells them how to pray to the Father in Heaven. The chiasmus, anaphora, and symmetry of the passage produce the *Chi rho* symbol in an identification of Jesus as the Christ

(Messiah) who is at one with the Father; anagogically, Jesus, teaching the word of God, IS the Word of God—he is what he teaches. What is spiritual here is, not the statement, but the presence of Language as it adds dimension to the statement and disturbs the listener or reader, as Wordsworth says, *with the joy of elevated thoughts*.

Aristotle begins his *Rhetoric* by establishing the correlativity of rhetoric and dialectic. He notes that this correlativity is common, in general, to all things and all persons. He shows the interdependence of antitheses and configures his introductory remarks with contrapuntal chiasmus and anaphora and figures like amphibologia (ambiguity: going in two different directions at the same time) and polyptoton (different forms of the same root-word; here, *amphoin* [in-both] and *amphoteros* [both]), the speech of the text participates successfully in Language, with the result that Language discloses that all things are in some way dyadic. Heidegger, to whose work Professor Denial rightly referred me, enabled me to grasp the extent to which figures of speech and syntax were on the way to Language.

Ovid's *Metamorphoses* opens with *In nova fert animus mutatas dicere formas / corpora*, which is consistently mistranslated as *My intent is to speak of bodies changed into new forms*; but *nova* (new) modifies *corpora* (bodies), and *mutatas* (changed) modifies *formas* (forms). The translator ought to begin with *Spirit* (animus) *impels* [me] *to speak of forms changed into new bodies*. It is the anagoge, wrought by the chiastic ratio, *new : changed :: forms : bodies*, that is misread by conventional translators, who annihilate the literal sense and nullify the dyad. One must begin with Plato's notion of pure (insubstantial) forms being variably reflected in material bodies; spirit (the rational soul) can then understand that forms can be changed into imitative reflections of themselves.

One then apprehends Language's presence in the antithetical and interdependent union of form and content, that is, the dyad, comprising *changed forms / new bodies*. Spirit (*animus*) is both rational (dialectic) and soul (rhetoric).

Kris rebuffed all of my attempts to interest her in my topic. As soon as I began to talk about anagoge, or anagogic openings like these, she would raise her eyebrows, move her open hands outward, and turn to Andy or to her housework. *Come on, BlissKris; it's my WORK.* She said, *Yes, it's what you do.* I asked her if it wasn't better than coal-mining. *Work is work,* she said. I went on feebly about coal-mining: suppose I wanted to talk to her about my breathing troubles—from coal dust and shaft gases. *You know I'll always listen to your troubles, Pete. Are you having troubles with what you're doing?* I said that I was not having troubles, really, but, well, difficulties, and, well, maybe I was troubled about maybe not being good enough for scholarly work. *You're a fine school-teacher, Pete; you don't need the high scholarly business. You ought to think about leveling off.* I said that I wouldn't, as long as Professor Landis believed I could do it. Then I asked her why she didn't believe in me. She stared at me, apparently stunned, then lowered her head and wiped her eyes with her wrist. *I do believe in you; in YOU.*

I sent a couple of my summaries to Blackie, ostensibly to let him know what I was doing, actually to try to impress him and win some praise. He sent a post-card message: *Please, Ped! PUH-LEEZE!! Love to Kris and Andy—Blackie.*

Sustenance lay in my weekly conferences with Professor Landis. Pipe in mouth, or in hand, he would go over my week's work, nod, ask questions, suggest improvements, recommend pertinent books and articles, and quietly inculcate in me a sense of worth. One Thursday, Professor

RAIN AND DARKNESS

Denial, having been asked by Professor Landis to read four of my pages on Ovid, joined the conference. He asked, jokingly, I hoped, although none of the three of us smiled or chuckled, if perhaps *shallow draughts* of Heidegger had *intoxicated my brain*. I promised to give enough thought to the matter *largely to sober* the brain *again*. I scored a point of approval by picking up his allusion to Alexander Pope. He asked me if, by taking *animus* as Logos, one could justify translating Ovid's line as, Language brings Forms, changed into new bodies, to speak. I supposed that one could justify the translation by noting that no possessive pronoun governed *animus* and that an intransitive use of *dicere* (*to speak*, instead of *to speak of*) would not abuse the text. Such a rendering, I added, would not be inconsonant with Heidegger's *Language is the saying of being*. I was afraid that I had given Professor Daniel his opportunity to demolish me with his erudition. That he did not do so was due probably to his courteous deference to Professor Landis. The conference ended pleasantly.

Marc M. Jelunac, one of my students at Uni High during my first year there and now a sophomore major in Classical Philology at the university, was the only person, other than Professor Landis, who listened with interest to my divagations on anagoge.

Once, sometimes twice, a week, we would have coffee and play chess in the Newman Hall cafeteria. This break in my library routine was welcome relaxation for me. Marc—wiry, red-haired, freckled—was intense and serious and determined to learn Greek and Latin. We were about equally matched at chess. He had asked me how we could know that Language exists apart from its speakers. I said that we couldn't know but that we gain intimations of its existence through great writing or real thinking, which enables us to experience

Being's saying being. I realized that Professor Denial was right about my shallow draughts.

Like Les Berg, Marc appreciated music, although his inclination was more toward modern than toward classical modes. Mezz Mezzrow, Jazz, Dixieland, Jacques Brel, Bix Beiderbecke, George Lewis. He was, at most, mild in his appreciation of Boogie Woogie, which he considered too formulaic. He admired Artie Shaw as a clarinet virtuoso. He had no time for any popular singers except Billie Holliday and Peggy Lee. I talked about Dick Haymes's evading the draft through his Argentinian citizenship and his being initially denied re-entry into the U.S.A. from Hawaii, where he made a movie, because of his draft-dodging. I commented with satisfaction upon his successful suit for re-entry. *Crooners*, Marc said, caring nothing about Haymes's alien status, *have only one register and a dip.* He allowed that Frank Sinatra had an impeccable vocal legato.

The burning glare returned to Kris's eyes when I told her about my lunching and chess-playing with Marc. Why couldn't I take a break from the dissertation routine by coming home for lunch? The walk would do me good, and she could use some help with Andy and the housework. The more heated our arguments became, the less they fostered any chance of being resolved. I would become angry; Kris would become bitter.

In a day or so, Marc met me at the library just before noon. *I'm going home for lunch today, Marc.* He said, *O.K., I'll walk you there.* We talked about Mann's *Doktor Faustus*. Marc tried to explain Schoenberg's serial music to me. I could relate the twelve-tone repetitions to anaphora, but not to Mann's novel, which I read as dyadic, with its many interdependently-configured antitheses. We concluded our discussion at the doorstep of the unit. As Marc turned to leave, Kris opened the screen door and said that we should both come in and have lunch. She set down some fruit and made coffee and sandwiches. She was gracious and put Marc at his ease. Andy was very friendly to Marc, as the four of us sat at the small table.

Kris asked Marc about his studies and his plans. He said that he was going to go to France at the end of the semester.

On the way back to the library, Marc was profuse with compliments about Kris—her kindness, her beautiful brown eyes, her beautiful smile, her production of an excellent lunch at short notice. He said that, if he were ever to marry, it would have to be someone like Kris.

That evening, I walked home in warm satisfaction, prepared to tell Kris how proud of her I was and to thank her. Her first words to me as I entered the unit were, *Don't you ever bring him here again!*

Thereafter, I walked alone to the unit for lunch with Kris and Andy. I cut my library work off at three-thirty on Tuesdays and Thursdays and spent an hour and a half on each of those days with Marc in Newman Hall. Usually we played chess on Tuesday and talked about literature or music on Thursday. To Kris I did not mention this arrangement. On the last Thursday in July, Marc and I said goodbye. He wished me luck on my final orals. I Novy-shouldered him and wished him all the best in his journey to France and in his proposed study at the Sorbonne. We promised to write to each other.

I submitted and defended my dissertation in mid-August. Professors Denial and Zloty were in Europe. Professors Landis and O'Neill were joined by the English professor with whom I had worked on mediaeval literature, by the German professor who liked my work, and by a Philosophy professor who was to check me out on Heidegger. The defense began at 5:00 p.m. on a Thursday. I did well with some questions; and, where I was obviously at some loss, my questioners provided me with clues or, in some instances, with recommendations that I do a bit of research in this or that area. The Philosophy professor was kind. He pointed out some errors that I had made and secured my promise to correct them. He asked me for my opinion on Heidegger's remaining silent and unapologetic about his membership in the Nazi Party. I said that his active membership did not exceed three years, that he had left the Party in disillusionment with Hitler's revealed sense of *Heimat*, and that his silence must have owed to his taking responsibility for his actions without making excuses for them.

My committee deliberated for twenty minutes, while I waited in another room. Finally, Professor Landis appeared. He smiled, shook my hand, and congratulated me. I returned to the conference room and received the handshakes and congratulations of the others.

With some uneasiness over my mediocre performance, but calmly satisfied that I now had my degree, I walked slowly on the long, now deserted, sidewalk back to the unit. *It's over, BlissKris. I made it.* She put her arms around my neck and kissed me. Andy said, *I made it.* We had a light meal. We gave Andy some cookies and milk as we shared French bread, blue cheese, and full-bodied Port wine. With darkness, we put Andy to bed, lit two blue candles, and listened to the radio. That was the extent of our celebration.

During the next week, we packed up and arranged for our move to the next state. We bought a new Chevrolet, with payments to be spread over four years. I paid my last visit to Professor Landis. *I think that the only way I can thank you, Professor Landis, is to do for one or more of my students what you have done for me.* He smiled and, almost imperceptibly, nodded.

Two days before we left the village of veterans' housing, a packet arrived from Paris. It was a copy of Mezz Mezzrow's *Really the Blues* (by Milton Mezzrow and Bernard Wolfe). There was an inscription written on the title page: *For I know you made it—Marc.*

49

From the university on the dull plain Kris, Andy, and I drove in our new car southeastward to the university lying amidst valleys and hills and outspreading woodlands. We settled into our rented lower storey of an old house that was just four blocks from campus. The fenced backyard sloped steeply down away from the house. There was an apple tree at the top of the slope and another one halfway down the slope. On the small screened back porch that was shaded by the nearest apple tree, I sat and read *Really the Blues*.

Reading in Mezzrow's book about a cat *named Stew*, I thought back to my dog named Shoe.

Professor Rittenhouse, whom we all addressed familiarly as *Ritt*, supported me and praised me often. The department's professor and associate professor were kind, helpful, and collegial. The untenured, an assistant professor and two instructors, resented my potential competition and contemned my lack of social graces. Kris resented and complained about my continued night work, now given over to class preparation. She disliked it when I would bring home a stack of blue examination booklets and devote evenings or weekends to them. We enjoyed being able to drive to movies, instead of taking a bus or walking, as we had done before. We enjoyed the two state parks that were within easy driving distance. Kris drove herself and Andy to church early every Sunday morning; the Catholic church was two and a half miles away from our home. We attended the requisite social gatherings; but Kris disliked academic people, and I was an awkward conversationalist. We never entertained; and soon, often pleading the unavailability of a baby-sitter, we missed many gatherings and dinners; after a while, it came to be accepted that we were not part of the social circle.

Advancement depended largely upon publication. My dissertation, rejected by three presses, I decided to shelve. During my first year and a half, I managed to publish only two notes on John Keats and nothing in Classical Philology. I wasted much time and work sending out poems that won no acceptance. The assistant professor published an enlarged version of his dissertation, and each of the two instructors published articles in refereed journals.

Teaching was my prime satisfaction. During my first year, I offered courses in Medical Terminology, Latin Poetry, and Mythology. Teaching the Greek and Latin elements of medical terms, I learned much about the concatenations of medical parlance. Lengthy terms, like hepaticocholangiocholecystenterostomy, were a source of pleasant satisfaction. In Latin poetry, Horace still gave me some trouble, but Vergil and the elegiac poets gave me a sense of command. Classical Mythology caught me up in its ramifications. The Greek and Roman philosophers taught that nothing can come from nothing (*nihil ex nihilo*); the Epicureans identified the smallest, the irreducible, parts of matter as atoms. Mythology, however, posited *nothing* as potential energy: asat, Nun, Chaos, tehom, Ginnungagap: this is complete entropy, totally devoid of information.

Potential energy kineticizes itself through consciousness. Potential energy is God the Father; potential energy's consciousness of itself is God the Mother: this is the cosmic androgyne. Energy is the male force of the universe; consciousness is the female force (the intellectual curiosity of Pandora and Eve; the intellectual *spiritus* of Athena). Kinetic energy is active; but consciousness is the activating impetus. Samuel Butler and Robert Graves articulate this effectively. The male, *frightened adjunct* to the female, as Graves puts it, coöpts consciousness as its own; the female allows the male to believe that the force of consciousness is male. This comported well with my ineradicable sense of inferiority to the female. Each of the Latin elegists was painfully inferior to his mistress: Catullus to his Lesbia, Propertius to his Cynthia, Gallus to his Lycoris . . . . Then, Dante to his Beatrice. Chivalry and the Courts of Love. Don Quixote to his Dulcinea, as Cervantes presented his version of this truth. The Romantics, wind-blown and cape-flown, nursing their passions' needs on dark promontories. Dmitri Karamazov rushing wildly to Grushenka.

Kris presented me with our daughter, Cyana Czarny (*Lucy Rebecca? Don't be silly*, Kris had said), to whom Anton, now six years old, became deeply and protectively devoted. Like her brother, Sharny grew a luxuriant head of dark brown hair and had deep burning-brown eyes.

Then came the color to rout the dullness. I am driving the two-year-old Chevrolet home from a supermarket, with milk, fruit, formula, breakfast food, tomatoes, lettuce, hamburger, and hamburger buns. I turn the car-radio on. I hear *Heartbreak Hotel*. Before the song is finished and the announcer identifies Elvis Presley, I have made a U-turn and am on my way to the record store. Clay, the clerk who just last week sold me a 33 1/3 of *Das Lied von der Erde*, which he had special-ordered for me, smiles and waves. He is completing a sale with two teenage girls. As they leave, I place my hands on the counter and say, *Heartbreak Hotel*. Clay brings me the 45 and says that out of two dozen he has only three left. I carry the treasure to the Chevrolet and drive home.

Kris listened approvingly and appreciatively as she held the bottle to Sharny's mouth. Andy moved about the little kitchen, turning in circles and half-circles, waving his arms and laughing. This was the quietus for crooning, the terminus for precise and articulate phrasing, for conventional euphony and euphemism. This was sinuous energy, activated by conscious sensuality, the insistent musical rendition of the pulse—not the heart, but the pulse. *Down at the end of Lonely Street.* The lyrics rolled into a continuum of immodest desire. There was something of this on the flip side, *I Was the One*, but it was not so pulsatingly intense.

Boogie Woogie had been the tag-end of classicism. Here was the end of *June-moon, home-roam*, and the nasal pretension of Vaughan Monroe. Elvis brought rain and darkness upon the bland perfection of Bing Crosby and Frank Sinatra, who now retreated to the fading folds of bold innocence. Dionysus and his wild hordes of thyrsi-wielding women and conscious androgynes are relegating Apollo to the sparkling of the ballroom and, ultimately, to the music of the spheres wherein he will violate his sister the Moon.

I Want You, I Need You, I Love You; Don't Be Cruel; Blue Suede Shoes. The imponderable and mellifluous catch of youth. I purchased each new single and album as soon as Clay had them in stock. Kris began to suggest that perhaps I was overdoing it. Still, she enjoyed the dark turn toward the jungle as much as I did. We bought Andy a pair of blue suede shoes. The gates of license [Not your gates, George] had been opened. Eisenhower voters were understandably unsettled.

Kris and I bought our first television set. We watched the sensual gyrations of Elvis. We saw the smile of this consummate entertainer who does not take himself seriously. The Apollonian *Colonel* Parker stepped in to contain and channel the rebellious and liberating music; but it had broken through. America began to stream through the gates, beyond the plains of replicated housing and apple-pie conformity into the colorful valleys and through the passes of wooded hills and over the mountain streams of decadence, with all of their variety and all of their vicissitudes. I resort to vicissitudinous metaphor, as I yielded to want instead of attending to need.

The proper state of need is to be just slightly behind the demands of necessity. Need is governed by necessity; want is governed by desire. I had an attractive family: a wife and two children, all with dark brown hair and burning-brown eyes. I had a respectable job, doing what I liked to do. I had a comfortable home and a reliable automobile. I was accepted by my colleagues, despite my being anti-social. The margin of necessity that kept me validly active encompassed my gaining poise and achieving basic skills in conversation; completing the payments on my Chevrolet, and ultimately being able to pay cash for a new automobile; owning instead of renting a home; publishing refereed articles and scholarly books so as to ensure promotions and tenure; and being a better father and a better husband. Want was consigned to soporific daydreams about Ulla Jacobssons's breasts, *Playboy's* nudes, and athletic and financial prowess. Then Elvis came into the day, and [Sorry, George] the black horse of my want took the trace and turned the white horse of my need.

One should be governed by what one needs and not by what one wants. Necessity can, with proportional effort, be placated; but Desire increases disproportionately with every satisfaction and, generating insatiable greed, grows morbidly obese.

    Sharny slept much less contentedly than Andy, as an infant, had. Andy's night-time crying had roused Kris or me no more than once a night, and during no more than three nights a week. Sharny screamed for attention at least twice every night of every week. I discovered, though, that I was not averse to getting up and picking up that soft, swaddled body and rocking it in my arms and, occasionally, feeding it from a bottle that had been warmed in a pan of water. After a few weeks, I would insist that Kris return to sleep and that the nighttime attendance upon Sharny was my task. I was neither led by Necessity nor prodded by Desire. I recalled the maternal affection that had made me happy. Then I would lay Sharny in her crib and rejoin Kris in bed; and then the daylight would come.

    There is a functional diaeresis in *I Want You, I Need You, I Love You:* the expletive bridge *uh-uh* serves also as an emphatic negative. *Well, I thought I could live without romance, uh-uh until you came along*: as Elvis sings it, we hear . . . *I thought I could . . . (but I couldn't) . . . until you came along*. Kris liked the song and the rendition as much as I did, and she would sing it to, and eventually with, Andy; but she cared not, nor shared any of my enthusiasm, for the mechanics of diaeresis. We should have been too old to be fans of Elvis, but his artistry eluded the bonds of age like that of Mozart or Rimbaud.

50

In the Business Office of the Administration Building, I was given a form to fill out so that Sharny would be listed as a dependent. The woman who took the form from me let slip a wisp of a smile as she caught me staring at the slight protrusions that her breasts made in her light blue blouse. An inexpensive—or, at best, unpretentious—wristwatch weighed loosely on her thin left wrist. On the third finger of her right hand a turquoise ring slanted loosely. She is a thin woman, but not short: her pale blue eyes are on a level with mine. Her straight hair, parted on the left and turning inward in a tentative page-boy curve, is light brown in color, with a dark low-light in places. Her face is thin and pale. Her lips, with a light touch of pink lipstick, are full. Tactlessly curious, I stare steadily at her and give up all pretense of indifference. She is not pretty; but the gravity of her presence is something strange and new to me. She looks over the form, then looks up and smiles; in an urgent need to touch her, I move my right hand toward her cheek and then withdraw it in open-mouthed embarrassment before there is contact.

This is a very interesting name, she says, displaying no notice of my awkward movement; *how do you pronounce it?*

See-AH-nah TCHAR-nee, I offer; *but we call her Sharny.*

That's beautiful, she says; *really different.*

What is YOUR name?

Anne. I continued to stare, my question suspended. *Anne Estelle Ihnat.*

To my drop-jawed blank expression she responded by printing her name on a note-pad. She removed the slip and slid it under the grille to me. I asked her if *Ihnat* (pronounced EYE-not) was Estonian or Lithuanian. She said it was Czechoslovakian. I did not want to leave; but my business was finished and I could devise no more small talk. I thanked her. She turned away and went off to a desk near a window.

Anxious confusion: what was this strong attraction that the thin, pale, blue-eyed, blue-bloused woman had for me? I walked slowly, mentally re-creating that short event in the Administration Building. I picked up Andy at school. We walked home, singing *Knick-knack paddy whack / Give a dog a bone.*

Kris is sitting in our maple rocker. She has cradled Sharny in her lap and, as she rocks slowly, softly sings Kipling's *Recessional*, Andy runs over to her and kisses Sharny and nestles into Kris's right-arm embrace.

Through the small round window, located about two feet below the ceiling, the afternoon sun pours a diffused golden light onto Kris's face. She looks up and smiles; and Language lets speech issue from me: *You're beautiful, Kris.*

Anne Ihnat is not beautiful. I cannot get her out of my thought. I know that I must see her again. I daydream about being in her presence forever. There was a strangeness that night. I held Kris in my arms as we drifted into sleep; but I saw in a world of warm, bright light the pale, thin woman with the pale blue eyes and the sensual lips behind the small, straight bronze bars of the grille.

In my classrooms the next day, I would find my vocabulary and go into my act; but, at each bell, the face of Anne Ihnat smiled into my mind. At 1:30, I stood before the grille. A woman who was not Anne Ihnat came forward and asked me if she could help me. I stuttered the name, *Miss Ihnat?* She said, *Just a moment,* and went behind a frosted-glass partition; and, shortly after, Anne Ihnat stood before me. I had not thought of what I was going to say. I grinned, stuttered, uttered a few vowels, and finally settled for *I'm sorry to bother you, Miss Ihnat—Anne?—I guess I just wanted to say hello.* She answered, *Anne, please.*

There's a staff lounge two doors down—she pointed to her right—*where we can have a cup of coffee.*

Sitting on blue-enameled wooden chairs at a black-enameled small, circular table, we drank black coffee. I stared at her and rested my hand, palms up, upon the table top. *I, uh, um, ah . . .* was the best that I could do. She said, *A friend of mine in the office took your Mythology course, Dr. Blaustern. She liked it very much and told me all about it, and about how handsome you were.* I asked her please to call me *Pete*, and I said that I was very glad to receive the compliments. At last, I felt relaxed. I began, with genuine curiosity, to ask her about herself. She answered all of my questions, without hesitation or inhibition. She asked me not one question about myself.

She lived in an apartment with her mother, who worked mornings as a maid at a motel. Her younger brother lived in Gary, where he worked at a steel mill. Her father had gone off to work on the Alcan highway and never returned. She was nine years younger than I. She had a B.A—History major, Biology minor. She had completed work on her M.A. in History; and her advisor had secured for her this job on the academic staff. She did not care for movies or for Elvis Presley, but she liked Dean Martin.

RAIN and DARKNESS

She abhorred writers of historical fiction, like Samuel Shellabarger, Thomas Costain, and quite a few others. She liked the novels of Jakob Wassermann and Louis-Ferdinand Céline, which she had read in translation. The time was gone; she had overstayed her twenty-minute break. *Tomorrow?* She answered, *Yes*. As we stood, we looked directly into each other's eyes: commitment. I reached out to grasp her hand; she let me do so and did not resist my affectionate pressure. Then she smiled, turned away, and was gone.

Tufts of grass were reaching up through the cracks in the sidewalk. I thought of a song, *Tomorrow is Forever*, from a movie. Claudette Colbert and Orson Welles were in it, I think. Soon I am singing, *This old man, he played eight, / He played knick-knack on my gate*. Then Andy and I sing together, *With a knick-knack paddy-whack, / Give a dog a bone*; and Andy sings, *This old man came rolling home*.

51

Of the books for which Anne had expressed a liking, the Library had only *Kerkhoven's Third Existence* (but not the German original), *Voyage au bout de la nuit*, and *Mort à crédit*. Anne was especially fond of *The World's Illusion*, which was a translation of Wassermann's *Christian Wahnschaffe*. She offered to lend me her copy of *The World's Illusion* and gazed slightly off to her left when I said that I wanted to read the original. Our coffee breaks took place now almost every day. One Friday, as another Anne-less weekend neared, she gazed again just slightly to her left and I felt what I have come to call a transfusive exaltation, the warmth of a desire that was its own satisfaction, a sense that all that I could ever need amounted to my living every moment within the presence of this thin, blue-eyed woman with the sensual lips that parted almost imperceptibly in her receptiveness to my surrender.

The feeling was so strong that I leaned toward her. She turned to look at me and, with a brightness in her eyes, smiled, almost imperceptibly again, in affirmation and placed her hand upon mine.

Anne, I said, *if I were free, I would propose to you.* She said, *You know what my answer would be.*

A colleague in the German department lent me his copy of *Christian Wahnschaffe*. The title is appropriate: a Christian (or, Christianity) misshapen by illusion. The truth of religion is love, not reward. Love is its own reward. It is not light; it is the divine darkness that defines light—as dark matter, presumably, defines matter. The pseudo-Dionysius must have meant this in writing about the superessential shining of the divine darkness. I read the translation of *Kerkhovens dritte Existenz*, which was the last novel that Wassermann completed before his death. Wassermann is an accomplished story-teller. His third-person narratives are what stories should be if the reader is to be caught up in the experiences of characters and in events and is made amenable to a profoundly simple theme: love is resident within and is nurtured by the darkness of faith and trust.

To turn from Wassermann's religious optimism to Céline's amoral pessimism was to indulge in a time-consuming excitement that cut deeply into my class-preparation time. Unlike veritable scholars, I am a very slow, meagerly retentive reader. I could not surrender to the light of any daily duties my sustained plunge into the darkness of Céline's night. Wassermann's darkness is a spiritual way of seeing; Céline's darkness is a seeing of the human way. In the limited healer Ferdinand Bardamu and his black-horse alter-ego Léon Robinson, I came again upon that necessary juxtaposition of two incompatible factors (the Camusian absurd, the tension-force of life, the dyad) that I had found in Melville's Ahab and the White Whale, and in Hardy's Jude Fawley and Sue Bridehead.

It came to me that Wassermann and Céline constituted a reading-dyad, a mental need that had been mysteriously recognized and satisfied. I told Anne how much both authors' works had come to mean to me; and I said that I could not help but prefer Céline. She said that she preferred Wassermann.

Kris was becoming increasingly impatient with my interminable reading and paper-work. I grew irritable and testy as she complained.

I would think of the difference between my life with Kris and a life with Anne; but then I would play some little game with Andy and listen to his laugh; or I would hold Sharny in my lap and feel her sacred warmth and stare at her infant-beauty; and I would know again that Kris and I were right (still, however, without knowing exactly what that meant). It was impossible to conceive of a Kris/Anne dyad, because the element of my self produced an irreducible triad.

Steadiness and escape from irresolution I found only in the classroom. Although there were mistakes and gaps that I was frequently at pains or at a loss to cover over, and while there was occasionally a student who disliked me for either my person or my inadequacy, I performed well and impressed many by my never looking to a single note. I had always resented teachers who relied upon their notes and yet denied students the use of notes in taking examinations. It was my determination to reverse that situation. Accordingly, my class preparation entailed considerable memorization. I was also learning that concerted belief in a student, such as Professor Landis and a few others had had in me, needed to be limited. One could believe in a student but not collectively in a large class. I needed to single students out; but I did so arbitrarily. Gradually, I increased the number of students that I could single out; and this was a source of satisfaction. Classes in advanced Latin or Greek were usually small—three to six students—and with these my dispensation of belief could be inclusive.

Anne's friend, the one who had taken my Mythology course, joined us for one of the coffee breaks. My apprehension and disappointment were overcome by her display of devotion to Anne and her profuse praise of my teaching. She had especially liked my presentation of the Female Force in Scandinavian myth: the androgyny of Loki, the dependence of Odin upon the Sibyl for knowledge, and, ultimately, the superiority of Brunhild and Kriemhild to Gunther and Siegfried. She asked me if I had read *Barabbas* by Pär Lagerkvist, the Swedish winner of the Nobel Prize for literature. I hadn't. She promised to bring her copy to work for Anne to carry to me. She said that she had to get back to work, thanked me for the coffee, excused herself, and gave Anne and me five or six minutes to be alone.

That was on a Friday. On Monday, Anne handed me a copy of the novel, translated from the Swedish into English. I knew no Swedish; but, after I had read the short novel, I began immediately, with a Swedish grammar and a Swedish-English dictionary, to gain the rudiments of a reading knowledge.

Lagerkvist's understanding of darkness seemed to me to go well beyond Céline's. For Céline, darkness is active—a way of life; for Lagerkvist, it is passive—the ground of life. I secured also an English-Swedish dictionary and, from my colleague in the German department a copy of *Barabbas* in the original. Swedish has much in common with German and English; but neither German nor English has the strange enclitic definite article. For example, *Dvärgen*, the Lagerkvist novel to which I next turned, is *The Dwarf*; the *-en* of the Swedish title is the definite article, *The*, of the English title. When an adjective is added, however, a separate prefatory definite article is added. *The eternal dwarf*, for example, would be *den eviga dvärgen; den* and *-en* (*the* and *-the*) constitute *The*. Kris listened politely, but without interest, when I told her about this. Anne shared my interest and said that the phenomenon should perhaps be called *articular insistence*.

At my urging, Anne read *Barabbas*, but she did not share my enthusiasm for it. I collected and read Lagerkvist's short stories, plays, and poems. Anne listened to my summaries and interpretations of them; but she preferred not to read them, turning instead to writers whom she eventually induced me to read: Unamuno, Camus, Sartre, and de Beauvoir. I told her about Blackie, who called me *Ped* (for *pedant*) and said that I was a loser because my need to be praised was greater than my willingness to praise. Did she think, I asked her, that this perhaps explained my penchant for passivity. She turned her head to her left, moved her chin toward her shoulder, and said, *Pete, it's never too late to lose.*

52

Anne had flexible working hours. She arranged for us to have more time together. She gave me a set of keys to her gun-metal-grey Ford, which she called her *Grey Fox*. After my two morning classes, I would stalk the Grey Fox and wait a few minutes in its passenger-seat for her. She would join me and drive to one of the six or seven huge parks beyond the city. We would hold hands, talk, and kiss. I said that I loved her. She did not respond. Anne was averse, possibly alien, to the conventional act or response. It was when I had no expectation of it, in the middle of something I was saying to her, that she smiled and said, *I love you, Pete*. By then, I knew enough not to say, *I love you too*. One Thursday, she drove to the motel at which her mother worked. I waited in the Grey Fox while she secured from her mother the key to a vacant unit. The room was small, dark, and seemed to me to be indescribably remote. Anne removed all of her clothing and lay supine on the bed. I knelt on the floor beside her. I am in the presence of Anne Estelle Ihnat, who does not ask for anything, who does not inquire about anything, who gives everything. This is the hour of completion, of utter perfection in dyadic tension with the light of the world outside and beyond the dark room's door. This is beyond happiness, which is chance; this is the radiance of the divine dark.

Back within the reality of the Grey Fox, I said that someday, somehow I would be free. I felt this to be true, even though I knew that it would not and could not be effected by divorce. *Life is a dirty trick*, Anne said. I asked her who, or what, the trickster was. *That's the dirty part*, she said: *there is no trickster*. In her pale blue eyes I saw the incipient return of that pain that our moment in the motel room had totally eliminated; and, feeling that pain with her, I understood that life's trickery is its momentary seizure of, and arbitrary rejection of, itself. Grounded in darkness.

Give a dog a bone.

Back home, I was filled with a guilt that brought no pain. Kris prepared an evening meal of creamed corn, American fried potatoes, and green beans. After the meal and the cleaning, I held Sharny while Kris and Andy worked on an educational jig-saw puzzle.

Kris's parents drove down from Hamtramck to see their new granddaughter and to spend Thanksgiving with us. They stayed at the motel where Anne's mother worked, the motel of my Elevation.

In December, Kris and I, bundling in Andy and Sharny, drove all the way to our home city for the Christmas holidays.

We stayed with Vera and Blackie. My mother was quite pleased to see her grandchildren. My father delighted Andy with fiddle-playing and managed to teach his grandson the words to a *Liedchen*. Paul, a Navy career man now, was home on leave. Kris visited her hotel; but only five of the thirteen people with whom she had worked were still there. A special party-reception was improvised for her. My uncle and I sat down to our cribbage game, as though no years had ever intervened; between games he tested me regularly on the state capitals: West Virginia? *Charleston*; Pennsylvania? *Harrisburg*.

Blackie and I spent the long part of an afternoon at Narducci's. Fred (Federico) Narducci, a friend of ours from grade-school and high-school, had his own Italian restaurant now. We sat in a candle-lit booth with hot dagos (Fred's spicy hot sauce was unique) and Hamm's beer. Blackie said that Jordy Klug was all over the chart these days, currently in Las Vegas supervising some demolition-and-reconstruction work. He was into munitions, plastics, gun-running, immigrant smuggling, South American drugs by way of Mexico, and National Rifle Association politics.

Trusting him not to confide in Vera, I told Blackie about Anne. It's not that Blackie was completely trustworthy, any more than I was; but I had to tell somebody. From what Anne had told me, I answered his questions. Anne and her brother worked full time and supported their mother, who worked part time and was not in good health. Anne went out now and then with other guys, one named Joe and one named Carl, but was neither intimate nor serious with either of them: yes, I believed her. Joe had been a high-school friend, who took it upon himself to be her protector. Carl was *just a friend*. She had told neither of them about me.

He said that, while I had passively yielded to Kris, I had been the active one in initiating the affair with Anne. *It's good for a passive guy to shift into the active, Ped, but it's also wrong.* He said that I shouldn't have done this to Kris and that, now, there are many things that I shouldn't be doing, but will necessarily be doing, to Anne. *Wrong can be good?* I asked. He assured me that good was a term of function, not of morality: something is good if it works, like light, as it was created by God, and bad if it doesn't. I recalled Lagerkvist, for whom the opposite of *evil* is, not *good*, but *love*. It was good, Blackie explained, that women could replace men in the factories during the war, but it was wrong. He waved aside my demurrer and said it's wrong to pound in a nail with a wrench or a screwdriver, if no hammer is available, but it's good to get the nail pounded in.

Women are part of the labor market now, a permanent part of the work force. WACS and WAVES and other military women will become part of the armed forces and, very likely, engage in combat sooner or later. It's all good for women, but it's wrong. If women will no longer be the subservient sex, that's goodbye to the family unit.

Women are better than men, I said.

Like Hell they are; but, say they are: all the more reason for them to be what they're built for—passivity, but with their need for praise balanced by a willingness to praise. That was insightful of Blackie. I thought of Ibsen's Hilda and Nora and Hedda and Rebecca—and of the tragedies to which their assertions of their inherent superiority led. Aeschylus's Clytemnestra, Euripides's Agave and Medea, Sophocles's Electra, even Aristophanes's Lysistrata. I mentioned these examples in support of his assertion; I added Jane Darwell's Ma Joad speech—men live by jerks; for women it's all one flow—at the end of *The Grapes of Wrath* movie. Blackie tipped his glass, refilled it with Hamm's, and said that I would become like Russell Simpson's Pa Joad if I didn't spend my time getting out articles and books instead of having affairs. Frame-lighted above the bar was the huge Anheuser-Busch lithograph of *Custer's Last Stand*, Otto Becker's adaptation of Cassilly Adams's oil painting. I raised my glass to it and said, *Well, here's to Errol*. Blackie raised his glass and added, *And to Arthur Kennedy.* We drank. Beginning then with Charley Grapewin and G.P. Huntley, Jr., we took turns in naming each member of the entire cast. I think we remembered them all: right through Minerva Urecal, Vera Lewis, Jack Mower, Joe Devlin, and Victor Zimmerman. I mentioned that Ian MacDonald had gone on to play Frank Miller in *High Noon*; but, for Blackie, that movie was a *Commie job by Carl Foreman*. We argued, pleasantly, about the House UnAmeican Activities Committee. He laughed me out of my recalled bitterness over Robert Taylor's sleazy slur of Howard DaSilva. He laughed when I related my bitter disappointment at learning that my father had voted for Eisenhower. *Ped*, he mused, with the kind of sympathy that no one else could ever have for me, *you're not strong enough for your romanticism.*

Although I didn't bring the conversation back to Anne, Blackie knew that I needed advice about my affair. *Anne has your heart*, he said; *she'll always be a deep part of your life; but Kris has your soul.* He made it clear that there was no way that I could leave Kris and the kids. As long as I was in that university town, I would continue to see Anne. One of us had to leave. It could not be Anne; the town was her home; her mother was not well. I was not likely to get tenure without getting down to the demanding business of professional scholarship from which my need for Anne, added to Kris's antipathy to my academic duties, would keep me. *Find a satisfying teaching job elsewhere, Peddo, where you don't have to publish or perish. Anne will always be yours and nobody else's and you know that.* Somehow, I did know that; but I tried to deny my vanity, my uncertain satisfaction in having the knowledge. A twinge of relief, along with increased pleasure in the spicy food and headed beer, signaled my decision to follow Blackie's advice.

53

The female force (I take the felicitous phrase from Richmond Lattimore's close-to-perfect translation of Aeschylus's *Agamemnon*) is deeper and nearer to Being than Virginia Woolf's *force of femininity*. The former is life, the latter a form of living. Woolf, a woman who wrote like a man, lived like a man, and looked like a man, said, *It would be a thousand pities if women wrote like men, or lived like men, or looked like men*. She begins paragraphs with *However*, uses phrases like *anyone in their senses*, and has *Nobody* serve as antecedent to *them*. She is nonetheless my guide: *a great mind is androgynous*; and *So long as you write what you wish to write, that is all that matters* . . . Only Joyce's *Ulysses* is peer to *Mrs. Dalloway*, *To the Lighthouse*, and *Between the Acts*. Among male and female lyricists, Sappho has no peer. Proust equals, perhaps, but does not surpass Lady Murasaki in greatness. Joyce, Woolf, Sappho, Proust, Lady Murasaki all—called *highbrow writers* by critics with malfunctioning cerebral hemispheres—have androgynous minds.

Many good writers, with, must one say, lower calibrations of brow, are womanly or manly, but are not Woolf's *womanly-manly*. I look up from this, my effortful, unrewarding prose, to which, at best, the Arnold Schwarzeneggerly term *girly-manly* might apply, to see the sunlight sprinkled on the corkscrew willow outside my window and to turn therefrom to

RAIN and DARKNESS

Anna Quindlen's *Black and Blue*, a first-person novel pocked with the inevitable omnimnemonism for verbatim dialogue. It's a good story, neatly wrought, but only womanly-womanly with its expatiations upon hair-do's, food displays, and clothing stylistics. The good guy, Mike Riordan, whose name is Irish, like that of the narrator, Frances née Flynn, is an even-tempered ne'er-do-wrong. The bad guy, Bobby Benedetto, has a manic Mediterranean temperament and beats his wife, the narrator, until she takes their son and runs away. I looked without success for intonations of the title more distant than the metaphor for discoloration caused by coagulations of blood beneath the surface of the skin; there was, unless my critical acumen is, as it may well be, errant, only the clever variant, *an onyx and lapis lazuli necklace of bruises*, a metaphor in three parts instead of two.

Quindlen accedes to convention in using aberrations that convention has made acceptable: like *different than* and *cesarean*, the latter so listed in medical dictionaries, which eschew the correct *Caesarean*. On one page, the aberration *didn't used to* appears three times in proximity; one doesn't say, for example, *didn't needed to*; one says *didn't need to* and should likewise say *didn't use to*. Intelligibility does not confer correctness upon shabby usage any more than longevity confers anything but longevity upon abuses of language. Is it Quindlen or Frances who is responsible for *the way the nuns made Grace and I do when we were young* and *Lt. Benedetto, who I'd met only once?* To a good writer the differentiation of herself or himself, as author, from her or his first-person narrator is not an impossibility.

Walter Benn Michaels ponders the supersession of English by Spanish, the evanescence and eventual disappearance of spoken English—disappearance, not death, because, as Professor Landis said, a language that has produced a literature that is still read is not dead. The English of *Beowulf* is still read, and that of Chaucer; both still participate in Language. As inflected English yielded to apocope and curtailed orthography, the language Michaels speaks will yield to *cheeseburger, pizzarama*, and the codified brevity of electronic mail. Resistance to such passage is civilizational heroism, futile but functional, which is to say, good.

Quindlen's Frances Flynn Benedetto runs away from her abusive husband and tries to change her identity. This, as Quindlen shows, is not the better course. Concerted resistance, the being of heroism, is the better course. And Quindlen herself should not have yielded to *cesarean* and *didn't used*.

My resistance to the radiant darkness of Anne should not have been a running away from the prospect of academic perishing. It should have been a firm stance by which I did what Professor Landis believed I could do and from which there would be no Anne for me. It would not be that firm stance, as Blackie knew it could not be.

Anne didn't praise me merely in words: in lending her presence to me and in requiting my love for her, she praised me ideally. Blackie, who essentially defined me in the context of praise, must have known how much I needed this ideal praise; and yet he counseled me against my need. He was advising me, I think, to do my duty, which was to praise Kris, and to live with my need unsatisfied, as great people do. I was not great; but, maybe, with my unsatisfied need and with Professor Landis's belief in me, I could at least achieve academic success. Professor Landis's belief in me was, after all, a form of praise; but I did not need it in the way and to the degree that I needed the presence of Anne. My passivity, then, could achieve its active meaning only in relinquishing the satisfaction of my need. This is probably the true nature of sacrifice. For what? The well-being of Kris, Andy, and Sharny. To what end? Language.

Elvis was then singing about wanting to be, not a tiger or a lion, but a Teddy Bear. Lions and tigers are great. Teddy Bears are not alive.

54

Ritt was surprised when I told him of my decision to leave the university. He asked me to give the matter further thought and not to act in haste. I promised to do as he suggested. He was confident that I could get a book contract within three years. This would ensure my receipt of tenure. He reminded me of my proven excellence in teaching and of my having earned a reduced teaching load in the interest of research. Kris urgently favored my adhering to the decision. She did not care for this university town or its academic life. If she had any suspicion of my infidelity, she fully suppressed it. Anne, at first, said nothing. When I told her about Blackie's advice and my strong inclination to accept it, she got up from the booth—we were having coffee in a roadside diner at some distance from the university—and put a Johnny Mathis song on the jukebox. She returned to the booth, reached across the table surface to put her hand on mine, and she smiled. Then she said, *Pete, the rose will always be in bloom.*

Anne's rose metaphor owed chiefly to her reading of Keats, many of whose poems and passages therefrom she had memorized. *Like rose leaves with the drip of summer rains.* Not infrequently, but never in celebration of an occasion, I would send her four long-stemmed roses. She said that she put these in a long-necked opaque white vase, beside which she would lay her volume of Keats. *Fair dewy roses brush against our faces, / And flowery laurels spring from diamond vases.* Our eyes would meet in a sober steadiness as we indulged in these sentimental flourishes. *Love, why wilt thou let / Darkness steal out upon the sleepy world / So wearily . . . ?* She described her evenings: preparing and eating an evening meal, while Johnny Mathis 45's played; cleaning up the dishes; her mother writing a letter to Anne's brother while Anne herself read Keats; watching television; and, then, Anne giving her mother the prescribed medications and seeing her to bed. Anne would read novels until she herself retired between ten-thirty and eleven. It may be that the opaque white vase was a metaphor for diamond vases—not a simile, which would have entailed correspondences (plurality, translucence, the strange upsurge of victory), but a metaphor that could not possibly be taken literally, improving thereby upon Keats's metaphor, which could, in fact, be taken literally. George Soros is right to define the false metaphor as one that is taken literally.

Robert Burns presented the newly sprung rose as a simile of his love (being both his emotion and his beloved); a second simile of this love is the *melodie, / That's sweetly played in tune.* Anne's primary metaphor is the rose that will always bloom.

With this, Ray Ellis and his orchestra play *All the Time*, sweetly and in tune; and Johnny Mathis sings, *I needed someone all the time* . . . Keats's laurels springing from diamond vases, Burns's rose *That's newly sprung in June*; Anne's roses in an opaque white vase; her one rose that has bloomed and will bloom all the time.

Jay Livingston and Ray Evans wrote *All the Time*. Anne quoted a line from it some weeks after our brief moment in the roadside diner. We were sitting on a rustic oak bench in a state park. Before us, a steep slope sank into a long, deep valley. Behind us stood a dense woodland, with only a few leaves, in the tall trees, turning color in the late October sun. I was holding her right hand on my lap. She reached over my lap and took my right hand in her other hand. With ease, and in peace, we stared at each other. Anne said, *You are the one love I am living for*. I knew that I did not have to reply. Then we kissed, and embraced, and sat quietly for many minutes. I recalled the smooth sound of Johnny Mathis's rendition of that line. Some of the lyrics work only because of the warm grace with which Johnny Mathis renders them. The two similes—comparing feelings to the warmth of May wine and to the width of the sea—must look barren in print; but Mathis translates them into a sound that is the intonation of Language. In Anne's embrace, in her presence, I was, as Heidegger understood Hölderlin to do, returning home.

Ritt came to understand that my need to change direction was not exclusively academic. *What's important is how you feel*, he said. *Follow your heart.* Yes, my feelings, which were not a matter of warmth and width, were important. Anne had given them meaning. *Heart* was quite different and more complex. Beyond *heorte* and *cardia* there is a primitive sense of giving trust. I had given trust to Kris and to Anne; and each requited my gift. Sustaining both the gift and its requital meant sacrificing Anne's presence (*And fare thee weel a while! . . . / . . . And I will come again*).

In November, over coffee, Anne, who liked my explanation of *dyad*, asked if *pair* would be a kindred term. Each is a singular noun denoting two interdependent constituent elements in opposition; remove one of the elements, and the application of the word disintegrates. I suggested that, while that was true for two words, it didn't work for actual things; remove one element of a dyad and both elements are destroyed, annihilated; remove one element of a pair, and one or both may continue to subsist in separation. *The truth, then, could be in the words*, she said. I nodded; if the words, as myths, were metaphors that could not be taken literally. *But,* she asked, *what about my word, which I have given you, and your word, which you have given me?*

 I didn't recall that we had pledged words in this way; but then it occurred to me that, of course, we had done so in the mutual gift of trust. Anne, who did not waste words, had taught me how not to waste them. She seemed intuitively to possess something of the wisdom that I was struggling to gain through my reading of Heidegger. Language tends to unfold itself when words are inherently alive.

 Ritt arranged for me to be interviewed at an unpretentious (not prestigious) university that, to Kris's delight, lay between our home city and Hamtramck. The interview and visit were to take place after the holidays.

55

The position would carry tenure and my offering of courses in both Classics and English, as I had been doing. The salary would almost generously exceed my current salary. My publications, few but moderately creditable and with some promise, along with my teaching record, enhanced my candidacy. The visit went well, because I sincerely wanted the position and had brought with me no vanity contingent upon my current employment by the much larger (and prestigious) university.

Between thirty and forty persons—faculty members and students—attended my lecture. There were posters advertising it: *Gallus: Texts, Text, and Speculation: A Lecture By Dr. Peter O. Blaustern*. The texts were the references to Gallus by writers in classical antiquity; the text was the small aggregate of lines ascribed to Gallus; and the speculation was based upon the *spuria* that I had culled from Jordy and Mischiato, including the possibility that in Egypt Gallus had originated the *Fundamentum*, an anarchic movement that eventually comprised conspiratorial unions from Ireland to China and from the Arctic circle to Cape Horn and the Cape of Good Hope.

There was a long and enthusiastic discussion; skeptics were more curious than scornful; and there was gratifying interest in my expressed hope to undertake a research quest for the *Heidelberg recension*.

Interest was centered on the speculation, the very groundlessness of which had impelled disinterested journal referees to recommend rejection of my article on Gallus. Had I possessed the genuinely scholarly mind of Professor Simon Schama, whose *Dead Certainties* would later justify the coloring of history with narrative fiction, I might have been able to include the speculations about Gallus in a theoretical argument. Being a performer, however, instead of a scholar, I was limited to entertainment outside the confines of enlightenment. Here I entertained successfully, as I had been doing in my classes, where most of my students approved my presentations and only a few were dubious about them. In grammar, translation, and standard biographical and chronological information, I stretched no facts or points; but in criticism and modes of interpretation, and in hypothetical biography and chronology, I tended toward the abuse of restraint.

When we were students, Blackie liked to say that teaching was just bullshit. Not in the cases of mathematics and foreign languages, I argued. He would tentatively concede, adding music and crafts, provided that the teachers were so good that they didn't have to teach. Professor Landis was certainly that good; and he had insisted that the teaching of Greek and Latin completed one's learning of them. If now, moreover, I agreed with Blackie that there were very few ways other than teaching by which one could earn a living with a mastery of Greek and Latin, he would doubtless say that that simply proves the inutility of *dead languages*. He had little patience with the Humanities, although he tolerated the superb framed print of Rubens's *Judgment of Paris* that Vera treasured and had hung on the wall above and behind their bed. I thought often of Professor Landis's elaboration upon the Judgment of Paris: it had to be right, but it was not textually justified by the earliest sources; the *Iliad* says only that Paris was offered *lust for which he would be sorry (mach'osyne alegeine)*, and the *Cypria*, naming Athena, Hera, and Aphrodite, says only that Aphrodite offered him marriage with Helen. Lucian's story, upon which Rubens based his painting, is quite late, following the *Iliad* by eight or nine hundred years. Lucian's tale is comic, with each goddess offering Paris a bribe.

Professor Landis said that the bribes were metaphors for the three ways of ancient Greek life: Rule (Hera's offering), Glory in War (Athena's), and Sensuality (Aphrodite's), the last, Paris's choice, being the least. Rule comprised sovereignty and philosophy; Glory in War comprised battle prowess and athletics; Sensuality comprised physical and aesthetic pleasures and the arts. This teaching I could not take as anything but undeniable. Hera imbued Agamemnon with sovereignty; Athena imbued Achilles with great battle prowess; and Aphrodite attended to the sensual needs of Paris. Teaching the recognition of the undeniable is not bullshit.

Implicit in the three ways of life as the offerings of goddesses, not male gods, is a fourth way: the worship of the source of the offerings, the female force. A man may pursue rule, championship, or sensual gratification; or he may worship the female force that makes the three pursuits possible. The pursuer needs three women: a wife or mother (to rule him), an intellectual activator (as soul mate), and a mistress (to fulfill his sensuality). Most fortunate is he who finds all three in one woman. The worshiper achieves greatness. The female force (threefold, like Robert Graves's White Goddess) IS greatness; her priestess needs no man, but she may condescend to be the object of one or more of the pursuits of any man. The female is triadic; the triad, taken with the male worshiper, constitutes the indefinite dyad (female-male), which is a variable tetrad (three-one). The tetrad—always a tetrad—is completion, or perfection: a man needs three women. The dyad is dyadic tension: a woman needs only one man.

Reading now Salley Vickers's *Instances of the Number 3*, I can see that her character Peter Hansome's first wife is merely protatic; his second wife, Bridget, is his Hera; his mistress, Frances, is his Athena; and the exotic Veronica is his Aphrodite. Not having worshiped the female force, he impotently wanders, posthumously lost, from the reality of darkness to the unreality of light. Peter is the equivalent of the ghostly Paris. I recall Pasternak's Doctor Zhivago, who had his Hera in Tonya and his Athena in Lara, but lacked an Aphrodite. The Three Graces of Botticelli's *La Primavera* grace the dust-jacket of Salley Vickers's book. Paris, who chose Aphrodite, had only Oenone and Helen; but, ultimately, if not in Homer, his was the thelycratic choice. The vast variety of sexual preferences, genetic sexual determinants, and forms of fidelity are disturbingly peripheral to the ultimate relationship of the female-male tetrad. The greatest writers aim at the perfection of the indefinite dyad. Vickers wanders, erring by hooking Peter up with a beautiful woman, Zelda, who is in fact a male named Zahin—this, despite Vickers's felicitous and wondrously unerring locution, *Very happy, as it happens*. Mishap, good hap.

Good writers, like Vickers (and Pasternak), aim at greatness. Vickers has a clause—*The air was sharp with the scent of incipient spring . . .*—that would be perfect had she not appended to it a rambling metaphor, *and the sun on the field was laying the lightest benediction on the pale ranks of spring wheat* . . . . After the three graces of *sharp*, *scent*, and *spring*, combined with the muted alliteration of the tumescent *incipient*, one doesn't want to contend with graded benediction and the leap from incipient spring to (full) spring (with wheat risen). Elsewhere, her *two kinds of person* is laudable; the philistines say *kinds of persons*, but on the next page (190) she has the correlative conjunction *neither* followed by three *nors*, instead of *neither . . . nor . . . or . . . or*. Worst, near the last words of the novel, there is *But no one defended themselves*. As narrator, she correctly writes *She seemed unable*; and, as author, she has a character incorrectly say *I never seem to be able*. I dislike the British aberration *different to* for *different from*. That I have to look up *trugfull*, *anorak*, and *bollards* owes to my own insufficiency. A trugfull is about three-fourths of a bushel, or, as she says, *more than enough for a single person*. I flip back to page 58, where Salley Vickers writes to *try and suggest*, and I conclude that this novel about life as a Dantean purgatorio, through which, with the help of Shakespeare's wit and theatre (wherein plays play plays and men play women, who may in turn play men) and the religious sensibility of John Donne, is, in its connection of love triangle with the Trinity and with its imperfect triads in pursuit of perfect tetrads, quaintly inferior to Heidegger's FOUR: earth and sky, divinities and mortals. She clarifies literature as a motive of life; Anne, with her Keats, and I, with my Wordsworth, would applaud that clarification.

(Anne would have been indifferent to William Safire's acceptance of *raised* as synonymous with *reared*. I cannot be.)

Anne's favorite memories were of Christmas Eves, when, before their heavily decorated and well-lit Christmas tree, she and her mother and brother opened their colorfully– and ribbon-tied presents. They would enjoy cookies that her mother had made and drink egg nog sprinkled with nutmeg. They would stay up late, playing *Hearts* or *Monopoly* or *India*. I told her about my pleasure in walking on the wet sidewalks past the high-piled winter snow, colored by the city's decorative Christmas lights, and about my shopping with my limited earnings for presents to give my parents, brothers, and sisters. I recalled the pleasant touch of my jacket collar against my cheek in the cold air. I mentioned too the cold, crisp Christmas days, with full sun on the high snow, in a bright emptiness that was totally remote from problems, troubles, and perplexities. I admitted that my presents were almost always the wrong choices. My mother and Paul (and my uncle, when he was part of our gathering) would feign pleasure at my purchases for them, like, respectively, chocolate covered cherries and a tie (and a carton of cigarettes); my father would say nothing beyond *Dank'* for his gift shirt; the younger kids would either moan or toss their gift toys or trinkets aside.

The fourth edition of *The American Heritage Dictionary of the English Language* defines *small talk* as *Casual or trivial conversation*. I think it is a social convention of talking for the sake of talking. It is good to know that Edward Hopper abhorred small talk. I tell myself that I abhor it; but I had let Anne know that I considered it a skill, like writing best-selling novels, that I fully lacked. Anne and I never talked just to be talking. Often we talked about trivial things—wrist watches, toy racing cars, watermelon seeds, the pointlessness of stamp-collecting—but never without interest. We talked amateurishly about painters. I praised the work of Edward Hopper and Jackson Pollock. She passed those over for Matisse and Georgia O'Keeffe. *Anne, I said, I prefer your very real labia to those variously depicted by O'Keefe in landscapes, along with her ovarian cattle bones.* She kissed me, long and meaningfully, and then said, *It's all one world, Pete, and this is all we have.* I was sure, at that time, that I knew what she meant; at this time, I have no clear sense of what she meant. Our casual or trivial conversation was not talk for the sake of talking. It was part of our being together, like our frequent long silences, during which I experienced the euphoria I had known within my mother's embrace when I was a child. I don't mean that Anne was a mother-figure for me. I didn't want her to mother me, as often I needed Kris to do. Rather, I had long waking dreams about her giving birth to a child of mine. I told her about these dreams. She smiled, stroked my wrist, and said, *My wish too—but not out of wedlock.*

Anne's ethical principles were not grounded in religion. They were traceable, I think, to an ancient, dark sense of responsibility to one's blood, to what the concept of *Blut und Boden* had disclosed to Heidegger. Like Lagerkvist and Camus, she refrained from denying the existence of God but insisted that God had no concern for humankind. And so it was strange that we should spend, in a huge, stone Catholic cathedral, our last hour together before my move to another state.

Holding hands, we sat in silence. We watched, as others, alone or in pairs, walked on the aisle, genuflected, made the Sign of the Cross, sat in the pews ahead of us, or knelt in prayer; some went on to light candles near the altar.

Anne and I knelt on the old wooden board and, somehow knowingly, prayed to each other. My prayer was, *Wait for me, Anne, so that you can bring our child into our life.*

Kris was practicality; Anne was fulfillment.

Kris was loving; Anne was love.

RAIN AND DARKNESS

Kris kept time to music with her left foot, Anne with the middle finger of her right hand. Hedwig had melded in memory with a Heidelberg I had never seen. I was married to Kris. I belonged to Anne.

In the Chevrolet, I look into Anne's pale blue eyes and place my right hand on her cheek. Her light brown hair has a few dark brown strands. There is a light touch of pink lipstick on her full lips. My Athena.

56

The move from the large to the small university was an appropriate descent. I fit in well, academically, if not socially, with my new colleagues. Kris and I rented the lower half of a well maintained duplex. The larger of its two alcoves became my study. Kris enjoyed a laundry room just off the kitchen. One of Blackie's fellow Field Artillery officers, Graydon Braham, is an associate professor of Art here. Blackie writes to him; and Grayber, as everyone calls him, helped us to get settled, arranged, and familiar with the town. He gave us one of his original oils, *Wayside Shrine*, to hang behind and above the sofa in the living room.

Graydon Corinth (Grayber) Braham, like Blackie, had been an OCS (Officer Candidate School) second lieutenant. He and Blackie served together in the same Field Artillery battalion in France and Germany; both had attained to the rank of captain. They kept up correspondence after the war and occasionally got together, their visits lessening considerably after Blackie married Vera. Upon receipt of tenure, Grayber had purchased a huge Victorian-style mansion, among the eighteen rooms of which was a ballroom. He removed the wall between two of the third-floor rooms and set the area up as a studio, open to the northern sky under a glass ceiling and a slanted wall of glass. One of the other rooms became a dark-room for photography. Another became a projection room for slides and films. Five rooms were inexpensively but tastefully furnished as guest rooms, one of which Vera and Blackie enjoyed when they came for a visit in August of that year.

It was an exceptional week. Kris and I renewed our good times with Vera and Blackie. We sank contentedly into Grayber's plush but not garish sofas and easy chairs. Grayber's gourmet meals were delectable. Andy and Sharny played in the ballroom and, outside, on the five acres that qualified the property for the status of a farm and the reduced taxation thereon.

Grayber's mansion had, in time, become the scene of a succession of parties. There were faculty members who disliked his shoulder-length hair, clothes-line-rope belts, moccasins, khaki pants, and buckskin vest over a pale blue shirt; but, if invited, they would not miss his parties.

He gratuitously befriended Kris and me, baby-sitting frequently for us, so that we were able once again to see as many movies as we liked. Andy and Sharny became devoted to him. At age ten and four, respectively, they sat in his studio for a portrait in pastel, which remains a treasure. He told them stories, taught them finger-painting and chalk-drawing, played *Old Maid* with them, and showed them how to win the loyalty of his three Siamese cats.

One of the movies we saw at that time was Stanley Kubrick's *Paths of Glory*. It had been released about two years earlier and was part of a double-feature at a nearby second-run theatre. Kris and I were amazed at the excellence of the movie: the photography of Georg Krause, the performance of heretofore mediocre Wayne Morris, the recognition of war as a diabolical constant in opposition to Being (or, as Kris had it, to human existence), and the magnificent rendition of *Der treue Husar* at the movie's conclusion. Susanne Christian, as the Fräulein whose singing restored humanity to the souls of the initially rowdy and salacious French infantrymen, married Kubrick, as we were later to learn. Pressing Grayber into a second night's baby-sitting, we returned the next night for a second viewing. I taught Kris the words to the *Volksweise*, and she sang it with melancholy clarity. *Paths of Glory* had been the second part of a double feature. We had gone to see the main attraction, the irritatingly grim *I Want to Live*, which we bothered not to watch again on our second trip. I wrote to Blackie about the film. He responded, saying that Vera had been greatly impressed by Ralph Meeker, whom they had seen on stage in *Picnic* during a stay in New York, and he admired the performances of Adolphe Menjou, Kirk Douglas, and George MacCready. Despite his interest in photography, Grayber was largely indifferent to Hollywood movies, and we could not persuade him to see the Kubrick film. He did, however, accompany Kris on his baby grand piano as she sang *Der treue Husar*. He went on to instruct Kris in the mysteries of the Gregorian Chant. He recounted to Andy, who was now enrolled in a Catholic school, the lives of the earliest saints. And he generously outlined to me the colors of light in Edward Hopper's work and the colors of tawdriness in Reginald Marsh's. I remember his saying that Marsh painted an America that had crowded itself into *garish bleakness* [not my phrase, George] and that Hopper was painting a post-ecclesiastical America that was living in a blue perpetual Sunday. He admired Hopper's celebration of the integrity of self-containment but had reservations about Marsh's *proletarian pugilism*. When I objected to *post-ecclesiastical* by reminding him that church-going Christians still constituted an American majority, including the Bible Belt and the office of the presidency, Grayber chuckled and likened the *spiritual hangover* to the British monarchy, with its outmoded Beefeater uniforms and gilded carriages, and to the retention of Latin instruction in the grade-schools of backward states like Indiana. I think he did not intend to scorn the study of Latin. He himself knew Latin better than I did. And by *backward* he meant *rooted in outworn tradition* as a guarantee of secure continuity, in keeping with T.S. Eliot's tentative definition of culture. The guarantee, however, while it might span epochs or eras, could not incorporate perpetuity. Kris and I hung Grayber's portrait of Andy and Sharny above our bed. Sharny had worn no jewelry during the sitting; but Grayber had painted her wearing a gold-cross necklace. This puzzled me but won Kris's enthusiastic approval. We both gradually came to understand that the necklace was a suggestive extension of the *Wayside Shrine*. Grayber esteemed the beauteous *simplicity of Christian imagery and iconography*, but had no use for Christianity's *organizational dogma and hierarchical rigidity*.

Within a year, Kris purchased just such a necklace for Sharny. As I placed the necklace on my pleased but quizzical daughter, I re-experienced, inexplicably, the sinking dread that had importuned me after the Russians launched Sputnik (this event, I had thought, was the repudiation of Nietzsche's metaphysical comfort; and I had envisaged a crumbling moon and a black extinction of life itself).

The Eisenhower years, punctuated by Sputnik and the jaggedly inchoate integration of the races in the South, were winding down. Blackie and Vera, on one of their visits, upheld the intelligence and competence of Richard Nixon. Kris, Grayber, and I argued in favor of John F. Kennedy. Blackie insisted that Kennedy was working with the Mafia. This he had learned, he said, from some unguarded remarks made contemptuously to him by Jordy Klug, at the mention of whose name Vera shuddered and Grayber, who knew about Jordy through his correspondence with Blackie, nodded. Kris and I, incredulous, smiled at each other.

When Kennedy won the election by taking the corruption-riddled Illinois vote, as Bill Clinton's successor would one day, with the aid of the Supreme Court, take the corruption-riddled Florida vote, Grayber said that Blackie had told us so. I was less convinced than pleased.

Kris and I had taken now to alternating our Christmases with her parents and mine. We would stay in her parents' home during the Hamtramck visits and with Blackie and Vera during the three or four days in our home city. During one Chistmas visit, I asked my mother if she knew anything about Jordy Klug's possible involvement with the Mafia. She said that Hildy had suspected that Jordy was connected with the Mafia. Over coffee, she and Hildy had asked Jordy about his two black-coated and black-hatted friends. *Hildy said, Are they mafoosee?* I corrected my mother: *Mafiosi?* She nodded and said that Jordy had laughed and had explained that the Mafia was a discredited arm of *ee fonamendo* [*Il fondamento?*, I asked; she nodded again.] that had been taken over by stupid Northmen when they invaded Sicily. I asked if Jordy had mentioned Harald Hardraði. She shook her head. Jordy had assured her and Hildy, she said, that, if they ever ran into big trouble, *il fondamento* would be there for them. She didn't use the phrase *be there for*, I think she had garbled another bit of Jordy's Italian, probably *in servizio*, or, more likely, *sempre in servizio* (always on call).

57

Grayber was interested in the connection of the Northmen with the Mafia. He traced his lineage to the Scandinavian Rus folk, who invented Russia; and he concurred with historians who traced the invention of Blackmail in Scotland and the definition of the Mafia in Sicily to Viking invaders. He was born Göran Sjögren Nilsson. His parents, Åke Nilsson and Anna Sjögren Nilsson, died in an automobile accident when he was two. Sent to an orphanage in Minneapolis, he was entered as Graydon Corinth by an immigrant Greek nurse, who, without immediate access to his surname, gave him the name of the small town, Braham, from which he had been sent. He learned about his parentage and provenience in his late teens, but retained his nurse-given identity. I joined him in the entertaining research into mediaeval Scandinavia and thoroughly enjoyed our discussions and sharing of findings. Talking with Grayber was as easy and exhilarating as talking with Anne had been. With these two, as with Blackie, I was completely at ease and not only held nothing in reserve but also had no inclination whatsoever to do so.

 He was interested in my account of the evening with Hedwig and Mischiato and prompted me to recall as many details as I could. He had never heard of *il fondamento* and said that challenging as the notion was, the term could suggest to him only the Italian word for asshole. He posited, only half jokingly, an international Manichaeism, in which an international aggregate of assholes nurtured a sense of goodness and light by slaughtering all proponents of the evil darkness of dissent. I objected that, while Manes would fit into the proposition, the Roman opposition to Manichaeism would not. He said that Rome initially was opposed, as well, to Christianity, of which it was to become virtually a synonym. I yielded. We then contrived an opposition as an international Aggregate of Pricks (*il pene*) nurturing justice and freedom through repression and aggression.

We invented a theory, then, of *historic eversion*: anal and penile potentates were, in fact, in league and constituted an alliance of violence in the interest of an anarchy that served their unlimited ambitions by subjecting the masses to control by molestation. It was a game in which I suspended my suspicion of metaphors. Our perverse laughter would echo through Grayber's mansion, or disturb colleagues in conference with students, or win the frowns of female and male waiters, or of counterwomen and countermen, as we disturbed other patrons, or, in the duplex, where Kris, smiling at our loud pleasure, would emerge from the kitchen to serve us coffee.

Fondamento, I would say, is a cognate of *fundament*, but it's not used in the same way in Italian. Grayber would laugh and say, so what: *apocalypse* means *revelation*, not *doom*, but it's used as though it meant that event itself of which it can be only a revelation; or, *embattled* and *beleaguered* are not synonyms, but they're used as such—*recto verso*, same page, same coin. I invoked Heidegger and said, *No: same book, same bank*. Grayber raised an eyebrow and grinned twistedly: *No matter; it's the darkness that counts. It's the background, or the turn of the back.* Like that eerie figure, to the viewer's leftmost rear in your Marsh's *Down at Jimmy Kelly's*: four lechers staring at the well-fleshed naked lady with the sad painted lips and the blonded hair; a bored, contemptuous waiter, moving off into the darkness; and that androgynous figure, female in scorn, male in presence, raising a *verre à pied* in solipsistic toast. Or the guy with his back to us in Hopper's *Nighthawks*.

Every now and then it's always the darkness, the figure therein, the rear. Fundamental, like in the beginning.

Every now and then it's always?

I can see why Blackie calls you Ped.

Black coffee. Grayber would settle for bouquet and sips. I would tend to drain every cup, as I would tend to consume every part of my every serving of my every meal. Grayber refrained from the derision to which I sensed that he felt impelled. In this he reminded me of Guinotte: gentility. Perhaps he intuited my having been conditioned to frugality and wastelessness by having known childhood in a large working-class family during the Depression years.

In all, we concurred about the sinistrous [Open the gates, George] figures in the rearward darkness.

We wondered, too, why painters generally eschewed the rain, while poets, songwriters, and movie-makers did not. Grayber said that his many attempts to paint the *stabbing rain* lacked the rhyme that came easily to *wordsmiths*. I suggested that he limit the rain to falling and that he forget about the metaphor. He chided me, rightly, about my own frequent notice of *falling darkness*. Nor does the darkness *come*: it simply is, and we are turned to it.

Grayber thought that my reservation about *wordsmith* was aberrant. I said that word-formation and the acid blaze of the forge were inconsistent; but he insisted that art consisted of such inconsistencies. He reminded me of Joyce's *to forge in the smithy of my soul the uncreated conscience of my race*, which, with its hyperbolic *for the millionth time*, had always seemed to me to be sophomoric and vapid. Did I object to the use of *forge*, as in to *forge a check?* No: *smith* in Old Norse denotes a worker in metal; but Latin *faber*, the source of *forge*, can denote a worker in any medium. I thought of the English assistant professor, Candace Schwarz-Bleiler, who told her students that T.S. Eliot's *il miglior fabbro* meant *my little brother*; one of her students offered this in my class when I asked if anyone knew the meaning of Eliot's Italian dedication of *The Waste Land*; my correction (*the better craftsman*) was reported to Schwarz-Bleiler, who thereafter despised me. I like to think that I was mature enough not to despise Grayber when he reminded me that we are limited to *faber* in translating *smith* into Latin, raising an eyebrow and waving aside my dim recall of Cicero's *opifex verborum* (manufacturer of words; wordsmith).

58

Thanksgiving was a week or so away. After lunch at the Union with two of my colleagues, who remained at coffee for an exchange of obscene jokes, I was walking across the campus back to my office.

The grass upon the mall was strangely green in the slant of the early afternoon sun. Walking toward me, on her way to either the library or the Union, a student from one of my Humanities classes stopped me with a wave of her arm. *Professor Blaustern, did you hear about President Kennedy?* She told me that he had been shot in Dallas and was not expected to live. I hurried back to my office. An older colleague came in to confirm that Kennedy had died. On this same day, I later learned, Aldous Huxley and C.S. Lewis also died.

Television's coverage of the events in Dallas and Washington, D.C. was dramatic. Kris, saddened, but less so than I, thought it was odd that Pope John XXIII should die in June and John F. Kennedy, the first Catholic President, should follow him in November. Then we watched as Jack Ruby shot Lee Harvey Oswald. I went on to watch as many replays of this event as I could; and during one replay I stood and shuddered as, scanning that crowd of men, I recognized, black-hatted and white-necked, Jordy Klug. Kris said that it was only my imagination, after I had managed to get her to view subsequent replays. I called Blackie, but I could get no confirmation from him, although he said that he wouldn't be surprised if Jordy had been somehow mixed up in all that mess. My mother was, in December, vaguely to say, in response to my questioning, that she thought Hildy had said something about Jordy's being in Texas around Thanksgiving.

Kris proceeded with the preparations for Thanksgiving, to which Grayber contributed much of his time and culinary talent.

At the Thanksgiving meal, Grayber, our guest, said Grace: *Domine in caelo, Tibi gratias agimus . . .* , turkey, stuffing, cranberries, yams, mashed potatoes and darkened gravy, coffee, and both pumpkin and mince pie. Kris, Grayber, and Andy cleaned up the dishes, while Sharny and I vacuum-cleaned and straightened up the dining area. Andy then worked on a jigsaw puzzle, an Utrillo scene, which he had spread out on our folding card table. Sharny played with her hendecarrhematic Chatty Cathy, giggling as she pulled the string and smiling as she stroked the hair—brunette hair, and brown eyes, *Just like Mommy.*

Kris, Grayber, and I followed on television the running account of the assassination. The event ultimately depressed me much more, I think, than it did either Kris or Grayber. Lincoln, Garfield, McKinley: there had been other assassinations, all by gun-wielders in gun-prone America; I thought of Jordy Klug and his .22 and his .45. Grayber and I immediately looked beyond the self-identified patsy, Oswald—Grayber to L.B.J. and I to the Republican Party. A sense of loss and the pain of meaninglessness tended to disorient me. Kennedy, youthful and visionary, was dead; and, once again, Jordy Klug stood at an intersection of history and in the strange, shallow recesses of my limited [Stunted, George?] imagination. Kris likened my *so-called glimpse* of Jordy to the sighting of a UFO and forbade my talking about it in the presence of Andy and Sharny. Grayber transferred his suspicion from L.B.J. to the CIA and the Mafia and expressed some concern about my *close to obsessive* insistence on having spotted Jordy Klug at the televised scene of Jack Ruby's murder of Lee Harvey Oswald. Blackie, when Kris and I stayed with him and Vera during the Christmas break of that year, expressed similar concern. *A hat and pale neck, Ped? Come on!* But it was the stance, the posture of secrecy, the baseness. I played with a line from *Othello*, changing it to *It is the base, it is the base, my soul.* Then I turned in thought to *Julius Caesar* and damaged a line so that it read, *It is not in our stars, dear Brutus, that we find the base of baseness, but in ourselves.* Unable to understand my own rumination or to convince anyone that my *sighting* had been accurate, I gradually assumed that I had been wrong. Illogically, I did not let that assumption displace my conviction.

The war had been followed by the black Republicanism of Senator Joseph McCarthy and General Douglas MacArthur and the bland white Republicanism of President Dwight D. Eisenhower. The decade of *Ike*, pot, LSD, the Beatniks, coffee-house poetry reading, and early Rock was succeeded by a decade that was defined by assassinations, the prolonged futility of the Vietnam War, and a counter-cultural movement that changed the customs of music and dress and the nature of higher education. The New Criticism, which had rightly propagated close reading and wrongly eschewed consideration of poets' biographies, was giving way to anthropologically-informed Structuralism and to post-modernist mis-readings of Heidegger. The air-brushed photos in Hugh Hefner's flourishing *Playboy* would soon be challenged by more graphic spreads in Larry Flint's inchoately pornographic *Hustler*. Elvis Presley's counter-cultural sexuality of musical movement, however, would be checked by *Colonel* Parker; and, after serving two years in the U.S. Army, marrying, and fathering a child, Elvis would make standard movies and continue his recording career on 45 rpm's and 33 1/3 rpm's; he would make a dramatic return, clad in black leather, to superstar stage status in the same year in which Robert Kennedy and Martin Luther King, Jr. were assassinated.

With the benefit of a relatively low-interest mortgage, Kris and I bought a small three-bedroom house; Andy and Sharny had their own separate rooms now. We bought a new car on a three-year financing plan. My meager and workaday publications, including two small books, sufficed for a full professorship. Carrie Coreghian had sent me a warmly inscribed copy of her 562-page masterly analysis of the turns given to English literature by Cartesian and Newtonian mathematics. I sent her neither of my books—an edition, with translation and commentary, of Vergil's *Bucolics*, and a monograph comparing Wordsworth's sense of Nature with Heidegger's *Sein/Seyn*—much less any of my reviews and articles, none of them remotely consonant in quality and significance with hers. By the time I had advanced to a full professorship, Carrie had achieved an international reputation and was the recipient of an endowed Chair. Ill-equipped though I was, and despite the disregard of my monograph, except for two strongly negative reviews, I continued to work on Wordsworth and Heidegger

Students, gratified, some perhaps by my devices of entertainment and others by my patent belief in themselves, kept up my discussions of, for example, intonations of futurity in the present participle, specifically when it governs an infinitive: going to see, going to know, going to be, even going to meet. Compare, for example, wanting to see, needing to know, having to be, or dying to meet. Generally,

RAIN AND DARKNESS

I would suggest, going, in this construction, is a being on the way (unterwegs). A student objects to the equation of a noun with an adverb. I propose that there is here a transformative process of the present becoming the future, as noun (static) becomes adverb (dynamic). In purposive going there is a being on the way to Being. We decided that *going to go* and *going to be going* were neither self-referential nor redundant. A recurring complaint in my course-and-teaching evaluations was my *going off on tangents*.

During one fall semester, I guided six high-school Latin teachers through Lucretius on Thursday evenings. Like Lagerkvist, Lucretius acknowledges the existence of deity and denies that the divine exerts any control over the human or responds to any human entreaties. I put forth the notion that Lucretius's *Venus genetrix* was the force of life itself that, like Lagerkvist's *Livet*, it means, but does not give meaning to, a living woman or man. What I enjoyed most about those Thursday classes was walking out of the building, after class, into the darkness and going slowly across campus to find my Buick in the faculty parking lot. Like Wordsworth, I could look up at a *lovely tree / Beneath a frosty moon*; and I could talk to Anne, as she walked with me in my easy dreaming: my own *solacia dulcia vitae*. There would be rain, and, later, snow; but every Thursday night I slowly walked with Anne.

59

... primum Veneris dulcedinis in cor
sillavit gutta et successit frigida cura.
—Lucretius

I have lived to mark
A new and unforeseen creation rise.
—Wordsworth

Ritt invited me to serve on a panel (Politics and Vergil's *Bucolics*) during a three-day Classics conference. Grayber agreed to help Kris with errands and the kids. I packed the shirts and the new shaving kit that Kris had given me for my recent birthday and, leaving about 3:00 a.m., drove through a foggy October morning. The city had changed: there was a new swath of freeway, new malls, and several designations of the old narrow streets as one-way. The modest motel at which Anne's mother had worked was now a huge Holiday Inn. I checked in and called Ritt. He came immediately and made me feel very welcome and actually important. We had lunch at the new Campus Club with Professor Landis.

A big-name Classicist from Columbia University delivered the opening address at 2:00. There was a reception at 3:30; and there was to be a dinner at 7:00. I was to share a table with Ritt, Professor Landis, and two of my fellow panelists.

At 4:40, forgoing the nap that I should have taken, I was in the Administration Building. Anne was now in charge of both Admissions and Fellowships. We had coffee in her office. We left at 5:00. Anne drove me to the Holiday Inn; and we renewed our selves in my room. Anne wept a bit, and I felt somewhat shaken. But we had found our world again. Anne had remained thin; and she was trim within the fit of her pale blue dress. There were some lines about her eyes and mouth. Her face was a bit pale, and she appeared, except for the brightness of her pale blue eyes, a little tired.

Her mother had died four years ago—breast cancer. Her brother, who was now a quality-control manager for a small-appliance manufacturer in Chicago, had taken two weeks off for the rites and to help Anne with the settlement of their mother's affairs. He offered Anne a business-correspondence job with his firm, but she declined. The two of them were unable to locate their father. Anne now shared the upper floor of a duplex with the woman who owned it and who rented out the lower floor.

We talked about novels and movies, about the assassination of JFK and the inane formality of the Warren Commission, and about the exponential nature of unhappiness. I held her hand; and the soft, cool pressure of her fingers made unhappiness irrelevant to me. There were moments when she would turn her face slightly to her left. These moments would be followed by the lengthy silence of a long embrace and the gift of her sensual lips.

She drove me back to campus. The dinner was the usual dull affair, with academic speeches and academic humor. Professor Landis drove me back to the Holiday Inn, where I slept until well after 10:00 the next morning. Anne came to pick me up for lunch.

During the afternoon, I participated in my panel and was complimented by Professor Landis, with whom I had a long talk over late afternoon coffee; his sight was failing and he was learning Braille *for the dark years ahead*. He asked if I had probed any more deeply into the Gallus area. He smiled broadly when I told him that I was having another note published about the political connections that Gallus had established in Egypt.

Anne and I drove that evening to a French restaurant twenty miles away and enjoyed breast of guinea hen and wild rice. Returning, we spent the entire night in my Holiday Inn room. *Here's one*, she said: *and all night long she slumbered thus before the ashy grate*. Iambic heptameter? Iambic, anyway. I knew it wasn't Wordsworth; and I knew that Anne was given more to novels than to poetry (except for Keats). Finally, I guessed, Hardy? She smiled, *Close: Dickens*. I should have remembered that Dickens was much more prone to metrical prose than Hardy was.

We talked about the Tet offensive and the vagaries of the war in Vietnam. We tried to understand the assassinations of Martin Luther King, Jr. and Robert Kennedy, the rioting at the Democratic convention in Chicago, and the Black Power salute by Tommy Smith and John Carlos at the recent Olympics. We concluded that the country was changing its direction, as Athens had when the Melians were massacred, as Rome had, not when Caesar crossed the Rubicon, but when Cicero was beheaded. Annus, she said; but what's the word for darkness? I offered *obscuritas*; but then I thought that *caligo* would be better. *Annus caliginosus*.

After breakfast in the motel, Anne returned to her workday and I to panels and uninspiring talks. There was

RAIN AND DARKNESS

a final banquet and a valedictory in Latin by one more big-name Classicist, this one from Texas. It was all over by 3:00. I said goodbyes to Professor Landis and Ritt and then picked up Anne at 5:00. We drove to a cafeteria, *The Frontier*, which had a rustic Old West decor and juke-music selection boxes in the booths. *All the Time* wasn't available; but Johnny Mathis's covers of *Those Were the Days* and *Love is Blue* served us well, along with a couple of Elvis's standards. Anne still had no particular liking for Elvis and had not seen his formidable comeback special in August. We talked about Ross Lockridge, Jr., his *Raintree County*, his suicide, and the laughable film version of the novel (with Elizabeth Taylor and Montgomery Clift, whose injury in an automobile crash during the filming would leave him thereafter with a distorted nose). Anne went over the Oedipal motif in the novel and thought that Lockridge's suicide had something to do with a maternal fixation. What was his mother's name? Elizabeth Shockley. I thought that he had seen through all the acclaim and best-seller status and, realizing that his intended Great American Novel was merely mediocre, had opted, in the crash of his dream, for carbon monoxide. Anne and I agreed that the Walt Whitman bit near the end of the novel is tacky and tedious. We liked the legato of the chapters, the last sentence of each chapter becoming part of the opening sentence of the next. It is, yes, a very fine, a masterly novel; but it is alien to the greatness that lies in deeper darkness.

We drove to Old Quarry Park and sat on a bench. Fog had settled in, and it was somewhat chilly. We remained warm in our lateral embrace; Anne's head rested on my shoulder. Recalling her enthusiasm for the poetry of Keats, I tried her with *And seal the hushed Casket of my Soul*. She laughed it off: *Sonnet: To sleep; I used to recite that to you.* I said that the metaphor, because it followed quietness, was much better than Joyce's *smithy of my soul*.

Yes, smithy carries noise, Anne said. LBJ is noisy too, against the quiet casket of JFK. Anne's interest in my unsettled notion that Jordy Klug was involved in the assassination prompted my telling her all about Jordy—his mugging and shooting at Blackie and me, his devotion to my mother, his parceling out the Gallus-like elegiac Latin and his stance within the aura of *il fondamento*.

Sadly, Anne whispered a laugh. She mentioned her mother and her brother and herself and me as the Tricked. There is Trickery and the Tricked, but no Trickster, except as a colorful personification of Trickery, like the comic antagonist of Batman, called the Joker. All the con artists in the world, all the Vikings and Tongs, all the Black Hands and Mafiosi and Cosae Nostrae, all forms of organized terrorism and organized crime, all calculating decadents, all cartels and killer-cold corporations, all left-wing and right-wing extremism: these constitute the ground, the foundation, of Trickery, the dirty trick that life must be, as meant we live, and die unmeant. We—the weak, the generally honest, the unsophisticated, the defenseless, the timorous, the *aestuantes intrinsecus*—make up the Tricked. Anne used one of Keats's similes to describe us: *Like sick eagles looking at the sky*. That's where metaphors and similes rightly live, in the infinite rigidity of romantic poetry. I mentioned and then summarized for her, since she had not read it, Melville's *The Confidence-Man: His Masquerade*. She laughed a number of times at Melville's exposition of truths. A great artist, she insisted, is always one of the Tricked who can articulate the Foundation.

We returned to the Buick. What we were to give each other would not, we knew, wait until we made it back to the Holiday Inn. There in the car, awkwardly, but with perspicuous understanding and consummate acquiescence, we freed ourselves from sickness and from all inclination to look at the sky.

After driving back to the University, we stood beside Anne's car and, in the heavy fog, talked about aims and goals.

It would be good to make a name for one's self; but neither of us felt sufficiently driven to do so. We talked about wanting something most in life. I said that maybe what I wanted most was to write a good novel. Anne said that maybe what she wanted most was freedom from a terminal disease, like the cancer that took her mother. Then I looked at Anne and said, *No, I know what I want most in life*. And Anne said, *Yes, and so do I*.

She drove away. I returned to the Holiday Inn.

It was still dark when I woke up. After packing my clothes and books and toilet articles, I checked out and had a breakfast of eggs, bacon, toast, and coffee. Then, in the morning fog, I took to the road. After about fifty miles, I turned on the windshield wiper, as the fog turned to rain.

Within a few weeks, Nixon would defeat Humphrey and would bring his dark scowl into the White House. Before the year would come to its end, Norman Thomas, John Steinbeck, and Tallulah Bankhead would cease to exist. I remembered Tallulah Bankhead's radio programs, to which Kris and I had listened every Sunday night during the time when I was working on my doctoral degree. The program would always end with the cast and guests singing Meredith Wilson's *May the good Lord bless and keep you*.

60

The rain gave way to sunshine. The two-lane road was bordered by fields and hills of easing brown, gentle yellow, and fading green. The freeway, 1-94, on which I would cover the final segment of my route, was about two and a half hours away. I drifted into reminiscence of Andy and Sharny. The years from Truman through LBJ had comprised their childhood. As brother and sister, they had known a calm compatibility.

Kris had reared them as well-indoctrinated Catholics and was a very good mother, always putting their interests and needs above her own, as she had let my academic pursuits prevail over her deepest wants and wishes. I knew that I had consistently given priority to my affairs, feeling bothered by, and frequently resentful of, my parental and marital duties.

Andy and Sharny are both dark-haired and burning-brown-eyed, like their mother. Andy was devoted to, and favored, his mother; oddly, despite my uncommunicativeness to both, Sharny favored and sided with me, always serving my defense when Kris railed against me (*Mama, don't yell at Daddy!*). They are both somewhat withdrawn, Andy in sullenness, Sharny in shyness. Kris and I had, during a summer of happiness, purchased a spinet for $500. Kris played well, and gave me a few lessons. Andy and Sharny did very well with their lessons from an instructor recommended by Grayber. Andy and I would play *Chopsticks* together;

Sharny would accompany me as I played *Ain't Dat a Shame?* (which Kris had taught me). Andy turned eventually to the clarinet; Sharny stayed with the piano. Andy became something of a rebel, showing a decided preference for the canon of Bob Dylan and looking with some disdain upon my predilection for Elvis. He collected Dylan's recordings and particularly liked *Ballad of a Thin Man* and *A Hard Rain's A-Gonna Fall*. Sharny sided with me; we played many of Elvis's LP's together, especially the hymns and, among these, especially *It Is No Secret*, which I sang soundlessly now as I drove. Kris now favored the Beatles, who, she said, really know something about music.

Sharny tolerated my habit of calling attention to and correcting lapses from English grammar and usage; and she always followed my pedagogical [pedantic, George?] instructions. Andy was resentful, however, and would persist with aberrations like *could have went* and *most everybody*. Both willingly benefitted from my attentions to their schoolwork compositions. Kris, whose lapses from English grammar and usage I had come studiously to refrain from correcting, approved of my helping the kids with their homework. One of Andy's high-school teachers, Mr. Neunzehn (Elmery P. Neunzehn), applauded the new trend of descriptive in place of prescriptive lexicography and preferred colloquial to formal composition. Academic justice seemed to me to have been served when he was fired, although he was terminated, not for incompetence, but for having stroked a student's inner thigh under her skirt; the student had informed her mother, who then complained to the Commissioner of Public Schools. This was, incidentally, the first shaking of my assumption that persons in positions of professional trust—teachers, physicians, psychiatrists, dentists, lawyers, clergy—did not abuse that trust, an assumption that in time, no one would be able rightly to hold.

Nineteen is Andy's age now, as he matriculates at the University of Minnesota. Sharny has just begun high school. The ramp to the freeway is two and a half miles ahead. [Open the gates, George.] The tires purr in approval of the freeway's smooth surface. Relaxing from my concentration upon the two-lane highway, I turn on the Buick's radio. Songs from the Twenties: . . . *Here I go, singing low / Bye bye, blackbird . . . Bluebird, bluebird, calling me far away / I've been longing for you* . . . I thought about the wedding photograph of my mother and father. They are young and very attractive, but stiff in their pose; and neither one is smiling. I thought about my brothers and sisters. All are married now and rearing children. Kris and I had traveled home for each of their weddings, except for Paul's, which had taken place in California. The freeway rises into hills and defines wide turns. Braced high over pines, a much-larger-than-life-sized model of a black bull marks the location of the Black Angus Café.

The restaurant is not crowded. There is a couple (early thirties) in one of the booths; there is a younger couple with a quiet child in another; there are three denim-wearing guys having sandwiches and beers at the counter. I take a stool at the counter, down and away from the guys in denim, and order coffee and a large hamburger with cheese. (I refuse to say *Cheeseburger* because I despise such hybrid compounds; there is no city named Cheeseburg.) The music, issuing from a speaker near the kitchen, is Elvis's *If I Can Dream*, to which only the quiet child—a boy about ten years old—and the waitress appear to be listening.

The Three Denims are noisy, but not boisterous, and the waitress fields their lechery without any show of contempt.

As she bends to pour their coffee, the round downthrust of her breasts is open to view, and she does nothing to deprive the trio of its appetitive gaze. She provides me with the same pleasure as she pours my coffee. Elvis is followed by Steppenwolf; and, as the Three Denims react appreciatively to the change, I, on impulse, ask the waitress if she has read Hermann Hesse's *Steppenwolf.* She nods, with a sigh that condemns my condescension.

On a ledge near the opening through which orders are passed from the kitchen, there is a red rose in a bud vase. I stare at it studiedly. It is important to me now to keep my eyes off of the dark red hair and lightly freckled face of the waitress. *Pretty?*, she asks, turning her heard leftward toward the rose as she refills my cup.

Odd place for it, is all that I can say. She says that she is working out the surface area of all the petals. Surprised, I laugh and ask her how she does that. She asks me if I have ever worked on topological vector spaces. To this I can react with neither a sigh nor a nod. The Three Denims ask for their check, pay it, and leave. I lower my head and sip my coffee. As she clears and wipes the counter after the departed customers, she says, *Hey!* I turn my heard up toward her. *You're not a dancer, are you?*—*No*, I admit, *I am not among those who move easiest.* I thought my allusion to Pope's couplet was clever, but I was too dispirited to try to gauge her familiarity with Pope.

When I paid my check, she smiled at me and said, *Just a minute*. She took the rose from the bud vase and gave it to me. The couple and the quiet boy were leaving their booth. As I was going out the door, she called to me, *Drive carefully*, and handed the couple their check. In the Buick, I laid the rose on the passenger seat.

Later, I turned off the freeway and drove along the old two-lane highway, passing through three small towns and stopping in one that was divided by a broad, swift river that reminded me of the Inn River. I carried the rose to the middle of the old bridge and, with what I felt to be a religious ceremony, dropped it into the rush of the dark water. The waitress was much prettier than Anne; but, with her slim body and sensual lips, she reminded me of Anne. When she smiled, though, I had felt the pang of pleasure I had known when Kris had, long ago, first smiled at me.

After driving through one more town, I made my way back to 1-94.

61

Patricia T. O'Conner has written a lucid review of two books on English usage, one by Ben Yagoda and one by David Crystal. Yagoda rightly dislikes the back formation *enthuse* but wrongly defends the use of *fun* as an adjective and the phrase *try and*; Crystal opposes the extremism of the prescriptivists; both tolerate the use of *they, them,* and *their* as singular pronouns. O'Conner courageously doubts that the singular *they* will gain acceptance in *educated writing in our lifetime*. Unfortunately, a lifetime is not a long time, and aberrant English usage continues to be justified by the distantly related fact that language changes. Thinking again of the red-haired waitress in the Black Angus, I recall that, while she did not speak much, she spoke with masterly precision. Nice bulbs, one of the Three Denims, staring down at her breasts, had said. After the other two finished laughing, she smiled and said, *Life hasn't been kind to you, has it?* And I, who had not learned to dance, was uneasy with Pope's adverbial use of *easiest*, correct though it was and is. *Born to Be Wild.* Topological vector spaces.

 The mathematics professor whom I asked about topological vector spaces managed not to enlighten me. I followed him well enough in his differentiation of planar and Euclidean spaces; but, when he had recourse to formulas, symbols, and diagrams—*Your rose petal, you see, as a coördinate system, is not orthogonal*—or to Set Theory, about which I knew only that Max Beberman's New Math was informed by it, then my interest was defeated. It was good, however, to learn that Simone Weil, whose essay on the *Iliad* as a poem of force had given me much to think about, was the sister of one of the professor's mentors at the University of Chicago.

Force. Simone de Beauvoir has published *La Force de l' âge* and *La Force des choses*: the prime of life, force of circumstances. A student has sent me a note in which angrily he insists that by giving him a C, I have forced him, in his prime of life, to die in Vietnam: a low grade-point average can nullify one's retention of draft deferment by way of college enrollment. From another university another student writes in anger about my negative review of his professor's translation of a Latin work; he says that my translation of the *Bucolics is forced and not so hot*. I note with some satisfaction that neither letter bothers me. I do not join in the protests against the Vietnam War. It started with Eisenhower, was carried on by Kennedy, became the burden of Johnson's administration, and is now being disingenuously carried on *sub rosa* by Nixon, a force of circumstances.

My daydreams and worries have nothing in common with those of the current countercultural radicals, although I'm in favor of making love, not war. I dream about flying an SE-5a, walking in parks with Anne, coaching the Detroit Lions through five seasons without a defeat, attending a concert by Elvis, writing a well-reviewed novel. I worry about Sharny's health: she is pale and underweight, lacking in energy.

One day in July, Sharny and I are watching the television coverage of the moon landing. Kris is in the kitchen. Andy is in the house of a friend, where he, his friend, and three coaevals are listening to Bob Dylan records and doing whatever else they do. The friend and one coaeval went to high school with him; the other two coaevals are fellow freshmen at the University of Minnesota. Sharny and I were sharing a plate of herring, blue cheese, pepperoni, anchovies, and soda crackers.

Michael Collins remained in Apollo 11. Neil Armstrong and Buzz Aldrin were bringing the lunar module slowly down to the surface of the moon. Can this be actually happening? Sharny stared, her head thrust forward. I gripped the edges of the easy chair's arms. Each statement from the module to Houston defined the distance of the module from the surface of the moon. I had known feelings comparable with this excitement at only a few other times: waiting in sleeplessness for Santa Claus, anticipating the one birthday party I had been given as a child, and moving toward Trish for my first kiss; I would know it again only as, a few years after the descent to the moon, I watched *Summer of '42* and waited, in vain, as it turned out, for Jennifer O'Neill to strip before Gary Grimes. Now there was a swirl of moon dust and the words, *Tranquillity base here: the Eagle has landed.* Sharny and I stood up and hugged each other. That was a moment of happiness, the full experience of spontaneous pleasure. The moon-walk itself was equally enjoyable but less exciting, Armstrong's utterance for history—*That was one small step for a man, one giant leap for mankind*—came through initially without the indefinite article, an omission that actually had made the pronouncement inane, although it was accepted, prior to its being eventually corrected, as a veritable profundity. For me, this was a second emotional witness to history, the first being my delivery of the morning newspaper that headlined FDR's election to a third term. These two events recur in thought to me as my *American moments*, one of which I knew in the pleasant solitude of a November dawn, the other of which I shared with Sharny on a summer afternoon.

Generalists who lack the genius of Renaissance men and women do not become effective scholars. My unchecked tendency to generalism precluded the specialism of the scholar, the expert. Two areas of specialism had been open to me, classicism and literary criticism. Only Jordy Klug, I believe, could have prodded me into the depths of classicism; and only notably successful and broad publication could have promoted me to the echelons of recognition. I adhered to the New Criticism and held my conviction that literary criticism should inform readers of what they had perhaps not grasped or understood about literary works. My essays, chiefly on the English Romantic poets, were few, slight, and attractive of either no notice or no positive reaction. My struggle for ingenuity in reviews was profitless effort. Structuralism, with its paradigms of metonymy and metaphor, was promising and pleasantly challenging. Word-play in Post-Structuralism and Deconstructionism was inspiring; but, as these movements transformed literary criticism into Theory, I turned away from the jargon of *valorize, resonate, always already, emblematic, privilege* (as a transitive verb) and all the tiresome anti-semantic and esoteric high nonsense and developed my own dilettantism of Heidegger and quantum mechanics, at the periphery of each of which I remained an intellectual fledgling, but, as a result of both of which, my classes became more entertaining: I accused the Deconstructionists of corrupting Heidegger's existentialism and Way to Language and I related Heisenberg's principle of uncertainty to modes of interpretation; but my career foundered. Blackie rightly puts me down as a loser in life; in addition, I see myself as a personal loser and as an academic failure.

I listen to Ray Charles: *Born to lose, / I've lived my life in vain. / Every dream / has only brought me pain* . . . And the Beatles give me this: *I'm a loser / and I'm not what I appear to be* . . .

What's left—quitting? I do not quit.

Poppa Neutrino, né David Pearlman, says to Alec Wilkinson, *If you don't attack, you're just receiving all the blows of life*. I have become proficient in the reception of blows. One can be ethically (that is, in keeping with one's character), but not morally (that is, with regard to one's responsibility to others) disposed to laziness, which is a predisposition to inactivity and a factor of academic failure. Inactivity (idleness, indolence) is non-dimensional passivity. The loser is dimensionally passive; the failure is prone to inactivity. The loser receives; the failure is not received.

Where is the *element of uncertainty*? In losing? In failing? The element of uncertainty rests with the princess in Stockton's story of the lady or the tiger. There is no element of certainty for Schrödinger's cat; but there might be if we knew whether the cat were female or male. Philo Judaeus claimed—knowingly, I think—that everything, to the extent that it lacks a woman, is incomplete and without a home. By the idea of home I understand the idea of certainty. If Schrödinger's cat is female, the unopened box in which it is enclosed is its home; if male, its box is its prison: home is life; prison is death. André Gide says that the female is ultimately independent of the male (and that the male, as a glorified sperm sac, ought to be free to indulge its own glory, like the peacock). Robert Graves sees the male as *frightened adjunct* of the female. Anne had established the certainty of my undefined dream. Kris was the certainty of my home.

J.C. Bradbury says that expansion ruined the certainty of baseball. Records were once made within the limits of the exclusively best talent. Expansion necessitated letting in the riffraff. Against mediocre hitters the best pitchers can accumulate three hundred strikeouts in a season for ten or eleven seasons. Against mediocre pitchers the best hitters can put down the home-run records of the past. Steroids and changes in rules (including the designated hitter) and technological enhancement of equipment aggravate the decline of the sport; but the main factor of deterioration is the dilution of talent by letting in the riffraff. This is the case, as well, with higher education. Through the GI Bill, hosts of the ultimately unqualified made their way into the professoriate (among them, me). Their passage was signaled by a transition from suits and ties to seersucker jackets and khaki pants to jeans and open collars. Formality yielded to informality. The classroom-student honorifics of *Miss, Mr.,* and *Mrs.* were abandoned in favor of first names. Among female faculty members, the certainties of conservative dresses changed, not as a result of the GI Bill, but in keeping with the Feminist movement, to pants-suits (now pantsuits) and various modes of immodest attire. The counter-cultural protests led to universities' orientation from student demands, influxes of insubstantial trendy courses, and course-and-teaching evaluations that produced universal grade inflation, as instructors sought popularity and inoffensiveness. Political correctness, *multiculturalism, diversity,* and cost-accounting contributed to the demise of the Liberal Arts, especially literature, as higher education moved toward the status of the trade school. *Multiculturalism* was ideological fakery. Properly to study a culture, one must know, or at least study, the language of the people.

The *multiculturalists*, however, discouraged and ridiculed the study of foreign languages. One of them, in chatter preceding a committee meeting, explained why the word *china*, referent to dishware, was not capitalized: *Metonymy; it takes the name of its provenience or originator and becomes a common noun. Like frankfurter or martini.* Someone said, *Speaking of frankfurters, what about the Coney Island?* She, Associate Professor Candace Schwarz-Bleiler, erstwhile Assistant Professor of *little brother* memory, added something about varying stages of transition and frozen caps. I earned her glare and sneer by disclaiming metonymy in favor of an English borrowing from the Persian word for *porcelain*, namely, *chini*, spelled *cheney* or *chiney* in the seventeenth century. She asked me if I knew where china was originally made and then smirked when I allowed that it very likely was China. There was a general resentful silence, followed by a change of subject and, then, the Chair's calling the meeting to order. I doodled: *The brewer skewered fewer newer sewer-viewers in bluer days gone by.* [And now, many, many years later, I doodle in thought, as, turning to this scattershot novel and away from coffee and *The New York Times*, where I read about his death, I recall Dennis Hopper, whom I admired for coming across in person as a very nice guy and for his stated belief in his having had the protection of a guardian angel.]

62

The FBI agent presented his identification, a card behind a plastic window with photograph and name. He was a short person, with thin grey hair. He wore a three-piece grey suit and well-shined black shoes. Kris invited him in, asked him to have a seat, and, then, as he began to question me, told him to wait for her to get our tape-recorder. He did not object to a taping of his questions and my answers.

>AGENT: *Would you say that Mr. Klug is a person of good moral character?*
>ME: *Yes.*
>AGENT: *Do you know anything about his connection with an organization called the Foundation?*
>ME: *No.*
>AGENT: *Have you ever heard of the Foundation or il Fondamento?*
>ME: *The University has a Foundation for the receipt of gifts and contributions.*
>AGENT: *I mean an international organization.*
>ME: *No.*
>AGENT: *To your knowledge, has Mr. Klug ever been in Dallas or Memphis?*
>ME: *No.*
>KRIS [calling from the kitchen]: *Is Jordy in some kind of trouble?*

AGENT: *No, Mrs. Blaustern; we're just doing a routine check. Mr. Blaustern, has Mr. Klug ever done you any kind of bodily injury or threatened you in any way? Or do you know of anyone he may have injured or threatened?*
ME: *Jordy? No. Not at all. Why do you ask?*
AGENT: *How long have you known Mr. Klug?*
ME: *For about as long as I can remember: his mother and mine have been very good friends.*
AGENT: *Were you and he good friends? Or are you now good friends?*
ME: *We were never particularly close, as friends; our interests have not really coincided.*
AGENT: *Do you have any addresses for Mr. Klug?—in, uh, Miami, New York, New Orleans, or any foreign addresses?*
ME: *No. Nothing like that. None at all. We don't correspond.*

The agent showed no frustration or impatience or disappointment. Kris served coffee and some of her raspberry-filled paczki and prune-filled oatmeal cookies. The agent took his coffee black. He complimented Kris on her cookies, but ate only one. I enjoyed a puffed-up paczek, having over a long period of time learned how to eat paczki without making a mess. He asked a few more questions, which I'll not bother to transcribe here. I continued to give only vague, non-committal, or negative responses.

When he asked if Jordy was homosexual, Kris angrily told him that that would be none of our business and that he, the agent, was perhaps out of line in asking us such a question. The agent sipped his coffee, asked two questions about my possible acquaintance with some of Jordy's associates, about whom I could honestly say I knew nothing, and, after a brief silence, rose to leave. Kris saw him to the door. He thanked us for our time, turned, and, with hunched shoulders, went out to his Oldsmobile Cutlass.

Kris and I embraced. Kris surpised me with her resentment of the agent, in that it amounted to a defense of Jordy, for whom she had no affection whatsoever. *That asshole had all the answers. He just wanted to be sure that we didn't know them.* That struck me as being close to right and led me to suspect that the agent was a phony sent by Jordy himself as a test of my *omertà*. If so, I had learned that lesson long before learning how to eat a paczek. Kris was sure, though, that he was an actual FBI *slime-sack*, surfacing in a three-piece grey suit and well-shined black shoes, as unsmilingly insidious as J. Edgar Hoover, who was out-powering those in power with ever-bulging files of their blackmailable transgressions. *Jordy and the FBI are both crooked and rotten*, Kris said, *but Jordy doesn't claim to be upholding law and order.*

Blackie, when I called him, said that he had been interrogated and had, like Kris and me, said nothing beyond the non-committal and the superficial. He did not, however, share our conviction that the FBI itself was devious and crooked. My mother wrote in answer to my letter that no FBI people had been to see her. If any of them should come, she said, she would simply tell them that Jordy had always been her friend and had always shown her kindness and respect. It was for this reason, perhaps, that I could never quite dislike Jordy Klug.

JFK had accepted full responsibility for the Bay of Pigs debacle and, by implication, for attempts to get Fidel Castro assassinated. LBJ did not admit to having underwritten the fabricated attack upon the U.S. destroyer *Maddox* in the Gulf of Tonkin. With the elongations of the conspiracy theory, involving JFK's assassins on the Grassy Knoll in Dallas, and the prolongations of the Vietnam War, united trust in the U.S. government was lost. My trust would vanish once the dirty tricks and the *segreti* of the Nixon administration were disclosed; although my own evasiveness with Three-piece Grey Suit and Shiny Black Shoes differed only in degree from the stonewalling of Nixon's Attorney General John Mitchell.

From how much more has been lost I distract myself by writing and by reading. I admire the title fashioned by Pinceton's Eddie S. Glaude, Jr., *In a Shade of Blue: Pragmatism and the Politics of Black America*. Or I turn to Andrew Butterfield's review of the Tintoretto exhibition at the Prado and wonder how so august an aesthete can defend his dangling participle: *Daunted by the practical challenges of doing a show about Tintoretto, no one has tried for the last seventy years.* How can this mean anything but that no one has been daunted by the untried challenges in question? Is there here ensconced some theory of an ellipse absolute? Now I look to a headline in *The New York Times* over a story by Lucinda Roy: Black Day in the Blue Ridge. It is from Blacksburg, Virginia, in the Blue Ridge Mountains and concerns the author of *Richard McBeef* and *Mr. Brownstone*. The author of the two works was an English major who shot and killed thirty-two people (students and faculty members) at Virginia Polytechnic Institute. He then killed himself. Was he a loser? If he was a loser, what kind was he? I couldn't identify myself with him. When, later, I e-mailed Blackie about this, he said that the guy was a quitter, not a loser, that he translated quitting into a moment of superiority by killing; and then he, by suicide, defined his departure from the game. The editorialists recalled the Austin sniper, the Columbine high-school shooters, the Scotland shooter, the Amish school shooter, and others; but Blackie said that the pattern had to be calculated resignation, followed by tentatively indiscriminate slaughter and suicide; the Columbine shooters had themselves been invoked by the VTI shooter. George Orwell has written that *any life when viewed from the inside is simply a series of defeats.* If this is true, then losers have at least this in common with winners and manage to recognize that they are genetically less endowed with tensile resistance to defeat, while quitters delude themselves by grasping at self-destruction as a means to spite defeat.

Grayber says that World War I was followed by the murderous gangsterism of the prohibition—and protection-rackets; that World War II was followed by the extremes of stultifying conformity and reactionary Rock music; and that the Vietnam War, in all its senselessness, has produced an epidemic of greed and perverse gratification. Blackie will say that the slaughter-suicide mode of quitting is, indeed, *perverse gratification*.

Sharny and I played *Seegolly*, our Faith-is-Substance game: One can lose faith, as Guinotte had maintained; but, so long as one has faith, one can lose nothing else. I asked her about the many contradictions and inconsistencies in the *New Testament*. She said that God's religions of belief—ancestors, pantheons, sacrifice—worked well enough within their requisite imperfections, but that a religion of faith could be imperfection itself. So God incarnated the Word and caused it to flourish among fishermen and poor people and prostitutes. Intimations of the Word were collected and written into books composed in a vulgar street language and rife with errors, contradictions, and inconsistencies, the acceptance of which could no longer be belief (as in the case of the old Jonah and the Whale story, which was at least consistent), but had to be faith. Belief requires a modicum of logic; faith requires no logic and thrives in freedom from it. *See?*, she would ask. Dutifully and happily, I would reply, *Golly.*

Sharny was quiet, undemonstrative, and very bright. I was proud of her; but, strangely, she made me proud of myself: in her presence I knew how to care and not to care, knew that my genuine care for her nullified my narcissism. In Sharny's presence I felt that I was an adult, knew what it was to be an adult, and took pride in the knowledge. She and another female student each had a full 4.0 grade-point average and were to be co-valedictorians in high school. The faculty committee decided, however, that the other student should be sole valedictorian because of her aggregate of extra-curricular activities and social accomplishments. Without complaint or bitterness, Sharny accepted the salutatorianship.

The valedictorian offered the usual head of lettuce: *Let us meet the challenges . . . Let us be diligent in our efforts . . . Let us go forth . . . .* Sharny, adjusting her new granny glasses, had said, shyly and with sober steadiness, *If we do not forestall the Silent Spring that Rachel Carson writes about, we shall one day be denied even the intoxicating shallow draughts of the Pierian Spring.* It was, I thought, an odd pun, but original. It was lost, in any event, upon the lettuce-nourished audience. I still look at the crease-worn manuscript, although I've long since memorized the speech. She differentiated belief from faith. Belief is in what one discerns by one's senses. Faith is in what lies beyond the senses. One can achieve creative belief in one's self only by achieving faith in what lies beyond all selves. Education enables us to believe enough to suspend disbelief and initiate the quest for faith by which we can ascend to the self that is the soul. My loud clapping brought about no swell in the polite applause.

Sharny was thin, myopic, and imbued with a sadness that I found myself capable of sharing and found myself, in the sharing, feeling a richness.

Now *Time* devotes much of its current issue to the Virginia Tech shooting: *Darkness Falls. One troubled student rains down death on a quiet campus* By Nancy Gibbs. And David von Drehle offers an essay in explanation of that student's narcissism, noting that *Freud explained narcissism as a failure to grow up.* Jeffrey Kluger is closer to Blackie's way of thinking: he writes that what the shooter, by his action, says is, in effect, *I surrender.* My rambling thought is that this adolescent gunman never had an inspiring Trish, was denied the stability provided by a Kris, and could not even dream of the reality embodied in the waking romance of an Anne. Equally important, he lacked the strength that Jordy gained from a perverse integrity.

63

The assassination of the Kennedys, Malcolm X, and Martin Luther King, Jr. had darkened the cultural landscape [Open the gates, George]. The counter-cultural protests, steeped in the opposition to the Vietnam War, and the postmodernist *raid on the articulate*, to abuse Eliot's observation, vulgarized the gentility of higher education, to which gentility I had tried to flatter myself that I belonged. At Kent State University, four students (two women and two men), who were protesting the Vietnam War, had been shot and killed by marksmen of the Ohio National Guard. Three protesters for peace had bombed Sterling Hall in Madison, Wisconsin, and Robert Fassnacht, a graduate student, was blown to death. President Nixon kept the Vietnam War alive and illegally ordered deadly incursions into Cambodia; and his criminal cover-up of criminal political burglaries and break-ins, including spy-novel attempts to discredit the individual who exposed the Pentagon Papers in discrediting the administration, led to his resignation in total disgrace. The country was discrediting itself.

Student protests against the war produced violent student activism for changes in the educational system, to which pusillanimous educators acceded. In keeping with the degradation of standards, critical theory politicized literature and strove to annihilate the echelons of meaning.

Pär Lagerkvist was taken into the darkness of death, about which he had written so much; and then Martin Heidegger turned his back to the darkness of non-being. I mourned them. As another summer turned in shadows toward its end, Andy came into my air-conditioned study, where I am putting together syllabuses for my approaching fall semester's courses, and asked me if I'd heard about Elvis. *No, what?* With real sympathy, he said, *He's dead.*

About a lustrum earlier, Andy, with Sharny's help, had purchased tickets to an Elvis performance and had driven Kris, Sharny, and me there. It was about an hour's drive. Our seats were high and away from the stage; but Andy had provided us with good binoculars. To me it was a magical evening, from *Po'k Chop Annie* to *I Can't Help Falling in Love with You*. Elvis's height surprised me. Most celebrities appear in motion pictures and on television to be taller than they are, like Alan Ladd and Paul Newman; the opposite was the case with Elvis—tall and stately on stage in his fringed and spangled white jump-suit.

Elvis was the complete entertainer, the greatest entertainer of the twentieth century, to which recognition his subsequent secular canonization attests. His rendition of *My Way* vaporized the egotistical version by Frank Sinatra. Paul Anka's *I ate them up and spit them out* were words that Sinatra enunciated too clearly; Elvis did not change them but mellifluously obscured them, so that one could hear, if one chose to do so, the more appropriate *I chewed them up and spit them out* or even *I ate them up and shit them out*. His darkly moving cover of Kris Kristofferson's *For the Good Times* easily outdistanced that of Ray Price. *Hear the whisper of the raindrops blowin' softly on the window.*

RAIN AND DARKNESS

To Andy (and Sharny) I owe my having seen Elvis perform in person. And now Andy has informed me that the King is dead. Andy gave me a pat on the shoulder and left. My shoulders trembled, and I wept. During the following week, some students signed and sent me a sympathy card.

My wish at this late moment is that I were a good enough writer properly and effectively to define and lend deep subjectivity to the fully realized career, lambent to blazing, of the effortlessly great Elvis.

I should like to be able to write like Florence Williams in her stunning review of Sara Wheeler's biography of Denys Finch Hatton: . . . *he liked drinking Chateau d'Yquem and wore a brown velvet smoking jacket when he wasn't in the bush shooting bongo and stalking dik-dik.* I consult my dictionary. A bongo is a large forest-dwelling antelope; a dik-dik is a small antelope. Williams has worked these names into a trochaic lyricism. Denys Finch Hatton, moreover, preceded Elvis in a dramatic natural grace (tantamount in quality to the gestural grace of Armando Galarraga, the tall, cool Venezuelan, who would smile uncomplainingly when Umpire Jim Joyce would admit to having erroneously deprived him of pitching a perfect game).

Finch Hatton and Elvis are dead. I first experienced the indefinability of death when Kris's father died. Kris, Andy, Sharny, and I drove to Hamtramck for the funeral, Andy and I doing the driving by turns. Lung cancer had taken Anton Skoczny-Nabodny to the darkness of death in this decade of death. Anton was alive; then Anton ceased to be alive, ceased to exist. *Zur Ruhe?* Death is not rest, or sleep. Those are states in which the blood flows. *Requiescat in pace.* Vain subjunctive. *Sov nu i ro.* Unheard imperative. Death is totally alien to similes and metaphors. The corpse—here, old Anton—may be *en soi*, or *an sich*, but the person *is* not, not even *is no more*. Vestiges of the person are only rosary-beads of memory [Otg, G].

Rosary-beads would be an elliptical metaphor; but it functions no more effectively than Lagerkvist's *mörker*, in which the dead wander meaninglessly through eternity and God saws wood by lantern-light. There is no darkness, visible or otherwise, not even black, not even not. The person is annihilated, totally eliminated from existence and from all evidence of his or her existence and from the memories of him or her. Elvis's music lives on, but Elvis does not live in his music or in our memory of his self-deprecating smile or in the pictures and motion pictures of that smile. No person, however great, participates in the immortality of her or his accomplishments.

Robert Graves was great in his accomplishments. He spent two days and a night on this campus. He insisted on having a room in the women's dormitory. I accompanied him there after his first day's activities, including a public evening-lecture at which I delivered a ten-minute introduction. I learned that he spent most of the night talking to young women gathered around him in the dormitory's reception room. On the way to the dormitory he had said to me, *Nothing really matters*. I picked him up in his room the following morning to take him to breakfast. On his night-stand was a small celluloid angel, curvaceously female in contour, from which he had removed the wings; he explained the dealate state: *Without wings, she doesn't leave me*.

At breakfast I expressed my appreciation of his poem, *Hercules at Nemea*, which I regularly presented to my mythology students. He said he should not have written the phrase, *maned like a lioness* because a lioness does not have a mane. That had never occurred to me. (For later editions and collections of his poems he changed the phrase to *fierce as a lioness*.) This memory is clear to me; it is *of* Robert Graves, but it *is not* Robert Graves, who ceased to exist in his ninetieth year of life.

Epicurus's conclusion offers nothing beyond flat fact. Diogenes Laertius ascribes to him the much repeated statement: While we exist, death is not present; but when death is present, we do not exist. In another ascription we read that death is nothing to us because it is the loss of perception, which is nothing. That, though, is the horror: nothing.

Even Heidegger, who posits Nothing as the ground of transcendent perception (through complete boredom, true love, or uncanny dread [*Angst*]), does not accord perception to those who have ceased to exist.

It is different for those who have faith, no matter what their religions may be, both in their approach to death and in faith's substantiation of their hopes and beliefs. I am satisfied that Kris and Sharny have faith. I am not sure about Andy or about myself. Anne, I know, does not have faith. Andy follows the rituals, but to their interiority he is, I think, indifferent. Anne contends with the *dirty trick*. I pray, when my insufficiency unto myself is painful.

Film noir and Edward Hopper's masterworks juxtapose shadow and light in depicting light as the prelude to death. Their juxtaposition is Nietzsche's and Lagerkvist's amalgamations of Dionysus and Apollo. Their light is an intruder into the prime of darkness, a claim of primacy for itself, a mask of Apollo (the Apollo of Veii, not the Apollo Belvedere). In its beneficence to life, light is a sanction imposed upon darkness by the Light-bringer (Lucifer, Phosphoros). In the constancy of its speed, in its undulant quanta, and in its curving, light is evil (upward-striving), as evil as Melville's resurgent white whale: *primum MOBI-le, DIC-tum sanctum*. Between the big black-hole bang and the bright blue sky of early June there must be light.

Elvis should have progressed from his black-leather comeback jeans and jacket to his white jumpsuit to his June-blue jumpsuit; but he put on his white jumpsuit last, his white clown-suit.

Hopper caught it all in *Soir Bleu*: black-clad absinthe drinkers, and a blue sky at twilight that is made pleasantly blue only where it absorbs the glow of death from a white-clad, white-faced, frowning clown. Two men wear black caps; one man and one woman have black hair: one man and one woman, seated nearest the clown, have brown hair, as though the clown-light had tempered black. At age thirty-two, when he painted *Soir Bleu*, which I think of as *Noir Bleu*, Hopper must have concluded, as Anne has concluded, that life is a dirty trick. *Soir Bleu* moves from the white clown to blue, to black, through and around to the central whiteness: *blanc, bleu, noir*. Holland Carter speaks of a *Hopper shtick* and says that Hopper *went with anxiety and longing and made them feel-good entertaining, like Hollywood films*. I can't compete with Carter in sophistication. I can only nurse the opinion that Hopper presents the mystery of indifference in such a way as to enable a viewer to achieve the indifference with which to oppose longing and despair. Albert Camus calls it *the deep nobility that is found in indifference*. Grayber says that, yes, we can see all this in the black-white-blue of Hopper's *Summertime*, but how do we then account for the mundane brown and dull yellow of the door-half, just beyond which the sensual young woman stands? He insists that I would do better closely to study Jackson Pollock's *Lucifer*, into which the Satanic force has thrown black, white, and blue, but, in doing so, has dulled the white to grey and corrupted the blue to a dark unpleasant green that is all but lost.

White-blue-black suits my reading of Heidegger. His Being is white, his realized potentiality of Death is black, and his Running-forward-in-thought-toward-Death is blue. Blue also is his To-be-toward-Death. This clarifies for me the mediaeval *Memento mori* (Keep death in mind) as *ut vitae conscius* [*vel conscia*] *sis* (so that you might be conscious of life). Heidegger's potentiality of Death intensifies life and gives a person the ability to ascend to his or her ownmost (*eigenst*) ownness (authenticity, *eigentlich Eigentlichkeit?*). This Blue Life, however, does not offer the means successfully to confront the black zero of the death of an Other who had been part of the Blue. While I did not weep for Kris's father, or become as depleted (or as sustained in faith) as Kris by his death, I suffered, as I was later to suffer in increasing measure, at being beset by the black zero.

Heidegger, the greatest thinker of the twentieth century, is derided for his short-lived membership in the Nazi Party and for his mandatory salutes to Hitler. His silence, unencumbered by excuses or exculpatory explanations, bespeaks, as I said in my response to the philosophy professor's question, his (Heidegger's) acceptance of responsibility for his actions.

The project of his academic career depended on Nazism; but, within this political tidal movement, it is his movement away from the limitation that matters. Initially, progression is a backward movement: a pitcher's rearing backward, a backward rocking of the spinning wheels of a car on ice. It is a matter of going forward by means of backward movement: Dante's going to Paradise by way of Hell, Parzival's approach to the Grail by leaving the Grail Castle. *Denn der Weg zum*

Nahen ist für uns Menschen jederzeit der weiteste und darum schwerste (For the way to the nearby is for us human beings always the most distant and accordingly the most difficult). *Die Inständigkeit in der Gelassenheit zur Gegnet . . .* (The inner-stability in a letting-go to the expanding-abode). *Gå utenom* (Go round about), the Bøyg tells Peer Gynt. One has to let the Self go out to the expanding-abode so that one may then ascend to it and fully realize it; kept close inside, it withers in the darkness of selfishness. Heidegger's *Heimkehr* (Homecoming) led him out beyond the caverns of the Third Reich. Cast it out, says the pseudo-Dionysius, and be carried up to the Divine Darkness, which is the fullness of Light. *Don't be afraid of the dark*, say Rodgers and Hammerstein: *walk on through the rain.*

How does Hopper's *Wise Tramp* (*A Woman in the Sun*) get to stand naked in a bright vacation room? She is the stripper of *Girlie Show*; she is the woman of the diner in *Nighthawks*, having gone there from the show place. Grayber laughs at this, reminding me that the stripper (1941) and the woman in the diner (1942) cannot be one and the same with the woman who stands naked in the sun (1961). Maybe not, but Heidegger lets me see it that way. Grayber says, *Look at how much older the woman in the diner is than the woman in the sun.* The difference, I insist, is not age—look at the hair, the nose—but light. The woman in the diner is holding her ticket [*Book of matches*, Grayber says] to get out of the city, the ticket possibly having been proffered by the aquiline-faced man sitting close beside her, a cigarette held between his index finger and middle finger, exactly as a cigarette is held by the woman in the sun. Grayber lets his conviction that I am in error be modified by his admission that the latitude for interpretation is broad. He smiles when I suggest that the woman in the sun has gone round about. Grayber is right; but, comforted by the inoffensive darkness of summer's nights, I find pleasure in seeing the three paintings as I want to see them.

My wanting to see things my way is not the same as needing to see things the right way. To right abounding wrongs, or to try to right them, or even properly to protest against them, one has to be inherently, genetically right and have no need of praise. Robert Hughes sees only two figures in Jackson Pollock's *Minotaur*. The painting has three figures. I point this out to Grayber, who, with his genetic rectitude, sees the work as Hughes sees it.

Maybe it's a matter of, not seeing, but feeling. In *A Rainy Night in Georgia*, Brook Benton sings of loneliness as producing a semblance of global rain and then a feeling that it's *rainin' all over the world* and then an asseveration that *it's rainin' all over the world*.

Recognizing how ill this digressive sixty-third unit—this clutter of ruminations—befits a novel, I send it, that is, all of the unit that precedes this paragraph, to Blackie, who writes that he can't really follow it and that, hey, Ped, isn't it kind of pretentious? (I've misplaced his letter and I don't recall his exact words.) He adds that Vera liked it and has read it three or four times and sends a line from Horace: *nonum . . . prematur in annum, membranis intus positis* (shelve it for a decade), a line I had long ago taught to her, when she showed me a poem she had written about gentians and roses left untended near a vacated house. She knew that I would not be offended, that, instead, I would be pleased at her remembering the line.

The vacated house of Vera's poem reminds me now of Dickens's *Bleak House* (about a house more pale than gloomy or somber, a house that offered few prospects). Dickens combines Esther Summerson's first-person narrative (in which her memory of lengthy conversations is, again, prodigious) with the more acceptable third-person omniscient narrative. Geoffrey Tillotson says, *It is possible that [Dickens] made a mistake here*. It is, indeed, a mistake; but the scope and depth of the novel are vast and viable, and there are such lines as *in maggot numbers, where the rain drips in* and *we heard thunder muttering in the distance and felt the large raindrops rattle through the leaves*. There is a dark ellipsis in feeling raindrops rattle. It is productive of a headache to turn from this to the noisy, rattled English of Newt Gingrich and William R. Forstchen in *Pearl Harbor: A Novel of December 8th*, as Janet Maslin makes clear in her account of this assault on grammar. It is better, in thinking about the nature of a novel as one tries to write a novel, to turn to Trezza Azzopardi's *Winterton Blue*, or to Cormac McCarthy's *All the Pretty Horses*, third-person-omniscient-narrative novels that are devoid of Summersonian quotation marks . . .

. . . devoid of quotation marks, as Hopper's paintings are devoid of depicted raindrops or fallen snow.

64

Sharny and I laugh at the clumsiness of Jerry Ford, his stumbling (and Chevy Chase's mimicry of it), and his wayward golf balls that now and then hit spectators; but his pardon of the miscreant Nixon is nothing to laugh at. We watch the replays on television of John Ford's movies, from *The Informer* through *The Man Who Shot Liberty Valance*. The expressionistic chiaroscuro is in keeping with *film noir*, but John Ford muses upon the passing of old orders and the melancholy inevitability of cultural transitions, although not upon destructive constancy, like that of the Lagerkvistian dwarf and executioner, emblems of the inextinguishability of evil. We tolerate the calibrations of cornball humor—the antics of rivalry by Ken Curtis and Jeffrey Hunter in *The Searchers*, for example, or the stock Irish humor of *The Quiet Man*, but we smile in gratitude for the music—*Blow the Man Down* and *Harbor Lights* in *The Long Voyage Home*, or *Red River Valley* in *The Grapes of Wrath*, or all the old-time hymns, or *Innisfree* and *The Wild Colonial Boy* in *The Quiet Man*. As presents (for Father's Day, my birthday, or Christmas), Sharny has given me books about John Ford's films and his career as a director.

Kris and I watch films directed by Stanley Kubrick, except for *Lolita*, which Kris dislikes. We sit through *Paths of Glory* whenever it appears on television. We go to one of the remaining movie houses or to a multiplex to see each new Kubrick film: *2001: A Space Odyssey*; *A Clockwork Orange*; *Barry Lyndon*; *The Shining*. We trace his theme of the misdirected human quest for perfection and technology's aggravation of that quest.

Kubrick's opposition to technologically enhanced selfishness, greed, and apathy is in accord with Kris's Catholic ethics. John Ford seems to recommend that the members of the old order that is passing away accept and abet the transition from their tradition to the new order that is coming about, as John Wayne's Tom Doniphon helped James Stewart's Ransom Stoddard to displace free-spirited gun-rule in favor of the strictures of law in *The Man Who Shot Liberty Valance*. I could not, however, and cannot accept and abet the transition in literary studies from edifying explication to nebulous and anarchic theory: I cling to the traditions of sublimity, to Matthew Arnold's propagation of the best that is written and thought, and to the close reading, although not the anti-biography, of the New Criticism.

Readily, however, did I accept and abet the transition from male dominance toward female equality, as it has been occasioned by the Feminist Movement, despite its being co-opted in the academic world by special interests, notably militant lesbianism and misandry, and post-modern jargonism. My promotion of the nobility of feminism was informed by my recognition of the Female Force. Even now the facts that Gide delivers in *Corydon* are iterated by the account of the parthenogenesis of a hammerhead shark in the Omaha zoo and similar incidents. As one of the five members of the Arts and Sciences Committee on Curricular Innovation, I voted in favor of the establishment of a University Women's Studies Program. The proposal passed; and our committee was charged with the selection of a director. Associate Professor Candace Schwarz-Bleiler was on the short list of three applicants, two of whom were disposed of by 5-0 and 4-1 votes. Although I had spoken against her, I finally voted in her favor; and the 3-2 vote gave her the directorship. I'm not sure why I ended by voting for her: too weary to go through another slate of candidates? indulging in a bit of perversity? deciding to believe in her despite my antipathy to her, based on her antipathy to me and my vestigial conviction that she was a shallow academician? I like to think it was the last, and that I was being true to the principles of Professor Landis. In any event, she learned of the 3-2 vote, but not of who voted how, and assumed that I was one of the two who voted against her. At least two of my colleagues told me of her bitter complaints about me in this matter. The odd satisfaction that I experienced in being disliked, perhaps despised, for something I hadn't done was akin to what I felt when I would like someone who overtly disliked me—Jordy, for instance. Schwarz-Bleiler was thin and somewhat tall, with an elongated face (similar to that of the young Edna May Oliver or the young Lily Tomlin, but less unattractive than either, or maybe just less attractive than Sarah Jessica Parker), and straight brown hair cut short.

Her nose, above thin lips, was a trifle too large and her neck a trifle too long. She consistently wore slacks or a pants-suit; very rarely she appeared in a calf-length dress or skirt. The UWSP flourished under her directorship; she was an able administrator, unregenerate, however, in her insistent use of those aberrations from grammar and usage that were not so much tolerated as flaunted by the English department. She used *contact* and *impact* as verbs, misused *empathy* as a synonym of, actually as a supersession of, *sympathy*, regularly confused *embattled* with *beleaguered*, accepted as correct *like I* and *most* for *almost*, and packed her memoranda with *absolutely, if you will, vast majority, in terms of,* split infinitives, and all the current epidemic clichés. She was, I think, apart from my near relatives, only the second female whom I could not consider in any sexual context; Eulalie in grade school was the first—Eulalie was my friend, Schwarz-Bleiler was my enemy.

She found her calling with UWSP. The position drew her into an active eddy of academic advancement, carrying her into contact with conference leaders and influential feminists. Her jargon-jammed publications increased in length and number, and her two books brought her a full professorship and national renown. She took opportunities, moreover, to comb my few reviews and articles for examples of sexism and male chauvinism, to which she called attention in various of her footnotes. She also found errors of fact in my work and corrected them in her work, off-handedly and with admirable objectivity. Needlessly, I thought, she also cited typographical errors, some of which had been due to my laxity and others to my not having been accorded the gratuity of proof-reading. My attempts, in two lengthy articles, to refute some of her argumentation and to repudiate her abuse of English were regularly rejected and returned without comment. Nothing in my mind seems now to oppose my admitting that she was sincere and justified in her contempt for me. She was following the direction that the English language was taking. She was part of a Ransom-Stoddard transition with which I was not Tom-Doniphon enough to coalesce. She was doing what she sincerely wanted to do.

Teaching was what I wanted to do; and I was doing that, but its concomitants were unpleasant academic chores, like committee work, self-justification reports, campus politics, and publication for the sake of publication. What I wanted most to do, however, was to write poetry, for which I had no gift, and to write novels, in which, like Dickens, I could with impunity have a Mr George get away with exclaiming, *By George!*

Tina Brown says, *Writing a book is one of the last chances to do what you want*. If I cannot write a veritable novel, shall I then write a book?

What is a veritable novel? Schwarz-Bleiler's expression was close to a sneer: if I had to ask, at this point in my work, how could I know? I asked her if she had read the stories of Longus or Petronius's *Satyricon*. Of course she had. In the original languages? Pedantry, she insisted: *There are good translations, which make the works virtually English for academic purposes.* Are they novels, I asked. She said not quite: they were prototypes. My argument was that they both belonged to and informed the genre, along with Sterne's *Tristram Shandy* and Melville's *Moby Dick*, Joyce's *Ulysses* and *Finnegans Wake*, Proust's *À la recherche du temps perdu* (at my French she let the tip of her tongue protrude from the left side of her mouth, moved her head from side to side, raised her eyebrows, and rolled her eyes), Woolf's *Mrs. Dalloway* and *Between the Acts*, Nabokov's *Pale Fire*, Pynchon's *V.*, and Dorfman's *Moros en la costa* (the same facial movements, expressing *Affectation!*). When I suggested that, given novelistic de-centeredness, non-linearity, and plotlessness, the novel need be defined only by newness and now-ness, she, in a flurry of indifference to etymology, flounced off.

Retiring to my office, I reached for my curling, worn, and yellowing copy of *Bleak House* and turned to one of my flagged passages: *Sir Leicester has . . . retired into the sanctuary of his blue coat. Mr. Tulkinghorn, an indistinct form against the dark street now dotted with lamps, looms in my Lady's view, bigger and blacker than before.* I resolved then to wear blue as much as possible and to think of Anne as my Lady Dedlock.

A headline, *Blue Water, Black Gold*, prompts me now to think again about the veritable novel. *Diana of the Crossways*, George Meredith's story, based on the marriage of Caroline and George Norton and Caroline's affair with Sidney Herbert, had to be officially identified as a work of fiction. Truman Capote's *In Cold Blood* presented, as a novel, the account of two executed killers, toward one of whom Capote is subsequently understood to have been erotically attracted. Laura Albert presents JT LeRoy as the fictional author of novels written by her (Albert). The exaggerations and invented events of James Frey's memoir resulted in its exclusion from that genre; it qualifies, I think, as a novel. In each case, the vagaries are new and are imbued with now. Daniel Shields contemplates the *blurring of any distinction between fiction and nonfiction* and says, *Anything processed by memory is fiction.*

In turn *The Search for Bridey Murphy* and Clifford Irving's autobiography of Howard Hughes, by default, may be considered novelistic. Contrary to the opinions of those who profess the death of the author (as artist, as the creator of her or his work), my opinion is that the author, in the case of the novel, *is* the novel. Neither, I believe, can the novel die (as a genre), as long as writers impose the effectively new upon a dimensional now. My conviction in this owes, most likely, to Mary McCarthy's review of *Pale Fire*. I admire Roland Barthes, Jacques Derrida, and Paul De Man, but I understand Mary McCarthy. For the difference between good novels and bad novels, I turn to James Wood, whose self informs his own first novel, *The Book Against God*, which I find to be both good and bad and which I continue to read for, among other qualities, phrases like *the relentless northern rain and the unrelieved blackness of my day*.

Wood's novel is a convincing depiction of a failure who is an inveterate liar. The first-person narrative is, however, the product of a very successful writer. Perhaps only the successful can succeed in writing about failures. Must it be, then, that only winners can succeed in writing about losers? Am I, then, to be frustrated in this attempt to portray myself? Rhetorical questions, to which I deny the answers. I infer from Wood, though, that writing fiction is lying, as opposed, say, to inventive entertainment. His narrator observes that the provision of metaphors is a bad habit. (I applaud that observation.)

Bad, I insist, are Wood's two uses of *I can't seem*, his narrator's recapitulation of page-lengthy speeches within quotation marks and without the justification of letter-writing or electronic recording, his use of *loaned* for *lent*, his qualified absolute (*rather empty*), and his composing this arty burst for his narrator's wife-to-be: *I can't argue it logically. All I can say is that I feel when I am utterly suffused in music, immersed in it, so responsive to it that, that . . . well, in some silly way I want to change colour like a chameleon does, and become the colour of music—when that happens I go through the music as if it is a cloud, and, yes, I believe, I believe.* I try to imagine Kris talking like that, or Anne, or even Schwarz-Bleiler. Well, Schwarz-Bleiler would say *like a chameleon does*.

What is compelling and convincing is Wood's novelistic preoccupation with death as a meaningless transformation of living human beings into nothing: *the dead go nowhere at all.* I nod at this iteration of the dirty trick that is life.

The trick made its dirty way into the world of music and comedy. Groucho Marx died three days after Elvis's death; then, in the following month, Leopold Stokowski died; and, in the month after that, Bing Crosby dropped dead on a golf course in Madrid. Elvis was forty-two, Stokowski ninety-five, and Bing Crosby seventy-three. Pondering the deaths of celebrities, while being draggingly moved only by the death of Elvis, I began to resist thoughts of my own mortality, unwillingly picturing Kris's and Sharny's mourning and envisaging Anne and Schwarz-Bleiler as blue and black angels attendant upon my disappearance into non-existence.

Blackie, in answer to a letter I had written him, in which I had described and asked for his opinion of Schwarz-Bleiler and her enmity toward me, wrote: *Her hostility is overt, Ped; and that's as close as you'll get to friendship in that Liberal Arts world of yours. Try to get her to collaborate on a book with you, if you can overcome your distaste for her so-called abuse of English. Or, get yourself into some other scholarly collaboration and avoid, as much as possible, contact with her. There is enmity and betrayal in business; but committed investments and advice provide a solid platform for friendship. You've got only the friends of your youth and you appeal, here and there, only to quiet women who wrap themselves in the gauze of your passivity.* His correct placement of *only* was, I think, a nod to my earlier needling; and I decided to overlook his odd metaphor, which, now that I re-read it, is less acceptable in a novel than the above-quoted prose jaunt of Wood's narrator's wife-to-be. Blackie went on in that letter to comment on the growing influence of the Christian Right in politics and on the Democrats' loss of the South to the Republicans, thanks to LBJ's Civil Rights legislation. He was both pleased and troubled by these developments: Liberalism was dying (good), but religion was beginning to define Conservative policy (bad). Did I know that Jordy Klug was spending a lot of time in Texas and Tennessee, working with the Religious Right? Blackie's information about Jordy was culled from his business associates in Florida, the Carolinas, Tennessee, Mississippi, and Texas and from my mother, whom he and Vera were kind enough to visit regularly. Jordy's activities in gerrymandering, vote-suppression tactics, and political conspiracies reminded me of Publius Clodius Pulcher and his gangs of hoods and hit-men in the employ of Julius Caesar. Blackie's information included no suggestive analogue for Caesar, however. Well, by extrapolation from the Watergate gangsters, maybe Nixon.

65

From the stack of 45's Kris plays Elvis's rendition of Don McClean's *And I Love Her So*. Then she plays Perry Como's cover. She asks me if I can be objective enough to admit that Perry Como's is the better version. Tone? Phrasing? Interpretation? She may be right; but I find myself unable to admit it. Sharny says that Como has the pleasant legato of ease and sunshine but that Elvis has the bittersweet catch of rain and darkness. Giving Sharny a hug, I tell Kris that I have to go with rain and darkness. Then Kris takes my hand and says, *We'll get by*.

Kris goes to the new table-desk in the living room and works on bill-payments and letters. Sharny and I play chess in the kitchen. The chessboard is a cherry-wood frame with black and white squares. The silver-plated (white) and onyx (black) pieces are mediaeval figures—tournament knights, spearmen pawns, mitred bishops, castle towers, a French king and queen (black), and an English king and queen (white). The set was a Christmas present to Sharny from Kris and me. After I checkmated Sharny, she stared at the board for rather a long time in silence. Then she stunned me with a question: *Dad, what can you tell me about Anne, or Hedwig, or both?* I did not look up, or expose my surprise. After a moment, I got up, poured myself a cup of coffee, sat down, and, looking into Sharny's brown eyes, said that I had known a Hedwig Nette a long time ago, during the war, in Austria.

Some of us, I lied, were quartered in the house in which she lived with her mother. I managed to transpose Hedwig and Frau Nette to Karl-Heinz and his mother.

Hedwig and her mother lived by the Inn River. Karl-Heinz and his mother lived near not even a stream. Creatively, I thought of them as standing where Guinotte had stood, on the bank of the Lech River, encouraging me as I struggled against the current but giving me none of the confidence that Guinotte had given me.

Sharny stared, calmly, I would say, into my silence.

And Anne? Well, I had known an Anne something or other who worked in Administration at the university where I did my first teaching. She helped me when I filled out a tax form to get you listed as a dependent. We had coffee a few times and became friends. *Did Mom know her?* No. *Was there an affair?* No, nothing like that. I am lying to my daughter.

How could Sharny have known the names? I had never mentioned the names to Kris, much less to Andy or to Sharny herself. Had I talked in my sleep or, somehow, unconsciously uttered the names? When I asked Sharny how she had come upon the names, she went up to her room and brought back an envelope. It was addressed to her and postmarked Las Vegas. I removed a letter and read: *Dear Cyana: It had to be blue, it had to be blue. I wandered around and finally found—the one proper hue, reflecting the true and making me glad just to be sad thinking it through. Some colors I've seen, might never lose sheen, might never shade gloss or sink in the Floss, but they wouldn't do. For no other hue, gave me a will—with all its tints, I need it still. It has to be blue, deep or light blue, it has to be blue.—Anne is your father's star.—Considerably, Hedwig.*

The complimentary close seemed ridiculous. The parody, or re-working, of the Kahn-Jones lyrics made little sense to me. The handwriting, though, or, actually, the printing, with its cuneiform angularity, I knew I had seen before. I said something like, *Moldy sarcasm*. Sharny corrected me: *Moody sarcasms*. And I was proud of her, although I had deliberately perverted the phrase from *The Mill On the Floss*. Sharny had read all of George Eliot and Jane Austen and Emily and Charlotte Brontë. I put the letter back in the envelope and held it out to Sharny. You keep it, Dad. She said she had no use for it.

The next day I went through my files and dissertation notes and stared, with something less than surprise, at Jordy's Gallus-verses, printed in the same wedge-like script. I read the letter again, trying industriously but vainly to fathom its import. It was easy enough to understand that Jordy wanted to hurt me, through Sharny; but why all this blue business? It had to be Anne? Anne, with her blue eyes? Was Jordy telling me, through Sharny, that *de profundis*, Anne's love had wrought my redemption? I placed the unfolded letter, along with the envelope, in the file with the Gallus-verses.

Then, a few months later, shortly after my birthday, Schwarz-Bleiler tossed me a letter, written in the same angular script, and said, *Keep your stupid jokes to yourself, Fart-mouth, or I'll file a complaint*.

She walked away before I could respond or ask what she was talking about. She had given me no envelope. This was the letter: *Sublimate your inferiority to POB by contemplating Cadmus, Jason, and St. George*. No salutation, no complimentary close, no signature. Just Jordy's cuneiform conundrum about three mythical figures who had something to do with dragons. I filed the thing with the Gallus-verses.

I knew, vaguely, that there was some connection between Jordy and Hedwig Nette. Jordy's intrusion into the mutual antipathy of Schwarz-Bleiler and me was something else; I had described it only to Blackie. A few of my colleagues were well aware of the hostility; but who among them would have been in contact with Jordy? Either Blackie had mentioned this to my mother, and she to Jordy, or Blackie had, unaccountably, been Jordy's direct informant. Resisting an impulse to call Blackie, I decided to write to him about the matter. Then I abandoned that decision. Whatever Blackie's motives may have been, if he were the informant, they were not meant to be known to me

That Jordy should know about Cadmus, Jason, and St. George seemed odd. He was, however, as I had come to understand, never to be underestimated. That he should assert my superiority to Schwarz-Bleiler, or to anyone, seemed very strange. Had Blackie managed to inculcate him with this judgment? Cadmus, Jason, and St. George slew dragons. Cadmus and Jason sowed the teeth of the dragons they had slain. The warriors that sprang from the sown teeth, in each case, confusedly fought each other. St. George's dragon was a Johannine allegory of evil. In this, was I the hero and Schwarz-Bleiler the dragon (like the Dragon Lady in Milton Caniff's *Terry and the Pirates*)? Hardly: each hero was ostensibly inferior to the monstrous and each hero prevailed over the monstrous, as it was probably intimated that Schwarz-Bleiler would prevail over me. Giving Jordy credit for setting up this riddle, I enjoyed a touch of pleasure in my confidence that Schwarz-Bleiler did not have the interpretative wherewithal to arrive at this conclusion. Her hasty and huffy disposal of the note by crumbling it and tossing it at me was, for me, evidence enough of her hebetude. I had smoothed the paper out and placed it in a book I was carrying.

When, during the following February, a massive valvular aneurysm ended the life of my brother Paul in his fiftieth year, Jordy attended the funeral and offered my mother more comfort and support than I had been able to offer her. Blackie and Vera not only attended the funeral but also arranged it and paid many of the expenses for it.

Jordy and I supported my mother, each holding a hand under her arm at the shoulder, in the funeral parlor and again at the cemetery. My sisters—Jane and Leanna—and my brothers—Henry, Luther, and Joseph—gathered about my father, whose dull stare, half-opened mouth, and hunched shoulders measured his distance from severe emotion. Kris, Andy, and Sharny remained with my brothers' wives and sisters' husbands and their children.

From a clear sky a radiance brightened the snow cover and the white geometry of the many lines of uniform military headstones. Wisps of breath-vapor issued from the Lutheran minister's mouth as he intoned the concluding rites: *in the sure and certain promise of everlasting life* . . . [redundancy, and the strange word *promise*]. The flag was lifted from the casket, folded smartly into triangular strata, and presented to Paul's wife. The honor guard fired its three shots. The bugler sounded the ineffably beautiful *Taps*. Paul was lowered into the earth and out of existence. Two young men—his sons—stood at the grave and saluted.

Jordy and I guided my mother to the funerary limousine and rode with her to the church, in the basement of which a very fine meal was served. Although it was not the place or the occasion to do so, I managed eventually to ask Jordy about the letters to Sharny and Schwarz-Bleiler. Addressing me without his customary sneer and obscene epithets, he said that the research of the base was constant and thorough. Did I think that with a taxpayers-provided salary anything I did could not be known? Could I never master the Latin language and the research-competence of a true Latinist? *But why the letters? Why?* Why did he have to send them? Because, he said, I was like most of the country, *passive and supinely egotistical.* I thought he may have meant *supremely.* He chuckled at that. No, he meant *supinely.*

Jordy seated my mother and himself at one of the card-table-size wooden tables. Blackie and I joined them. Kris and Vera had taken a table with Andy and Sharny. My mother was opposite me at our table. Jordy, to my right, sat close to her and appeared to be protecting her from me. Blackie sat to my left. My mother gazed distractedly and ate very little of the food that Jordy had placed before her. The German potato salad, fried cod, and cole slaw were excellent. Jordy, still on his obscenity-free behavior, complimented Blackie on his choice of caterer and menu. After a short spell of silence at the table, I, avoiding any mention of Sharny, asked Jordy what he meant by that blue business in his note. His sneer turned into a smile as he turned to my mother and said, *Stella, your son names his daughter Cyana and then calls her by her middle name.*

Before I could object that the naming and the calling originated with Kris, Jordy asked me if, as a classical scholar, I knew the meaning of *Cyana.* I said that it came from the Greek for *blue.*

My mother looked up, smiled, and said, *Oh, that's nice. And what does Sharny mean?* Up to then, I had never given any thought to the etymology of my daughter's middle name, chosen by Kris. My reaction to my mother's question was to think of Steinbeck's Rosasharn (Rose of Sharon). Jordy gave me a moment to answer: and, when I said nothing, he spoke, somehow both gently to my mother and contemptuously to me: *The name Czarny is Polish for black.* To my involuntary affection for Jordy was now added a new degree of involuntary admiration. Blackie, impressed, asked Jordy if he knew Polish. Jordy replied, enigmatically, that he knew what needed to be known. My mother placed her hand on Jordy's arm, patted his arm, and then turned, with discovered appetite, to her food. Luther and his wife and daughter were getting my father to smile; the daughter wiped some cole slaw from his lapel.

Jordy addressed Blackie and me, not, I thought, unsympathetically, and yet with deep scorn: *You guys are really out of it.* He said that the country had turned the corner with the death of JFK, that the base (the details of which he did not disclose) was now manipulating opposition to, and eclectic encouragement of, an ethos of self-destruction informed by greed and apathy. His actual words were simpler than my paraphrase; and they were courteously coarse. He admitted, too, that his use of a .22 in his teens was as unnecessary as it was unwise. Now, in middle age, he had put away much of his impetuousness, he claimed. That I had somehow stumbled through the war was perplexing to him; but my adherence to my conventional ideas about the U.S. was to his mind as ill-advised as his waywardness with the .22. Then he said that the Nazis had assumed that the Jews were the base, or the foundation. Intent upon annihilating the Jews and supplanting them as the base, the Nazis, had they succeeded, would have set the work of the *fondamento* back by a century. Hitler and his nutbags could never have established themselves as the base, which could not subsist as an ethnic ideal, insofar as an ethnic ideal, like Aryans, had to be a target, not an aim, of a definitely multinational foundation.

Blackie seemed to be understanding Jordy. I could not understand him. I asked, nonetheless, if Gallus had invented the base. No, Jordy said, he was the first successfully to bring Europe into the network . . . (I am, of course, correcting Jordy's split infinitive in my quotation.).

Jordy stood up then, kissed my mother on the forehead and said, I*'m really sorry about Paul, Stell'*. Turning to me, he said, *I do offer you my condolences*. Then he walked quickly away. Blackie went off to get another serving of cod for my mother.

Advenio has miseras, frater, ad inferias.

66

Paul had lived for only eleven years after his retirement from the Navy. He'd had a good job as a quality-control engineer with a company that manufactured precision tools. His Navy pension and his new salary made it possible for him to pay for a house built to his liking, with a fully equipped wood– and metal-working shop, on a suburban acre. I knew him better than I had known my other brothers and sisters, but still not well enough properly to mourn and rightly to remember. Now he was gone, and many years were gone, years that I cannot fully or easily account for as I collect the fragments of my memories. Paul's death reminded me of how much of my life had been lived and of how little I had accomplished. A score of years had faded into academic schedules, preparations of syllabuses, classroom routines, addiction to television, going to bed by night and being eased into sleep by a routine set of daydreams, and constant reading without absorption (except of numerous fanciful notions that I could use to enliven my lectures: von Däniken's *Erinnerung an die Zukunft* [*Memory of the Future*; published in English as *Chariots of the Gods?*], the Higgs boson, Jean Bruller's *Les Animaux dénaturés* [the definition of *human being* consists in religious instinct], ring-composition, my obsession with Heidegger's concept of Language [despite my lack of the ability logically and properly to understand it and alienate it from fancy]).

RAIN AND DARKNESS

My father was, and still is, a fiddler and an accomplished mechanic; Paul had been a manual artisan, a precise technician; I laid a wavering hand upon the infirmity of drift.

Pope Paul VI, firmly purposed successor to the magnanimous ecumenicist John XXIII, died and was succeeded by John Paul I, whose thirty-four-day reign was exceeded in brevity only by the two-day-tenure of Stephen II. All things Pauline—Paul Simon; Paul Anka; Peter, Paul, and Marry; and Pope John Paul II—turned my mind to my capable brother, whom life had Lagerkvistianly ceased to mean before he could meaningfully survive me, as he should have done.

Apart from genuine fraternal affection, Paul and I had very little in common. He was practical, active, and imbued with integrity. He had no interest in movies, although, prodded by Kris and me during one of his leaves, he saw *Paths of Glory*; he was moved by it, and he praised the stirring finale, fashioned by *Der treue Husar*, which our father's fiddling and our familial singing had made known to him. He expressed admiration for my framed print of Hopper's *Nighthawks*, and I bought one for him as a present after his retirement from the Navy. He couldn't understand why I thought the woman at the counter was holding a ticket. When I said that Grayber saw it as a book of matches, he said that women, even tough women, do not light cigarettes for men. *She's holding a sandwich*, he said. Gail Levin corroborates his observation, as Professor Walter Wells corroborates Grayber's. I'm quite alone with my interpretation, *sub specie paganorum*. Paul's wife did not like the print and, I was saddened to learn, gave it away not long after Paul died.

The years just before and all during the Decade of Greed were years of death, or, years during which the instances of death were illumined by the equivocal Hopperesque light that followed the evil light of *film noir*. Jacques Brel had died. Sid Vicious fatally stabbed his Nancy and then died himself four months later. Twenty-year-old Dorothy Stratten, *Playboy* Playmate of 1980, had been murdered by her ex-husband, twenty-nine-year old Paul Snider, who then committed suicide. Jim Jones's more than nine hundred followers followed his instructions and drank fatal potions of poisoned Kool-Aid. Giorgio de Chirico and Norman Rockwell, painters respectively of the shadowed and the shallow, died, along with Margaret Mead and Golda Meir. Nelson Rockefeller died, reportedly in the embrace of a woman who was not his wife. Cancer took out John Wayne. Death came for Herbert Marcuse, who had vainly entreated Heidegger publicly to repudiate his past Nazi affiliation, and for James T. Farrell, whose Studs Lonigan lost his Lucy [Wordsworth, too, had long ago lost a Lucy] and knocked up his Catherine [Hemingway's Lt. Henry, too, had knocked up his Catherine in a novel slightly earlier than Farrell's].

Jean Seberg, who played Joan of Arc, married Romain Gary, and wrote *Blue Jeans*, died while sitting in her car, having apparently taken intentionally an excess of drugs. Al Capp, Henry Miller, and Jimmy Durante were followed out of existence by Roland Barthes and Jean-Paul Sartre. Alfred Hitchcock died; likewise Josip Broz, the Tito whom the Četniks hated. Steve McQueen died five days after Reagan was elected. Seven months later, once the Decade of Greed had seen its inception, Pope John Paul II took a would-be assassin's bullet and survived to forgive publicly the man who tried to kill him. Two years before my brother Paul died, and three years before the death of Marcuse, Martin Heidegger ceased to be. Two years before the end of Heidegger's running in thought *zum Tode*, Pär Lagerkvist had followed his Blue Lady through Eveningland.

Lagerkvist's Holy Land is the equivalent of Heidegger's ascent to the self: it is the quest (as pilgrimage) for true love (the human being to whom one consecrates one's innermost self) and the spiritual fulfillment of being (represented in the West by the Virgin Mary): Lagerkvist's pilgrim, Tobias, transcends time, as his beloved (in her blue flaxen dress), who had died in early youth, re-informs his self, to which he is ascending, and completes his spiritual fulfillment (his virgin Mary): his beloved and the Virgin Mary become one (the Blue Lady). Later, Javier Sierra will have his pilgrim, Carlos Albert, seek transcendence of space. His *sor Maria Jesús de Ágreda* will have achieved *bilocación* (being in two places, distant from each other, at one time), which for Carlos, will be proof that nothing is a matter of chance and that there is, by that fact itself, a *Programador* (Programmer). His Sister Maria Jesús is *La Dama Azul* (The Blue Lady), representative of the human being and not to be confused with the Virgin Mary. Sierra's angelic orders among humanity take the form of human beings who are bilocational by nature—in particular, in his novel, *una mujer vestida de negro* (a lady dressed in black). Under *la Estrella Azul* (the Blue Star), it is for the pilgrim to become angelic through the achievement of bilocation in a programmed universe; this is *el milagro azul* (the blue miracle). Dickens is more like Lagerkvist: *The line of demarcation between the two colors, black and blue, showed the point which the pure sea would not pass; but it lay as quiet as the abominable pool, with which it never mixed.* Lagerkvist, though, shows *two* worlds of blue (love and being) against the black ground of darkness (*mörkret*).

Sierra posits a programmatic miracle by which the blue and the black are atoned. I must prefer to dream in Aftonland, where time gives way to being and where those whom I have loved, and those who have loved me, can wander in eternity.

The many deaths that occurred during the Decade of Greed led me to incur losses of aspiration: *What's the use? What's the point?* I suffered, as well, a sense of the inchoate decay of the country as Reagan loosed the dogs of aggression and fed the gluttons of corporate plutocracy: programs unleashed by deregulation that gained maturity during the first decade of the new century, the Decade of Torture. [Open the gates, George.] History and death brought me to bleakness; but the sustenance I found in literature's subordination of death led me to appreciate a kind of holiness in the written word.

The *good old days* are the days of youth and upward striving. Once life begins to edit its meaning of a human being, there is mainly inertia and entropy. Ignorantly, I had looked forward to the new decade, expecting changes for the better and reasons for equanimity; but what became the Decade of Greed was for me a personal decade of death. Leanna, the younger of my sisters and the baby of the family, died from ovarian cancer. The death of Hildy, Jordy's mother, also hurt my mother deeply. At the funeral, I shook Jordy's hand, and he Novy-shouldered me. Then my mother herself died from cancer of the liver. At the funeral, Jordy shook my hand. Blackie's father died, and I wept as I embraced the fading Rebecca. My father sank into Alzheimer's and had to be placed in a nursing home, which is actually just a way-station for expedited moribundity. He lost his recognition of everyone and everything, except the playing of the fiddle; but, two weeks after he laid his fiddle down for the last time, he closed his oddly staring eyes and breathed no more. All these deaths came about during a period of eighteen years; but they are relative in general to the Decade of Greed.

My father had written a simple will, revised to exclude my mother after she had preceded him in death. He had bequeathed his house and his possessions to Jane, Henry, Luther, Joseph, and me. With the sale of the house and the settlement of debts, this amounted to a few thousand dollars for each of us. One specific item in his will moved me with a force that I had never before experienced: *To my son Peter Oktober Blaustern, the Hardanger Fiddle.* He must have known that I would maintain the instrument in keeping with the Teutonic dignity that had informed his ownership of it.

When Sharny was twelve, he had taught her to play a Norwegian *slått* (tune) on his *hardingfele*. She had learned it well, and she played it at his funeral. After we returned home, she became its custodian. Grayber, who admired the Hardanger fiddle very much, arranged for her to take lessons with a violinist in the Music Department. Eventually, Sharny explained to Kris and me the nature of the fiddle's polyphony.

Whom have I loved? My parents, Paul, Kris, Andy, Sharny, Anne, Trish—each in a different way. To my younger brothers and sisters, whom I have hardly known, I have had, perhaps, devotion or familial affection. Who are those who loved me? The same, except for Trish. Erratically, but vividly, my parents, Paul, and Leanna appear to me in dreams. At times, in dreams, I am surprised to see them because they have died; at times, there is no surprise and it is as if they are rightly alive. There is, in almost every instance, an even sequence of being that is followed by an abruptly terminated sequence of presence. The dream changes, or I come out of sleep. It seems to me that the loved ones can direct their currents of being to me only briefly and can function only as waves that do not collapse into particularity. The existence of loved ones in dreams is in a pleasant ambience. My memories of their physical existence are never severed from sadness. I have tended to think of heaven as an infinity of soul-waves, and of love as the wave-function of souls. *Die Liebe nahm kein Ende mehr.*

Sometimes, in dreams, my mother is the young girl she was before I had been born; sometimes Paul appears in clothing I had never seen him wear; and sometimes Leanna is older than I am and gently scolds me for my selfishness, the end of which, she says, is emptiness. She had never spoken to me in this way while she was alive. Her thinking has perhaps survived her existence. There must be a reality in dreams that issues, not from the *Unbewusst* (Freud's Unconscioused), but in *Erschlossenheit* (Heidegger's *was being* that discloses itself).

67

Sixty-seven! Dickens's *Bleak House* comprises sixty-seven chapters that cover 865 pages of small type in my New American Library Signet edition. In these few pages of mine, I have been brooding over something like six, close to seven decades. My earliest memories: getting out of a bed by a low window and hurrying to stand in a spot of warm morning sunlight, at age three or four; and, within a year from that stream of sunshine, watching my brother Paul take his first steps early one evening as my parents cheered him on. *Kleine Schrift*. The forward action of *Bleak House* is limited to less than one decade, as I recall. So let it be: I am composing neither *Bleak House* nor the *Iliad* (with its forward action of a mere seven weeks). Then there's *Little Dorrit*, with seventy chapters in 845 Penguin-edition pages, with Arthur Clennam *glad he had resolved not to fall in love with Pet*, while his jealousy of Henry Gowan's attraction to Pet (Minnie Meagle) belied his resolution.

How can a person effectively resolve to love or not to love? Dickens must be satirizing the notion of determining such resolves. Love, like faith and Language, is there (*ist da*; Dadaist): it may unfold itself to us; we can predispose ourselves to a reception of it; but love is not subject to will or decision. Often I wondered if my inability to dislike Jordy Klug was a form of love (familial, fraternal, or self-identificational). There was something of an answer for me at my mother's funeral.

My brothers and sisters and I had pooled our money for a huge floral funeral spray with the banner *Mother*. Vera and Blackie contributed an impressive floral spray with the banner *Dear Friend*. Other sprays were bannered *Beloved Wife*, *Aunt*, *Grandmother*, and *Sister*. The grandest and most majestic of the floral sprays carried the banner *Godmother*. There was no card to identify the godchild. When I asked the funeral director about the identity of the donor, he checked his file and gave me the name, Giordano G. Scaltro. I then envisaged my mother holding the infant Jordy up to the baptismal font and taking for him the vow *to renounce the Devil and all his works and all his ways*. My mother and Hildy Klug had been best friends during most of their lives. This explained, in large measure, Jordy's devotion to my mother and perhaps, to some extent, my persistent inclination of forbearance toward a guy who had taken shots at me. *In spiritu fratres.* At least I knew, at that moment in the funeral parlor, that those shots, which had only wounded Blackie, would not have been, and may not have been intended to be, fatal: two .22-caliber bullets at long range by an expert marksman.

A question I had never asked myself before presented itself now: Had Blackie been the actual target?

Kris and I had stayed with Vera and Blackie for a few days after my mother's funeral. On the day before we were to leave, Blackie received a telephone call from Jordy: Would the capitalist and the tax-supported new orphan join him at his club for drinks that afternoon? Blackie accepted for both us, came back from his office at about 4:30, changed into casual clothes, and told Vera and Kris that we'd be back in a couple of hours, that we were going to the Habsburg Club for cocktails with Ped's godbrother.

It's not like he's just a member of the club, Blackie told me, as we drove away; Jordy owns the Habsburg.

A valet parked Blackie's Lincoln. An attendant escorted us to Jordy's office. Jordy greeted us with his familiar ungrammatical condescension and conducted us by elevator to a soundless, plush-carpeted corridor and into a tastefully lavish clubroom, richly carpeted, with mahogany tables and blue leather-upholstered chairs. At one end of the room, a very attractive young woman, wearing nothing above her waist, tended a massive mahogany bar. When she came to our table to take our orders, Jordy smiled as I stared at the bare breasts. Blackie, apparently accustomed to toplessness, maintained a sophisticated indifference. Jordy ordered a bottle of Lacrima Christi; Blackie had a Boodles Martini; I asked for Black Label Scotch. [Yes, George, there is now a Blue Label, and that is what I ask for now.]

Jordy waved away my thanks for his attendance at my mother's funeral and his magnificent floral tribute: *Your mother is a magic lady; she deserved a first son so much better than you.* Blackie thanked Jordy for the invitation and his hospitality. Jordy's acceptance of his gratitude was strangely civil. After a few drinks, we were talking and laughing in the manner of old friends at a valued reunion. This, too, was strange. Jordy asked Blackie why he never had kids. Blackie's childlessness was none of Jordy's business; but *That's none of your business* was a statement that was not meant to find its way into this symposium. Blackie said that Vera had undergone a hysterectomy in conjunction with cervical cancer and that she and he had decided against adoption. Blackie then asked Jordy why he'd never married.

Jordy offered a long, generally misogynistic answer: women had the one celestial thing that all straight guys needed, and it was their main *bargaining chip*; unless you could really love a woman, it was silly to pay the enslaving price when you could stay free and pay only the monetary price (his actual words were far less formal); love was a good but very rare thing, something he could not experience, and, in evidence of its rareness, the family unit, was now disintegrating under the trends of no-fault divorce, cohabitation without marriage, pre-nuptial contracts, the play of instant gratification, and the recognition of homosexuality as a genetic disposition.

He surprised me by likening himself to an unregenerate Ivan Karamazov, Blackie to Dmitri Karamazov in a troika, and me to an Alyosha constantly in the presence of a putrefying Father Zosima. Overcoming my surprise, particularly at the image of Blackie as Dmitri, I thanked him for at least not identifying me with Smerdyakov. Then he surprised me anew by saying that our Smerdyakov was somewhere about, that there had always to be a fourth, in this case, imperfection added to reason, emotion, and religion: *Imperfection is our brother, Stinking Lizaveta our devil-mother.*

At this, I said, *Who the hell are you, Jordy? And what is this Scaltro business?* He said that I knew who he was but that I was too weak to live in my Pre-conscious: I was confined to my Conscious and led by my Id; I could not retrieve from my deeper Pre-conscious anything that I really knew. I asked him where he had learned about Dostoevsky and Freud. He said, *I don't need to go to college to be taught how to read.*

Blackie asked him if he had gained any of his obvious wealth honestly. Jordy smiled and said that his *honos pugnae* was more evolutionarily sound than the rapine of *honest business. Capitalist is a telling term, Capitalist: after you shove your rods up people's asses, you cut of their heads with your duplicit axes.* I thought that the remark was tentatively clever, and I caught the allusion to Lucretius's *fasces et secures*. I was unsure of the *honor of battle* (or *military glory*, as translators have it). I asked Jordy if the phrase was Horatian. *It's from Vergil, Mr. Herr Doktor Professor.* My rejoinder: *Well, I know that pax, pecunia, and pugna all have the same root.* Jordy gave me what I can call only a look of ungrudging approval: *You're right, Peter. That's good. And what's the fourth?* I knew this too: *Pagus.* Jordy squinted, half-smiled, and did a thumbs-up.

To our questions about the base, or the foundation, Jordy responded by asking us to try to imagine it as a benign tumor spontaneously striving parthenogenetically to change its consistency into that of a divisible quantum of energy. *Impossible*, said Blackie, apparently understanding what Jordy was talking about, as I could not. Jordy offered no argument to the contrary; but he went on to speak at quite some length. My attention was already stunted by the flow of Scotch. My summary has to be general, and mainly in spotty paraphrase, marked by a translation of most of Jordy's profanity and obscenity into plain talk. He began by complimenting me on my note about the radix of peace, money, war, and property, the four constituents of civilization, which it is the proper impulse of the foundation to confound. The impulse is attended by the poets of damaging darkness (*emotive agents who storm the trends and slash the tents of convention*)—Archilocus, Gallus, Mohammed, François Villon, Joseph Smith, T.S. Eliot . . .

Jordy caught my surprise at his mention of Eliot and went on for a few moments about Shantih, Bleistein (and Ezra Pound's millionaires farting through *silk handkerchiefs*), Stetson . . . at Mylae, and setting *my lands in order*.

He said that we could use Plato's example of the charioteer and two horses: the charioteer (reason) was the foundation, taking control of the white horse (energy) and the black horse (unreason, fanaticism). Being Greek, Plato stopped at three and ignored the fourth element, the chariot (the moving platform of technology). The white horse has become oil-business. The black horse has become uncompromising fundamentalism (*frozen-shit religion*). *Under the shit-roof of the ol' religion*, the family unit will splinter into single parenthood and X-rated movies. Television will curtail our attention-span and reduce information and news to a flow of entertainment (*a piss-river of dumb students watching the Three Stooges*). The foundation, with Orwellian instruments of control, will institute a functional fascism founded in fear; it will shoot down functional capitalism with unregulated corporate acquisitiveness and it will shoot down liberal education with stringent cost-accounting.

With his thumb and forefinger, Blackie rotated the stem of his verre à pied and smilingly watched the troubled float of the pitted olive. He seemed not at all surprised at Jordy's predictions. I sipped my Scotch and, with my head downturned in silence, affected a lack of surprise at Jordy's sophistication, folded though it was in the vile language that I have here sought to mitigate and minimize.

Finally, Blackie asked Jordy what exactly his position in the foundation was. *Heritage, man*, Jordy said. *From Gallus?*, I asked. His silence I interpreted as consent. Then, taking advantage of this feast of frankness [Sorry, George!], I, managing to hold my weak blue gaze against Jordy's diabolically black stare, asked him if he had full access to the carmina of Gallus. His answer, which I interpreted as affirmative, was indirect but in no way evasive: *They're only occasionally good, Herr Doktor LackLatin; he brought out more than Catullus but less than Propertius.* I checked my urge to beg him for information about securing the canon. He had already indicated in many ways that I had missed my shot at this. Blackie turned away from the subject and, reverting to the mention of his childlessness, told the joke about the married MBA's, each specializing in cost-accounting. Their house was precisely neat, their lives unerringly organized, and their actions exactingly practical. They wanted children, however, and, after five years of disappointed endeavor, consulted a doctor, who found them both physically fine and normally fertile. *What position do you assume in lovemaking?*, he asked them. *Why, the normal doggy position, said the wife; I kneel on the plush carpet and he approaches me from behind.* The doctor rubbed his ear and said, *Hmm, I'd recommend the missionary position in bed.* The cost-effective couple looked startled and blurted out in unison, *What! And miss television?* Blackie waved me in; but the best that I could summon was Woody Allen's joke about his wife, who was so immature that she would come into the bathroom while he was in the tub and would sink all his boats.

Jordy offered a joke about Pedro and Pablo, who, while taking a siesta, watched a deputy post a notice of reward for information leading to the capture of Two-Gun Juan. Pablo asks Pedro if he knows Two-Gun Juan. Pedro says that, while eating a burrito one afternoon, he was held up by Two-Gun Juan, who took his few pesos, ate his burrito, and then ordered him to eat the shit of his (Juan's) horse. *Do I know Two-Gone Juan? Si, Pablo, we had launch toGATHer.* Jordy's Spanish accent sounded Italianate.

Before you guys go, Jordy said, by way of letting us know that the symposium was about over, *I got a few words here for Herr Doktor Professor.* He had the waitress bring another round and a notepad and ball-point pen. He wrote down the following and handed it to me: *Mundus per spatium nigrum vehitur mihi cordis caeruleus dominae coram ego languidulus in terra mihi non locus est sed caelo in opaco intueor nequiquam caeruleos oculos.*

It took me only a few moments to scan out two elegiac distichs and to get the sense of the passage. Jordy asked me to translate it. I asked him to read it out loud. He read it in perfect scansion; and I complimented him. *Translate it*, he ordered. I wrote my effort down and then read it aloud: *A blue world is borne through the black space of my mistress's heart, in the presence of which I am weak; there is no place for me on her earth, but, in her dark sky I gaze in vain at her dark eyes.*

Jordy said, *Close enough; you've improved.* I said that the passage was not classical and asked for its source. He asked why it wasn't classical. I said that the image of earth in space was much too early and the *mens* (mind), not *cor* (heart), should be the seat of emotion. He then quoted Ovid's *nec circumfuso pendebat in aere tellus ponderibus librata suis* (before the globe of earth hung in the surrounding air balanced by its own inertia) and insisted that *mens* was generally located in the *cor*. Here I lacked the wherewithal and depth of argument; and I sipped my Scotch in silence. Blackie stared curiously at the two of us.

With a change of mind, or a change of heart, or for whatever reason, Jordy ordered another round. He and Blackie talked about OPEC and the problems of international oil supply. I stared at the waitress's breasts, which by now appeared to me to be less erotic than adipose and loosely appendant. Blackie's speech was beginning to slur. My eyesight was beginning to blur. Another round.

RAIN AND DARKNESS

Jordy arranged for a limo-driver to take Blackie and me home, and he had another driver follow in Blackie's Lincoln. Vera had kept the evening meal warm for us; but neither Blackie nor I had any appetite for food. In the guest room, I removed one of my blue suede loafers. I remember nothing beyond that.

Vera and Kris put together a full breakfast: fried eggs, bacon, pork sausages, toast, jam, orange juice, and coffee. Kris and I began our drive back at about ten o'clock, with Kris at the wheel; she drove until we stopped for lunch at a Burger King, where I ate my Whopper and half of Kris's. I drove the rest of the way, enduring Kris's slowly waning anger over my spending an afternoon getting drunk and her occasional complaints about my lack of consideration.

68

Sharny had been too ill to journey to my mother's funeral. Andy had attended and had gone his own way after the rites; he had given Kris a note for Sharny along with a get-well card. Kris's displeasure with my *Habsburg orgy*, as she called it, softened to indifference under her concern for Sharny and upon Sharny's defense of me: *After all, Mom, Dad should be entitled to a wango after his mother's funeral.* What bothered Kris more than the drunkenness was the camaraderie with Jordy, in whom she saw deep evil. Grayber, who had been caring for Sharny in our absence, was not surprised about Jordy's hospitality and affluence (or about the waitress, whom I mentioned only to him).

Grayber was interested in the Latin distichs and intoned *It's a blue world* as he read them. I had typed them out:

> Mundus per spatium nigrum vehitur mihi cordis
>   caeruleus dominae coram ego languidulus.
> In terra mihi non locus est sed caelo in opaco
>   intueor nequiquam caeruleos oculos.

He asked for a Xerox copy. At his suggestion, I sent a copy to Professor Landis, who was now *emeritus*. Professor Landis wrote after a week or two: *Dear Peter, thanks for the elegiac passage, which is less pedestrian than the other fragments and, I think, less identifiably classical. The image of the domina*

RAIN AND DARKNESS

as a macrocosm has no Graeco-Roman precedent that I know of. I've tried without success to see it as an extrapolation from Hesiod by way of Ovid. If you cannot press Mr. Klug to divulge his source, we shall just have to conclude that Mr. Klug is the author. With all good wishes, L. I had just about reached the conclusion that Jordy was intelligent enough and inventive enough to have contrived the schemata about the foundation and the Latin verses; but the tentative conclusion would go for naught in the darkness of the recollected evening I had spent in the presence of Hedwig and Mischiato. Resignedly, I added the distichs to my file of Gallus material.

Could the macrocosm consist of Gaea (Earth) giving birth to, and then coupling with, Ouranos (Sky), as Hesiod tells the story? Black earth, blue sky: but the lines have blue earth and black sky. Would Professor Landis allow a metathetic transference of epithets? Ovid writes about forms changed into new bodies; most readers translate this as bodies changed into new forms. Gallus's domina is Lycoris: is she *dominatrix* or *domina matrix?* Lyricism, by both semantic and sonant paronomasia, generates verbal dyads. Baudelaire's *symboles qui l'observent* (symbols that observe him) is, in sound, the same as the more ordinary *symboles qu'il observe* (symbols that he observes). Does the *Lyc—of Lycoris* intone *wolf* or *light?* In sound, why not both? Grayber, when I discussed this with him, preferred the conservative position of Professor Landis: one must not read too much into a text. Against that cautionary commandment I am always in revolt. The postmodernists would carry it to another dismal point: there is no text beyond the tentative ideology of a writing's textual presumption. Wrong! Texts exist; and we can't read them objectively without subjectively reading into them.

Gallus set up the generic situation of a mistress dominating the poet who is in love with her, or ardently desirous of her. His Lycoris was followed by Catullus's Lesbia, Tibullus's Delia, Propertius's Cynthia, and Ovid's Corinna. This is a version of the Female Force. Gallus, I'm sure, or rather, I suspect, had the broadest and the most immediate experience of it. During the many symposium rounds at the Habsburg orgy, Jordy had said something about the *force expressed by Gallus* finding its way into the Italian opera, and into the best of German opera (Mozart, not Wagner) and coming through in a soprano like Elizabeth Schwarzkopf and lyric tenors like Enrico Caruso and, especially, Luciano Pavarotti. The *Forza del Destino* is ultimately the Female Force as both the destroyer (of the coöpted foundation and all things male) and the destroyed (by perverted consciousness) *in saecula saeculorum* (forever and ever).

Turning from this rambling narrative [Open the gates, George] to recent events, I ponder the death of Pavarotti and the death, less recent, of Elizabeth Schwarzkopf. The portly Pavarotti and the white-headed Schwarzkopf (well, white-*haired* when elderly) have ceased to exist. Their voices continue to exist on recordings, but neither of the possessors of those offices can appreciate the fact. Only the living can appreciate what those who have died have created and produced and left on record.

Losers must anticipate their own eventual loss of existence and their lack of leaving evidence of anything of greatness on record; but, in the nothing of non-existence, how can it matter? Heidegger defeated non-existence in his receipt of the unfolding of Being. Without his strength and his capacity for complete thought, I can do no more than to admire his mind and to fashion, in my fashion, an existence

RAIN AND DARKNESS

grounded in that elusive uniqueness that can be accredited to neither genes nor super-ego.

Listening to Pavarotti sing *Nessun dorma*, to Schwarzkopf sing *Es gibt ein Reich*, I relive a moment with Trish in a summer night; I relieve my ignorance with a sense of what Heidegger means in his explanation of *es gibt*. It gives. It is given. A thing is the gift of itself in the action of giving itself. I see that George Grizzard, with whom, as I recall, I once spoke briefly, has died of lung cancer, survived by his partner of forty years, William Tynan. Grizzard's last movie (or, the movie in which I last saw him) was one in which he played the role of a dying man. Jane Wyman, magically cute in *Magic Town*, has also died. She was the talented first wife of the second-rate actor who played the dying *Gipper* (George Gipp) and went on to expropriate the role and the words, *Win one for the Gipper*, as he presided over the Decade of Greed. An actor is a thief of gifts.

Gipp, Heidegger, Schwarzkopf, Wyman, and Grizzard are all survived by their works but, no longer in existence, have no sense whatsoever of their being survived by any thing. Back, then, early in the Decade of Greed, in the chilling drizzle of early April nights, I would walk over wet sidewalks made less abrasive by the light rain and carry my day's disappointments home toward the quietness of black coffee with a somewhat sullen Kris and crossword puzzles with a weary Sharny. A decade of greed, a decade of death, my attempt to chronicle which in what I wanted to call a novel would be now adjudged by Blackie as a manifesto of mediocrity. Nonetheless, he encourages me, without believing in me, as Grayber believes in me without encouraging me. This, I shall insist, is a novel that makes no point, carries no message, professes no moral, says only what I have to say, independent of any neatly defined plot, the kind of novel that W.G. Sebald might have written if he had been without talent. There is no talent evident in the few poems that I have managed to get accepted for publication or in the two novels that lie long unpublished and shelved away in a recess of the basement.

Talent alone can compensate for insufficiencies of character. Charles McGrath, reviewing David Michaelis's biography of Charles Schulz, includes the suggestion that the great cartoonist may have had *essentially an arrested sensibility, locked in adolescent longing and self-absorption.*

Blackie may well have said that about me, had his expression been as precise as McGrath's. Michaelis's *Schulz and Peanuts: A Biography* presents, according to McGrath, an artist whom success did not make happy. Maybe not; but it justified him, adolescent longing and all. At least I have learned—from Theognis, Sophocles, and Heidegger—that happiness (the abstraction of chance, which itself is abstract) is not a valid human goal. The true goal is justice, the events and actions that even out a life and provide a compensation for being alive:

Πάντων μὲν μὴ φῦναι ἐπιχθονίοισιν ἄριστον
μηδ' ἐσιδεῖν αὐγὰς ὀξέος ἠελίου,
φύντα δ' ὅπως ὤκιστα πύλας ᾿Αΐδαο περῆσαι
καὶ κεῖσθαι πολλὴν γῆν ἐπιεσσάμενον.

(Not to have gone through birth is best of all for those on earth, and not to have gazed at the rays of the blazing sun; or, if one has been born, to pass in the fastest way through Hades's gates and lie enshrouded deep within the ground.—THEOGNIS)

Without talent, I cannot be justified. Without talent, I cannot be just. Lagerkvist sees longing (*längtan*) as the concerted wish that is its own satisfaction; and, with his talent properly to express longing, he was among the just. Justice is a universal law of adjustment; Theognis's elegiac distichs point out the only path away from the need for it.

While writing my dissertation under Professor Landis's direction, I took the time, at Professor Landis's urging, to participate in a university theatrical production: I had the role of Armand in *Le Voyage de Monsieur Perrichon*. The rehearsal and the performances were, for me, exhilarating. Mrs. Landis, who attended one of the performances with Professor Landis, said that I had missed my calling. She meant it, perhaps, as a kind of joke; but she may have been right. Kris has always considered me a performer. Perhaps I had a talent for acting. If so, I should have nurtured it on the stage and not in the classroom. It occurs to me now that the Landises, at that time, may have been gently nudging me to recognize and heed my proper calling. It is doubtful, though, that Professor Landis would have compromised his belief in my academic competence.

69

In the same issue of *The New York Times* in which the review of the Schulz biography appears, William Satire mentions Jacques Barzun's reminding him that *boggle* is an intransitive verb that has joined the many other words that have been bereft of their integrity. Descriptive lexica now list its transitive uses, like *boggle the mind*. This reminds me of my argument with Schwarz-Bleiler in the middle of the Decade of Greed. Politically correct and adamantly postmodernist, Schwarz-Bleiler had used the clause, *a concept that boggles the mind*, in a committee meeting. The mind, I said, may boggle when confronted by a concept, but a concept cannot *boggle the mind*; it can only cause the mind to boggle. Glaring in open fury, she invoked the descriptive lexical entries and said that I ought to keep up with the times. *Language is a living thing, Mr. Blaustern: it changes.*

Citing Heidegger, above Schwarz-Bleiler's groan, I said that Language is the saying of Being in which languages, as living entities, participate in accordance with the Geworfenheit of its speakers, that is, the language systems into which its speakers are thrown. Living entities change, but they must resist those changes that precipitate decay and death. So, said Schwarz-Bleiler with a smile, languages need diets and exercise?

Despising the metaphor, I nonetheless extended it: diets and exercise constitute our efforts to remain alive for as long as possible, to resist the changes of forms that move our bodies toward death. She likened the inevitability of death to the inevitability of language change and language mortality. But that, I countered, is the point. We ought to resist death at every juncture—the death of the body, the death of the English language. She laughed and said that the two deaths were not logically related. I claimed that they were inseparably related, that we live by language as much as we live by food and physicality.

As she argued, all the gestures and neologisms that I deplore came into play. She laid the little finger of her left hand along her lower lip; or, she placed the tip of her right forefinger upon the midpoint of her closed lips, or along the line of her upper lip, as David Caruso would later do in the wretched movie *Jade*, and as television news reporters have come increasingly to do in feigning interest in the hastily unheeded replies of those whom they would interview; the hackneyed words of pretentious parlance all recurred: *proactive* (a meaningless neo-antonym of *reactive*), *vast majority*, *absolutely* (hyperbole for *definitely* or *exactly*), *most* (for *almost*), *thrust*, *clout*, and the inevitable *impact* and *contact* as verbs. One of the committee members occasionally nodded slightly in my favor, but the others visibly and with mild interjections sided with Schwarz-Bleiler and grew impatient, not only with our irrelevant dispute, but also and mainly with my opposition to the jargon and language-abuse to which they had been bred.

Schwarz-Bleiler belonged to the new English-department order of politically correct ideologues. Their basic Marxist leftism had crumbled into an inconclusive academic anarchism: intensified ethnic diversity that eschewed integration; multiculturalism that scorned the study of foreign languages; misandry-based feminism; and a sustained opposition to the classical elements of the traditional liberal education. It was my great displeasure, in adhering conservatively to Homer, Aristotle, Vergil, Augustine, the mediaeval trivium and quadrivium, Chaucer, Milton, Shakespeare, Dickens, and the logical niceties of English grammar and syntax, to discover that my allies in this conservatism were, in general, political conservatives who favored Republicans and the rigid Right. Blackie wrote that it was time for me to leave the morass of the Democratic Party. He said Democrat Party, in keeping with the current Republican propensity for terminological insult.

That it was not possible for me to outdo Blackie in raillery contests or to prevail over Schwarz-Bleiler in open argument owed to my having fallen short of *aretē* (□ρετή: fulfilling one's self in combat, fulfilling one's self as a man, as a human being; excellence [in morality, in art]; fulfillment of function), a virtue which can amount to the meaning of life. The *aretē* of a race-horse is that it wins races, of a light-bulb that it unfailingly provides needed light, of a chair that it adequately supports a seated person, of a scholar that he or she maintains precision and integrity in research, of a teacher that he or she provides clear and unerring instruction, of a human being that he or she be human (a thinking biped that lives because he or she is alive). As a performer, I belonged on the stage, not in the library, classroom, or at an academic committee meeting. Without scholarly depth or instructional acuity, I lacked the substance of argument, debate, and, more important, conviction. *Virtus rerum essentia; homo suam virtutem facit. Aretē* is the essence of things; it is the predetermined function of each thing; a human being, according to Heidegger and the Existentialists, has no predetermined function but determines, while existing, her or his essence (or function). Andrew Kern, a true scholar, expresses it well in speaking of *a teleology that sees the perfection of a thing's nature as its purpose.* My need of praise, an entertainer's need of applause, precluded my having an academic purpose that would have enabled me to put Schwarz-Bleiler in her mediocre horse-faced place. Not being a complete master of the impeccable English that I pedantically championed, not being in infallible command of it, I could not rise beyond pretentiousness.

70

A good antidote to the confabulation of Schwarz-Bleiler was the company of Grayber. There were evenings like the one in which he brought me a remarkably good print of Gustave Caillebotte's *Paris Street, Rainy Day*. He had helped Kris prepare a Friday supper of fried cod, cole slaw, and placki ziemniaczane (Polfish potato pancakes), during which he cheered us both with his witticisms about the lethargic actor who was performing a role as President instead of genuinely serving as President. He takes his lines, Grayber said, from the movies—*Gipper, evil empire, Make my day*—instead of drawing them from a fund of statesmanship.

Relaxing with the Lacrima Christi wine that Grayber had brought, he and I, while Kris cleaned up the dishes in the kitchen, studied Caillebotte's blue umbrellas (grey in most prints), the black coats and stovepipe hats on the men, the blue points and projections of the buildings, and the glistening cobblestones.

The red carriage-wheels fit in, I thought, but not the green lamp-post. Grayber liked the anaphora of the red carriage-wheels, green lamp-post, maroon clothing of the woman, and green building panel. It's the *useless rain of your films noirs*, he suggested, with earth deserted in favor of functional red and green. The umbrellas are all opened and functioning, I observe; but the rain is not visible. We concluded that the blue umbrellas' keeping the rain away from the pedestrians served sensually to keep the rain from our eyes. The defeat of rain; the darkness of garments. The leaden-sky-colored umbrellas fulfilled their function; the cobblestones and the blue-accented buildings fulfilled their function: to keep the rain and the earth from fulfilling their function of fertility in union. From Heidegger's *Four*, divinities and earth had been excluded, sky had given its blue to the umbrellas, and only mortals remained.

Grayber nodded toward my copy of Gail Levin's *Edward Hopper* on the shelf near the sofa. We resumed our study of the self-portrait he had painted in his mid-forties: a middle-aged man, quizzically resolute in a large brown hat, dark green suit-jacket shadowed from collar-top and shoulder into total black, seriously firm blue shirt, and dark green tie dipped in black shadow. He is framed by a wall the indefinite off-white of which is tinged with suggestions of light green and light blue from contiguity with the light bluish-green moldings and door. The color of the floor approximates that of the hat. The brown gives ease to the viewers' eyes; the blue and the shadowed black take the academic viewer's mind back to *bhel-*, the Indo-European root of the words *blue* and *black*, a dyad of positive and negative radiance. The portrait would come to adorn the cover of *Edward Hopper: cinquanta poemes sobre la seva obra pictòrica* by Ernest Farrés, a Catalan poet; the fifty poems are ekphrases of fifty Hopper paintings. The portrait itself, on the cover, is bordered in blue, with a black transversal from edge to edge of the cover. Grayber and I pondered all the paradoxical *connotations of blue* (including Puritan priggishness and night-club-comic obscenity) and the achromatic depths of black, until Kris came into the room to watch her evening television programs. With the Caillebotte and the Hopper book, we retired to the kitchen, where Kris had made coffee for us. We spread the glossy Levin page before us.

Full, settled lips, and eyes discernibly blue in the hat-brim's shadow; strong, straight nose; eyebrows slightly raised.

Proud, indifferent, and questioningly scornful of critical disapproval that is invested with an inchoate sense of superiority. Yes, coffee-brown and nightbush-green are at odds with Mediterranean evening-blue; but the hat, covering the bald head, and the running patch of floor are extraneous to the Self; the shadow, in alliance with the vivid blue, has brought the green to complementary black: I wear my bruise and discipline my lechery and wonder, without caring, who in Hell you think you are.

And so Hopper had died in the year that Farrés was born, and Faye Dunaway played a horny Bonnie to Warren Beatty's impotent Clyde, and Sidney Poitier outshone a bilious world. To paint like Hopper, to govern like FDR (whom Hopper despised), to look and sing and entertain like Elvis, to write like Anthony Burgess, to brood like Lagerkvist and think like Heidegger: distracting daydreams in a dying century, dulling and denying a Self, like (to use Ross Douthat's exceptionally acceptable simile) *the custodian of a . . . politically correct English department at a fading liberal arts college.*

Blackie had written that daydreams were symptomatic of failure and were ensigns of losing. Grayber, pouring a second cup of coffee, said that Blackie called it somewhat short, that the problem was not daydreaming itself but daydreams themselves: daydreams, like desires, can fail; and, when they do, black can no longer complement blue, and the mysteries of blue become untenable and improbable.

Grayber and I have agreed that a greed has grasped this decade. [Sorry, George.] The Victorian era (with Dickens,

Melville), the Gay Nineties, and the Edwardian period (the Wright Brothers, Einstein, Picasso, Henry Ford) had been punctuated by World War I and followed by the Roaring Twenties (James Joyce, T.S. Eliot, Marcel Proust), the Depression of the thirties, World War II of the forties, the Grey Flannel generation of the fifties (rudely ripped by Little Richard, Elvis the Pelvis, Hugh Hefner's *Playboy*, the influx of ex-GI's into the academic world, and the Beats). Postmodernism tolled the knell for the New Criticism and filled the interstices of the counter-cultural sixties and the trash-night seventies. Morning in America meant a prevailing hangover pervading the Greedy Eighties. And here we are, as Grayber and I were to learn, on the eve of another Gay Nineties (Don't Ask, Don't Tell; out and Out). Norman Rockwell, Thomas Hart Benton, and Grant Wood had been set aside for Edward Hopper, Reginald Marsh, Jackson Pollock, and Andy Warhol.

After Grayber and I said Goodnight, under a surprisingly bright North Star, I joined Kris and watched The Tonight show with her. Kris dried her tears again, as we sat in our recurrent fury at Sharny's having been diagnosed with leukemia. It was impossible for me to accommodate my thoughts of emptiness and non-existence to any reality of life.

71

Blackie and Vera, Grayber, and Jordy Klug were all present at the funeral service for Sharny. She had not wanted to lie, in lifelessness, exposed to view. Her embalmed body lay in a closed casket that was centered amidst floral sprays of roses and carnations. Placed atop the softly and gently blue-colored casket was an 8x10 black-framed photograph of Sharny playing the Hardanger fiddle.

Five eulogies preceded mine. Copies of each of them had been given to me the day before the funeral service. The first was by her high-school principal. There were two from her close friends. Grayber's was the fourth. Andy's was the fifth; and his remarks moved me the most and puzzled me. This part, in particular: *Giordano Klug, who has become a kind of uncle to me, told me that people are pained by feelings of incompleteness. I said that, while I had such feelings, they did not really pain me. That, he said, is because you have a sister named Cyana Czarny. I'm not quite sure what he meant, except that I know my sister has been my complement—not because of her name (she will always be simply Sharny to me), but because of, as my Dad will say, her being. Jordy insisted that it was in her name that I could know that marriage is a partnership, while the relationship of sister and brother is a conclusion. A wife, he said is tied to the logic of the flesh, and a sister, whose name is imbued with the depths of earth and sky, is proof of spiritual identity.*

RAIN AND DARKNESS

My Dad has tried to teach me that the spiritual depths of earth-sky manifest the perfection that is Four. He also suggested, when I was studying the Industrial Revolution and the technological corruption of the human being, that I read Dickens's DOMBEY AND SON. *I did this; but I found my attention to the Industrial Revolution giving way entirely to the relationship of young Paul Dombey and his older sister Florence, which disclosed the nature of conclusion that Jordy had talked about. Florence survived her kid brother, who died in his seventh year, as I now survive my kid sister, who has died in her thirty-first year. Her smile, like Florence Dombey's, dispels despair. Her touch is a shelter from fear and sadness. She is music. Because of her, I am among the Fortunate men who live on earth and see the sky. I have a sister.*

It surprised me that Andy had grasped and retained my infrequent and heterodox comments to him about Heidegger's Four. It disappointed me that he had learned as much, if not much more, from Jordy Klug, my own attempts to understand whom had been increasingly frustrated. It disturbed me a little that Andy should have found in Jordy Klug an avuncular companion; and, when I recalled my own uncle, who guided much of my unsettled youth, it saddened me.

Then, mumbling and bumbling, I began to read the pretentious eulogy that I had composed: *Living on the surface of experience and with the tentative comfort of denial, one cannot probe the pain-giving depths of acceptance. Kris, Andy, and I stand smiling in the April sunshine, as Sharny runs across the playground to us, her arms outstretched toward us. In autumn twilight, between Kris and me, she skips on the sidewalk and, swinging her arms, sings,* TWINKLE, TWINKLE, LITTLE STAR, *as Venus appears in brightness. Now, replete with love, and finally abandoning pain, she departs in body, at the age of thirty-one,* *from her parents, her brother, and her friends. Her departure brings to a resisted end the shallow summer of my passing life and exposes me to the untenable responsibilities of acceptance and the rare futility of denial. My adult life has been a dim extension of immaturity. Distantly, I've walked past soldiers killed in combat, attended obsequies of parents, relatives, and friends, and noted the mortality of celebrated entertainers and empowered leaders; but, until now, I have not really known the searing, cutting pain of bitter loss, nothing like the agony that visits me on Sharny's passage from existence. She was too intelligent to attempt dismissal of the loneliness that a long undetermined illness instilled in her. She knew truths that many others could not, and cannot, even think about. She loved music, and it was her means to a happiness that life and nature had otherwise refrained from apportioning to her. On my father's Norwegian fiddle she played many waltzes for me—*La Golondrina, The Blue Skirt, The Blue Danube, *and others. Once, when I told her of my disappointment about the Danube, about its being, not blue, but repellent green, she said,* Dad, one day you will find a river that is truly blue, one that will not wind in weariness to the safety of the sea, and you will merely smile at Swinburne's melancholy. *This is Sharny's promise . . .*

Here, my voice came to a stuttering stop. I thought of Sharny, alive and smiling, of how well she understood me, of how much she cared for me. I could not go on. The three pages that I had been holding fell to the floor. I could see Kris's tears, and Andy's uneasiness; but I just remained standing, head bent, shoulders lowered. After a few moments, Blackie came forward, picked up the three pages, and led me back to my chair beside Kris, who put her arm around me.

The priest spoke, informally offering solace and formally intoning a prayer. A young man, enlisted from the congregation, picked up the Hardanger and played, with considerable skill, *La Golondrina*. Seeking shelter, and finding none: *Buscand' abrig' y no l'encontrará*. There was also in my mind that line from the *Pervigilium Veneris: Quando fiam uti chelidon, ut tacere desinam*? When shall I become like the swallow, so as to end my silence? In life's equivalent of springtime, a very short period of venal expression is prelude to the shallow summer; and the fall that follows is always too late, the long winter of deaths too coldly intrusive.

Vera and Blackie supported Kris and me during the ritual at the cemetery. As the blue casket was eased into the black earth, my knees bent in weakness, and Blackie steadied me. Kris stood straight and firm, rigid in her faith, holding my left hand, while Vera's right arm embraced her. The mid-May sky had deepened from Infantry blue to Riviera blue, as it and its white masses of cumulus purity paid homage to Sharny.

Andy had invited Jordy Klug to both the funeral and the reception at the house. Kris accepted Jordy's condolences, which seemed to me to be anything but insincere and for which I found myself to be grateful. Blackie remained close to me, and Vera watched over Kris, who managed frequently to smile, as I neither could nor desired to do. Andy, very attentive to his mother, embraced her and kissed her cheek and forehead, rather often. Later, he spent most of his time in active conversation with Grayber and Jordy Klug.

After the slow and even departure of the guests, Andy put his arms around me and said, *Bear up, Dad*; he hugged his mother and exchanged many kisses with her; then, to my pained surprise, left with Jordy. Blackie and Vera, despite the long drive ahead of them, were among the last to take their leave. Grayber, having cleared the tables and taken care of the entire cleaning of dishes and utensils, played a few soothing tunes on the piano, and left, assuring us that he would look in on us the following day.

 Kris and I sat together on the sofa that we had long planned but never managed to replace. *It's getting dark,* she said. *Yes,* I said, and added, *It was a good blue and white day.* She agreed. Homophonous, I thought: *empty nest and emptiness*—well, almost.

72

Kris shared my inability to accept, but not my bitterness over, the loss of Sharny. Her faith was impressive. It gave her, even in painful sadness, an equanimity that somehow contributed to my own sense of stability. It strengthened me, although I was not a sharer in it. Never, during our life together, has Kris, in any way or by any means of suggestion, sought or urged my conversion to Catholicism. It has been as though her faith, in her mind, or in her heart, is quite enough for the two of us. She respects my distaste for organized religion, especially for all the costumery and hierarchical absolutism of the Roman Catholic church, but she insists that there is an ancillary and necessary order in organization. Evidence of there being many pedophiles among Roman Catholic priests had begun to appear in the media, along with the scandals and perversions of some television-evangelists and terrorist jihads of radical Islam. *Nothing is perfect, Hon'*. She added that every pill we take has destructive side-effects, every virtue is a seedling of vice, and life itself is a form of dying.

I thought of Dickens's Mr Morin: *vices are sometimes only virtues carried to excess*. We are all, like Kafka's Joseph K. or Camus's Meursault, under a sentence of death, without being duly aware of the crime with which we are charged. Pedophile priests and papal red shoes are excesses of, respectively, propagating faith and wearing humble sandals.

Kris told me about Gerda Weissmann, a Polish girl, whose story Kris's parents had told her. Gerda, in her teens, having endured a death march of some 350 miles from a labor camp (at Grünberg, Kris believed) to Volary in Czechoslovakia, attributed her survival of three years in labor camps to her creative imagination—looking beyond the present to parties and activities after her return to a life in freedom. That seemed to me to be a kind of denial. Kris claimed that denial was a refusal to acknowledge the present reality, but that looking beyond the acknowledged present reality to an imagined good was, not denial, but faith. She reminded me of my having told her of my own looking ahead from the reality of combat to a forthcoming birthday. Had I, in the darkness, pretended that there was no incoming rain of 88's or of Nebelwerfer shells? No; and then I remembered my conversation with Guinotte and my looking ahead to a sudden end to the war in the Pacific theatre and VJ Day. There was, as well, a talk I had heard Viktor Frankl give: he said that he survived the concentration camps by constantly thinking ahead to the completion of a book he was composing. *Was Gerda Weissmann Jewish?* Kris said Yes, she was—and surely I didn't suppose that faith was *peculiar to Christianity*: *it's universal, Pete.* She said that any organized religion, whatever its imperfections, was a good channel for the spirituality of faith but, in no case, an exclusive proprietor of it. (What she actually said, I think, was, All religions have faults, but any religion makes it easier to gain and retain faith, and nobody, no religion, owns faith.) *We'll see Sharny again.* Her saying this made me feel better; but I could not look far enough ahead to envisage that reunion.

 Kris's notion of faith had to be—has to be—right. It also clarifies in large part the artist's projection of an accepted present reality toward a transcendent reality tangent to

RAIN AND DARKNESS

Being. In my passivity, I had not the capacity for either mode of holiness: Sharny had ceased to exist and had become only a painfully beautiful memory; I would not succeed at artistry in writing. I could only publish my pedantry and continue to try to compose poetry and to turn my life into a novel. Sharny's death, along with our aging, was bringing Kris and me closer together.

Andy now wrote regularly—about every three weeks. *Dear Mom and Dad*—he spoke in his letters, however, almost exclusively to his mother, constantly offering solace for the loss of Sharny. He wrote from Miami, Washington, D.C, New York, and from Hamburg, London, Oslo, and Naples. He wrote much about Jordy, of whom, it was obvious, he had become a disciple. Kris was more disturbed by this discipleship than I. My apprehensiveness about Jordy was gradually giving way to a sense that, since my mother's death, his relationship to the Blausterns was something akin to wardership. Grayber and Blackie, particularly Blackie, in his letters to me, advised skepticism and restraint: Jordy Klug was not to be trusted.

Skimming Andy's letters, I muse over snippets: . . . *The Bay of Naples is a big, easy inlet. You'd like Neapolitan pizza, Mom; it's topped by anchovies, uncut boiled eggs, octopus. Dad, Jordy says I should mention a papyrus roll of Galli carmina, available to an elect few, from Herculaneum . . .*

Pines, snow, and the mysteriously uneasy fiord of Oslo; Grandpa would have loved it here, and Sharny too. Lots of fiddles. Jordy and I made three visits to the Akershus castle, met two of the base guys from Napoli. We'll go by boat with them to London . . . Very busy here in what must be the dirtiest parts of London. Jordy knows all of the Dickens sites. With tears and a heavy mind I think of Sharny as we trace the haunts of Florence Dombey. Jordy tells me to remind Dad of Lady Tippins['s] black list and blue list of lovers. So, Dad, maybe you know what he's talking about. The pines and fiddles of Oslo give way to daily rains and dreary darkness here . . . Like in London, there are dark, narrow streets here in Hamburg. Always we meet our base connections in shadows and narrowness. Jordy's German is as good as his Italian and Norwegian. What's the word, Dad? Polyglot? I know you don't like him, Mom; but he's way out of the ordinary; and he reveres Grandma Blaustern and Sharny. He has attacks of sciatica and incapacitating headaches. I wish you and Grandpa had taught me more German, Dad. Jordy and three serious guys from Yemen are trying to teach me Arabic. Nice vocalic language, but I have no ear for it; and the letters have different forms depending upon their place in each word . . . Here in the Big Apple we find again dark, narrow, dirty streets, and more Arabians. Met a couple of Polish guys. They started singing when I told them Sharny's name . . . The Declaration of Independence, in its showcase, is really illegible. Too many years beyond the original ink. Jordy sneers and calls my attention to the inhumane statements in it about the Indians. Hardly legible; but Jordy, of course, knows the document by heart . . .

The letters included more information about the base, or the foundation, than I thought Jordy, who would certainly have known about the contents of the letters, would have tolerated. Clearly, Jordy must have not only tolerated but actually have also encouraged the provision of information. Frequently Andy spoke of *Uncle Jordy*. This did not fail to disappoint Kris and me.

Have we lost both of our kids, Kris? Kris said that, of course, we hadn't. Sharny had completed a life, wholly: holy, sancta; she had fulfilled her life, as herself, as our daughter. Andy was making his own choices, not acceding to our choices.

RAIN AND DARKNESS

Nonetheless, as I looked at the strands of grey in Kris's hair and patted my incipiently protruding mid-section, I felt that much had been lost.

[My ability to invoke you, George, proves only an ability to invoke; it proves neither your existence nor mine. Come dream-bent down this gorge toward those gates that gleam in rain and darkness.]

73

In his criticism, Kazin was always alert to a novelist's failure to grant personal reality to any character other than his own stand-in (this was his recurring complaint against Saul Bellow), and in his journals he was often alert to his own failure to grant personal reality to wives, lovers, and friend.—EDWARD MENDELSON

Blackie owned four motels—the Blue Year and the Green Dreams in his state (our home state), the Brownfield and Blackwater in the neighbor-state (in which Kris and I now lived). The Blackwater was almost exactly half-way between the Konshaks' house and ours. Some months after Sharny's death, he invited me to spend a weekend with him at Blackwater. We had good meals, drank good liquor, walked down dirt roads and over park-land fields, and talked through the evening and into the night. We recalled the old movies, speculated about Jordy Klug, argued about politics, compared the capitalist's with the academician's style of living, and tacitly appreciated the nature of friendship. We realized the restorative quality of the meeting and made it an annual affair: *Same time next year.*

During the first year of George H.W. Bush's presidency, we talked almost exclusively about his predecessor, whom Blackie extolled and I despised. In his Hollywood roles, Ronald Reagan had rather appealed to me; but, as he carried his acting into the White House, my resentment dissipated that appeal; and his Hollywood performances increasingly seemed to me to have been mediocre elements. He came vaingloriously to identify himself with George Gipp, the Notre Dame football player, whom he portrayed in the movie about Knute Rockne. He called himself (as I've already noted) the Gipper, as though he had become the avatar of that football player's virtues. He borrowed, from then contemporary movies, catch-phrases—*Evil Empire; Go ahead, make my day*—so as to make people believe in him through make-believe. Rapt in swaddled awe, his followers elevated his cornball expressions—*I forgot to duck*; *There you go again*—to the status of original epigrams. Blackie insisted that my disaffection here was the infection of prejudice and that Reagan's facile mundaneness and ready Hollywoodism were parts of his style. That he had style and an articulateness that eluded mere glibness I preferred not to deny.

We shared contempt for the attempt by John Hinckley, Jr. to assassinate Reagan; but Blackie would not second my notion that Hinckley's act, in his intent therewith to impress the actress Jodie Foster, was appropriately within the context of Reagan's Hollywoodism. *That's sick, Ped.* Yes, maybe it was.

Reagan's ending the strike of the air-traffic controllers by having all the strikers fired had been lauded at the time by both Blackie and me. The labor unions had become bloated with crooked administrators and corrupted by the pursuits of political power. The well-being of workers had become subordinated to the greediness and power-hunger of the workers' self-serving advocates. The consequences of Reagan's fiat, however, were the movements toward the elimination of workers' well-being and that of the middle class itself. Blackie was not unhappy with those consequences nor with Reagan's ultimately successful drive to annihilate governmental regulation, the consequences of which would be a national financial disaster during the first decade of the next century.

Nancy Reagan's *War on Drugs*, one of the current misuses of the word *war*, was about as productive of good results as her reliance on astrology. *Come on, Ped; she meant well; and who doesn't accept his [or her] sign?* With that, Blackie gave me much that I, a Libra, continue to think about.

Insisting that Reagan, by accepting responsibility for the deaths of 241 suicide-bombed Marines in a Beirut barracks, should have resigned his office, I had to acknowledge the validity of Blackie's argument that the responsibility was, in fact, met by Reagan's immediate abandonment of an ill-conceived military mission.

A night-attendant placed more Scotch, ice, rice chips, and caviar on the small table between us. We toasted Vera and Kris. The lake beyond our veranda, spotted with starlight, grew moderately undulant beneath a dark northeastern breeze. The navy-blue night sky disclosed a meteor shower—the Perseids, seemingly emergent from the Milky Way. Attempting a joke, I invoked the Marxist Medusa slain by *Perseus Reagan on gigantic Grenada and the Andromedan* medical students he rescued. His *Weiss-Scheiss* retort proved to be funnier. A reply constructed around *Stokes-no jokes* seemed appropriate, but I was unable to fashion the conceit.

We argued about Reagan's successful Supreme Court appointment of the brilliant (but, to my mind, benighted) Antonin Scalia and Reagan's unsuccessful Supreme Court nomination of the Nixonian Robert Bork. Blackie was much better at arguing than I; he was also louder and more forceful; and he was effectively intimidating; but, like Guinotte, he respected whatever I had to say and never resorted to browbeating, even when I ranted, as loud and forcefully and unsubmissively as I could, about the treachery and injustice of Reagan's presiding over the sale of arms to Iran as a means of funding the Nicaraguan Contras. Blackie insisted that Reagan had no advance knowledge of the deal; I was convinced that such ignorance would have been impossible for a chief executive and that, again, Reagan was false to his own responsibility. Oddly, though, Blackie agreed with me that Lieutenant Colonel Ollie North was an upper-echelon asshole.

To concur with Blackie that Reagan deserved credit for winning the Cold War was beyond the capacity of my temperament; but I conceded that the Cold War ended during Ronnie's watch.

We had more Scotch, and a pot of coffee. The night breeze became cooler. We talked about computers, new movies, Cadillacs, and nuns. Finally, we recalled the night that Jordy shot at us; and we went on to reminisce about our days in high school and college.

74

Kris has never shared my antipathy to Ollie North. She thinks he's a nice-looking guy who did his best to do what he thought was right. When I question the morality and Constitutionality of selling war materiel to a hostile Iran as a means of financing the Nicaraguan Contra rebellion, she says I'm naive to believe that the Government is ever really on the level. *What about Kennedy's Bay of Pigs debacle, or the Government's interference in the affairs of Chile?* She says that the military-industrial complex that Eisenhower warned us about has fully materialized, and that corporations have become the *de facto* sovereignty. My repeating Blackie's objection to a good Marine's having dishonored himself, by obeying orders that entailed criminal activity and by lying to his President about what he had done, simply makes Kris chuckle. She reminds me about my insistence that Reagan had full knowledge of the entire affair and presided over it and that his firing of North was purely *pro forma*. Reagan was the villain, she maintains, not Ollie North.

Grayber tended to agree with Kris. A good soldier, a good Marine, obeys orders: North obeyed Reagan's orders and served as a scapegoat for him. The Nürnberg defendants, I remonstrated, did not get away with that. But they, Grayber explained, failed to draw the line at moral imperatives: a soldier ordered to commit murder or rape or torture must disobey; North's obedience entailed only a conflation of military and political strategy.

It entailed treason, I almost shouted [Open the gates, George]—or maybe I said it somewhat above a whimper. Grayber smiled and said that North was convicted of obstructing a congressional inquiry, accepting illegal gifts, and destroying evidence. The ACLU managed to get the conviction vacated on the grounds that his testimony had been given under the promise of immunity. Kris laughed and sought to soothe my sensibility by recalling North's defeat as a candidate for senator.

We were otherwise enjoying Grayber's Black Forest Chocolate Cake, which he had baked for Kris's birthday, the one we celebrated a month after my meteor-spangled night in Blackwater. The dessert was Kris's favorite. My gift to Kris had been a silver bracelet studded with three blue sapphires. She was pleased more with my giving her the bracelet than with the gift itself. She wore the bracelet during the birthday celebration but never, so far as I've noticed, again thereafter. At gift-giving I am a chronic failure. Kris was delighted, however, with the bouquet of red roses that Andy had wired her. The celebration included our playing of *I'll Get By* four or five times. The old 45-rpm Dick Haymes single had held up well over the years. . . . *rain, and darkness too* . . . .

Grayber asked if we'd ever heard the Frank Sinatra version; and we, in surprise, admitted that we had not, that we had heard other versions, but not Sinatra's, neither of us being aware that Sinatra had actually covered the song, despite its being the kind of song that he was born to sing. Grayber explained that Sinatra had performed it on a radio variety show. He had heard a recording of the show and would see if he could secure a copy for us.

Grayber was true to his promise. When the three of us celebrated my birthday, three weeks later, he had brought over the recorded program. We played the Dick Haymes 45. Then we listened to the Sinatra recording on our tape player. Kris dabbed at her eyes and reached for my hand. Four words seemed to translate themselves into something substantial within my consciousness: that old black magic.

The difference? In the 1952 movie, *Stars and Stripes Forever*, Clifton Webb, as John Philip Sousa, auditions aspirants to his band. A trumpet player renders a very enjoyable riff of *Carnival in Venice*. Webb/Sousa (/Harry James), by way of constructive criticism, renders the same segment, with triple-tonguing and contrapuntal flourishes. The applicant, in despair, picks up his horn and walks out. The astonishing difference in quality and moving charm is equivalent to the superiority of Sinatra's to Dick Haymes's *I'll Get By*.

The competent baritone of Haymes's rendition is smooth, melodic, steady, and mellifluous. Sinatra, however, with seeming effortlessness, creates horripilative variations, slides, drops, and easy subtleties in perfect legato. One can almost see Haymes picking up his music and making his exit. Much as I, in general, dislike Sinatra, I cannot deny that, with songs like *I'll Get By* and *Summer Wind*, he has no peer, he is the maestro.

Kris and I were pleased and grateful when Grayber made to us a gift of the Sinatra tape. We knew that we wanted to have it; but we have never played it again. In fact, we never played our Dick Haymes 45 again on birthdays or anniversaries. For some reason, which neither of us could articulate, we played it only intermittently, although frequently—particularly

RAIN AND DARKNESS

when black clouds darkened a day or when a steady rain fell from a twilight-blue sky.

When, a few years later, I confessed to Grayber our apparent ingratitude for his gift, he smiled and nodded. He said that Proust would call it *la garde du temps protégé*. That means, I think, watching over protected time, a kind of emotional proprietorship of, in this case, *our song* and the time during which it had been provided by Dick Haymes and not by Frank Sinatra.

My understanding of Grayber's understanding deepened later on, when Kris and I attended an exhibition of thirty-four of his paintings in Chicago. Twenty-three of the paintings sold readily for the price posted in the catalogue. Bids were placed on eight others, for which prices were not posted. Three were not to be sold. One of these was entitled *Rain and Darkness*. Kris and I spent what may have amounted to hours looking at it, studying it, returning to it, and sitting before it.

The oil on canvas is large (34"x21"). On it, a row of city houses rises in silhouette through a dark grey day toward an angry black thundercloud that fills the upper sky. Slanting from the lower sky to the base of the canvas, and across the entire canvas, were piercingly thin lines of blue rain. Grayber came up behind us during an afternoon hour, as Kris and I sat before the painting. He put his right hand on Kris's right shoulder and his left hand on my right shoulder. As Kris took my hand, I said to Grayber, *You've painted rain*. After a long moment, he said, *And darkness too*.

Grayber led Kris away to meet some ladies and to have some wine and cheese with Melba toast. They seemed to know that I wanted to be alone with the painting for a while. It almost startled me that Grayber had, in his composition, thoroughly caught the colors of my disposition—of my subjectivity. Blackie knew me as a winner knows a loser, to whom the winner is nonetheless a devoted friend.

Grayber knew me in a different, deeper sense, as an artist knows the person whose portrait he or she is painting, as Robert Hayden had come in retrospect to know his father: *Sundays too my father got up early / and put his clothes on in the blueblack cold . . . / . . . of love's austere and lonely offices.* Blackie knew me objectively and accepted me subjectively. Grayber knew me subjectively and expressed me objectively, on a level at which winning and losing were irrelevant. This is the level at which the introspective Andy Razaf saw the meaninglessness of racial prejudice in a world that obliquely insisted that prejudice was genetically meaningful: . . . *Wish I could fade, can't make the grade, / Nothing but dark days in sight . . . / . . . When you are near, they laugh and sneer, / Set you aside and you're denied, / What did I do, to be so Black and Blue?*

Razaf and Hayden nurtured their sensibilities, not in striving to succeed to or to achieve superiority, but in an ascent to their respective selves. T.S. Eliot has it right: The poetry does not matter. A road map does not matter, once you have reached your destination; and *the end of all our exploring / Will be to arrive where we started / and know the place for the first time.* [Much quoted lines, George, but always applicable.] Heidegger's statement flowed upward through Grayber's blue rain: *der Weg, der uns dahin gelangen lässt, wo wir schon sind* (the way that makes it possible to get to that place where we already are). Moving toward Being, and not toward being something, is the ascent to the self.

It doesn't matter at whom Jordy was shooting: Blackie took his two bullets for me. It doesn't matter that Grayber

RAIN AND DARKNESS

retrieved the Frank Sinatra recording: he painted *Rain and Darkness*. Later that week, I tried again, as fruitlessly as ever, to write poetry, confidently unconcerned now that the poetry does not matter.

75

No, the poetry does not matter: it has no specific value. It is what a poem says to itself that is of importance: this is Language speaking; and Language, according to Heidegger, is the saying of Being. There are Razaf's specific words, the particles: *could... can't.... Nothing... dark days... you... they... aside... denied... did... do... Black.... Blue.*

The antitheses generate the tension that elevates particles to the wave of Language. The reader, the listener (to the score by Fats Waller and Harry Brooks) graduates from the tension of unresolved prejudice to Language's undulant provision of death's prejudice against life. Woody Allen catches it in the black humor of his cinematic and musical blues: *There's nothing good about getting older.... Death is a no-win proposition... You die.... and you're gone. That's it... It's one strike, and you're out.* Dickens knows all about it: he has his Baron of Grogzwig peremptorily dismiss the Genius of Despair and Suicide, who has *coarse dark hair* and wears *a tunic of a dull bluish colour*.

Grayber told Kris and me that *Rain and Darkness* had become his personal favorite. We were both pleased to learn this; but Kris caught from my facial expression the fact that I had taken this as praise. In bed that night, she said a bit peevishly that Grayber's understanding of the reason why couples had favorite songs and his understanding of us through our favorite song was not praise. To be understood is not to be praised. Hitler's favoring the *Horst Wessel* song was a clue to his character; but to know this was not to praise him. There was something wrong with Kris's argument, but I couldn't work it out. Horst Wessel, the artist, certainly pleased Hitler by composing the song, which reflected Hitler's temperament. Wasn't that an accolade? Still, I didn't say anything, except to concede that Kris was right to contest my smugness.

There was that argument we'd had when we saw the movie *Hud*. At that time, I hadn't yet learned the unprofitability of trying to win an argument with one's wife. Paul Newman's character, Hud Bannon, is an unregenerate miscreant—a self-centered, promiscuous, adulterous, and generally vile person. His affection for his nephew Lon, played by Brandon de Wilde, who looks up to him as a *macho* hero, is blunted by his contempt for the nephew's conventional sensibility. He scorns and contemns the noble ethics of his father, played by an aged Melvyn Douglas. Alma, the housekeeper on the Bannon ranch, played by a very attractive Patricia Neal, is jaded but moral; she is drawn to Hud but leaves the ranch after he rapes her. Hud's father dies; his nephew leaves the ranch in disillusionment, and Hud is left alone.

Unrepentant and disdainful of remorse, he slams the door of his house and, as he turns his back on the world, pulls down the door-shade, carrying his smirk and shrug into his chosen world. To my observation that Hud knew and accepted himself and was authentic in wanting to be what he had found himself to be, in being what he had learned he was, Kris responded with anger: Hud had no redeeming quality whatsoever; he was evil and inhumane; he was simply an example of what happens to a person who cannot care about anyone but himself.

Forty years afterward, when I happened to discuss *Hud* with Grayber, I used my coinage *bio-litotes* to denote the affirming of one's self by negatively turning one's back on those who oppose that self. Grayber did not like my pretentious neologism, but he agreed with me that Hud's amoral denial was not necessarily puerile. He showed me a print of Arnold Schönberg's *Selbstporträt*: the subject is walking away from the viewer, his hands behind his back, holding a walking stick. Schönberg was about thirty-seven when he painted the self-portrait, but his depicted carriage is that of a resolute old man, bald, with sloping shoulders held stiffly straight. His suit, head, and hands are shades of brown touched with black, matching the color of the strong, old tree that fills the left third of the picture. The sketchy ground is light brown, variegated with a darker brown and tinged with the suggestion of green. The thin, almost imperceptible lines of green on the dark brown tree are like the lines of blue against the black of Grayber's *Rain and Darkness*. The autumnal cast of the oil, with its intimations of defeat, is belied by the intimations of springtime resilience. I renewed my take on Hud's back-turning, when the dust-jacket photo for Rüdiger Saranski's biography of Heidegger showed the black-hatted, blue-coated Heidegger seated on a bench with his back to the viewer; he is looking out over a blue valley, toward which he holds out a walking stick, in answer, perhaps, to the critics he has put behind him and in acceptance of the dimly defined valley's unfolding of itself to him, the valley valleying.

Stephen Holden writes, *It is said that as we age, we become more and more ourselves.* This is the case, possibly, because, if, in our youth or prime, we cannot ascend to the self and accept and assert it, that unaccepted and unasserted self will emerge when age removes the barriers to its manifestation.

RAIN AND DARKNESS

J. Hillis Miller, commenting on *Our Mutual Friend*, says, *Dickens remains true to his feelings that each man or woman has a fixed nature, a selfhood which may be obscured or distorted but never essentially altered.*

Beneath its limitations (lack of talent, lack of meriting praise, obtuseness, shyness, lack of dexterity, inability to dance), is a self, a true self that can accept and accommodate those limitations and enable one to turn one's back upon a world that defines one by one's limitations.

With age, the limitations broaden and solidify. Generational genes may have accounted for my managing with little trouble to teach myself the use of the typewriter: it was part of growing up in a world that saw the ball-point pen succeed the fountain pen, which had earlier succeeded the inkwell-pen and the quill. The ability to type lent itself well to the word-processing elements of the computer but not to the increasingly complex intricacies of the computer as an informational source. The computer became a tool the mastery of which lodged itself within the generational genes of the young and the very young but eluded those of most of us typewriter-age senescents. Wholly welcome was the passing away of carbon-paper, whiteout fluid, and all the tedium-generative accoutrements of both the manual and electric typewriters, which themselves became obsolete. Once multinational fonts, including classical Greek and Biblical Hebrew, became common, the production of my personal texts developed into a gratifying task.

E-mail correspondence was another much appreciated electronic gift. Once I had a couple of screen names (commercial and educational), the renewal of some old connections followed. The most unexpected renewal was correspondence with Carrie Coreghian. Carrie now had an endowed chair at a prestigious Eastern university. Her books and articles had won for her guest professorships in Canada and Europe. She had so far outdistanced me in academic accomplishments that I was almost embarrassed to answer her first e-letter, which, with great surprise, one morning I had received. After the initial exchange of e-letters, however, our old conversation resumed with ease and pleasure. Carrie, despite her patent intellectual superiority to me, still looked to me as a mentor and an authority, still praised me with an effusiveness that met my need for praise. We were both delighted to learn that we had selected the same number for our screen names: carcor52 and peblau52.

Receiving Carrie's suggestion that we meet at one of the annual academic conferences, I had regrettably to admit that I never attended any. She understood and went on to compliment me on avoiding the fulsome pretentiousness that characterized them, including, she said, sincerely, I'm sure, the papers she read routinely at them. Ominously, she confided to me that she was being treated for cervical cancer, as a survivor of five years.

Our e-letters were informed by an affability and spontaneity that matched our lunch-conversations of many years past. Carrie's constant praise of my person and my academic performance was a tonic to my self-esteem. The praise was not merited; but, most important, it was never insincere. When I asked her why she had never married, she said that, in her heart and mind, no one had yet measured up to me. My vanity, nurtured in this way, easily overcame my incredulity. We wrote to each other for about three years. During the third year, our e-letters became daily exchanges. Then:

RAIN AND DARKNESS

I'm retiring in May, Pete. The evil crab has found its way to my lungs, even though I gave up smoking ten years ago. I'm into chemo again. I'd like to have one more Robert Nathan-like spring, but I've laid my chips on Red 25 and the ball has rolled into Black 29. Your poem, BLUE STONE IN OCTOBER, which I recite to myself every day, means much more to me now—rivers and sand.

Without any gift or talent for poetry, I had persisted in attempts to write poems, most of which were rejected by the journals or magazines to which I had submitted them. Sending samples of them to Carrie was a kind of consolation. She received them gratefully and complimented me on their composition and, sometimes, but infrequently, recommended minor changes in a line or outlined ways to develop and bring a theme to a challenging conclusion. With some concern, I wrote:

Hang in there, Carrie. Cancer's not the death sentence it used to be. Retirement's a good idea. We're both now well within the retirement range. In a couple of years, I'll be retiring too. We'll write longer letters then . . .

In her last letter, she wished me a happy birthday. The letters stopped coming, and I knew she was gone; nonetheless, I continued sending daily letters, until someone, writing as *Carrie's computer nanny*, sent this:

Dear Professor Blaustern, Carrie died peacefully in her sleep three days ago. She was laid to rest yesterday. She wanted me to be sure to let you know and to offer to return to you all of your e-mail letters to her. She had printed out and saved every one. I await your instructions.

Roy Arthur Swanson

In answer, I wrote:

Dear Friend, thank you for your kindness. The letters belonged to Carrie, and she is gone. Please burn all of them. With heart-felt gratitude . . .

At that time, as I now in guilt admit, I was sorrier, perhaps, for the loss of Carrie's daily praise than for the loss of Carrie herself. What bothers me as much as this crescent guilt is my inability to understand Carrie's admiration of me and her strong affection for me. That I deserved neither in no way curtailed my ready acceptance of both. More unsettled by this unfeelingness than I am now by my ascribing to Kris phrases that she never used, like *pro forma* and *de facto* (accurate paraphrases, though, of what she actually said), I wrote, in our twice-yearly exchange of snail-mail letters, to Blackie, asking him if unwillingness to praise entailed inability to care. He answered:

Ped, I'm still sorry that we didn't learn of Carrie's death in time to attend her funeral. She would have been a good wife to you, if you had been sensible enough to her feelings to have loved her; but Kris, of course, has proved to be the right wife for you. Yes, insensibility to the feelings of others goes along with unwillingness sincerely to praise [I've corrected Blackie's to sincerely praise*] others; but she accepted that trait in you, just as I have always done. It's part of losing, Ped. You'll have to accept that, and you'll have to accept being bothered by that. Isn't that what your unrepentant Nazi Heidegger would have you do? Carrie once told me—and she was sighing and kind of misty-eyed when she did—that she saw a dark depth of loneliness in your eyes and that she wished she could replace* *it with a well of courage and confidence. I think that maybe you'll never have any idea of what you have lost here. Love to Kris. Vera has fully recovered from her double mastectomy; she sends her love to you both.—B.*

76

Kris has her health problems too, but nothing like the need for a mastectomy. She has had heart-bypass surgery, gallstone removal, and laser removal of cataracts. In general, she is aging well. She is heavier, wears thick bifocals, and jousts with arthritic flare-ups; but her complexion remains clear and smooth; and, with skillfully applied dark hair-coloring, she has lost little of her attractiveness. Now and again, I think of Anne and wonder if she has changed. She is always there in living recess, waiting, I believe, as I am indefinably and somehow not deniably waiting. The forms of denial are many: that is certain. The extent to which one, consciously or unconsciously, sustains them is a measure of one's ineffectuality. A loser is not necessarily ineffectual; but ineffectuality does necessitate loss.

Blackie and I enjoy moderately good health. We're slowing down but not quite ready to yield to retirement. Jordy Klug is exceptional: he does not show the ravages of age—not one grey hair, while Andy, his constant acolyte, is already greying. Jordy is still, despite his ailments, trim. He accompanies Andy on each of Andy's visits home, and continues to manifest both his phenomenal disgust with me and his mysterious connection to me, to which my reaction has remained an apparently genetic inability to dislike him. He has never belittled me in front of Andy; but when Andy would accompany his mother on one of her errands, and

RAIN AND DARKNESS

Jordy and I were left alone, Jordy would come at me with his arcane mixture of contempt and tentative edification. *So, squandered sperm, are you any closer to the Apennine holiness of Latin?* I had a vague sense of what he meant, and I asked *Dicisne linguae originem?* He smiled mid said that Language (*capital L, Heidegger's* SPRACHE *to you*) all begins in mountain snow; the Norse gods, the Aesir, descended the Himalayas and migrated to Scandinavia, where they conceived blue-clad Odin, who gave up his eye to master language, the runes. This was not new to me: I included such speculation in my Comparative Mythology course.
From the Sibyl, I asked.
From the Volva, ancestress of your mother. Volva, yes; ancestress I couldn't fathom.

Gallus, he said, saw the Language in deep mountain snows and mastered language in full reduplication. It's in the elegies, which he said I had not the keenness of mind to retrieve. *You can't ingrain the blue Female Force by way of adolescent lechery.* Gallus's Lycoris is his conception of the force; and his foundation is the best male approach to it. Christianity and Islam twist its political surfaces into fanatic conquests. The true roots, the mountain snows of politics lie actively in Lingua Domina, deeply undisclosed beneath the futile language of material conquest. Gallus's foundation has been coöpted by Islam and the Mafiosi; repressing the work of the Woman, they cause their golden galleons to run aground in greed. *Hey, Peter Oktober, do you know the etymology of greed?* Well, I suggested, there's the Indo-European *gher*—meaning dig, Old Norse *gjordh* meaning *girdle* or *clasp*, Latin *hortus* (*garden*) . . .
Less or more, he said, grinning without his usual contempt: the *chastity belt in the Edenic garden of the vaginal fig; the belt is removed and studded with gold; gher—becomes ghel—* . . .

Who ARE you, Jordy?
A presbyter of your mother, Periphery Pete, and your enemy in time.

Eventually we would talk about Reagan's initiating the decline of America with his well-intentioned attack on the New Deal; we would eat huge, heavily salted Bavarian pretzels and drink bottle after bottle of Heineken's beer until Kris and Andy came back.

Blackie was less puzzled than monitory when I wrote and asked him what he thought of Jordy's uncanny insight into my academic themes and his inexplicable reverence for my mother that continued now, long after her death. He answered with a very long letter that I just don't want to reproduce here in full. This, though, is the part that I constantly re-read and have largely memorized:

> *. . . and we've learned that he's a genius, Ped—a genius, but perverse and spooky. The friendship of his mother and your mother must have been some kind of holy bond, and his DNA must carry on from ancient Rome. Somehow he needs to kill his need of you. He would nurture that need if you were a genius and a winner. He knows, as we do, that your high intelligence is not enough to dispel the darkness through which you'll always walk. Andy has sparks of genius and the Luciferian will that Jordy can accommodate. Andy is closer than you to your mother in all but immediate birth. But birth is Jordy's criterion. I'm glad that Carrie never met Jordy. She would have tried to drive a stake through his heart. Tolerate him, ol' buddy, for Andy's sake. And learn from him as much as you can. He has a hell of a lot he can teach you, and he'll keep doing it, grudgingly, as long you use that darkness of yours as a sanctuary . . . .*

77

There were thirty-two movie theaters in the city when Kris, the kids, and I took up our off-campus residence here. There were also four outlying drive-in theaters. The oldest and largest of the movie theaters was the palatial Lake Park, at the south end of Crane Lake Park. It had been built in the 1920's, during the trend of luxuriously ornate movie palaces. Its Egyptian motif included, in its half-acre lobby, a pyramid fountain, Isis and Osiris wall paintings, a brightly painted limestone statue of a pharaoh on his throne, cylindrical pillars on which were painted Red Crowns, White Crowns, the Khepresh Blue Crowns, Shuti Crowns, Atef Crowns, and Pschent Double Crowns. The screen was framed by a massive wood carving, fluted and gold-flaked. Above the thick-plush silent seats rose huge velvet hangings; and the vaulted ceiling sparkled with stars against a deep blue field of sky. All that ostentatious glory is now no more. The Lake Park is now a *multiplex* divided into eight sterile, overly lighted compartments, each with its own screen. Five of the other movie theatres remain, as specialty houses or rentals. The drive-ins, despite their noble rear-guard championship by Joe Bob Briggs, have all disappeared.

Grayber (with one of his gorgeous teaching assistants—mini-skirted, corn-blonde waist-length hair, skin-tight jeans), Kris, and I went to one of the eight Lake Park screens to see *Groundhog Day*. Lilac Gustave (changed from Lillian Gustafsson), the T.A., and Kris got along quite well, in a kind of daughter-mother way. Kris liked the movie, because it showed the importance of learning how to care. Lilac was interested in facial contours and bodily movements; she thought that Marita Geraghty, as Nancy Taylor, was magnificent in both respects. Grayber and I saw Bill Murray's Phil as an inauthentic Hud, untrue to his real self as he yielded to the mandatory expectations of the Other. We all liked the Ray Charles background-singing: *but you don't know me*. We all liked the crisp rendition of Paganini's variation on a theme by Rachmaninov.

What got most immediately to me was the episode in which Andie Macdowell as Rita confessed her study of Nineteenth-Century French Poetry. My academic introduction to this body of poetry had been brief but adhesive. Victor Hugo was unarguably Olympian, alone on the seacoast, the night filled with stars. The Romantics, the Realists, the Parnassians, the Symbolists, and the Decadents—waves of lyricism, to which for the following few days I returned in reading and in recollection. Lamartine, weary of hope and rowing in silence; de Vigny, seeing Jesus among the olive trees that sough in the wind [in the fourth grade we used to sing, *Winds through the olive trees, softly they blow*]; de Musset, arriving too late in a world too old; Gautier, urging the artist to fashion blue mermaids; Leconte de Lisle: the sun addresses you sublimely; ensconce yourself in its verbal flame; go down to the lowest cities, your breast steeped sevenfold in the divine nothing [echo of Dionysius the Areopagite, adumbration of Heidegger]; Baudelaire, whose sky was as sad and beautiful as a great cemetery; and

Verlaine, with his strange, penetrating dream of an unknown woman who requited his love.

One nineteenth-century French poem had, in spell-casting intensity, committed itself to my memory: Arthur Rimbaud's *Sensation*:

> *Par les soirs bleus d'été, j'irai dans les sentiers,*
> *Picoté par les blés, fouler l'herbe menue:*
> *Rêveur, j'en sentirai la fraicheur à mes pieds.*
> *Je laisserai le vent baigner ma tête nue.*
>
> *Je ne parlerai pas, je ne penserai rien:*
> *Mais l'amour infini me montera dans l'âme,*
> *Et j'irai loin, bien loin, comme un bohémien,*
> *Par la Nature, heureux comme avec une femme.*

Rimbaud wrote the poem when he was fifteen. At that age, I was delivering newspapers at dawn and daydreaming of sensual fulfillment with a girl (sometimes an unknown girl, who walked beside me and smiled as the sunlight melted the morning mist). Rimbaud's poem assured me that my daydreaming was qualitative and not insubstantial. Over the years, I've tried very many times to produce a good translation of the poem, surrendering finally to my inability to render the alexandrines, with their abab rhyme scheme, in ninety-six English syllables with attendant rhymes. This infelicitous effort is representative:

> Through summer evenings all blue, on paths of retreat
> I'll go, tickled by grainstalks, to tread silky grass:
> In something like dreams, I'll feel cool under my feet.
> I shall let the wind bathe my bare head as I pass.

I shall not speak nor shall I be pondering:
Infinite love will surge in my soul and ascend,
And I shall go quite far, a Gypsy wandering
Through Nature, as happy as if with a woman.

The chiasmus, *Through . . . I . . . I . . . Through* [for *Par . . . Je . . . Je . . . Par*], works well enough; but *ascend* and *woman* do not rhyme, nor does the *n* of each effectively qualify as off-rhyme; and the fourth line of the first stanza, exclusively in monosyllables, is one *That*, as Alexander Pope says, *like a wounded snake, drags its slow length along*. Even Pope's bad example, though, includes two disyllables. To desist from further attempts is, however, not to be thought of. And, in my own blue summer evenings, as I walk alone along the paths of Crane Lake, I recite *Sensation* [Excitement] and change *une femme* [a woman] to *mon Anne* [my Anne].

Crane Lake was named after its shape, a fairly regular ellipse with a bay at the north end, from which juts eastward a long narrow beak-like extension. The lake-crane has no legs; but its discernible beak, especially appreciable from hill-site lookouts farther north, is a delight to tourists, locals, and art classes, including Grayber's. Lilac Gustave's painting of it, in blue, grey, green, and dark brown, won a national award. In winter, the lake-beak freezes solid quickly and thoroughly; and it invites throngs of skaters.

In summer there are many patches of rye-spears on the green paths of soft grass, and Rimbaud's poem sings itself to me as I stroll in the blue evenings and daydream about a Bohemian life with Anne. The years have muted my memory of her voice and blurred the contours of her pale face; but they have, proportionately, sharpened and highlighted my insight into a happiness-with-Anne that has become in my imagination an ideal song.

Grayber introduced me to the beak-paths during a summer weekend when Kris was gone on a visit to her sister. After her return, Kris accompanied me along the paths, but they had not for her the inscrutable charm with which they compellingly tempted me. She encouraged me to take the occasional evening walks alone, given my warm enjoyment of them. It turned out, on my part, to be a kind of infidelity: by way of the summer-evening air and the rustling leaves, my imagination brought Anne to me—Anne and blue visions of fourfold perfection. The paths were never crowded; the few persons, if any, to be encountered were intent on their own reflections. There was never an exchange of greetings; at least I was never engaged in any. Now, many years later, the paths are empty at night, except for patrols by police officers, in recent wakes of drug pushing, sexual predation, and rapes.

On the first blue evening that I walked on one of the paths alone, I re-experienced the mysteries of the Gift of the Konshaks and the Austrian night with Hedwig and Mischiato. Thereafter, however, a walk along the lake-beak was a walk with Anne, as, over and again, *Sensation* recited itself to me. Wondering in depth if Anne really existed, I would remind myself that Jordy had written of her to Sharny. But how did Jordy know of her existence? And, as far as that goes, who is Jordy? Well, Blackie can answer that. Maybe.

The cool grass paths, the crepuscular sky, my sense of myself, and the visitation of memory all came together in a Heideggerian fourfold: earth, sky, mortals, divinities: this creative coalescence of myself with nature seemed to be what Rimbaud meant by *infinite love*, or *endless love*. This, I thought, might be the fundamental religious experience: atonement with nature in a surging of love, the simultaneous general love of all and the particular love of one that Lagerkvist, the *religious atheist*, has written about, the holy land of his Blue Lady in Aftonland. There is likewise the particular love expressed in *I'll Walk Alone* [*I'll always be near you . . . Till you're walking beside me*] and there is also the general love expressed in *You'll Never Walk Alone* [*. . . don't be afraid of the dark . . . Walk on through the rain*].

There were long, solitary walks when I was fifteen: the paper route, the Sunday sidewalks of the city, the after-movie nights, the walks beyond the river caves and across the Levee, the walks to and into city parks. These were idle, self-indulgent, sentimental, but satisfying walks. During these walks, I stayed within myself and dreamed of sensual grace and winning.

During the lake-beak walks, I dreamed of Anne and multiplied my self fourfold. Without talent, however, in dance or song; with only passive ability (to gain the affection of certain quiet women or a determinedly attentive friend); without presence or strength of personality; I remained a loser, like Edward Hopper's solitary man sitting alone on a bench in his *Night in the Park* or crossing a deserted street in his *Night Shadows*, or like his ghostly clown in *Soir Bleu*.

To *Groundhog Day*, then, I owe the melancholy depth of what is to me this dusky, strange, and not unwelcome reverie.

78

Through a late-summer blue evening at the Blackwater, Blackie and I drank beer and talked about George H.W. Bush's successful Gulf War campaign, Operation Desert Storm (or something like that). Surprisingly (to me, but not to Blackie), Bush had mustered a grand alliance, rescued Kuwait from the aggression of Saddam Hussein, and terminated the campaign with brilliant finesse. The military decision not to pursue Hussein to Baghdad was a move of effective statesmanship. Leaving the Kurds to their disastrous fate at the ravages of Hussein was something else, however. Blackie figured that it was the necessary price for the clean cut of the victory. He allowed my point that the slaughter was a dehumanizing element of a war fought principally for oil. *But oil is the grail in the Middle East, Ped.*

Bad metaphor, Blackie: oil is liquid, the Grail is a solid

I'm using the compound symbol you gave Carrie and me; Holy Grail and royal blood.

Carrie, I remembered, was the one who had given it to both of us: *san gréal* and *sang réal*. At the time, I found it exciting; but, measuring it in comparative mythology, I came to conclude that it was irresponsible wordplay. Still, as I now acknowledged, the wordplay suited Blackie's usage: oil, the object of a transcendentally material quest, has become the royal blood of the OPEC. (And Mary Magdalene, as progenitor of divinely royal blood and sharer of the Eucharist blood from the holy chalice, has become the subject of best sellers).

The night's humidity, punctuated by intermittent dark rain from a cloud-black sky, had kept us inside the lodge in air-conditioned ease. At a table near ours, two attractive over-thirty women, with glowing highlights in their hair and partially exposed breasts, to whom I strove weakly to be as indifferent as Blackie was to them, directed inviting glances to us. One wore a blue, and the other a red, cutaway blouse. My undisciplined and poorly concealed gazing at Blue Blouse was fully taken in by her. They left, after Red Blouse went to the phone and returned to her friend, smiling and nodding.

Our Blackwater meetings, which once had taken place in late July, were now regularly deferred to late August. Blackie's summers were largely taken up with his new business ventures, among them a car dealership (KK & AT Buick-Pontiac-Subaru). A.T. was his partner, Arnaut Trenteneuf, a Parisian stockbroker who had relocated to a well-known brokerage firm in New York and then to the executive office of its branch in the Midwest. He had become Blackie's broker, and the two became friends. With the profit margin of Green Dreams narrowing because of its inconvenient distance from a new freeway, Blackie, taking A.T.'s advice, sold the property to a real estate developer and, in partnership with A.T., purchased the car dealership. The advertising for KK & AT was informed by early-twentieth-century Americana: on the radio, a jingle based on the song, *K-K-Katie*; on television, manipulations of the *Krazy Kat* cartoons; and, in the newspapers, juxtapositions of old *Vat 69* illustrations with *Kat 39* motifs.

Blackie, Vera, and A.T. regularly spent the second week of August in Detroit.

A.T., who was multilingual (French, Spanish, Italian, German, Danish, and English), had successfully tutored Blackie in French; and, as Blackie and I tried conversing in French, it soon became clear that his oral French was better than mine, all except for my enviable perfection of the uvular r.

He would Novy-shoulder me and smile sympathetically at my gaffes; and he once expressed what I took to be sincere gratitude for my not carrying my English-language pedantry over into French.

We talked then about pedantry *versus* intellectualism. Since I rather disliked the term *intellectual* and had never considered myself to be an intellectual, I did not resent his equating intellectuals with winners—*Carrie was an intellectual, Ped*—and pedants, or pedagogues (*Like you, Ped*), with losers.

He said that an intellectual is governed by the conception of words and governs their growth and maturation and that a pedant adheres to the arrangement and denotation of words and welcomes their stases, like a mortician rubbing his hands at his prospects. Apart from the simile, which I found abhorrent, the differentiation seemed valid: it came close to Heidegger's observations. This August argument, made palatable by Dutch beer, recurs to me as I now read Nicholas D. Kristof's differentiation of the true intellectual from the *pedant*. Speaking of President Clinton's *fulgent brain*, and making reference to Sophocles, Kristof says that an *intellectual is a person interested in ideas and comfortable with complexity and a pedant is a supercilious show-off who drops references to Sophocles and masks his shallowness by using words like* fulgent *and* supercilious. The tone of self-deprecation seems effectively to underscore the validity of the observation.

Blackie allowed that Bill Clinton measured up to the standards of an intellectual and that President George H.W. Bush, despite his patrician lineage and Harvard education, did not quite measure up to those standards. He insisted, nonetheless, that Bush was not a pedant and could indeed serve as President more efficaciously than, say, *faux*-Bubba Clinton. Blackie was feeling the effects of a severe downturn in the economy; but he and A.T. had full confidence in Bush's ability to retrieve national solvency. Bush's broken promise *(Read my lips; no new taxes)* was an act of courage, not a betrayal of principle. As a knee-jerk Democrat, I had nothing with which to counter Blackie's apologia beyond my dislike of Bush's twangy wimpiness and my admiration of Clinton's comfort with complexity and skill in simplicity of expression and my emotional inability to vote for anyone who was not a Democrat.

In November, owing largely to the draining away of Conservative votes by a likable third-party candidate, Clinton, to my great satisfaction and Blackie's muted consternation, became our forty-second President. And, for the next eight years, KK & AT Buick-Pontiac-Subaru prospered.

Despite the business upswing and Clinton's center-right position, Blackie and Vera detested him. They drove down to spend a Thanksgiving holiday with Kris, Grayber, and me; and, while all was mellow and well during our recollections of old times, the conversation about Clinton became bitter and recriminative. Vera despised the philandering Clinton and came close to screaming, as Grayber and I defended him. My only complaint about Clinton was his termination of the Texas accelerator project. His extramarital activities were his own private affairs, as far as Grayber and I were concerned. Kris took Vera's side, until Vera became shrill and had to be restrained by Blackie. The holiday ended abruptly, as Vera, in a rage, walked out of the house, with Blackie following her and then driving her back home.

79

Candace Schwarz-Bleiler crowned her national eminence in Women's Studies with a third book, which became something of an instant popular and academic classic. It won for her an endowed chair at a highly prestigious university in California. Shortly after its publication, she brought a copy to my office and, with a disarmingly warm smile, made a gift of it to me. Beyond my congratulating and thanking her, there was no conversation. The academic year was ending; and her departure from my office was the last of what I was to see of her in this setting. On the title page she had inscribed *To Peter, the better craftsman*. This was her ultimate payback; but it had also to be her gracious concession to me as her superior in English-language usage and in the translation of *il miglior fabbro*. At the bottom of the same page, she had written, *fn. 59—any relation?*

The 441-page study of men's historic victimization of women was entitled *Put Out the Starlight; The Male Trail of Transferred Betrayal*.

The epigraph to her book, encapsulating her thesis, was taken from Shakespeare:

It is the cause, it is the cause, my soul:
Let me not name it to you, you chaste stars!
It is the cause. Yet I'll not shed her blood,

RAIN and DARKNESS

Nor scar that whiter skin of hers than snow
And smooth as monumental alabaster.
Yet she must die, else she'll betray more men.
Put out the light, and then put out the light . . . .

The lines are part of Othello's soliloquy as he prepares to strangle his wife Desdemona. The *cause* is her supposed infidelity, which has been related to him in falsity and malice. Desdemona is as chaste as the invoked stars. Othello's regret centers on her physical attributes, on his loss of a prized object, with which he identifies his love. The death sentence is severe and perversely noble in its service to other men as a preventative of their being betrayed. He will blow out the candle and then put out the light that is Desdemona's life. The true light of Desdemona is the illimitable light of the chaste stars. Othello's ridiculous chauvinism is standard perennial male presumption, grounded in an incalculable male need to objectify and victimize the female. Schwarz-Bleiler takes up these points with many examples from myth, legend, history, and literature: Eve, Pandora, Eurydice, Cassandra, Antigone, Alcestis, the Sabine Women, Hypatia, Caesar's wife, Joan of Arc, Anne Boleyn, Blackbeard's wives, Thomas Hardy's heroines, and several twentieth-century figures (including Eleanor Roosevelt, Jean Harlow, Marilyn Monroe, and Sharon Tate). She posits the male need of a victim to be based upon the male's compensation for his inferiority by claiming to be victimized by the female: Iago is the embodiment of male self-delusion.

With her not entirely original thesis I had little fault to find. What disturbed me was the mass of postmodernist jargon and the total reliance upon translations for non-English citations. After seeing that the footnotes included no foreign-language material beyond titles, I skimmed the book without checking them out. They are not footnotes, actually, but endnotes—all at the back of the volume.

Initially, I must have skimmed over the passage to which footnote 59 was referent. In time, seeking it out, I read:

G. Scaltro traces the transfer of an ancient base, striving to valorize the female, from Roman counter-imperialism to eastern proclivities that maintained and profoundly aggrandized the subjection of the female to moral, mental and physical degradation.

Preferring that there be a comma after *mental*, I turned to the endnotes:

Scaltro, G., La Storia del fondamento espropriato di Gallo, *Rome: L'Erma di Bretschneider, 1994; transl. A. Blaustern,* The Perverted Base, *Chicago: Chandelle, 1995, pp. 43, 45, 59, 116.*

The juxtaposition of *Scaltro* and *A. Blaustern* was jolting. There could be no coincidence here. This had to be a project or product of Jordy and Andy. It made no sense to me that Jordy would have needed anyone else, much less Andy, to translate his own Italian. The only conclusion to which I could come was that, if this was the work of Jordy Klug and Anton Blaustern, Jordy had assigned the translation to Andy as an exercise. My need to obtain a copy of the book became as urgent as my weakness of spirit and my sadness (over a sense of betrayal) had become painful.

The university library had no copy. To write to Schwarz-Bleiler, now in California, was somehow not an option. My e-mail and subsequent USPS (snail-mail) letters to L'Erma di Bretschneider were neither answered nor acknowledged. Grayber located a copy of the translation on the Internet and ordered it for me. He said it was very strange that no copy of the original Italian was available from any source. He would continue his search, however. His interest in the book was almost as strong as mine. Neither of us mentioned it to Kris. It was my intent, however, to show her the book, once I had received and read it.

Grayber brought me the unopened package and refused to accept any payment from me. The pocket-size (duodecimo) volume was a 193-page paperback in 10-point print. The cover was in pastel blue with heavy black Roman lettering. A. Blaustern's page of acknowledgements included a dedication of his translation *To Gretchen, for her support and patience*. G. Scaltro's dedication page staggered me: *In memoriam—Anne Estelle Ihnat [1934-1994]*. For a moment I seemed to be blind, as my chest burned with pain. Sitting at my desk, stunned, I turned no page. Daylight turned to dusk; but I did not turn my desk-lamp on.

Kris brought me coffee. She turned the desk-lamp on. Handing the book to her, I asked if Andy had ever mentioned it to her. She looked at the cover and then the title page and then the beginning of the text. *Are you sure that this is Andy's work?* When I nodded, she said that Andy had mentioned to us his doing language work: *But who is G. Scaltro?* That, I told her, is G. Klug in Italian. She asked me if Andy or Jordy Klug had sent the book. Showing her Schwarz-Bleiler's book and pointing out footnote 59, I gave her the brief story of its acquisition. She showed no interest in reading the text or in the identity of Gretchen or, to my relief, in the identity of Anne Estelle Ihnat. Handing the book back to me, she kissed my forehead and returned to the kitchen.

80

Grayber had given me leave to enter his house at any time, except, he had said, on Thursday afternoons, when he liked to spend the hours from two o'clock to four o'clock painting without interruption in his studio. Today was Thursday, shortly after three o'clock. My classes had gone well and had kept my mind off of the Scaltro dedication. As soon as the last class was over, however, I hurried unthinkingly to Grayber's. He was not in his living room or kitchen; so I went straight into his studio. He looked back angrily from his canvas. Seated nude before him, on a green-velvet-covered chair, was Lilac Gustave, her legs spread wide in a Rodinesque pose. Unconcerned, she smiled, as I gazed steadily and lecherously at her. Grayber growled, *God damn it, Pete!* as he put down his brush. Managing finally to look away from Lilac, I stuttered and, failing to express myself, I held out toward him the Scaltro-Blaustern book. My pallor and pain got to him then; and, waving a break to Lilac, he Novy-shouldered me into the living room. Lilac put on a lavender-colored silk robe, followed us, and then poured out a service-round of Scotch.

When I pointed out the Scaltro dedication, Grayber steered me into his study area. Lilac did not accompany us. Grayber initiated a search on his computer. He brought up two pages on *Anne Estelle Ihnat*. There was her date of birth: *26 December 1934*. Various addresses (including the address of her brother in Flint, Michigan), dates, and a list of supervisory positions appeared. A bibliography included two articles in *Technolog*, four in *Feminist Account Record*, and reviews of three Feminist books.

Grayber said that he would probably be able to find and copy all of these for me. Then, the date of death: *30 January 1994*. My hand shook, and I dropped *The Perverted Base*. Grayber picked it up, slipped it into my briefcase, and patted my arm. He printed out the two pages and slipped them, as well, into the briefcase. *She's the* âme bleue *you told me about?* I nodded.

Here ended, then, the sustenance of a constant dream, the daydream of a life with Anne that was never to have been, *but always to be*. Here was the black emptiness of a blue futility. Never had I factored into this dream the element of death. Now here it was, in an undeniability with which I lacked the stamina to cope. Anne is dead. The dream is gone.

Grayber led me back into the living-room area. Lilac, completely dressed now, served another round of Scotch (*Hudson's Bay*, Grayber's favorite—Blackie's too). And another. Lilac had prepared a platter of canapés; these and the Scotch were moderately restorative. Grayber and Lilac saw me to the door.

Returning home an hour later than usual, I was met at the door by Kris. She said that Grayber had phoned to tell her that I, feeling a bit sickish, had stopped at his place and had perked up somewhat with a snack and some Scotch. *Are you O.K., now?* I nodded. Kris had prepared a pot of baked beans and some hamburgers with fried onions. Restored by my favorite meal and by Kris's unquestioning attentiveness, I was ready now to cope with the death of my dream.

Jordy Klug's deep reach into my life and affairs was no longer a cause for any kind of surprise. The Scaltro dedication must surely have been another deliberate means of eliciting my anguish. He had become a spectral enemy, an aura of evil from which I could not disassociate myself because it was consonant with my troll (or my id, or my Old Adam). He would know that the book would find me. Was Schwarz-Bleiler his lieutenant in this thrust? There was no way by which I could work this out; and Jordy would have known the pain that my attempts to do so would bring to me. Worse than either Jordy's creative malice or Schwarz-Bleiler's probable conspiracy was the possibility that Andy may have been a knowing participant in Jordy's diabolism.

In the weeks that followed, I regained emotional equilibrium, but not equanimity. There was now a dead spot that had to be carried and could not be excised. It infected every effort in which I would ordinarily take pleasure. There was still pleasure, but no longer enough in which to lose myself.

One good change, I guess, was my new sense of security and unity in the presence of Kris. It could not have been part of Jordy's intent to imbue me with this sense, much as I came to want to think that it was.

Andy, writing in answer to my questions about the book, explained that it was Jordy's way of answering his (Andy's) own persistent questions about the foundation, in work concerning which Jordy and he were engaged in considerable traveling. Jordy wrote it in Italian and assigned him the English translation of it. Gretchen Moehring was the widow of a Polizeikommisar (some kind of German police inspector). Fluent in Italian, as well as in French, English, and the Scandinavian languages, she had guided him in his work.

RAIN AND DARKNESS

Das Geschichtsbuch by day, *die Liebesgeschichte* by night. He did not know the identity of Anne Estelle Ihnat: he assumed that she was some relative or friend or mistress of Jordy. He didn't think that his mother or I would be interested in the book; but he was pleased that I had come upon it in my research. Yes, he would autograph it when next he was home. After I shared the letter with Kris, and then with Grayber, I slipped it into the book. In August, I would show the book to Blackie. It was not until late July, well before that year's Blackwater respite, that I began to read *The Perverted Base.*

81

Si bene jam faciam mihi, cara, semper, Lycoris,
sint tenebrae et pluviae et sanguineae caligae
in caligone in glacie sub montibus noctis...

With pride in Andy's work, but as a duty, Kris had read about thirty pages of the book and then had set it aside in a loss of interest. Grayber said that he would like to read it, but not until after I had done so.

The work began with an odd mythological prelude: *Set's imprisoning his brother Osiris in a coffin was not enough: he eventually butchered Osiris and threw the remains out into a whirling world. Osiris's sister-wife Isis traveled widely to gather up the pieces and reassemble them, all of the pieces except the elusive genitals, which she ultimately found in a distant tree, removed therefrom, and completed the assemblage. Breathing her brother-husband back to life, she instituted her own pregnancy, sent Osiris to reign over the dead in the underworld, and gave birth to Horus, who would effect revenge upon his evil uncle. The story reflects a movement toward Woman's reassertion of Her vital superiority and the physiological truth of the extraneousness of the male.*

Here is the opening of *The Perverted Base*:

Augustus Caesar's prefect of Egypt, C. Cornelius Gallus, found the Isis-reflections to be in accord with his elegiac expression of Woman's dominance. Lycoris is the name that he conferred upon his mistress-superior. Parthenius and Virgil admired Gallus as a friend and poet. Catullus, an older contemporary poet, caught up Gallus's elegiac spirit and called his own mistress-superior Lesbia. Tibullus followed with Delia/Nemesis, Propertius with Cynthia, and Ovid with Corinna. Only Gallus, however, related the concept of mistress-superior to a clandestine world order, which he propagated and developed as the fundamentum. The base, or ground, of existence was appreciated as a divine stream of female power, untenable by male strength, which was to be nurtured as a means of self-destruction, a recognizably futile opposition to the Female that would result ultimately in translating masculinity into fertile darkness kept alive in death by sister-rain.

The movement spread outward from Gallus's army, outward in all directions from the Mediterranean. Augustus curtailed it by despatching a praetorian squad to put Gallus to death. The murder was covered up as a decree of the Senate against Gallus's ambition. Gallus, like all prefects, had aggrandized his position in stone epigraphy and by periodic proclamations. He was executed, however, for establishing a religio-political force that has persisted, with vast variations, through medieval and modern times, and is now entrained, through antithetical perversion, in a profound anti-feminism.

Time magazine lay *zuhanden*. Tearing out one of its inner-stapled subscription postcards, I placed it in the book to mark my place (page 1), and closed the book, vaguely thinking now that Professor Landis's interest in Jordy Klug's Latin passages had led to his directing my dissertation and to my employment as a teacher, an employment that fulfilled, not promise of, for instance, a brilliant career, but, in actuality, Professor Landis's belief in my ability to teach.

Jordy, my natural enemy (my anti-self), had been the *causae radices* of my livelihood. There was a negative-positive connection between Jordy Klug and Professor Landis. Odd ramifications began to fit, to fall into order—except that Jordy had called Kris a *Polack cunt* (because she was *a complainer?*). A tinnitus became the sound of the rushing Lech; no, the rushing sound of the Inn; and Hedwig walked quietly in the night.

Professor Landis would have been very much interested in *The Perverted Base*. He had written to me, in as much excitement as his scholarly objectivity permitted, about a Qasr Ibrîm papyrus, edited by Anderson, Parsons, and Nisbet (Nesbet?), which closely reflected, if not literally reproduced, what he had called a demotic inscription among the Klug lines. My preoccupation with Gallus, which had waned while Professor Landis's had grown, now reasserted itself.

One of my Gallus folders enclosed handwritten and typed notes; the other enclosed Xerox-copied articles and chapters. Nothing had been added to either folder for about eleven years. Professor Landis's letter was in the first folder; I read it over (Nisbet, right).

Gallus came from Forum Julii in the Province, or southeastern Gaul, what is now Frejus on the French Riviera. His friend Vergil, like Catullus, was from northern Italy. Catullus was born about 84 B.C., Vergil about 70, and Gallus a few months later than Vergil. Parthenius, a poet of the sophisticated Alexandrian school, tutored Vergil and Gallus in Greek and presented Gallus with a collection of his short prose summaries of romantic myths and legends, so that Gallus, in masterly composition, might develop them as elegiac poems or even epics. He includes, for example, the story of Blue Horse, son of Pharax. The beautiful White Delight requited the love of Blue Horse; and they were married. Blue Horse was an inveterate hunter. He went out each day with his hunting dogs and returned too late to do anything but retire. White Delight decided to follow him one day to check up on his activities; she was attacked and killed by his dogs, grown savage in their having become totally inured to the hunt.

Also among the friends of Vergil and Gallus were L. Varius Rufus, a poet and dramatist, whose highly lauded tragedy *Thyestes* has not survived, and Asinius Pollio, another dramatist of great repute, whose works have not survived and who arranged for Cicero to meet Gallus, much to Cicero's pleasure. Cicero had attended a stage performance in which the actress Cytheris, whom Gallus will celebrate in his poetry as his dominating mistress Lycoris, sings Vergil's sixth eclogue, in which Gallus is presented as being patronized by all nine of the Muses.

Besides being a skilled and well regarded poet, Gallus was a successful politician and a commanding-general. During the redistribution of lands subsequent to the assassination of Julius Caesar and the proscriptive execution of Cicero, he was commissioned by Octavian to apportion the Transpadane territories, winning the profound gratitude of Vergil by enabling him to retain his estate.

Cytheris, who had been Antony's mistress, became Gallus's elegiac beloved, only to leave him for another military man. Antony lost to Gallus, not only his mistress, but also, in Egypt, much of his armed forces and naval fleet. Gallus, having taken and fortified a harbor town on the western edge of Alexandria, frustrated Antony's attempts to recall to his service soldiers who had once been in his command but now served Octavian and Gallus. When Antony tried to call to them outside the fortifications, Gallus had his trumpeters drown out the human sounds. Gallus left the harbor apparently undefended but had secretly laid chains across the sea-bottom of the harbor's entrance. When Antony's ships entered the harbor, the chains were pulled up by machines and the invading ships were captured or destroyed.

Octavian made Gallus the Prefect of Egypt; and Gallus maintained order effectively. He successfully put down an insurgency at Thebes and advertised his accomplishments with monuments and public inscriptions. Valerius Largus, Gallus's companion and second-in-command, reported this self-aggrandizement to Rome as arrogance and insolent disrespect for Octavian, who is now Augustus Princeps. The Senate decreed Gallus's disenfranchisement and exile. Gallus then, according to Suetonius and Dio Cassius, committed suicide.

Vergil's tenth eclogue is an accolade to Gallus, who is lovesick after Lycoris has left him to follow another soldier to icy mountain regions. He writes a hymn of Gallus's regret: *Where does it end? Love is indifferent, cruel, and as far from satisfied with tears as grass is with streams or bees with clover, or goats with green leaves. No matter! Arcadians, sing my demise to your mountains, as only you Arcadians can. If you can pipe the song of my bygone love, my bones will rest in gentle peace. If only I had lived among you as a simple shepherd or a vintner. I could have made out with a Phyllis, Amyntas, or some other hot-blooded honey. So what, if Amyntas is dark: violets and blueberries are dark: and she'd live with me under the willows or vines, and sing to me; or Phyllis would bring me flowers. Oh, Lycoris—here were cooling springs and restful meadows and a grove, with only time opposing us. But, no, the silly dedication to devastating war keeps me in battle, dodging spears thrown by the enemy.*

RAIN AND DARKNESS

And you—far from home and free from me—look in loneliness at Alpine snow and the frozen Rhine. I hate to think about it, or believe it. I hope the cold does you no harm and that the sharp-edged ice does not cut into your tender feet. Ah, let me come and play for you upon a Sicilian shepherd's pipe and sing my Chalcidian songs, the songs that I've arranged for you! No, I have to settle for suffering in the woods amidst the dens of beasts and carve my messages of love in the bark of sapling trees: and then my love will grow as those young trees will grow. Or shall I follow nymphs along the heights of Maenalus, or hunt wild bristling boars? Cold would not curtail my ranging the Parthenian glades with hunting dogs. Why, I seem already to run the rocks and hear the sounds of hunting in the groves—it's good to let the Cretan arrows fly off a Parthian bow—not that this could ease an aching heart or teach alleviation of human hurts to Amor. Neither Hamadryads nor my songs can do a thing; the very forest fails: goodbye to that. I cannot influence Amor, not though I drank the Hebrus dry or put up with its winter's cold and stood against the stinging sleet of Sithonian storms; not though, when dying elm-bark dies on high, I should drive sheep through deserts in the height of summer. Love beats everything; so I surrender now to Love.

Servius claims that Vergil had worked these words from Gallus's own poetry into his tenth eclogue. If he is right, then the famous *omnia vincit amor* (love conquers all; love beats everything) is ultimately the work of Gallus. Servius also claims that Vergil's conclusion of his fourth Georgic, a love story about Gallus, was censored by Augustus and that Vergil replaced it with the story of Orpheus and Eurydice.

Gallus lost his Lycoris and the rewards of his military achievements. He had won high admiration for his poetry and high advancement for his military victories. He was divested of his noteworthy prefecture, and his poems have not survived. He was, then, a loser. Vergil was a winner. Vergil had great talent; he also had great admiration for Gallus.

82

The Perverted Base recapitulated much of the material that my notes included, but it denied that Gallus had committed suicide and added the strange story of Gallus's international *fundamentum potestatis* (power base). It included an account of Gallus's Alpine pursuit of Volumnia in an unsuccessful attempt to win back his Lycoris: Vergil, in this account, fashioned a statement in sympathy with his friend, a statement he was later to use in his epic—*uarium et mutabile semper femina* (the female is flighty and fickle forever). The statement, however, may have been a rejoinder to one that Gallus had made: *omnipotens omnino et durior semper / femina* (the female is always stronger and all-powerful in all ways); so writes Scaltro. There are no footnotes, no endnotes; there is no documentation.

The urge to reproduce large sections of the book must be resisted, if not to retain some balance in what is supposed to be a novel, then, realistically, to avoid infringement of copyright: the book is still in print; and, somehow, I'm not up to asking my own son for permission, or to arrange the receipt of permission, to exceed fair use.

Brief paraphrasing of signal points, however, serves as accessory to a loser's plot.

In the Isis cult, Gallus found a salutary outlet for his instinctive submission to the female force. It was an instinct that needed to be nurtured by resistance. [A natural dyad, George?]: *dominatricis crudelitas, voluntas victimae* (the combination of a willing victim and the severity of a dominatrix). The world order should be that of insurgent male subjection to universal female sovereignty: a paradoxical sovereignty, subjectively hierarchic and objectively anarchic. Antony would still be an imperator, Gallus a prefect; but Cleopatra and Volumnia would hover in ordinal power. There would be no male *princeps*: Augustus would prevail among Romans at the behest of Livia. In same-sex union, the *cinaeda* would bend away to the *pathica, cinaedus* to *pathicus,* the praxic to the pathic. The active must learn passivity without yielding to it; the passive must accept his passivity while striving against it. The active is divine; the passive can, at best, attain to nobility.

Something echoed here, the faint pop-pop of a .22: Jordy doubtless knew that I could never attain to nobility. That would be his analysis of my being a loser. Hector knew, in his innermost being, that he could not defeat the Theteic Achilles; but, without once denying what he knew, he died trying.

Gallus's Isisism spread covertly, enhanced ineluctably by secret priestesses and cadres of male acolytes, west to Rome, Gaul, and Britannia, and east to Philistia, Persia, and India. What Valerius Largus actually reported to Augustus was this thelycratic threat to imperial *divinitas*. As a matter of administrative dominion, Augustus encouraged self-promotion and self-aggrandizement among his prefects and procurators, but the new order of a spiritual lamina elevating the female force had to be put away. Gallus was recalled to Rome, tried for undue ambition, and sentenced to exile. The trial was as false as the charge, the sentence a sham. A murder squad put him to death; and his demise was publicized as suicide. In melancholy, the aging Volumnia smiled and touched her sagging breasts with an arthritic left hand.

The spiritual lamination persisted, as all such movements always do, losing its motive, as all such movements always do, but retaining its force, now translated into its antithesis. The Christians picked it up, but Mother Mary and Mary Magdalene were transmogrified into mystic vagaries. Once perverted, the base overtly establishes its masculinity and the spiritual wave collapses into an imperial paternalism: Hypatia is murdered, and there is no spin or cover-up.

There are seemingly nine waves in all. The Isis wave could not have been the first. As the vestiges of the Christian wave elevated a tendentious Mariolatry, the Islamic wave succeeded and established a ferocious paternalism, or patriarchy. Fractious Christianity and uncompromising Islam demarcated West and East. The Christian remnants of the perverted base foundered finally in papal presumption and protestantism; and the eastern perversion prevailed as the undulant foundation. The female is tortured or killed in punishment for having been raped.

The East retains the laminal wave: the West has learned how to utilize that retention.

83

That the book is consistent with Schwarz-Bleiler's feminism did not displease me; indeed, it coincides with my own predilections in that regard. The weird notion of a laminal base or undulant foundation, however, has to be itself a perversion of quantum physics. Had I any genuine respect for the book at all, I should not have attempted to reduce its 193 pages to a needlessly embellished epitome.

Increasingly troubled by Andy's textual collusion—that is, he must have approved the content that he had translated—I asked Kris for her reaction to Andy's involvement in the patently anti-Catholic text.

Kris was not disturbed by any of it; she reminded me again of my inability intelligently to understand the depths of Catholic faith. My reactions, she suggested, were like those of Jack Lemmon in *Cowboy*: ethically perplexed when the trail riders did nothing while Strother Martin died from a snakebite and studiedly indifferent when the riders are deeply moved by the suicide of Brian Donlevy. The cowboys' principle, which Lemmon cannot understand, is faith: one accepts the life that is taken as having been fully lived; one mourns, as a failure of Life, the life that takes itself. Sharny's life, as an example, was taken; Andy has learned how to ride the trail. Here I embellish Kris's much simpler vocabulary, as I have somewhat embellished the blunt theses of *The Perverted Base*. While I see indoctrination, dogma, and ritual (especially the Sign of the Cross, which I saw a pitcher in professional baseball make before each pitch) as inhibiting life, Kris knows, or seems to know, that they forestall and oppose the failure of Life.

Grayber read *The Perverted Base* with more surprise than skepticism. He was especially interested in its apparent provision of a detail that I felt unwilling to dwell upon. The text states that two editions of Gallus's work are still extant. Papyri, *Galli poetae volumina*, having survived the concerted destruction of Gallus's works by order of Augustus, remain hidden in Libya. A fourth-century codex, copied from these rolls, was moved within Heidelberg after World War II to an undisclosed location in that city. When I had read this, I recalled Jordy's taunt about my failure to secure the treasure in Heidelberg; but, even over Professor Landis's awakened interest in the possibility of the treasure's existence, I had adjudged the matter to be purely fictional. Jordy was wise and intellectually acute beyond my comprehension; this I had come to understand; but he was also a consummate liar. The undocumented Scaltro book had a tenuous relation to legend but none to fact.

Schwarz-Bleiler betrayed a lapse from scholarship in giving it the dignity of citation.

A book published by L'Erma di Bretschneider, in which extant texts of Gallus were mentioned, would have brought the world of classical scholars into exhaustive pursuit, if there were any substance to the statement. Learned journals and classical conferences had given the book no notice or credence, not even bothering to ridicule it. Unlike myself, most classicists were thorough bibliographers and would certainly have known about the existence of the book. If

Schwarz-Bleiler cited it, and if, as the case was, it had a Library of Congress number, it should have been known to scrupulous classical scholars; but it had been given not even the angrily repudiative attention that Velikovsky's or von Däniken's wild surmises had received.

Don't give it serious thought, I said to Grayber; *it's fiction.*

He quoted a line from *What Maisie Knew: . . . fiction, through which indeed there flowed the blue river of truth.*

Not the fiction of refuge, Grayber—the fiction of deviousness, I rather weakly retorted.

Grayber thought that the lines quoted from Gallus's elegies were compelling. The few lines from Gallus that have been adjudged genuine are not, I objected, very good; any competent Latinist could invent lines of equal merit. Still, I lacked the conviction that would have satisfied my friend. A recollection of Mischiato's darkness and of Hedwig's dark smile inhibited me.

Grayber was taken, as well, however, with the Scaltro notion of undulant foundation. It is, he said, like the urban grey that informs Andrew Wyeth's rural current. My plan to take the book to Blackwater to get Blackie's reaction had to be changed. Vera was seiously ill. Blackie had taken her to the Mayo Clinic, where she was diagnosed with Alzheimer's disease. Shortly after the summer solstice, Kris and I packed a suitcase and two satchels and flew to the home city. Blackie had hired a live-in nurse; she was in her late fifties, stocky, grey, and dark complexioned. Her name was Nancy Sunday, and she had gladly come out of a dull retirement to devote herself to Vera. A day-cook-and-housekeeper was also hired, Rosario Sueña, an illegal immigrant—and a young mother of two boys born in the U.S.A.; she was also dark complexioned. Nancy was cheerful, always smiling, and gracefully slow of movement. Rosie was sullen, with lips constantly downturned, and abruptly quick of movement.

Rosie took our suitcase and satchels, as Blackie, having transported us from the airport, showed us in. Vera, seated in a wheelchair near a sunlit window, beamed slightly, as she saw Kris, and then turned away, as she saw me.

Kris embraced her and kissed her cheeks and forehead.

During the next ten days, Kris and Nancy became mutually affectionate; I learned a bit of colloquial Spanish from Rosie; and Blackie and I talked and drank at extended length. Blackie made it clear that he would never surrender Vera to a nursing home. One night, late, when the women were all sleeping, he wept and thanked me for being there.

Vera had moments of clarity; and we all, even Rosie (albeit unsmilingly), would lean toward her to lend her our good feeling. The spaces of blankness, when Vera stared upward, with her mouth partly open and her hands in her lap, were jaggedly disturbing to us, but most of all to Kris, whose rosary and silent prayers seemed not to provide her with their usual solace.

Three days before Kris and I were to leave—it was a Friday—I asked Blackie to read *The Perverted Base*, while I helped Rosie with some of her chores: dusting, and folding laundry. Kris helped her with the evening meal, after which Blackie was in a reasonably good mood; and, enjoying Scotch and mixed nuts and pretzel sticks, we talked about the book. Blackie was almost angrily skeptical; he was amused by what he took to be Jordy Klug's talents for sheer deception and angry that he had enlisted Andy in an unhealthy enterprise. *This is, of course, all bullshit, Ped.* I countered with extended mention of Jordy's apparently multilingual genius and his eerie familiarity with C. Cornelius Gallus. *Look*, Blackie insisted, *we didn't dig deeply enough into Jordy's real existence, but he's no Wandering Wop or Journeying Jerry or whatever.* Blackie thought that he was probably some kind of intellectual stalker, independently wealthy and internationally sophisticated; that he had singled me out for his personal attention, or as his personal victim, was doubtless due to his very real affection of my mother. *Real attachment*, I thought, although I did not consider Jordy to be totally incapable of affection.

Rosie's sons were American citizens; and Blackie, through contacts he had made in business, and, by indirection, politics, was arranging for Rosie's ultimate receipt of citizenship. Her son Manuel, eight, had been conceived in Mexico and had been born in Arizona. Her son John, six, whom she called Juan, was born in Kansas; his father had been Rosie's employer, who, already married and the father of two girls and a boy, had relieved Rosie of her housekeeping job, secretly saw her through childbirth, and sent her north with a generous sum of money. Her sons were now legitimate schoolchildren, and she had a moderate bank account. She avoided the informality that I had encouraged and steadfastly called me Señor Pedro; but I did get her to join Kris in singing *La Golondrina* to an unresponsive Vera.

On the Monday afternoon when Blackie was to drive us to the airport, Kris and I said goodbye to Vera, who raised her right arm in a vague wave, to Nancy, who kissed us both, and to Rosie, who simply nodded but then surprised me deeply by saying *¡Adiós, Pedro!*

During the short flight, above the green and brown squares of farmland, I thought about Shannon Estrella and wondered if she still existed.

84

Sitting in September on a bench beside the lake, I listened to the waves that were being pushed in by a northeastern breeze: Heimdal's amniotic waves in crescent nines: from slipping wash through serried splashes to a crashing break. Over and over. Again and again. *With nine times nine, and nine times over,* as Dickens wrote. The ninth wave is the big one, always a crash. It may be that history moves in series of nine waves.

The Crash of 1857 could have been a Ninth Wave, followed by Depression, waves of the Secession movement, Civil War, Reconstruction, the Gay Nineties, World War I, the global Flu pandemic, the Roaring Twenties, and, then, the Crash of 1929. Next came the wave of the Great Depression, World War II, the Thermonuclear-Bomb Anxiety, the Civil Rights movement, the sustained wave of Rock and Roll, the Sixties' Counterculture, the Feminist and Gay movements (achieving some culmination in the Nineties) . . . the Eighth and Ninth Waves?

[The Eighth and Ninth Waves, I would learn, would follow: Terror, and the Crash of 2008 (along with its great Recession).]

There were interwaves, perhaps: contrapuntal, or intercalary, like the assassination event (Lincoln, Garfield, McKinley, JFK, MLK, RFK, and three failed attempts: Truman, Ford, Reagan); cinematic, automotive, aeronautic, relativistic, Freudian, Nixonian Watergate, computer-development, Reagan-greed.

What are the Nines one dresses to? Why is a cat accredited with Nine Lives? Are the nine stitches saved by a Stitch in Time to be found in a parallel universe? Could any symphony (Mahler's Second, or Eighth?) possibly supersede Beethoven's Ninth? Horace's tenth year, the year until which one should put away one's literary efforts, is, in accordance with Roman numeration, literally *in novum annum* (to the ninth year). Like the last of the gestational months (Heimdal's waves, the nine Maidens of *Balder's Dreams*), September is the ninth month (not the seventh, as its name declares).

The Nine Muses wait in vain for a ninth note beyond the octave. Chaucer called it: *Eke wonder last but nine daies never in town.* Lars Porsena swore by the Nine Gods. Pease porridge in the pot is nine days old. Nine she-camel hairs are said to be an aid to memory; so writes Marianne Moore. And William Butler Yeats will have nine bean-rows on the Lake Isle of Innisfree. The three witches in Shakespeare's *Macbeth* go about: *Thrice to thine, and thrice to mine, And thrice again, to make up nine.*

Two, the green number of dyadic tension; three, the red number of logic and reason; and four, the blue number of completion: these are the numbers of particularity. In concert, they add up to nine, the number of undulance. Heidegger fashions my thoughts, but I cannot think like Heidegger. The splashes of the depression-waves set me at ease; the crashes of the ninth waves make me uneasy. Two students, a young woman in a white sweatshirt and yellow shorts and a young man in a grey sweatshirt and matching sweat-pants, jog by along the lakeshore path. The afternoon passes. Taking a last

RAIN and DARKNESS

look at the lake, from shore to horizon, I leave the bench and walk southwestward, in the direction of the sun, and go home to Kris.

It was Sunday. Kris had enjoyed lunch with her St. Veronica's Compassion group and had spent the afternoon at the home of one of the members. It was about two months since the group had met at our house. The group had grown to fourteen members and was looking for a reasonably priced rental hall. It began with just five women, who embroidered handkerchiefs and sold them for charitable contributions. Then it grew larger and began to deliver Thanksgiving dinners, and Christmas boxes, and Easter baskets to the poor, the jobless, and the homeless. Many Sundays, however, particularly late-summer Sundays, were given over to current talk, exchanges of recipes, and sharing of personal problems.

Kris, dressed now in blue slacks, white blouse, and rose-patterned apron, was cutting up carrots, onions, lettuce, peppers, and mushrooms to put into a beef stew. My moderately ailing memory, somewhere beyond retirement age, sent me to review and check over my preparation for Monday's classes. Where, I wondered, could I work in some nine-waves material. My Advanced Latin students were doing a rhetorical analysis of Cicero's *Somnium Scipionis*. Scipio's Dream: digress to Rip van Winkle's double-decade of dreamless sleep, and work in ninepins? No, I would have to re-read the story, and I preferred not to. To bolster my Sunday spiritualism, I played some Elvis tapes: *How Great Thou Art* and *Peace in the Valley*. Kris called out and asked me to play *It Is No Secret*.

Sunday dinner: beef stew, red wine, hot biscuits (with butter and Smucker's red raspberry preserves), and Folger's coffee. Having learned not to read at the table during a meal that had required more than cursory preparation, I put the *New York Times* book-review section off to a later time, and, after Kris's saying of Grace, asked her about the St. Veronica activities; and, when she had related her news and descriptions (*Janie Martin is going to have a knee-replacement Thursday*) and her silence signaled my turn, I pieced out my bench-reverie. Kris allowed that the sequence of nine waves might, like fallen leaves' always blowing counterclockwise, have some scientific basis; but history, she insisted, cannot really be shown to move in sequences of nine waves. She reminded me that I was always coming up with groundless and romantic theories of waves and patterns. How could I formulate contrapuntal waves of history when I am tone-deaf and have no musical talent, when I never take her dancing or try to master the simplest dance steps? My predilection for (her actual words were *hang-ups on*) Boogie, Beethoven, and Elvis was just a confusion of music with melody, like confusing a recipe with an ingredient. Kris meant well; she was not mean, merely impatient with my penchant for impractical fascination.

Complimenting her on the delicious stew and the light, flaky biscuits made from scratch, I changed the subject. We talked about movies and television programs. Later, washing and wiping the dishes while Kris watched a television program (a re-run of *Wheel of Fortune*), I thought about Austin Farrer's *A Study in Mark*. Farrer showed how *Mark* framed single episodes with two episodes similar to each other but not to the centerpieces. This had reminded me of the editorial arrangement of Catullus's poems in sequences of lyrical balance; in *Mark*, the sequences were in spiritual balance.

Mark needed no resurrection episode because the anagogic sequences themselves made it clear that there had to be a resurrection. My excitement over Farrer's book and my delight in its presentations were later flattened by an article that repudiated Farrer's idea of patterned sequences. The author of the article was, I think, Elizabeth Hardwick; I'll have to look it up again one day. If patterns are what we are looking for, she wrote, patterns are what we shall find—something like that. If they're found, I wanted to believe, it has to be because they are there.

Today, years later, as the Western world celebrates the 200th birthday of Charles Darwin and Abraham Lincoln, David M. Shribman, executive editor of the *Pittsburgh Post-Gazette*, asks, *Can there be a poetry to history?* He ponders:

> ... [*W*]*hat are we to make of this week's 200th anniversary of the birth of Abraham Lincoln, coming as it does in the first month of the administration of Barack Obama, the first black president? Mere coincidence? Or some celestial mystery whose message we dare not ignore?*

When I read this to Kris, who is trying with little success to figure out the workings of the digital camera that Andy gave her on Mother's Day, she allows that coincidences are the handiwork of God but insists that the handiwork of God cannot be reduced to human formulations or decipherable patterns.

Why not? My conviction persists, despite my inability effectively to defend it. Doesn't the attempt to understand the patterns of celestial mystery bring us closer to the Divine? Doesn't invention, along with the improvement of the human situation, result from the discovery of patterns? Art, I think, is the creation of patterns; but it derives from the discovery and appreciation of patterns.

Amy Lowell's *patterned garden-paths* and all the patterns of restrictive convention *lead but*, as Thomas Grey observed, *to the grave*: her beloved soldier died in World War I. She calls upon the Divine (imploringly or profanely?), *Christ! What are patterns for?* War, in its ineluctable recurrence, is certainly a pattern, the mysterious celestial message of which humankind dares to ignore and the secular application of which Sun Tzu and von Clausewitz seek to formulate. Patterns may not be *for* anything; they may simply *be*—as language discernible by poets who experience Heidegger's Four (earth, sky, divinities, mortals). Positive or negative, they speak to understanding, not to purpose.

My spiritualism, such as it is, includes a guardian angel. As an admitted loser, I could not have lived so long and so moderately well without a guardian angel.

Jordy's bullets missed me. World War II tolerated my survival without even a wound. Kris and Anne nurtured my passivity. Professor Landis guided me to a livelihood. Falls, accidents, illnesses, and failures have thus far not proved fatal. On this matter Kris agrees with me: *Well, of course, everyone has a guardian angel!*

Back to the evening of my bench-reverie: having put away the dishes, I joined Kris in the living room before the television set.

85

Blackie's letters have come regularly to include a dispiriting report on Vera's decline. He is maintaining a strength and determination that his devotion to her provides. Karla and Katie are uncommonly helpful to him. Karla flies in from Cleveland once each month. Katie, whose husband's stroke necessitated his retirement and her constant attention to him, spends each weekend with Blackie, Vera, and Nancy. Rosie's fine services continue. Denial, always easy for me, is no option for Blackie. Watching his wife wither toward nothingness, he salvages, unrelentingly, the importance to him of a life that is now limited to breathing and slight movements. His letters turn secondly to his genuine concern for the well-being and activities of Kris, Grayber, and me. They conclude with his assessments of the current political situation, trends aggrandized by the media, and restatements of his essential conservatism.

He fully supports the impeachment of Clinton and fears that the Senate will fail to rid the White House of its promiscuous interloper. My defense of Clinton—a separation of crotch and state—is based upon my conviction that any politician is entitled to a private life, no matter how lewd or low it may be.

Blackie racks this up to my lechery-leaning, another characteristic of the loser: dreaming instead of doing, aching instead of acting. Against my view of Ken Starr as morally, physically, and intellectually reprehensible, he sees a dedicated and upright lawyer of inestimable benefit to the country.

 Up to Clinton, each of us could admit some good in the presidents of our lifetime, beginning with Franklin Delano Roosevelt. Blackie allowed that FDR led the country well during World War II and served a generation admirably in enacting the GI Bill. He thought that Truman was boorish and low-class but that his presiding over the Marshall Plan complemented, in foreign policy, the domestic achievement of the GI Bill. My admiration for Eisenhower, particularly in his insistence that America had no second-class citizens and in his sending troops to Little Rock to uphold that insistence, grew ultimately to be ungrudging. Blackie approved of Kennedy's style and his space program. He liked Johnson's civil-rights legislation, chiefly because it transferred the solidity of the South from the Democrats to the Republicans. Nixon's removal of the bars to China won my support. Blackie liked Carter's intelligence and genteel morality. And I liked Reagan's style and articulateness. We both applauded George H.W. Bush's swift and sure handling of the Gulf War. But, while I could see only some venial failures by Clinton, Blackie could see nothing but total failure. The reverse of those attitudes would prove to be the case with Clinton's successor.

 Grayber was, and continues to be, more objective than either Blackie or I. He is more logical than Blackie, less emotional than I. Values, he claims, should derive from art and science, not from chance and politics. What we get from Hamsun and Céline has finally nothing at all to do with the Nazi proclivities of either and everything to do with the dark truths of their narratives. Great leadership is artistic and is

RAIN AND DARKNESS

grounded in scientific principles. Plato was right about the philosopher-king as the best ruler: Marcus Aurelius came close to being proof of that. Alexander the Great, Pericles, Jesus, Augustus, Mohammed, Charlemagne, Washington, Lincoln, Queen Victoria, Gandhi, DeGaulle—he named quite a few others, most of them beyond my concerns—these were the artists of geometrical precision and the scientists of the soul; none was a professional politician.

It was in this frame that he called my attention to the paintings of Edvard Munch. In Expressionism, color speaks with the boldness and accuracy of an undefeated prizefighter. Maybe he said *efficacy* instead of *accuracy*—maybe he said both. In *The Scream*, truth is the blue and black flow of the fjörd; I added, the flow celebrated by Ma Joad in *The Grapes of Wrath*. The red, yellow, brown, and olive noises constitute *false mortality*.

Where black or blue is separate (clothing, for example) or caught up in the loud coloration, it becomes false. Blue/black is the truth of darkness; noise is the coloration of deceit, the *palette of politics and perverse purpose, the loss of information.* Grayber especially admired Munch's *Kiss by the Window*, in which linear green window-wood and wan olive lights are defeated by a spectrum of blue/black, with the faces of the lovers taking on a blue that will suffuse the kiss by which they merge.

There's THE GETTYSBURG ADDRESS, Pete: the truth is the black of burial merged with the blue of limited resurrection; men living and dead—our poor powers—new birth of freedom. The blue I didn't see; but Grayber said that blue is inherent in all the gradations of sadness; *The Kiss by the Window* is awash in a cleansing and regenerative sadness. *What do you mean by limited resurrection, Grayber?* He said, *Judaism has it down: the winter rains, the spring rains, and the early dew of political renewal.* He added that he was beginning to see it all in the true music of the Blacks, the music of the dispossessed that is rightly called the Blues. Politics can have no true purpose outside of its derivation from art. Plato expressed his opposition to art within the constructs of art; he should have admitted this. Cesare Borgia was as inept a student of DaVinci as Lorenzo was of Macchiavelli.

Grayber gave me a stunning print of *Kiss by the Window*. Kris liked it, when I showed it to her; but she snickered somewhat contemptuously at my paraphrasing of Grayber's critique. His notion of limited resurrection, she said, was just *silly fiddly-doodling* with *Hosea*. Later, while she watched television, I read *Hosea* and began to see what Grayber may have meant.

86

• • • The azalea plant is great, Ped. My thanks to you, Kris and Grayber. Nancy says it's the brightest, healthiest red she's ever seen. Rosie has placed it on a stand within Vera's line of vision and she keeps it watered. She always talks to Vera—in Spanish—as she tends to it. Rosie's a full-fledged U.S. citizen now, oath-taking ceremony three weeks ago. Vera doesn't talk any more. Her eyes move, though. And she gestures with her arms. She sips soup and orange juice now and then, but Nancy has her on I-V most of the time. I keep hoping that she'll come out of this. Nancy encourages me with her talk of miracles and Rosie prays by her bedside every day. I'm leaning on hope, I know. But what else is there? You say that guardian angels are probably bound to the genes of the guarded and serve in limited gradations. Come on, that doesn't make much sense. Does Kris go along with that? Vera may well have been genetically programmed for Alzheimer's—but I can't buy the idea of spiritual genes. I may have a guardian angel, given my business successes, but Vera can hardly have had one—not during these past few years, no way!

So, I imagine you're celebrating the Senate's acquittal of Blowjob Bill. Specter ought to switch to the Democrat party. Most presidents have some seedy sex lives, but it's part of their job to preclude exposure and ridicule. Especially now, with the media catering to high horniness. A president should be able to resist opposition with dignity and strength, but when he loses dignity and respect and resorts openly to lying, he ought to be forced to resign. How high does a misdemeanor have to be? Are the criteria supposed to be *both* high crimes *and* misdemeanors?

No, I haven't seen many movies lately. I've got most of our old favorites on videocassette, but it's not good to sit and watch them alone. I watch news programs, and Nancy watches medical programs and cooking programs. Sometimes we watch a movie on TCM, but I can't get Nancy interested in character actors or their names or even in featured actors' names.

Reading? Not much beyond Ayn Rand and *The Wall Street Journal*, as you know. I'm still puzzling over *The Perverted Base*. You'll have to send some more details about your Gallus guy. Love to Kris, with thanks for her prayers—B.

87

*D*ear Dad,
    The news about Vera is sad. I know that she means a lot to Mom and that, as your best friend's wife, she's of great concern to you. Jordy, I'm sorry to say, couldn't care less. The flag-draper's got his problems, he says, and I've got mine. He does have problems. Near crippling arthritis and arrhythmia, along with testicular cancer. He's under the care of a team of doctors here in Rome right now. Doesn't trust the Naples doctors. Most of them listen to the Cammoristi. Cammora has almost annihilated the Galloni (Chevrons) in Naples. We've been working with the Basque ETA and a few other groups to undermine the C. It's hopeless, but Jordy won't quit. We're getting a little help even from some jihadists, despite the Islamic perversion of the Base. Jordy can be ruthless. I watched him shoot two Cammoristi in their ears. But I also watched him save a young girl, about fourteen, from being raped. He cared for her and is now the only family she has. This letter may take a while to get to you. I give my mail to Gretchen. She takes it to Heidelberg and posts it from there. Oh yes, Jordy says here's a Neapolitan verse in memoriam Ihnat, says you'll know what he means: *Vicin' 'o lago, facimm' ammore, a cuore a cuore, pe' se spassa.* Says he changed "mare" to "lago." I'm kind of getting on to the Neapolitan dialect. Kiss Mom for me, *cuore a cuore. Love, Andy*
    The Neapolitan verse I made out as something like *Let's enjoy ourselves, in making love beside the lake.* Jordy has

a weird sensibility; I chose to be pleased by his message. The Chevrons, Andy would later explain, were a mere vestige of the foundation, which was now all but absorbed by the various ideological movements that had reversed its feminism completely. Jordy's health problems surprised and curiously disheartened me. He was, in some figurative way, the antithesis of my guardian angel; but I had learned by now that life pretty much depended on the sustenance of the antithetical tension.

Grayber says that this is the vibrant tension of art. Look at a Hopper, he says; the individuals, either alone (divested of communication) or in a frame with one or two others, may be ineffectively communicative; but they are *not* lonely.

Hopper himself did not understand how all this loneliness business came about in interpretations of his work. The need and the inability to communicate undergo resolution, through heightened acceptance of the tension, in the authentic person. Great art is fully authentic human expression. Of all this I managed at least an inchoate sense. It occurred to me that, if I had become a disciple of Jordy, as Andy had so become, I might have gained a real mastery of languages—and an ability better to comprehend Heidegger; but, no, Jordy would always be my enemy, as Blackie always would be my friend.

A *true enemy*, writes Fanny Howe, *sees you as symbol rather than a whole*. To Jordy I must represent, or may represent, that fragment of himself susceptible to the fatal infection of imperfection. Does Howe postulate a true friend? Not in what I have read of her work thus far. She writes in a soft, flowing, lucid prose that is not without faults. Passivity does not set her up securely as perhaps it may do for me: . . . *I was handed a book by a French writer* . . . Did someone hand her a book that was written by a French person, or, did a French person hand her a book? The ambiguity is resolved by the remainder of the sentence; but it gets the sentence off to a limp. Why not *Someone gave me a book that was the work of a French writer?* The active voice precludes the stumbling ambiguity. She does not attempt to retreat from the trying *try and stay*. She cites a Benedictine monk's citation of Bartrhari's *grammar leads* to *God*. It is important, now, that I secure an exposition of the fifth-century Indian philosopher's work. My guardian angel presides over the sanctity of infinitives. It would be good to know Fanny Howe, who, thrice married, is fifteen years my junior. As a teacher, *she walked a lot along along / The river bank*. Am I meant to ask if *along along* should be *alone along*, as at the non-conclusion of *Finnegans Wake?*

Kris would not like the writings of Fanny Howe, who posits the indisputable mortality of Jesus. Kris would have been, however, long before Howe's *The Winter Sun* appeared, interested in Andy's letter; but she was off to see her ailing sister, undergoing radiation treatment after chemotherapy. Kris's parents had joined my parents in death; and she, with her sister, long ensconced in religious orders, were, apart from a childless widower uncle, who was fading away in a Cleveland nursing home, the last of the Skoczny-Nadobnys.

With Kris gone, the house, despite the glow of floor– and end-table-lamps, was dark. The silence was dark. It helped somewhat to play Elvis's *Sentimental Me* and Haymes's *I'll Get By*.

Gradually, though, the pain of emptiness urged me out. The September night was chilly with the promise of fall. Past the closing shops and brightly lit fast-food stops, I walked alone along the lakeshore. Tentative daydreams gave way to the insistent realization that much was now long gone and beyond any kind of recovery save that of re-imagining. The many options of youth and maturity no longer existed. Death was editing my existence. [Open the gates, George.] Family members, acquaintances, friends, and celebrities, those with whom I had identified my interests, were ceasing to exist. The Christmas-card list grew shorter, with fewer additions now than deletions.

 The sky above the trees and over the lake was black with night-cloud. It was chilly, but I sat on a bench and watched a thin thread of lightning signal a soft roll of thunder. My night thoughts led, not to philosophic introspection, but to a recollection of Gloria Holden as *Dracula's Daughter*. Was Nan Grey in that movie? Yes—as a deliciously pretty victim; she must have been in her late teens then. And pale Irving Pichel. And old reliable Edward Van Sloan, Blackie's favorite. Even Hedda Hopper. Fear-fat Billy Bevan. Stately, dull Halliwell Hobbes. Vampires, a Hollywood element, in steady demand. I thought of Anne Rice's ingenious juxtaposition of *expect* and *except*, a literal metathesis, just right in the context of vampirescence. She shouldn't have followed it, though, with the redundant *luminous sheen*. One letter-change would have elevated the context: *numinous sheen*. Still, *new and strange*, evoking Shakespeare's *sea change*, is just right. It began to rain.

 The sprinkling was light. Walking back to town, I felt painfully empty again, alone and longing for a Kris who was away, for an Anne who was no more, and for a Blackie whose sole preoccupation now was with Vera, as she slipped away. *Sue Gill's Bar and Grill* was open. As the rain increased to nettlesome pellets, I went in and sat at a small table by the front window. There was only one other customer. He was drinking beer at the bar and shaking dice with the bartender. The kitchen-woman, doubling as waitress, brought me a

RAIN AND DARKNESS

menu; I waved it off and said I wanted only a chilled vodka, straight up with a twist, and some pretzel sticks.

The rain came down finally in fierce lines, turned cobalt in color by the red and blue neon lights of *Sue Gill's*. As the wind brought it against the windows, I thought of vicious vampire teeth, narrowed to sliver-fangs, piercing the earth and drawing out its pale blood. *Sue Gill: sugillare* (to taunt, revile; to beat black and blue). Guardian angels, I decided, cannot dispel despair; their protection is limited to the maintenance of physical well-being. The dark angels of reptile rapture are free to induce despair, to suggilate the soul.

After I'd had two more vodkas, the rain moved out. Two laughing and chattering couples came in, brushing off and shaking their wet clothes. Their noise was all wrong for my melancholy—I paid the waitress and left. The rain-wet streets glowed under the streetlights and reminded me of my lonely homeward walks from late-night movies long ago. Brown leaves fallen from birch and maple trees were glued by rain to the sidewalks. There were no streetlights near my house, which was dark and empty as I entered it.

88

Lilian Pizzichini has entitled her biography of Jean Rhys *The Blue Hour*; this was the name of Rhys's preferred perfume and it denoted the twilight hour, when Rhys the lapdog became Rhys the wolf—and *blue* intoned gloom. For a long time I thought of the September evening at the *Sue Gillis* as a blue hour; but, just as the Pfaffenhofen dawn changed from a grey to a silver memory, so that Blue Hour became the Black Hour: a night of Three Vodkas, after which I was never quite the same—actually, the moment in which I felt fully the irreversibility of age. Kris was away; she would come back; the black hole [Open the gates, George] that developed in her absence drew all my ambition-informed options irretrievably toward a light-incarcerating singularity. The words that Catullus gave to Ariadne came to mind: *nulla fugae ratio, nulla spes; omnia muta, omnia sunt deserta, ostentant omnia letum*: no relief, no hope: everything's changed, everything's empty, everything reeks of ruin.

A dream I'd had at the beginning of Reagan's reign also came to mind: bound and held prostrate in the dark, I knew that a bullet was to be fired into my head; there was a soft thump as it was fired into the back of my neck; but I did not die, and there was no pain; the act of dreaming, even of one's death, is a hold on life.

Likewise, that September night's realization of loss, along with the depression it brought, was a hold on life.

RAIN AND DARKNESS

Before the retreat to that grey dawn of Pfaffenhofen, there had been the strident screeching of shells shot from 88's as we clawed the cold ground and then heard the explosions about a half-mile behind us. Then closer. You don't hear the one that hits you, we had learned. In the hearing, as in the realization and the dreaming, one holds life at mind's length.

Between the grey dawn and the Black Hour, a life had gone by—long in calendar years, short in temporal grasp. Is the realization of loss something other than loss, as the dreaming of one's execution is something other than death? One cannot die within a dream; one cannot dream within death. One can continue to play the game, within the realization that one is a loser: everything's different, everything's hollow, everything's a sign of death.

It had been possible to imbue students with abilities they otherwise did not have by convincing them that I believed they had those abilities. This was the way by which Professor Landis led me through my doctoral work. This became the way of my teaching. When those students, many of them, went on to surpass me in scholarship and accomplishment, I could follow through with merited praise only reluctantly and in pretense. Jealousy? Perhaps. It is more, though, of what Blackie said: a need for praise that is greater than a willingness to praise. During a rainy night, my need foundered in darkness. Kris was away. Blackie was attending his dying wife. Grayber was making out with another of his model-assistants. *Omnia sunt deserta.*

Sleep came that night, but with it came my recurrent dream of being unable to find the car that I had parked and the frustration that caused me to wake up and get up just before three in the morning. Taking my 100-proof Smirnoff's from the freezer, I made my belated fourth vodka and put on a tape of Ariadne's prayer in Strauss's *Ariadne auf Naxos*. Ariadne envisages Bacchus in the Death-realm and calls upon him to transport her there, where all is pure, because *Hier ist nichts rein; hier kam alles zu allem* (Nothing is pure here; everything is ended here). She wants Bacchus, as the god of Darkness, to lie upon her eyes and in her heart *(Dunkel wird auf meinen Augen und in meinem Herzen sein)*. Bacchus/Dionysus, the god of wine, of Darkness, of vodka . . . . blue darkness: blue (sadness, perfection); darkness (death, perfection).

After turning off the tape and taking the stem glass to the kitchen, I sat back in the recliner and found at last the ease of a long sleep.

Now I read Lilian Pizzichini's account of Jean Rhys's return to Dominica: . . . *everything always changes . . . Her thoughts were of death . . . There was nothing left*. But that return was in February, 1936; and Jean Rhys was to live for forty-six more years, dying in May, three months before her eighty-ninth birthday.

Sunday morning sunshine, making a long Hopperesque yellow rectangle across the brown carpet, was pleasant in its bleakness as I oriented myself upon waking. There was Kris Kristofferson's *somethin' in a Sunday makes a body feel alone*—especially if one is alone. And Wallace Stevens's *Sunday Morning: . . . We live in an old chaos of the sun . . .* There was Lou Reed's *It's nothing at all / Sunday Morning / Sunday Morning*. Hopper's Apollonian sunshine, lavishing its lecherous light upon a nude Daphnean world . . .

In the kitchen, as the stem glass waited for its wash, I made some strong coffee and drank it black. Two fried eggs, with sliced raw onions and French's yellow mustard, sandwiched into slices of fresh white bread, completed my breakfast. As I

RAIN AND DARKNESS

was idling through the Sunday paper, Grayber called to invite me to a late lunch: *2:30, 3:00, veal parmigiana, Chianti, nuts, maybe some spumoni.*

After a long, hot shower; dressing in black flannel slacks and a loose-fitting light blue sweatshirt; and spending an hour with Stevens's *The Man With the Blue Guitar* in the leather-cushioned wicker chair on the sun-warmed porch, I felt prepared *to meet the day*, as Kristofferson did, in song, and even to hear *a lonely bell* echoing from the lakeside *like the disappearin' dreams of yesterday.*

Grayber's excellent meal and his grin-inducing, sometimes cachinnating, conversation were restoratives. He saw my Stevensian sinking *downward to darkness* as akin to Bunyan's *slough of despond* or San Juan de la Cruz's *noche oscura*. But it wasn't a matter of sin or the soul, as I tried to explain it. We settled on the nausea of Sartre's Roquentin as he confronted the roots of the chestnut tree: masses of meaningless existence, tons and tons of it. We agreed that loneliness is the meaninglessness of being alone. Grayber went to his library-room and returned with his copy of Sartre's novel. We checked out a number of passages. Grayber likes the episode of the autodidact and the Corsican. My interest is always in the word choices: the mauve suspenders *enfouies* (hidden away) in Adolphe's blue shirt; *un mur chocolat* (a wall that looked like chocolate); a black neck; a Negress singing *Some of these days / You'll miss me, honey* (Grayber and I agree that Sartre doesn't have the song quite right: it's probably, *One of these days you're gonna miss me, Honey*—or is it *Some one of these days . . . ?*); *. . . je vis que l'écorce était restée noire* (I saw that the bark stayed black); *. . . le noir, comme le cercle, n'existait pas* (like the circle, black didn't exist); *. . . on pouvait* *croire qu'il y avait au monde du vrai blue* (one might believe that there was, in the world, true blue}.

    Grayber poured out the last of the Chianti and toasted Black, which doesn't exist. Raising my glass, I said, *To black, which is non-existence—and to blue, and the blues.* We moved to the comfortable bergères in the living room, where we turned to chilled Boodles (straight up, with a twist). Grayber had succeeded in removing me from what we decided to call my chestnut slough. We talked on past twilight—about movies, modern artists, Heidegger's Four, Sartre's *en soi* and *pour soi*, Milton's lost eyesight, and Beethoven's lost hearing. It was a little after 8:00 when Grayber walked me home, the Boodles having made me far less steady than it made my host, upon whom it seemed to have had no effect beyond heightened geniality. Books and notes lay ready on the study table; but there would be no preparation for tomorrow's classes. No matter: winging it had long by now become a bent of second nature. My sleep that night was deep and dream-free.

    Monday morning's first class, at 10:30, was the Seminar: Caesar (four graduate students and two seniors). We were just over midway through the first book of the *Gallic War*; but I yielded to mood and asked the students to turn ahead to Book Five: *Omnes vero se Britanni vitro inficiunt, quod caeruleum efficit colorem, atque hoc horridiores sunt in pugna aspectu* (Now, all the Britons paint themselves with a mustard-plant dye that produces a blue coloring, and in this way become more frightening in combat). We noted, first, the music of the triple alliteration: *vero . . . vitro-caeruleum . . . colorem-hoc horridiores.* with its emphatic umbilicus, *blue . . . coloring.* Somehow, I needed to talk about *blue*: the color that terrifies (in battle), deceives (Odin's disguise), sanctifies (Krishna, the Virgin Mary, Israel, Georg

Trakl's poetry), and, as Holiness, transcends all things holy (Heidegger). The class was apparently with me, going so far as to find, if not magic in Walter Donaldson's music, then perhaps profundity in George Whiting's lyrics: *A turn to the right / A little white light /// . . . lead . . . to My Blue Heaven . . . . / . . . a smiling face, / A fire-place, a cozy room, / A little nest . . . where the roses bloom* . . . Heaven (holiness) is, not the blue sky, but the coziness of a warm room in the vicinity of blooming roses. Sentimental slush? Maybe, in the Roaring Twenties, in the hard-boiled prose of Ernest Hemingway and his one-dimensional use of the n-word, but not in the multidimensional thought of Joyce, Eliot, de Beauvoir, and Heidegger.

We compare the etymologies: *caeruleus* is from Latin *caelum* (sky); it also means *dark* and can be used negatively, as Vergil uses it. The Greek for *blue* is *cyanos* (a dark blue substance), *cyane* (a blue, grainfield flower; a bachelor's button); it can also mean *black*.

Seeing at length that the students were following this digression only politely and patiently, I turned back to our place in the narrative: *In castris Helvetiorum tabulae repertae sunt litteris Graecis confectae* . . . (In the camp of the Helvetii some lists written in Greek letters were found . . .). Why is there Greek transcription in this area that would come to be called Switzerland? This question interested the students much more than the nowhere-ness of *My Blue Heaven*. Did it relate to the Aryan wave northwestward to Scandinavia, to Asians and Aesir, to bovine holiness and Audhumla? The discussion became lively; and the active classroom, after Grayber's good cheer, had brought me back from emptiness.

During the next two weeks, I worked well. Completing an article on Caesasr's *nostros* (use of the first-person plural in third-person narrative), I felt satisfied enough to submit it to a refereed journal. (Later, after it had been rejected by two refereed journals *as lacking in scholarly substance* and *misreading a matter of narrative convention*, I still look back with pleasure to the feeling of satisfaction its completion had conferred upon me.) Grayber, having invited some colleagues and graduate students, arranged a birthday party for me.

Kris returned in late October. We drove home from the airport in a cold rain. Grayber brought a casserole of scalloped potatoes and ham, baked cod, freshly baked dinner rolls, and *Blue Nun* wine. He did not stay to enjoy his meal with us; he had rightly assumed that Kris would be too tired for conversation. Kris was pale and weary, but not disheartened. The prognosis for her sister was tentatively good. In any event, both she and her sister were fully sustained by their faith. For them, death, admittedly sad in the Earthly City, was ineluctably a glorious passage to the Heavenly City. When I told her that I had missed her to the point of depression, she smiled and patted my arm. She went to bed, after taking a long, hot shower. It was too early for me; I read for an hour, watched the late evening news on television, and then joined her. She was snoring lightly. It bothered me that my heavy, stertorous, apneic snoring might later wake her, as it often did. But, warm beside her, I was secure from the October darkness and the rain. We were together. We were right. In the morning, after breakfast, Kris went to 8:30 mass, while I drank coffee and read the home-delivery edition of *The New York Times*.

89

Kris, Grayber, and I were not enthusiastic about Al Gore. That he lacked star appeal was not negative: there had been enough of star-flash with Reagan the Right-wing Deregulator and Clinton the Right-leaning Centrist. What was wrong was Gore's prudish desertion of the man who had put him into the Vice-presidency and his compounding the desertion by enlisting as running mate the Holy Joe who had joined the spite-incited condylocephalics in their hollow hypocritical howls of protest against an infidelity in the White House that differed from many earlier infidelities only in its being sleazily and salaciously publicized. Joe, the Democrat In Name Only, the DINO sore-ass.

The Republican ticket invalidated our reservations: Fratboy and Sneer. So, we bent in to the narrow-mindedness of name-calling that characterized the kind of opposition we opposed. Blackie's letters, written beside Vera's sickbed, appealed rationally to Grayber and Kris, both of whom, nonetheless, grew stronger in their support of Gore as they moderated their displeasure with Right-wingers, while I remained wildly obstinate in my unwillingness to see any modicum of *upright Christian manhood* in Fratboy or *patriotic rectitude* in Sneer. To this day, even though I have learned and admitted that my knee-jerk attitude, like my unwillingness to praise, was and is wrong, I stand secure within the shelter of what I am: *Be what you have learned you are*, says Pindar;

No excuses, say the Existentialists; and Heidegger intones the *eigentlich* (the *own-ly*, the authentic) as inherent in the *eigenst* (one's *own-most* being). My own-most being is, when I am honest enough to admit it, passive. The passivity incorporates egoism, praise-neediness, proneness to denial, insecure lechery, predisposition to bias, and baseless vanity.

Anything positive? A potential for compassion, an awareness of my intellectual limitations, the guiding principle of teaching that I learned from Professor Landis and successfully honored.

Perhaps passivity was positive in my receipt of the friendship of Blackie and Grayber, of the devotion of Kris, the fealty of Carrie, and the love of Anne.

Except for the pleasantly appealing visages of the candidates' wives, the campaign was dark and grotesquely dreadful. Gore's words were mis-contextualized. Fratboy's duty-dodging was translated into heroism. Kris grew impatient with the profanity and sick moods into which the campaign caused me to plunge. *Pete, for Heaven's sake, don't hate so much.* Grayber, too, urged me to try to lighten up. He drove Kris and me out to River Forest, where we enjoyed a picnic and looked for blue flowers along the river-bank. *Was den blauen Fluss hinab untergeht* (What, moving down the blue river, goes under), writes Heidegger, reading Georg Trakl, who says *Das geht in Ruh und Schweigen unter* (goes under in peace and silence). We looked for blue flowers along the blue river of truth. *Die Blaue ... ist ob ihrer versammelnden, in der Verhüllung erst scheinenden Tiefe das Heilige* (Blueness ... in its gathering profundity, by which it shines out only as it conceals itself, is the Holy). For Heidegger, as for the followers of four-limbed Krishna, Blueness is Holiness. We found no blue flowers; but, in looking for them, we found the peace and silence of the blue river.

The election, owing to the gross illegalities of balloting in Florida, was a debacle. Gore won the popular vote; but the Supreme Court, by a politically partiisan vote of five to four (on12-12-00), removed from the country the protection long afforded it by the Constitution, and gave the election to Fratboy and Sneer, who were promptly to assume a non-existent mandate and initiate the brutal decline of Roman America. Grayber and Kris, and the experience of the blue river (the river that Sharny had promised me?), helped me to get by. But, on that most telling of days in American history, Tuesday, December 12, 2000, a new personal sadness prevailed: Vera Kirk Konshak died. A friend and business associate of Blackie's called to relay the news. Through a deepening snow, I walked with Kris to her church, where she lit a candle. Grayber and I arranged for teaching assistants to take over our classes. We would be returning from the funeral on the following weekend and be back in time for exam week. The weather was not good for travel. Kris did not want to fly. Grayber did not want to drive, nor did I. Long journeys by bus were trying. We settled for Amtrak. Delays, re-routings, and all the many local stops lengthened the trip to over six hours. Blackie's business associate met us at the depot and drove us to Blackie's luxurious home, where rooms had been prepared for us.

Blackie had been unwilling to leave the funeral home, where Vera lay in gorgeous state. He slept in an office there and took his meals there. He rose from his chair near the casket and greeted us with a weary smile of patent gratitude. He kissed Kris on the cheek and embraced her, and then shook hands with Grayber and me. He had gained weight, but his face was narrowed by years of concern and three days of incessant grief. What little there was that could be said was said by Kris, whose soft words of condolence seemed genuinely to comfort Blackie. Karla and widowed Katie (my *Gift of the Konshaks* of long ago) separated themselves from their sons and daughters and from Karla's husband to greet Kris and me. Katie took my hand and briefly held it in both of hers.

The service on the following day was quite long. A string quartet at the funeral home played darkly vibrant music that I did not recognize. The priest, quietly and with unaffected emotion summarized Vera's exemplary Christian life. Grayber and I joined three of Blackie's business associates and Karla's husband as pallbearers. In the cathedral, the priest intoned all the assurances of sure and certain resurrection and eternal life; There were four eulogies, the last being delivered on behalf of her brother, her sister, and herself by Karla. She spoke *of the rings of sanctity that constitute halos of familial certainty in a world of love that chaos and loss cannot impair.* Then Kris and I were delightedly astonished to see Andy approach the altar, genuflect, making the Sign of the Cross, and turn to recite Longfellow's sonnet on the death of his wife. He added these words: *Vera is not LONG dead, having been taken from us only a few days ago; but those here who love her now live in pale light and look upon a world defined by a sun-defying cross of snow.* Andy then took his seat with Kris and me, as Kris embraced and kissed him.

When I had e-mailed Andy about Vera's death, I assumed that he was in Europe; but he was actually in New York. Jordy, he later told us, was in Washington, D.C. The service was concluded by rites at the mausoleum, which Blackie, who sternly forbade any earth-burial of his wife, would thereafter visit daily, for at least a year, and then every Sunday, Tuesday, and Thursday. My many years of friendship with Blackie had not prepared me for his singularly uncompromising devotion to Vera. That they had been warmly content together had been obvious; but Blackie's absolute refusal to place Vera in a nursing home or hospice and his determination that her body not be committed to the ground seemed to me to be strangely undue. When I told Kris about my puzzlement, she said, *Pete, you've always been able to care, but you've never really understood the nature of caring.*

 She smiled at my unspoken plea for an explanation of what she meant; and I let the matter drop.
 Nancy and Rosie attended the services at the funeral home and the cathedral. They did not go the mausoleum. They went back to Blackie's house to open it and initiate the reception. They had become a permanent part of Blackie's household and were to remain at the residence and in his pay indefinitely.
 This was not the time to talk to Blackie about the Supreme Court's political decision against Gore, although I should have liked to have done that, believing that Blackie, for all of his conservatism, would not have approved of this breach of the Constitution.
 After the reception, Grayber, Kris, Andy, and I spent the evening with Blackie, with Nancy and Rosie doing all of the housekeeping and occasionally joining in the talk and reminiscing. They made up a sleeper-sofa for Andy in the guest-room set up for Grayber.
 Nancy and Rosie prepared an 8:30 a.m. breakfast. Then we left Blackie to the security of their attentiveness. Andy

Roy Arthur Swanson

drove Grayber, Kris, and me the long, cold distance home in his leased Cadillac. He drove expertly and confidently, even through a ten-mile stretch of sleet and an iced-over road. He stayed at home with Kris and me for the next four days.

90

Blackie's inability—if that's what it was—to let his Vera go somehow led me to think about Gilgamesh's inability to understand or accept the death of his friend Enkidu and his futile quest to find the means of eliminating death: futile, because being human precluded immortality. Vera was not the equivalent of Enkidu, but her death was the equivalent of Enkidu's death: death is death, the passage from existence into non-existence.

Nor was I his Enkidu; although, in this context of Death, I knew that much had passed away from me. [Open the gates, George.]

The twentieth century had passed into the twenty-first century. My delayed retirement from teaching was only a year or two away, as my weakened senses and increasingly fallible memory reminded me. The America I had known was now obsolescent. The two-party system of government had decayed into a neo-fascist Right and a right-of center Left. The Supreme Court had become politically partisan, with the Right in the majority. Higher education had become business-oriented, with cost-accounting and job-training informing its values. The Humanities and the Liberal Arts were being marginalized and dependent for survival upon trendy courses and grade-inflation. Students' rights and privileges superseded academic depth and thoroughness; and the dignity of the professoriate gave way to denim, slacks, and first-name address. English departments were taken over by politically correct ideologues, who preached diversity and multiculturalism and paradoxically eschewed formal grammar and syntax and the study of foreign languages (how could one study any culture, much less many cultures, without firm grounding in the language of the culture?). Rock and Roll had subsided into demon-wailing and unintelligible lyricism, along with the protestant savagery of Rap and the cadent collocations of Hip Hop. It was a Declaration of Irresponsible Independence: Death, Libertinism, and the Pursuit of Puerility.

The narrow-minded and nonsensical intolerance that is Political Correctness is wrongly taken to be Liberalism. Ever since my father denounced Landon's opposition to Roosevelt, I have considered myself a liberal. PC (weirdly analogous to the non-communicative information glut of the Personal Computer) is archly conservative of its own implosive rectitude; there is nothing liberal about breeding ethnicist provincialism while decrying the formal study of languages, about demeaning the canons of great literature as political oppression fostered by white males, and about a reactionary politicizing of the liberal-arts curricula.

Andy not only shared my views but also framed them with a rationale. His explanations must have followed, in large part, the strange thinking of Jordy Klug. The essence of his summary comes easily and disturbingly to mind. Giraffe-skin clad T.S. Eliot, with his twisted Anglo-Catholic anti-Semitism, exemplifies his own *mélange adultère* (perverted mixture), as well as that of the East-twisted West *de Damas jusqu'à Omaha* (from Golgotha by way of Damascus to Omaha). Four executions establish the cardinal points of an unhinged West: Socrates, Jesus, Gallus, and

Hypatia—the uncompromised male intellect guided by the alogical demon, the uncompromised male-comprising-female soul guided by the paternal demon, the uncompromising female-male political mind guided by the erotic demon, and the uncompromising female intellect guided by the logical demon.

Love of Wisdom, love of God, love of Love, wisdom of Love. All four twisted into the negativity that produces poison, torture, the sword, the feminicide. Anti-Semitism (more specifically, anti-Judaism), Crusades, Inquisitions, Fascism. *This is the full perversion of your Heideggerian Four; Dad; and it is in volatile foment now in Washington. Jordy's correctiveness is contaminated by the lack of a corrective to his own extremism; he saw the potential corrective in Grandma and needed to have it materialize in you.* But it did not.

Apparently, having recourse to Andy was Jordy's best option, but Andy was a generation late. Not much of this made any sense to me; and Kris said it was all *just plain spooky*. Andy did his best to explain the *transcendent Isis strain* and *Romano-Teutonic genetic elitism*, the latter having been politically coöpted by the Italian and German Fascists.

What's important, he insisted, is the alacrity with which the *corporate open range* and *the right-wing Evangelicals* have incorporated the perversion. Eisenhower saw the inception of the perversion in the *military-industrial complex. Reagan and Clinton killed regulation, Dad, and your Fratboy and Sneer are going to kill something much more important.*

Jordy Klug would join Andy in New York, where they would work with a Stem Group to try to undercut some religio-political ties being made between Eastern and Western perversions of the foundation.

Kris asked Andy how he was earning a living and keeping up his high style. Andy said that it was all foundation money, that the foundation had endlessly sufficient funds but insufficient power. More accurately, he explained, the power, in simultaneity with its vastness, is coöpted by antithetical movements. He reminded me of my old comparative-mythology lectures, with arguments borrowed from Teilhard de Chardin, Lévi-Strauss, and others: from potential energy to kinetic energy to matter to the biosphere (the sphere of life) to the noösphere (the sphere of mind) the transition continues toward the theosphere (Plato's sphere of pure forms—the gods who dispose). Gallus had caught the creative feminist principle of the noösphere as the universal foundation, only to have it subsequently masculinized by waves of phallic universalism: dark Zeus sends the rain of his sperm through the Towered aperture and into the Danaëan orifice.

As Kris moved her arms outward, palms up, in a gesture of bewilderment, I tried to clarify the mythological physics by recalling our appreciation of John Ford's movies, in which an old effective, but obsolescent, order contributed its own demise to a new and better form of order. In *The Man Who Shot Liberty Valance*, as we had noted before, John Wayne, representing the old Wild West vigilante order, turns that order against itself so that the new order, law and civil stability, represented by James Stewart, can be established. Kris sighed, smiled, and went out to the kitchen to prepare a pot of fresh coffee.

In this *Liberty Valance* context, perhaps, it has been incumbent upon me to sacrifice my academic methods in the interest of establishing Political Correctness and anti-canonism. Wayne's character, however, had at least to intuit inevitability and betterment in advancing the taming of the Wild West by murdering Liberty Valance (the remnant values of lawlessness), as depicted by Lee Marvin; but my intuition signaled no providential inevitability or higher value in the ideology of PC and the disestablishment of the Western literary traditions.

The very nature, however, of the foundational values with which Jordy Klug had indoctrinated Andy was perennial opposition to the imperialistic perversion of those values. Andy admitted that he had inherited too much of my passivity to be fully up to the essentially active, but almost wholly negative, task and that Jordy's activism had long been permeated by the same depths of negativity that predisposed peaceniks and Pro-Lifers to murderous sedition: the peaceniks blew up Bob Fassnacht, and the Pro-Lifers have murdered, at this writing, seven doctors who performed abortions in accordance with the medical needs of patients, the most recent having been shot to death in his own church.

Jordy and Andy's oppositional efforts are akin to my pedagogical conservatism. Both constitute integers of what I have called the Polar Conceit, a constrictive predilection for an order that is precluded from being superseded by aberrant new orders. The agent of preclusion is *das Ewig-Weibliche* (Goethe's Eternal Feminine, Gallus's Isis Strain, Robert Graves's White Goddess), my heart-borne glimpse of which had been Anne.

For some reason, as it had become clear to me, Jordy had made no mention of Anne to Andy. How Jordy had known, and all that he had known, about Anne remains to this day an impenetrable mystery to me; and my unwillingness to probe, much less solve, the mystery is a measure of my ungrudging gratitude to a prevailing darkness.

Kris returned, humming *I'll Get By*, with a service of aromatic coffee and Polish poppy-seed cakes.

91

Around a small artificial tree, rather hastily set up and decorated, Kris, Andy, and I celebrated an early Christmas. Andy gave his mother a gold cross on an eighteen-inch gold chain; he gave me a strikingly clear recording of my father's fiddle-playing (transferred from an old vinyl recording to magnetic tape). Kris and I gave him a new pigskin wallet, tailored to his special preference in the rare leatherwork that he particularly prized. We sang the old German songs in concert with the fiddle-music and then the old Christmas carols and songs, as Kris played the piano. We called Blackie, each of us speaking with him and wishing him the best of a season that he said would, thanks to Nancy and Rosie, not be painfully sad for him.

There was no more talk about Jordy during Andy's short stay, although, during brief moments when Kris was not present, he let me know that he and Jordy performed some highly paid adjunct services for the CIA, providing information about the Mafia wars in Italy and about other matters concerning European terrorist cells, the details of which he could not disclose. Up to now, he had suffered no injuries or wounds; Jordy, however, had been shot in his right shoulder and had once been subjected to torture. Gretchen, as a militant anti-terrorist in northern Germany, had gained high skills in weaponry.

RAIN AND DARKNESS

The three of us visited Sharny's grave and laid three red roses on the snow that covered it.

Grayber invited us to his home for part of an afternoon, and treated us to glögg and lutefisk. He entertained us with informal comparisons of Correggio's religious and pagan paintings and with a detailed comparison of Correggio's and Titian's *Danaë*s.

He opened a huge sheaf stuffed with Danaë prints and set out a tray full of Correggio slides. Titian completed three, maybe four, oil canvases of Zeus, in the form of a golden mist, seducing Danaë; there are two versions: in one, Danaë is attended by a seated, fully clad mature woman; in the other, by a standing nude Cupid. In both versions, Danaë is herself mature and stares up invitingly at the sperm cloud; in both, she is reclining, with her head to the viewer's left and facing right. The standing-Cupid version is the earlier of the two. Why did Titian supplant the Cupid with the mature woman? Correggio's patently virginal Danaë is reclining with her head to the viewer's right and facing left; her head is lowered, looking away from the sperm cloud, with her gaze directed to her pubis as it is being uncovered by a seated Cupid that is staring directly up at the sperm cloud; two unconcerned infant and wingless Cupids amuse themselves on the floor and beside the bed. Why do the two mid-sixteenth-century painters have their reclining subject facing in opposite directions?

Jan Grossaert's earlier-sixteenth-century Danaë is seated, unattended, with her blue gown hiked a bit above her knees, as she looks vaguely upward. Jacques Blanchard's early-seventeeth-century Danaë sleeps in pallor, while a Cupid and a dark-clad, cowled serving woman sets her up for the golden rain. Kris, Andy, and I hadn't known that the subject had attracted a host of artists: Goltzius, Tiepolo, Tintoret, Van Dyck, Rembrandt, Girodet, Klimt, Wertmuller, Burne-Jones.... Kris supposed that the subject was just palatable pornography. In support of her supposition, Grayber displayed a vivid print of Lovis Corinth's *Danaë and the Golden Rain*. In further support, he said that the same was true of artistic renditions of Leda and Daphne; but Correggio's Leda, like his Danaë, demeaned Zeus on the Loose and exalted the Eternal Feminine.

Did she put on his knowledge with his power . . . ? Yeats, he insisted, had the question wrong. It should be, *Did he add to his knowledge from her power?* As Odin added to his knowledge from the Sibyl's power. Correggio's Danaë is, not modest, but indifferent (more so than the beak of Yeats's Zeus): let Necessity avail itself of what it needs, as Time sends its meaninglessness into Infinity.

As the perverters persist in their twist of the foundation, said Andy. *As speech, seeking to choke Language, throttles itself,* I added.

Grayber quoted Shakespeare: *Age cannot wither her, nor custom stale / Her infinite variety.*

Kris smiled and studied her fingernails.

Later that night, warmly back home, as snow fell lightly outside, Andy played for Kris and me his videocassette of *The Decade of Decadence* (Reagan's Greedy Eighties) and explained the *level mettle of Heavy Metal*. Mick Marrs, Nikki Sixx, Vince Neil, Tommy Lee. He had sent the videocassette, along with two CD's (*Generation Swine* and *New Tattoo*), from Miami, but Kris and I had got through not even the whole of *Live Wire*. We learned now about unregenerate re-generation. About Nikki and Nicole's nicking themselves with heroin. About Mick and his groupies. Tommy and

Heather and Honey. Vince's vibes and his Lovey Leah. Andy explained quite well the appeal of raucous sonance and the heavy charge of aural aura. My interest in masculine electric's spiralling out of control in pursuit of the bitch of heaven was more than inchoate. Kris's appreciation of all this shit was limited to her delight in her son's presence and his impenetrable eloquence.

Andy repaid our attentiveness by watching and listening to the grey-bearded pre-Rock favorites that Kris and I had recorded on a videocassette: Judy Garland and Gene Kelly harmonizing on *For Me and My Gal*; Judy Garland and Connie Boswell harmonizing on *Every Little Movement*; Ethel Waters, Julie Harris, and Brandon de Wilde harmonizing on *His Eye Is On the Sparrow*; *Here's a Toast to the Dead Already* in both versions of *The Dawn Patrol*; the musical conclusion of Kubrick's *Paths of Glory*; Dean Martin and Jerry Lewis doing *That Old Calliope*; the *Panzerlied* in *The Battle of the Bulge*; *Just a Closer Walk With Thee*, at the beginning of *Heavenly Creatures*; and three or four other such *beautiful chestnuts* (as Andy called them).

On the day of his departure, we drove Andy to the airport and watched as he began, in sunshine, his flight to Washington, D.C. Christmas was just two and half days away. At the kitchen table that evening, in the early darkness, Kris and I dined silently on bread, sausage, cheese, and wine. After clearing away the dishes and straightening up the table, we went into the living room and turned on the tree lights. We sat silently and looked out at the night. A light snow had begun to fall. There were echoes now of Elvis's memories: *of quiet nights and gentle days.*

92

The first year of Fratboy and Sneer marked the end of America as I had known it. The shortcomings and faults of the country during the past century had been many; but, steadily, reforms and movements—the New Deal, the NRA, fiscal regulations, anti-trust laws enforced, Civil Rights, the Women's movements, the incipient recognition of homosexuality as a genetic reality—countered moral and corporate mediaevalism. Corruption, indeed, followed every mode of power, especially in unionism and party politics, and higher education had yielded its stability to Political Correctness and to distorted Affirmative Action and Deconstructionism; but there was still space for resistance and correction. Now, however, the destruction of the New Deal and the elimination of fiscal regulation, initiated by Reagan (and sustained by his two immediate successors) constituted ineluctable policy, along with a calculated curtailment of the Constitution. The armory of plutocracy had its inexhaustible supply of dumb-dumb bullets [Open the gates, George]. The country, growing addicted to *instant gratification*, has become dumbed down and numbed, enjoying Old Rome's *bread and circuses* and eating Marie Antoinette's *cake*.

Blackie, in retirement, retained many of his business contacts; he profited from them and enjoyed the advantages of inside information, creditable payoffs, limousine service, and private air travel. A leased jet brought him on visits to Kris, Grayber, and me in the spring and again in midsummer. He remained steadfast in his conservatism and considered Fratboy to be a *fine upstanding Christian man* and Sneer to be a *no-nonsense realist*. Grayber and I were more amused than discouraged by our attempts to convince him that he was in error; and Blackie similarly placed our *irrational intransigence* into a context of humor. Kris remained neutral. Blackie knew more about meteorology than any of us, and managed to prevail, without convincing us in the least, in his argument that *global warming*, or *climate change*, was neither exceptional nor induced by humans.

Andy's letters from Washington, D.C., which are becoming puzzling and ominous, I share with Grayber and Kris but not with Blackie. *Read about Rasputin, Dad, and the Grey Eminence, and the many versions of The Power Behind the Throne. Jordy and I can't make it here. We're off to New York, as soon as Jordy ends his current hospital stay. The Near East has coöpted the foundation, irreversibly, it seems. Childe Roland to the Dark Tower* . . .

Grayber has decided to retire this year. He has two young models living with him. He earned over $60,000 last year on sales of his paintings, three of which were versions of Danaë and two of which were variations on the Leda theme. Blackie, whose Nancy and Rosie secure his home life, while his investments and business contacts increase his affluence, asks me why I haven't retired. The reason, I suppose, is that I cannot quite envisage myself outside the classroom situation and the academic routine. *It won't be long, though, Blackie: Higher Education has become Hire Education* (I spell out the vapid pun) *and the constant reviews and required written justifications of one's position and status are mind-mushing and humiliating.*

Blackie reminded me that my own higher education amounted to training for the work by which I had found my livelihood and that tenure should not exclude accountability. At this, Grayber nodded but argued that salaried professionals, as opposed to wage-earning workers, skilled and unskilled, were accredited with proving themselves and subscribed to an ethics that entailed self-accountability. My own rejoinder centered on the concept of the baccalaureate as designating the completion of broad and varied learning that left the graduate free to choose higher endeavor.

Right, laughed Blackie, *in graduate school, where my M.B.A. and your Ph.D. certified completion of training for business and teaching, respectively.* Here, I looked to Grayber; but he just shrugged and said, that, while Graduate School was job-oriented, the four-year baccalaureate really ought not to be.

Blackie argued that even four years of Liberal Arts ought rightly to be [He said *ought to rightly be*.] imbued with professional direction. He was secure and articulate, without being smug, while talking about politics, education, and morality; but a turn to personal matters led him to dullness of glance and vagueness. He would speak of Vera, as though she were still alive. He would stare amorously at Kris, as though he were extracting from her presence the substance of the Vera that had been her friend. Kris sensed this, in part; but, sensitively, she would strive to remove her fingers, deformed by arthritis, from his line of vision.

The new movies, with their non-linearity and computerized gimmickry, held no interest for Blackie. The great black-and-white movies and the character actors of the years long gone by were eluding his memory.

RAIN AND DARKNESS

He lapsed into misty-eyed silence as Grayber and I traced the careers of Alfred Hitchcock and Stanley Kubrick. Cinematic reminiscence was now one of the childish things that Blackie had put away in favor of the maturity he found in the Republican resurgence and his belated adherence to the uncompromising morality of the Religious Right.

Grayber made some eerie charcoal sketches of Blackie as Gilgamesh failing to sleep for six days and seven nights and weeping after a snake devoured the prickly plant that he had secured from deep water: the lesson of Utnapishtim, the Sumerian Noah, held that the human mind cannot by itself exceed the limits of human physicality. Grayber gave the sketches to Kris, who put them in her scrapbook, adding them to her pressed oak leaves, old theater stubs, and photographs of relatives and friends, including those of her sister, her parents, and Vera.

That particular summer had brought a drought; and, though the days were seldom sunlit, the heavy dark clouds, through which the blue sky could not declare its cheer, belied their angry promise of rain. Elm, aspen, ash, and maple trees protected themselves by shriveling their leaves. The grass turned brown. The lake shore broadened, as the water receded. Cracks and fissures in the light brown soil appeared as miniature canyons. In Texas, Fratboy played golf and cleared brush from his ranch.

93

On the third or fourth Christmas after the war, my mother had given me a blue sweater. Strangely, the present that Kris and I had selected for her that year was a blue sweater. My mother and I smiled at the coincidence; but we enjoyed, in the moment behind our smiling, an ineffable junction of understanding.

It was after my seventh birthday, I think, that my mother had informed me that my color was blue. Without knowing fully what she meant, I knew that she was indelibly right. On that Christmas of the Blue Sweaters, I knew, in a wave of insight, which I could neither explain nor articulate, just what she had meant. For me thereafter blue became, conventionally, my favorite color, but, informatively, a way of ascending to my self, an ascent the nature of which is disclosed in Heidegger's sequences of thought: returning to where one has always been and, again, as T.S. Eliot would adumbrate, knowing it for the first time.

Blackie seemed, without my ever having to talk to him about it, to recognize this propensity of mine for blue. Just before boarding his plane, after his second visit that summer, he handed me a little package gift-wrapped in blue. *Here's an early present for your birthday*, he said. It was an iridescent opal, framed by blue chrome, set into a silver ring. I slid it onto the third finger of my right hand. *Perfect fit*, said Kris. Grayber added, *Perfect friend.*

The ring still fits, after almost a decade. The sweater has, long since that distant Christmas, become too snug; but it continues to hang, clean and buttoned up, in my closet. Heidegger, on his way to Language, cites Georg Trakl's residence in the realm of the reality of Blue: *die ehrwürdige Sage des blauen Quells* (the sacred Saying of the blue source). The abyssal reality of Nietzsche's Dionysianism, the abyssal horror into which Conrad's Mr. Kurtz gazed, the abyss into which Jehovah brought light—these are the same, an entropic meaningless black. Light, however, is the mask of Apollo, a deception, apparently meaningful, but equally meaningless. Beyond essential black and intrusive light is the blue source that says reality, that Meaning says. Intimations of it abound: positively in Odin's color, which exposes enlightenment as deception, in the Virgin Mary's color, which substantiates grief as the spear of love, in Krishna's color, which establishes perfection as the dynamic tension of mutually dependent and mutually incompatible factors, in the flag of Israel, which encapsulates the color of planet Earth as seen from outer space and denotes election as the spear of the I Am; negatively, in blue's being ascribed to loneliness, emptiness, and the pornographic. Blackness is the fullness of Nothing. Whiteness is the deception of light. Blue is the fullness of deception as perfection. From Russia, синевá, годубóй, and сúний (blue, light blue, and dark blue). From the moon, *blue genesis*.

The Mask of Apollo is deception divorced from perfection. Dionysian Dark is perfection as complete entropy. Nietzsche and Lagerkvist knew that life depends upon their sustained juxtaposition.

Novalis, Trakl, and Heidegger knew that the spring, the source of this sustenance, is blue: the blue flower, the blue river in blue twilight, the Blue Lady of Aftonland (*Sov nu i ro*). Mundane though the association was, it seemed to me to be soulfully satisfying that the states' political divisions came to be represented by red (Republican) and blue (Democratic). Jack Benny and Frank Sinatra took public pride in their blue eyes. Paul Newman's magnetic good looks were enhanced, in public admiration, by his blue eyes, in which he took no public pride, but which he acknowledged as a gift. It isn't just the eyes, of course: violet-colored eyes (like Elizabeth Taylor's), hazel eyes, green eyes, brown eyes, and eyes whose irises are as black as their pupils all have their tones of beauty. It is the coincidence of active blue with a benign physical complexity that marks a particular appropriation. The inactive blue of the dying body is false; the definitive black of the corpse is true; The black and blue of a bruise is a sign of injury and a symptom of healing.

Kris and I sat in the back seat, as Grayber drove. Dusk had indeed turned the world blue: Aftonland (Sleep now in peace), Abendland, Eveningland. Kris held my right hand and turned my new ring from right to left, from left to right.

Relaxed at home, with soft lamplight inside and summer darkness outside, we said little. Humming *I'll Get By*, Kris prepared some refreshments. As she served tea and crust-free club sandwiches, Grayber told a story about an RH-factor blue baby born to an Italian couple. The mother had a dream about an angel who visited Earth in the form of the color blue and became strong by absorbing blue as it moved over land and water. *I shall gather strength from your infant girl if you bring her to me,* the angel told the mother. *I am in the grotto that has filled itself with me; what I am must remain here;*

what I can be may leave here only with the strength that your infant daughter can provide. The parents took their daughter to the Blue Grotto of Capri, where the infant became a healthy pink. Rejoicing, they returned home and named their daughter Azzurina; the angel, having fulfilled a mission of resurgence that it did not need to understand, became Azzurina's guardian and prevailed thereafter in self-fulfilling potentiality.

Kris liked the story but not the concept of pure, insubstantial blue. *What kind of a blob would that be,* she asked. *Think of a color,* said Grayber, *like brown.* Then he asked her if she saw a brown thing or a brown blob. Kris said, *No, just brown.* Grayber explained that the brown of her thought was pure brown, that the angel became, not a blue angel, but the blue that can be summoned by a person's thinking of blue.

Kris turned her head slightly to one side, tucking her chin down toward her shoulder, smiled wistfully, and poured tea.

When I asked Grayber whether he began his paintings by studying objects or by thinking of colors, he said, *I always begin with pure blue.* I wondered, Even when he painted nudes? He said that, when he painted female nudes, he began with *pure blue, pure four, and abyssal black.* Kris asked him if he ever painted male nudes. He said that he frequently painted male nudes but that they were no challenge, that the female nude was ultimately impossible for him fully to capture, that, so far as he could understand, only Correggio and Picasso had succeeded in doing so. *Not Courbet?,* I asked. *Courbet must have begun with abyssal black*, he suggested, *and fallen therefrom into pornographic dreaming.*

Blue dreaming; not blue thinking.

94

Downward to darkness, on extended wings.
—Wallace Stevens

The new semester began, and I was close to the top of my routine. Fifty-one years of teaching had made my entrance into a classroom transformative: however bad or ill or worried or unprepared I may have felt, once I walked through the door and took my stance before a group of students, I was imbued with health, energy, confidence, and a fully impressive vocabulary. The subject of the course was there for me to talk about—easily, entertainingly, and, to a moderate degree, informatively, partly as a perennial student learning from my own discourse, partly as a stand-up comic who could, when a number of students had no response to a question on the assigned material, say, *Well, we are singularly uninformed this morning.*

Close to the top of my routine, but not at the top of it, because my lessened sense of hearing and my curious lapses of recollection were nudging me toward retirement. There was an awareness, neither unpleasant nor pleasant, that the long, colorless flux of years between my earliest and my current days of teaching had simply disappeared, leaving no demarcated account of themselves. And so they have been given no substance in this attempt at translating loss into a novel.

RAIN and DARKNESS

The indifference/interest dyad remained fresh in my lectures: complete interest combined with total indifference to the satisfaction of that interest. Unilateral love: Dante's complete interest in Beatrice and his total indifference to her non-requital; Don Quixote's love of Dulcinea, along with his indifference to her ignorance of that love. It is enough to love; requital offers a profound and unexpected joy, but non-requital does nothing to diminish the love. To say *I love you* is not an emotional investment in expectation of returns (*I love you too*), with pouting, and silent treatment, and anger consequent upon the disappointed expectation. To love is to contribute one's own upward striving to the upward striving of another; a complete contribution would be dying for the beloved, and greater love than that there is not This I taught as a great theme of literature, not as a virtue of which I was even remotely capable.

Bob, whose last name I can't recall, asked if Gallus possessed interested indifference. My answer: *Yes; he was the first to formulate it as a basis of government.* Marcella Dorinelli, waving away the question and the answer, addressed the small class:*Dante, Don Quixote, Gallus-poets, fiction!—men can't love that way; some women, maybe; but never a man.* There came to me no argument with which to gainsay the outburst. *What you say*, I said, simply to break the embarrassing silence, *is perhaps the real clue to our need to study literature.* Going on to compare Gallus to Catullus, I said that Catullus, deeply pained by Lesbia's infidelity, resorted to invective, while Gallus, learning that Lycoris had left him for another soldier, worried about her feet getting cold and wet. But ultimately, what both poets, like, later, Dante and Cervantes/Quixote, had the capacity to know was the inspiration of the Eternal Feminine manifest in the Word (Heidegger's *Saying of Being*).

Robert Graves shows men to be the *frightened adjuncts* of women, who carry the divinity of the White Goddess, whose priests men become by producing literature.

Marcella asked if I were saying that women cannot produce literature. They can, of course, I mused; and, when they do, it is always deeply superior and infinitely more precise than anything men can do—but, in order to do so, they absent themselves, either temporarily or permanently, from their divinity. Great literature, as Heidegger maintains, re-calls the gods (the divinities, the divine): it is holy. Running on in this way, I saw that I had lost the interest of the class—Bob, Marcella, and others were doodling—and so I returned to our text, Lucretius, the poet who invoked Venus.

After the class period ended, I secured black coffee from the vending machine and went to my office, where, for a time, I daydreamed about satisfying myself sensually with Ann Sheridan (dead much too soon, one month before her fifty-second year and twenty months before Neil Armstrong first stepped into moon-dust) and then turned my thoughts exclusively to Gallus.

About a week later, on a Monday night, there was a strange phone call from Andy. He was in New York: *Dad, Jordy says you should have made that trip to Heidelberg so you could understand the new perversion of the perversions of the foundation. Stay home tomorrow, if you can, and watch CNN or one of the news programs. Got to go now.* The dial tone sounded as I was in mid-question.

My schedule included no Tuesday classes, and I usually went to the university on Tuesdays only for faculty or committee meetings or, occasionally, to work with microfilm or microfiche at the library; so, I would have been home, as a matter of habit.

Kris and I had our usual, somewhat late Tuesday breakfast and then sat down before the television set to watch *Good Morning America*. Diane Sawyer and her group were talking about mysterious black smoke issuing from the North Tower of the World Trade Center, to which the camera repeatedly returned. The consensus was that something had *hit* the tower. Not connecting this with Andy's telephone call, and being bored, as I always was by the gabby-chatty vapid program, I left the living room—to make fresh coffee, intending also to check some notes on Gallus, and initiate preparation for Wednesday's classes. Returning with coffee for Kris and me, I saw on the television screen an airliner flying very close to the WTC. Diane Sawyer said something like *There's an airplane.* The plane disappeared behind the towers and, shortly thereafter, a huge burst of orange flame appeared. *My God!* was Sawyer's reaction. *What's THAT?* Kris said in something like a loud whisper. Slow to react, I stared at the screen and tried to get some mental purchase on what had happened.

Finally, I began to think about the many passengers on that plane, and the crew, and about their crashing into that building, the South Tower, and being burnt to ashes. Then began the long day of recorded bloodshed on American soil unmatched in quantity since the Civil War: the crash into the Pentagon; the straight-fall of the South Tower; the crash of United Flight 93 near Shanksville, Pennsylvania; the straight-fall of the North Tower. It was odd that the South Tower should fall before the earlier stricken North Tower. New York citizens running through the streets ahead of huge dust billows and a rain of flying papers, as in a scene from a 1950's disaster movie. Peter Jennings assumed commentary on ABC, and regular programming was abandoned.

Fratboy, reading *The Pet Goat* with the second-grade students of Emma E. Booker Elementary School in Sarasota, Florida, received the news of the disaster and was an inertly unheroic model of passivity, more interested, apparently, in seeing how *The Pet Goat* ended than in leaping to the activity incumbent upon a commander-in-chief. Eventually he thanked the *folks* at the elementary school and vowed to find and punish the *folks* responsible for the mass murder. From Sarasota, Air Force One carried Fratboy to the Barksdale Air Force Base near Shreveport, Louisiana, and from there to the Offutt Air Force Base near Omaha, Nebraska. At distressing length, well after Sneer had set up a command post in the White House bunker, Fratboy returned to Andrews Air Force Base in Washington, D.C. Remembering Roosevelt, Truman, and Eisenhower as commanders-in-chief, I realized the depth to which the Presidency had fallen.

Sitting in the same corner, but in a different chair, and watching a different television set, I had seen, almost thirty-two years earlier, America at its best, as the *Eagle* landed at *Tranquillity Base* on the Moon—the beginning, I had thought, of a great age for the country; but, following the assassinations during the Sixties, the countercultural ravages of the Sixties and preceding those of the Seventies, and then the Greed of the Eighties, along with the religiously right-wing insidiousness of the Nineties, it became clear that the Moon-landing had marked the end of true American greatness. This bright blue September day was the culmination of a darkness for America, a corrosive Dark Side.

RAIN and DARKNESS

Near the end of that day, I realized, with agitation, that much of the day's horror had been intimated by Andy in his telephone call. How had he known about this in advance of its occurrence? After beginning an e-mail to Blackie about the events, I gave it up and called him by telephone.

He said he said he was convinced that *the President* had not made a cowardly retreat; in fact, he laughed at my asking him if he thought this was the case: No, the protective entourage had to ensure the safety of the President; everything had been done in accordance with necessary procedures. The good Christian President was a courageous *two-fisted* Texan; and his vice-president was bravely doing his duty. My disbelief was countered by Blackie's reassurances and by my finding satisfaction in his calm confidence. When I told him about Andy's phone call, he seemed somewhat surprised; but he concluded that Jordy would have prompted Andy's calling and that Jordy could very possibly have had some connection to the plot. *Ped, I wish you could get Andy away from that guy.* At this, I felt a strange shudder of loyalty to our old tormentor, to whom Andy was, from my perspective, more of a ward than a lackey. Moreover, from what Andy had been saying, he and Jordy Klug were engaged in opposition to the forces of *perversion*. Still, it was good to have talked to Blackie.

On the day following the destruction of the towers, the filmed rendition of which reminded me of the Tower of the Tarot Cards, I offered the students in each of my three classes the opportunity to comment on or discuss the catastrophe. Their disinclination to do so was not particularly surprising.

Grayber shared my views and suspicions. He knew that the jet-fuel fire would not have been hot enough to bend skyscraper steel and that, if it had been, the buildings would have listed sideways in collapsing and not fallen straight down and that the tower that was hit second would, very likely, not have fallen before the one that was hit first. On Friday night of that week, he invited Kris and me over for a dinner of spaghetti and mushrooms, Chianti, and garlic bread. His two companions were out for the evening. We talked for rather a long time about the towers and about Fratboy's convenient and extended distance from the scene. Kris became bored and suggested that we watch a movie. *The Godfather* was to be replayed on a satellite-television channel. Kris and I helped Grayber with clearing the table and cleaning the dishes. Then we relaxed before the large-screen Panasonic television set.

This was the fourth time I had seen the movie. This time, though, I recognized the Italian passage in Al Martino's rendition of *I Have But One Heart*. The lines were those that Andy had relayed from Jordy Klug to me, in which *lago* was substituted for *mare*. This served the more to deepen my thoughts about Jordy and Andy's connection to the destruction of the towers.

Ambiguities: the sympathetic characters of murderous gangsters in the film; my strangely growing affection for the reprehensible Jordy Klug. My attention drifted to thoughts of the popular canonization of the bank-robbing killers, Bonnie and Clyde, and John Dillinger—and of women, like the *Lolita* star, Sue Lyon, who married an incarcerated felon. The attraction of the demonstrably evil for those morally committed to law and order must lie, I supposed, in an aspiration toward a knowledge necessarily resident in darkness: the tree-shadowed serpent in the day-lit Garden. Fratboy, unequivocally a villain, with his smirking disingenuousness, was, apart from the partisan approval of Republicans like Blackie, gaining from wishful non-thinkers a heroic status that was overtly belied by his evasion of military duty as an erratic member of the Air Force Reserve and his undeniable retreat from the immediate duty of a commander-in-chief in a time of crisis.

My ineffective attempts to resolve these problems of moral ambiguities and contradictions were compounded the following week by troublings of another, but not unrelated, sort: my former colleague, *Emeritus* Cormac C. McKnight Professor of Comparative Literature, J. Kieran O'Connor (the *J.* for *Jeremiah*), known to his family and close friends as *Jake* and to most of the academic world as *J.K.*, died after suffering for a little over three months from some unnamed muscular disease. He was an internationally celebrated scholar, the author of nineteen books and hundreds of articles and reviews. His works on Catholic novelists have become standards. Although never a close friend, he was friendly to me and helped me on a number of occasions to place articles for publication. Now, suddenly, he had ceased to exist. The huge memorial service and all of the accolades did nothing to dispel for me the utter blackness of his non-existence. My mourning was, not for a friend, or even for a much respected colleague, but for the goodness of existence that is inseparable from the evil of extinction.

J.K. and I had agreed that Charles Simic's proposed predilection for *an sich* (being in itself) in his poem, *Stone*, was misguided: *I am happy to be a stone.* If one is a stone, there is no *I* and there is no *happy*. Again: *The stone sinks, slow, unperturbed.* A stone cannot be, or is not, intrinsically slow, or slow by nature; although it can sink *slowly*; and, although a stone can be perturbed (dislodged, or scattered with other stones by an external force), it cannot be unperturbed (serene or calm—that is, in a pleasant emotional state). Simic may be expropriating the self-contained world of a stone's molecular activity or atomic motion, but to implant his own consciousness in this mass is to abuse poetic license and misconstrue metaphor. Worst, however, is its celebration of *an sich* as superior to *für sich* (being for itself).

Human existence is being-for-itself; inanimate existence is being-in-itself. To die is to be reduced to inanimate existence, to cease, as a human being, to exist. J.K. said that Simic was here compounding the perversion that John Ruskin called the *pathetic fallacy* (imbuing the inanimate with emotions). J.K. was now a stone. All his many accomplishments and contributions to literary studies survived him; but, much as I wanted to believe that he existed for himself in his words, I could feel only bitterness, as I recalled the dynamic scholar who was no more and the folly of Simic's nihilistic foray into the fallible figurative [Open the gates, George].

Before he retired, J.K. had yielded to the support of a cane. He chose one suited to his habits of style—silk shirts, cashmere jackets, ascots—a black T-shaped stick with two pearls embedded in the stem. At first, he swung it about jauntily, as though it were merely a fashion accessory; but, by the time of the retirement ceremony, his dependence upon it was acute; and he wore a special glove, attached to the cane, which his palsied hand was otherwise prone to drop.

After retirement, he remained, academically and socially, very active and much in demand. Like Grayber, he was a constant party-thrower and party-goer. He delivered a couple of lectures on Utopian Literature. By e-mail, he continued his argument with me about generic pronouns. Although endorsing my stodgy conservatism in English usage and grammar, he insisted that I was wrong to oppose the generic masculine ("Let every citizen contribute *his* share") and the generic plural ("Let every citizen contribute *their* share"). Where I maintained that the English language permitted only *his or her* (or *her or his*), he upheld the idea that we work with what we've got: if there is no pronoun referent to both genders, we assign that duty to existing pronouns (*he, him, his; they, them, their*), as Chaucer, Byron, Thackeray, George Eliot, and others have done. Arguments from precedent and longevity never seemed valid to me. What is definitively wrong cannot be justified by former or extended performance: masculine pronouns are masculine; plural pronouns are plural.

With J.K.'s death, however, it all began to seem pointless. Why bother? Fratboy was using non-words, like *misunderestimate*, and generally mangling the language that Franklin Delano Roosevelt had used with patrician precision. Like everything else, languages are variable, decadent, and mortal. The Greek of ancient Athens gave way to Koinê and modern Greek (with its loss of the aspirate and its reduction of vowels to the iota sound); Latin gave way to the Romance languages; Old English disappeared into a mélange of Celtic, Norse, Latin, Greek, Norman French, and borrowings from many other languages.

My belief that rules of grammar, usage, and syntax stabilize a language and, with the integrity of denotation achieved, forestall its demise was already being overwhelmingly challenged by inundations of technological jargon and computerese.

Walking across campus on a dark, overcast day, I fashioned an imaginary picture: J.K. is standing on the deck of the *USS Constitution* (*Old Ironsides*) on a black night, as

Roy Arthur Swanson

both he and the ship sink silently into a sea made indistinct by an impenetrable darkness that fully conceals Fratboy and Sneer, who stand and applaud from the no longer demarcated shore.

95

As moviegoers, Blackie and I had been most interested in the actors: the leads and the supporting players. His favorite leads were Rosalind Russell, Bette Davis, Jean Arthur, Ronald Reagan, George Murphy, and John Wayne; mine were Ann Sheridan, Olivia de Havilland, Hedy Lamarr, Errol Flynn, Fred Astaire, and William Holden. We didn't have idealized favorites among the supporting players and character actors; but we tried constantly to learn the identities of all of them. Photography didn't interest us much until we saw *The Grapes of Wrath*, *The Long Voyage Home*, and, in my case, *Citizen Kane* and came to appreciate the artistry of Gregg Toland. After the war, we began to study the ways in which Hollywood got around the restrictions of the decency codes and presented sexual intimations through *double entendre*, homosexuality through various forms of male or female bonding (not to mention the classic flair of Franklin Pangborn, Grady Sutton, or Clifton Webb), and Marxism and politics through theme and innuendo. We still rehearse vestiges of those days in letters and when we get together.

For Kris and me, the movies meant, chiefly, the *noir* elements, the career of Stanley Kubrick, the songs and music (like the theme from *Limelight* and, especially, Elvis Presley's singing).

Grayber tries occasionally to initiate us into the intricacies of high cinematic art; but he is sensitive to Kris's yawns and my feigned attentiveness and neither persists in his attempts to elevate our consciousness nor shows disappointment, calling thereby to my mind the gentility of Guinotte. Grayber's first consideration is always the director: Jules Dassin, Jean-Luc Godard, Volker Schlondorff, Andrei Tarkovsky, Satyajit Ray, Pier Paolo Pasolini, Michelangelo Antonioni, Peter Greenaway, Alexander Mackendrick, Akira Kurosawa, Bernardo Bertolucci—it's a long list. He doesn't care much for American directors, except for Sam Peckinpah and Quentin Tarantino. One night, after a fine dinner that he had prepared for us, he played his DVD of Tarkovsky's *Solaris*. I found the long takes and the painfully slow pace hard to bear, although the intellectual morality gave me much to think about—more than I could handle, really—and Kris fell asleep before the film had run its full two hours and forty-five minutes. Grayber's critique, though, was enthusiastic and edifying. (A shorter version, ninety-eight minutes, has been made, some thirty years after the original, directed by Steven Soderbergh and staring George Clooney and Natascha McElhone. Grayber found it greatly wanting; but it got to me, because it reminded me of Blackie's devotion to Vera.)

Grayber elaborates on *mise en scène*, script, cutting, sound editing, and other elements of cinematography that are, while I know them to be aesthetically and artistically important, of no demanding concern to me. He delights in the de-centered and non-linear films, which Kris and I, with a few exceptions—like *Pulp Fiction* and *Once Upon A Time In America*—take to be needlessly complex. When I express admiration for Ronald Colman's voice, Grayber explains that the mellow tonality is actually enhanced by the key light upon the angle of Colman's facial inclination.

How about Frank Overton's perfect voice? That, he points out, is a matter of contrast: Overton maintains a stiff facial posture which transforms his easy baritone into mellifluousness, the way Hopper's darknesses transform his easy colors into moods. Grayber's almost boyish pleasure in these matters precludes the possibility of his being a snob or a pretentious elitist; and the calibration of his brow can become exceedingly low, as when he watches hardcore pornography with his two mistresses, Angie Ledd and Chloe Tilsen—or so he tells me.

Apart from its vacuous vulgarity, pornography serves a practical purpose, Grayber insists: it stimulates lubriciousness and erectility when such stimulation is needed. It need not pretend to do anything else. The introduction of nudity into mainstream movies, however, exceeded its initial artistic intent and came to do service only to lechery.

Kris and I agreed with him, although privately I reserved my own predilection for lechery. Nudity for the sake of nudity, according to Grayber, is as bad as art for the sake of art; ethical sensibility calls for nudity for the sake of art—and art for the sake of life (*ars gratia vitae*). The trend in popular movies, beginning during the Greedy Eighties, has been that of schlock shock: misplaced pornography, gratuitous scenes of sexual activity, unchecked use of the so-called *four-letter words* (especially *fuck*, which becomes punctuative and a tmetic element), overextended car-chases (never equivalent to the classically orchestrated car-chase in *Bullitt*), massive explosions with Big Bang fireballs, and computer-generated images that send imagination to the cartoon-shed and blunt the reality of the fall of the World Trade Center towers.

96

The towers, along with WTC-7, fell because they were systematically destroyed by controlled demolition. This is the *conspiracy theory*, which is discredited, even laughed at, owing to what people want to believe and are conditioned to believe. Similarly, the Grassy Knoll assassins who brought down JFK have become figures of myth. *It's like the official report of Gallus's suicide,* Andy informed Kris, Grayber, and me on his extended visit home after Fratboy's flight-deck dance on the *Abraham Lincoln* under the *Mission Accomplished* banner. Gaea gave birth to Uranus and then made the mistake of cohabiting with him, who then became the tide that can be taken at the flood only by presumptive male force. He sired Kronus, who, taken to her bed by his sister Rhea, ate his own Olympian children in order to sustain the power he had usurped by emasculating Uranus. Rhea saved her youngest, Zeus, by feeding Kronus a swaddled stone and giving Zeus into the care of the female force (diminished, but undulant). Achieving maturity, Zeus caused his father to regurgitate the undigested siblings and took to wife his sister Hera, who was able to check but not coöpt his power. Always: Life-and-Consciousness (Gaea, Eve, Pandora, Isis, Freya . . .) projects, nourishes, checks, and is opposed by Energy-and-Power (Uranus, Cain, Epimetheus, Osiris, Odin . . .).

RAIN AND DARKNESS

This universal tension of incompatibly interdependent forces had disclosed itself to me in my own teaching of mythology. Andy got it, though, from Jordy Klug, the mystery of whom had now become too deep for me even inceptively to resolve. Kris was listening, out of love for her son. Grayber was listening, with nods and some skepticism. My listening was a matter more of despair than of interest, the sort of feeling I underwent when, some nine or ten years earlier, Grayber had shown me an unfunny joke: Arthur Dove's mucilaginous pastiche of baby-shit-colored spaghetti-like twigs on verdigris and glass, depicting an off-centered phallic blob, detumescent in descent from a dark-green panty-like triangle, a skillfully obnoxious sneer that Dove had entitled *Rain*. Andy spoke through a long afternoon.

There had been Hitler, Goebbels, Goering, Himmler, and Speer; now there were Fratboy, Turdblossom, Subtractington, Rummler, and Sneer. Above all, Sneer, the architect of De-Constitutionalism. The flying-but-not-landing lessons had been completed by identified but untouched Near-Eastern operatives. The interior explosives had been expertly emplaced. The Intelligence warnings and Presidential briefings about an imminent terrorist attack had been received and ignored, as Fratboy enjoyed part of his long vacation. The profitable, power-provident crisis was *zuhanden*. Fratboy was safely sent away to the Sarasota elementary school, and Sneer had hunkered down in a bunker command post. The efforts of the foundation, to whose well-financed but politically powerless members this was all easily known, to alert or alarm the responsible officials, and to forestall or prevent the blazing event, were futile. Only flight 93, as a weapon of mass destruction, was taken out of action—shot down by an F-26 before it could complete its mission to crash into the Capitol. The heroism of the passengers is a fact; but there is no way that they could have breached the door to the pilots' compartment. Andy had all the specifications of collapse, steel, and stress. Gallus's base, a tenuous string of history, had been translated into a radical male Foundation, powerfully entrenched by Egyptians, Saudi Arabians, and religious fanatics.

With regard to the discredited *conspiracy theory*, it cannot be denied that there was a conspiracy, not by the Twigs of the Belt-line, but by forces in opposition to the U.S.A. as the Great Satan. In this, my own reading, inspirited by a vague recollection of the indecent Dove, the Twigs attached themselves advantageously to the obscene verdigris.

And so Fratboy came to play the Turdblossom Passacaglia on his bullhorn; and the debilitating PATRIOT Act initiated the decimation of the civil rights of American citizens; and air travel became a comedy of incontinent constraint, while ports and borders were almost willfully neglected; and the threat of biological terrorism produced only a Munchian scream; and the politicized Justice department was purged of objectivity; and the agglomerative appointment of incompetents guaranteed the deterioration of government, while those entrusted with government despoiled the country of its monetary substance through billions wasted on an illegal war, mediaeval systems of torture, and total deregulation. This was a killer regime (one of its roots being evident in Fratboy's jocular mockery of Karla Faye Tucker, whose execution he had refused to commute), sunken in secrecy, devoted to darkness, and oriented toward absolute power.

Certified and well-researched strands of this devious, infernal descent would appear In Barton Gelbmann's *Angler* and Jane Mayer's *The Dark Side*. Mayer mentions Cofer Black's preparing for the new administration a *Blue Sky Memo*, detailing plans for unorthodox lethal procedures in preventive action against Al Qaeda, plans that were ultimately diverted from a proper to an improper target (from Osama Bin Laden to Saddam Hussein). She points out the poorly directed payments of huge sums of cash to *an infamous Afghan warlord, Rashid Dostum, a blue-turbaned tyrant with* [a] *bushy jet-black mustache and eyebrows*. She describes the interrogation of the young American Taliban, John Walker Lindh, by Johnny Spann and Dave Tyson, the former wearing blue jeans and *a black sweatshirt*. Eerie chords: black and blue, bushy, Walker—DARKNESS.

Blackie has his well-reasoned and conservative answers to conspiracy theories, *Angler, black sites* (Mayer), and my own poetics of a disastrous departure from responsible government. Terrorism cannot be opposed without limitation of civil rights, intrusive surveillance, repression of freedom, and favoritism of private enterprise in military production, endeavors, and contracts. The administration may be uncouth, to some extent, and uncommunicative, through necessity, but it is ultimately with the best concerns for the country. Our discussions were limited to exchanges of handwritten letters; Blackie would not have us committing our opinions to e-mail or computers. When I put to him Andy's advance knowledge of the events of that day in September of 2001, he wrote that this could mean only one thing: *Andy is under Jordy's wing, Ped. If Jordy knew what was going to happen, he had to be part of it. His so-called foundation had to be with al-Qa'Ida, not against it. After all, didn't you yourself tell me that al-Qa'Ida means the base or the foundation? If it weren't for Andy, I'd be pushing you hard to report this to the FBI.*

Even Grayber thought that Blackie might have some credence here. Considerably shaken up by the possibility, I nonetheless remained unable to shake my conviction, derivative from mythology and questionable history, that Andy and Jordy were contesting the maleficent darkness, as I am convinced that Heidegger was doing, despite Emmanuel Faye's current insistence that Heidegger's existentialism is Nazi ideology.

The new century, then, begins with a decade of darkness. Near the end of the decade, Robert Novak, *the Prince of Darkness*, will die; but Rush Limbaugh, Bill O'Reilly, and Glenn Beck will carry on. Blackwater will change its name to XE, but Erik Prince's organization of mercenaries, paid by the government, will remain as a cadre of the religiously revolutionary Right Wing. The shadows of Sneer's Dark Side will not disperse. Benighted Democrats will spring a litter of anti-liberal Blue Dogs (Cyanocynics).

Critics insisted that terror, like drug traffic, is properly the object of police-work, not the responsibility of uniformed armed forces. *The War on Terror* was a misnomer conceived in arrogance and devious power-seeking. The term initially affixed to the illegal invasion of Iraq was *Operation Eternal Freedom*, so seriously at odds with secular articulation that it was changed to the comically ambiguous *Operation Enduring Freedom*. Fratboy's *Freedom*, though, was indeed something to be endured. Added to the pernicious comedy was a color-code for terror: posted daily, as a gauge for alertness against the kind of terrorist activity that Sneer and Fratboy had been instrumental in ignoring, were graded colors—Red (severe), Orange (high), Yellow (elevated), Blue (guarded), and Green (low). Sneer and Fratboy propagated a politically beneficial Orange quotient, with frequent flashes of Red calculated to enhance their prospects of re-election. Fear furthered their tenure and successfully obscured their disastrous economic and foreign-affairs policies.

Sneer's Dark-Sided institution of military tribunals, indefinite detainment of suspects given no legal redress, torture-enhanced interrogation, and suspension of *habeas corpus* produced a country greatly in opposition to its Constitution and the democratic aims of its founders: a new death of freedom, over which a corporate plutocracy presided and to which the communications media lent tolerant approval.

The first year of the Sneer-Fratboy administration's second term was marked, like the first year of the first term, with a calamity.

Hurricane Katrina ravaged the Mississippi and Louisiana coast, forcing a breach in the fragile New Orleans levee and inundating its Ninth Ward and much of the below-sea-level city. Thousands of African-American inhabitants, taking refuge in the athletic stadium, were inadequately fed and quartered. The ordeal was shown on televised news, while Fratboy dawdled out West and offered idle condolences, deigning eventually to fly over the city and pose pensively in observation. The incompetence and crass indifference of the administration was exposed indelibly and indubitably to view. The corpse of an old woman was shown on television; she was seated in a chair outside the stadium and covered with a blanket. The television cameras caught corpses floating in the flood-waters. Even Blackie recognized the administration's dereliction of preparedness and response, although he would not acknowledge that it was largely due to irresponsible administrative appointments and cronyism.

97

Thanks for 96, Ped. As you said, it's not at all to my liking. Standard Liberal formulas, shrill and pointless. Your novel would be better without this segment for two reasons: (1) the sheer editorialism is distracting and dull; (2) the narrative variant makes the work much more the memoir that it continues to strike me as being than the novel that you continue to insist that it is. Again, when are you at least going to fictionalize our names? FRATBOY and SNEER would be a start, if they weren't so god-damned obvious and silly. Now that you're well beyond page 200, I wish you'd shown it to Grayber and asked for his professional opinion. Even if you don't plan to publish it, you ought to get some appraisal of its artistic merit from some colleague. You may not try to get it published, but you sure don't plan to destroy it; and those unchanged names can cause trouble somewhere along the route.

Not to mention its finding its way somehow or other, some day, to Kris or Andy—although you do well enough by both of them, as you do by me, even with your Liberal prejudices (or, as you prefer, knee-jerk convictions).

I've been thinking about your title. BLACK AND BLUE covers your initial theme and works out the meaning of the shots Jordy Klug took at us, at Ronald Reagan and Errol Flynn. But your memoir advances beyond that, into the clouds that have both threatened and protected the life that

RAIN AND DARKNESS

Kris and you have led. Your title really ought to be RAIN AND DARKNESS.

Here's something you might want to slip into one of your segments. Just as King David had the beautiful young Abishag the Shunammite to keep him warm in his old age, so I now have the attractive middle-aged American citizen Rosario to keep me warm in mine. I know you'll understand that this in no way betrays Vera. There are ways to nurse a cold. There's only one way to nurse Cold.

Any news from Andy about Klug-doings?
Love to Kris,
B.

98

Blackie, speaking of Grayber in context past, had received all twelve paragraphs of segment 96. Between the eighth and ninth paragraphs, there had been a break, signaled by white space. That white space (now eliminated) was to have represented about eighteen months of time, during which I had about decided to abandon this novel; and I wrote nothing, turning instead to a re-reading of the novels and short stories and poems of Herman Melville and to a vain attempt to write poetry.

My intention had been to write a quiet novel about non-special people leading unspectacular lives in mundane settings, a novel about *getting by*, about the persistence of friendships and enmities in a country whose democratic principles somehow prevailed over racism, hatred, and rottenness. Coming to terms with death, however, increasingly engaged my sense of futility. Sneer has been an Ahab; his Moby Dick is Constitutional resistance to political religion; he has monomaniacally wrecked the *Pequod* (the ship of state). Deaths of family members and friends constitute a moral noise that cannot be integrated into the serial tones of a quiet life. As Dickens says, in *Hard Times*, . . . *of all the casualties of this existence upon earth, not one was dealt out with so unequal a hand as Death.* And he scratchingly contrasts *a bright blue sky* with *a dark mist*.

RAIN AND DARKNESS

My narrative was anagogically to have accepted time as neither linear nor de-centered, and life as not defined by beginning, middle, and end; it was to have known time as timing, and life as being: being is, the time times. But I have not had Heidegger's capacity for thinking or Kris's capacity for faith. Nor have I developed the degree of talent that could nullify the need for praise, the need that Blackie has astutely identified as the loser's mace. My determined and genuine attempts to praise—to praise students, for example, as Professor Landis had praised me—have been matters, not of willingness, but of will. Four shards of spirit remain: my guardian angel; the divinity of women; language as the saying of Being; and the Blue that underlies all passing.

In *The Old Curiosity Shop*, Dickens concluded his third chapter by choosing to switch his narrative from first-person to omniscient third-person. That is what I should like to do here, now that I have tentatively decided to complete this work. That would provide the added advantage of unlimited direct discourse and its permissive accoutrements. It's too late to do that, though; and, in fact, there is not much left to say and not much left to do. Then, too, eight or nine years after completing his tragedy of Little Nell, Dickens chose not to relieve his autobiographical *David Copperfield* of the first-person invalidity of narrative that has bothered me since my time in high school.

On a cold morning in May, as I was enjoying a breakfast of fried eggs, bacon, buttered toast, and grape juice, Kris's short cry, *Oh no!*, came from the living room. As I was getting up from my chair, she came into the kitchen with the morning's paper. Grayber's photo was on the front page. The headline was, ART PROFESSOR FOUND DEAD / MULTIPLE STAB WOUNDS. It was not a long article: the cleaning lady, arriving in the early afternoon the day before, discovered him on his bedroom floor and called the police; many valuables had been taken from his safe and from his desk; at least twelve of his artworks and a large number of objets d'art were missing, along with his SUV, a Cadillac Escalade; two residents, Angeline Ledd and Chloe Tilsen were being sought for questioning.

Kris put her arms around me until my shaking eased down. Graydon Corinth Braham, né Göran Sjögren Nilsson, *Emeritus* Professor of Art and Art History, internationally celebrated artist . . .

Only three days earlier, Grayber had come over with his newly acquired volume of Ernest Farrés's volume of poems about Hopper's paintings. Kris had prepared a satisfying lunch of cod cheeks, French fries, sweet pickles, Macadamia nuts, and the Lacrima Christi wine with which Grayber kept us supplied. The afternoon sun warmed the kitchen; the living room held the morning chill; so, seated by a small fire in the fireplace, we had checked prints of Hopper's paintings against Farrés's lyrical ekphrases. And now Grayber has ceased to exist. He is no more. Life, *the dirty trick*, rips open again what Simone de Beauvoir, quietly enraged by her septuagenarian mother's death from cancer, calls *le rideau rassurant de la banalité quotidienne* (the calmative curtain of trite routine). Death, she writes, is always *une violence indue* (an unwarranted act of violence). Whether it would be, I add, the result of old age, leukemia, or murder.

The unusual springtime cold was offset by sunshine and lack of rain, high pressure and low humidity. Blackie made the journey to the funeral in his new silver-colored Infiniti. He stayed with Kris and me for about ten days and did much to enable me to cope with the blistering shock. He wrote and delivered an admirably condolent eulogy and helped me to compress my thoughts and memories into a collegial eulogy that I managed to deliver without breaking down. After the hugely attended funeral service, there was a memorial service at the university; Blackie helped me to compose a testimonial, which I delivered for both of us.

The campus police, in concert with the municipal police, questioned all of Grayber's colleagues and close friends. Tilsen and Ledd had matriculated at the university, taking some of Grayber's courses and serving as his assistants before his retirement; but there were no available photographs of them. Grayber's sketches of them and his oil portraits of them, along with his portraits of Lilac Gustave, had been either destroyed or removed. The detailed description of the SUV, including its license number, brought in no reports.

Under courteous interrogation, I provided the police with nothing they didn't already know. Tilsen had dark brown hair, a broad forehead, firm chin, was a head shorter than Grayber, and usually wore slacks and a long-sleeved turtleneck sweater . . . .

My meetings with the pair had been infrequent and always merely peripheral to my visits with Grayber. A few weeks back, he had invited us in as he received with pleasure a batch of chruoeciki that Kris had made. The two housemates were there, Tilsen in navy-blue slacks and a powder-blue turtleneck sweater, and Ledd, with her abundant red hair brushed lustrously back from her small oval face (perfectly complexioned and with a sprinkle of light brown freckles across the bridge of her nose), wearing her usual tweed miniskirt and yellow T-shirt over her taut, unsupported breasts (the nipples in high definition); she was petite and, sitting high on a bar stool that day in leg-parted posture, revealed, deliberately, as usual, her unpantied pudenda. Kris ignored my entranced gazing thereto; but, after our return home, her tirade in disgust about my shameful gawking was followed by some seventy-two hours of righteous wrath, which I endured in silence, aware that denials and weak demurrals would be futile in the wake of my guilt, until she, as she always did, forgave me by forgetting the incident. To my descriptions of the physical attractiveness of Tilsen and Ledd, I added my opinion that Tilsen seemed more reserved and less of a sensual exhibitionist than Ledd. Kris, questioned separately, corroborated my statement that we had last seen Grayber three days before his death.

99

The local and national television news programs featured Grayber's murder for a few days. There were comments by the police chief, two members of the Art department, a neighbor, and the president of the university. Blackie and I were briefly visible on CNN as part of the funeral cortège. The media had tagged Tilsen and Ledd, the alleged killers, as the *Thelma and Louise* couple. This seemed to me to be inappropriate, in that the flight of the movie pair followed largely from the attempted rape of one of them.

Blackie, who had known Grayber much longer than I had, could not be sure that he was entirely innocent of wrongdoing toward the two younger women. At my expression of disbelief, he said that I could not really get to know people because my caring for others was always displaced by my self-interest, that such was my nature. That Kris offered no objection to Blackie's observation about me did not surprise me: she, as well as I, knew that he was right. My consolation lay in knowing that neither Kris nor Blackie cared less for me because of my nature or even wanted me, for any reason, to try to change my nature. What bothered me was the possibility that Grayber may have had a dark side, of which I had never been aware.

Would not the French Papin sisters, Christine and Lee, have been more analogous to this case? In the early 1930's they had butchered their employers and wallowed in the corpses' blood. Jean Genet based his play *Les Bonnes* (The Maids) upon their crime, challenging his viewing audiences to try to understand the concentric and descending levels of motivation and pretense. Kris turned away from my account of the crime and the play. Blackie agreed that the Papin affair was closer to what Tilsen and Ledd had done but added that too few in this country could make the connection, while everyone knew about *Thelma and Louise*, and the coincidence of the initials, T and L, was a lock. He laughed and slapped the chair's arm-rest when I said, *I do hope there are no unsuspected dark levels to Rosie and Nancy.*

Birger Lovberg, a professor of Greek at a Lutheran seminary in northern Indiana, was Grayber's nearest relative, a maternal cousin. He served as a pallbearer and had been named executor of his intestate cousin's property. The cousins regularly exchanged letters with their customary Christmas greetings. Birger had saved all of his received letters and informed Kris and me of six paintings that Grayber had intended eventually to give us; they would be of great market value now; but, unfortunately, they were all among the varied large canvases with which his killers had absconded.

For two weeks and three days, during which Birger wrestled with the probate court, set up an estate sale, and worked out details for the sale of Grayber's mansion, he spent many hours with Blackie, Kris, and me. Blackie was impressed by his business acumen. Kris found him charming and admired his Missouri Synod devoutness. His literary and linguistic erudition, which he modestly displayed with grace and unpretentious ease, awakened in me a sense of the ideal that I had enjoyed before only in Professor Landis, as

RAIN AND DARKNESS

a man of letters, and in Elvis Presley, as an entertainer. He confirmed and extended my observations of Attic figuration in *New Testament* Greek; and he studied with professional interest my research work on Gallus, supporting with surprising logic my theory of Augustus's contract on the poet-soldier.

He disagreed, however, with the suppositions about Gallus's Isis-foundation; nor would he subscribe to the notion of the singular divinity of women. He saw human divinity as resident substantially in the soul of each human being, male or female.

Birger, moreover, could not share my critical approval of the works of Pär Lagerkvist, *whose dark humanism and unkempt Lutheranism* he found to be fitful and faulty. He much preferred Graham Greene, for whom sin was the *felix culpa* of faith, and William Butler Yeats, who berated humankind for its attempts to humanize God. Disturbingly, he placed Grayber in the post-midnight of Yeats's fourth age of Man: *Now his wars on God begin / At stroke of midnight God shall win*. Birger paraphrased: *His war on God had well begun / At stroke of midnight God had won.* Like Blackie, Birger had sensed in Grayber a darkness that, if it were real, had fully eluded me. Novy-shouldering me, Birger commended me on my friendship with his cousin and, in doing so, provided me with the deep, genuine consolation that I had desperately needed. He was more than twenty years younger than I, but I felt his comforting to be that of an old and wise paraclete.

On one occasion, an early evening during which we were all enjoying Kris's service of Martinis, Birger praised the performance of Blackie's Infiniti. *It's the right car for me*, Blackie said; *when I think about Ped, I get into it and split*. Kris concealed her laughter by lowering her head and placing her hand over her mouth; but her shoulders shook enough to give her away. Birger, perhaps because of my rueful smile and his awareness of my inability to take the joke, did not smile, but made a rejoinder that pleased and amused me greatly: *Of course, like all material possessions, it displaces the Why with an I.* Blackie appeared not quite to get the pun; and Kris was still recovering from her appreciation of Blackie's joke; but I was restored to ease and raised my glass to Birger.

100

They're here in Ajijic, Dad. We learned about the killing from television and the POST. Jordy knew that, with a stolen SUV and stolen artworks, they'd head for Mexico by way of a chop shop and a c dealer. We flew to Tucson. The SUV was there—repainted, newly registered, new serial number, Arizona plates. The c guy had already shipped the paintings to Marseilles and Caracas. He had given the women a pile of good cash and a clean night flight to Guadalajara. We tracked them from a private landing strip near G. to a *casa de huéspedes* in G. that offered *cobijo* and medical attention. They both had stitches removed from facial and other cuts. They must have been stitched up fairly early in their flight. The media said nothing about their wounds, only about the painter's being stabbed. We still haven't learned whether it was the painter or the women who acted in self-defense. From Guadalajara they moved here, a resort town on Lake Chapala. Nice place, ideal weather. They're in a private villa, owned by a friend of the shorter woman—Ledd—who speaks fluent Spanish, by the way. I'm here alone, in a resort hotel—Jordy is taking it easy with his arrhythmia in G. I use different rental cars and can keep onto them every day. They don't leave the villa very often. Right now, they both have dyed-black butch haircuts and wear slacks and light jerseys, kind of like twins, except for their heights. I've noticed that two other guys are tailing them. I called Jordy, and he said they're definitely not foundation guys—probably FBI and probably haven't noticed me yet, or they would have been on me. Anyway, Dad, Jordy says (1) we can get the foundation to take the women out, since they've misused their force and the painter was your father's friend, (2) we can alert the FBI, either the guys here, if we learn that they are FBI, or with a call to D.C., or (3) we can work out a way to get the money they made—some 60K—and send it to the painter's cousin in Valparaiso. Jordy says he'll let you decide—you, not, as he says, the flag-draper. So, I said I'd see if you had any preference. I've got my laptop here. Just send an e-mail (the yahoo address) and write 1, 2, or 3. Love to Mom,—A.

The letter, I somehow managed to realize, was written by my son and was not a joke; nor should I have saved it—not with local and federal police still making inquiries here. What I did do, immediately, was to send Andy an e-mail: *The number is 2*. Andy's e-mail response came later that same day: *Took my snail-mail longer to reach you than I thought. The 2 guys were what we thought. 2 took place independently yesterday.*

Then, during the following afternoon, it was breaking news on television. The FBI, with the coöperation of the Mexican *federales* had apprehended the *Thelma and Louise killers* (the headlines, but not the stories, omitted *alleged*). There they were, handcuffed, doing the *perp walk*, looking just as Andy had described them, but both were now also wearing sunglasses. The media were, for a few days, as glib and excessive as they usually are with sensational material; but the slant was toward the defense: sex slaves of a sadistic professor. National interest waned in favor of the *Barbie Bandits*, two attractive teenage girls who stole about $11,000 from a bank in Atlanta and, later, O.J. Simpson's involvement in an armed-robbery attempt, in Las Vegas, to recover property that had once been his.

Tilsen and Ledd, eventually, were saved from the death penalty, as it seemed, by their very real wounds. The defense lawyers contrived successfully to give the *self defense* claim primacy over the factual flight from the scene of the crime, grand theft of property, and traffic in stolen goods. The prosecution gained points by comparing to the relatively slight wounds of the women, the fatally brutal wounds of the victim and by emphasizing the theft and traffic as motives instead of vengeful exaction of payment for enslavement. But the jury would not be convinced that the women's wounds, especially those that scarred their faces, were self-inflicted as the basis for a plea of self-defense. The verdict, *guilty of aggravated assault and grand larceny*, was to bring in a sentence of twenty-five years. By *snail mail*, Blackie and I agreed that, in this trial, justice had become a fiction.

We could not agree, however, that this was the tenor of the injustice that Sneer and Fratboy were imposing upon the country. Blackie applauded the PATRIOT Act and was a *Support the Troops* advocate of the illegal war of aggression waged upon Iraq. He saw nothing un-American in Sneer's program of *extraordinary rendition*, indefinite detention of profiled suspects, and institution of torture, warrantless wiretaps, and all the other grotesque wrongdoings of a *Dark Side* sustained by disproportionately numerous *signing statements*, pusillanimous Democrats, and a dumbed-down populace. Our polarity, though, was at least congenial: we had what the polarized country lacked, a bond of symbiotic friendship.

After Kris and I returned, one afternoon, from placing a violet nosegay on Sharny's grave and four roses on Grayber's,

I showed her Andy's letter. My fear that she would be worried or shocked by the possibility of his having been an accessory to violence was dispelled by her asking me what number I had sent and then concluding that Andy must ethically have taken my advice despite his disclaimer of his having received it after the fact. She was miffed, though, at my not having shown her the letter upon my receipt of it.

At my explanation that I was just too shaken up to ask her to share my painful discomfiture she shrugged and complained again—rightfully, I now realize—about my erratic self-absorption. It was November; but over the graves there had been no snow, and swatches of the cemetery lawn had been still green, as the sun drew bright lines along the leafless branches of the oak and aspen trees.

Now, as we turned on the kitchen and living-room lights against the early evening shadows, Kris said, *Poor Grayber, murdered by benighted bitches who will live out their lives as though they were only randy thieves.* Musingly, I reminded her of Jordy's conclusion that Tilsen and Redd had *misused* the female *force*; and I explained, once again, the theory, to which, indeed, I subscribed, about thelycratism and the divinity of women; to this I added my aversion to capital punishment and my thought that the sentence should have been life without parole. Kris, like Blackie, approved of capital punishment and believed that the guilty bitches should have been executed. And, *That theory is silly, Pete; it's just horny male vanity putting women on a pedestal so that men can enjoy the freedom they think women deprive them of; otherwise, they put women in the pit—never at eye level, never on equal ground.* Although she had perhaps never read Simone de Beauvoir, she had summed up rather well what de Beauvoir calls *alterity* (justifying one's grossly negative view of *the other* by positing an ideal compensatory antithesis of *the other*—like saying that Black people are sub-human but super dancers or super athletes, or that Jews are money-grubbers but great intellects).

Lemondrop.com Monday 21 June
By *Peter O. Blaustern*
Women are divine. I am grateful for whatever attention a woman gives me and for however long she allows me the gift of her presence. I have loved and lost, but because I have known the touch and the smile of Woman I have lived.

Reply By Fran
Good for you! A man who is able to discern the Goddess in every woman will be amply rewarded—with love and inspiration. This is where true poets have always come from. Read Robert Graves' *The White Goddess* for further details!

Reply By Nick
Don't make me gag! Women could be divine. They'd just rather be selfish bitches.

By *lost* I meant Trish and Anne. The tension of the response seemed to me to be dyadic: *blue* Fran, *black* Nick. [Did you, George, arrange for this falling into place?]

Grayber had ceased to exist. There was no way to adjust to it. Kris prayed for his soul and had no problems with the fact of death. She would rise each morning well before 6:00 and find freshness in orange juice, buttered toast, and well-creamed coffee. For me, every morning was a stale ejection from the darkness of sleep into grey disorientation: what day is it? Is Grayber really gone? The reality of his presence in the precise studios of my dreams had to be externalized as realistic fiction. To me, each iron-grey morning entailed an urgent bladder, arthritic inhibitions, and an oneirectomy.

There was the pain-filled solace of Emily Dickinson's perfect simile: . . . *like the Distance / On the look of Death*—. Similes, if they work at all, serve best in comparisons of unseen forces with unknown things. Burns's love is only sonantally, not inherently, like a *red, red rose*. Love is more like the spectral force of a coloring that substantiates the unique fragrance of a rose; it is equivalent, in Kris's religious contentment, to the faith that substantiates hopes—and to Dickinson's deep *Blue to Blue* power of the *brain* to absorb the sea. And so . . . *a Fly*—, says Dickinson in her substantially imagined death, *With Blue* . . .

Kris was not unsettled by my lack of faith or by my inability to understand her religious contentment. She insisted that she had enough faith for both of us and that she relied upon my guardian angel to cordon me off from nothingness. She assured me that my irrefragable belief in my guardian angel fully complemented her faith. My feeling was that the guardian angel constantly protected me from the accidents and failures to which I was prone (Jordy's bullets, shipment to an Infantry replacement depot, incoming mortar and .88 shells, breaches of grammar and syntax, automobile fatality, cancer, and serious matters that could terminate my existence) but that this angel did not guarantee that I would gain eternal life. Kris nodded when I asked her if guardian angels were imbued with gender. *Your guardian angel is whatever you know him in your heart to be,* she said. Somewhat to my own surprise, I said that I had always—*always*—felt my guardian angel to be female and to have a name. *What is her name, Pete?* With easy warmth and with a pleasant sense of spiritual approval, I said, *Her name is George.* Kris smiled, grasped my right hand in both of hers, and said that this was true to the character of conventual reality: men in religious orders, from monks to popes, never assume names that are recognizably female; but nuns take names that Grace, through Truth, has freed from gender and, in consolidating male and female, has re-engendered.

Kris spoke at greater length and in simpler words; but this is how I recall the sense of what she serenely had explained.

Isn't this, I asked her, proof of the divinity of women. *Pete, that's like saying that the aroma of Folger's in the morning is proof of the divinity of coffee beans.* (That, I observed to myself, is one horseshit simile.)

101

The recollection of certain times and certain events can be a pleasant activity, although it's not really an activity, since recollection is a passive indulgence, like daydreaming. The recollection of error, failure, or death is not pleasant nor, since it brings up resistance to the pains of regret, is it passive. Denial is one of the modes of such resistance; but denial, as a quest for passivity, is generally a retreat from the ills of the present. At this time, my resistance must induce a retreat from the past to the present. The year of Grayber's death was a bad year in a bad decade. Have there been good decades? The Roaring Twenties—ending in a Crash. The Fabulous Fifties—pocked by HUAC and generative of the violent Sixties. The bubbling Nineties—leading to Fratboy's fatal first decade of the new century, the decade during which Grayber died at the hands of two women, who find my thoughts now only in the form of some imagined graphic novel. Escape from the present into the past generates, in its prolongation, the need to escape from the past back into the present. Activity seems always to intrude unceremoniously into passivity, as losers learn.

In his review of Morris Dickstein's . . . *Cultural History of the Great Depression* (quite timely in the current recession wrought by Fratboy's reaping the ruin wrought by Reagan's deregulation), Adam Begley questions the

RAIN AND DARKNESS

validity of slicing history into 10-year *chunks*— . . . *the Mauve Decade . . . the Roaring Twenties . . . the Hungry Thirties . . . the convention-bound '50s, the subversive '60s, the cringe-inducing '70s, the avaricious '80s.* Thanks, though, to our Graeco-Roman heritage, *decade* (Greek *deka* = ten) and *decadent* (Vulgar Latin *de+cadere* = to decay) coalesce; and each half-generation, overlapping with its successor, rises and declines within an almost eerily ordained current of ripeness to rottenness. With the Iraq War and the prodigal squandering of the inherited surplus, Sneer and Fratboy, politicizing patriotism and pulverizing fiscal responsibility by means of puerile privatizing of federal sustenance, expedited the putrefaction of the Run-down Ones (or whatever one calls the first ten years of a new century: the Digits? The Units?). Thus, I turn from a bad past year of this decade of descent to an equally bad present year.

It is the year in which we lose William Safire, one of the last fair-minded and articulately intellectual Conservatives and one of the few remaining champions of English grammar, syntax, and usage. It was depressing to lose Edwin Newman, the last news commentator to pronounce *covert* correctly. And now Safire leaves a tragically fading echo of linguistic integrity. It is greatly to be hoped that someone like Jack Rosenthal, filling in for Safire with the last *On Language* column before Safire's death, will carry on the necessary work. (But no: *On Language* will cease to be, in 2011.)

Rosenthal's essay deals with *phantonyms*, an effective coinage for *Words that look as if they mean one thing but mean another: fulsome*, misused by Obama as meaning *full*, when, in fact, it means *disgusting* or *insincere*; *noisome*, which has nothing to do with *noise*; *enormity*, denoting only *a great wickedness* or *a monstrous act*; *disinterested*, *enervated*, *fortuitous, penultimate, presently, restive*—all consistently misused. Other *phantonyms* that could be added include *embattled* (prepared for battle), which properly ought not to be confused with *beleaguered* (beset, besieged), as descriptive dictionaries and careless news writers allow it to be; *empathy* (physical subjectivity, like matching one's facial expressions to those of actors in a movie), which is different from *sympathy* (compassion, sharing the emotions or pains of other persons); and *convince* (which ought not to be followed by an infinitive; one convinces *of* or *that*; and which does not mean *persuade* [which is properly followed by an infinitive; one persuades *to*]).

A bad past year, and an equally bad present year: but neither is quite so bad as the year of Grayber's death, the year that deprived me of a companionship upon which, unconsciously, I had come to depend. We had been enthusiastically engaged in the study and discussion of Ernest Farrés's poems about Edward Hopper. Grayber had spent three years in Barcelona and was fluent in Catalan; I have only a spotty reading knowledge of peninsular Spanish. Turning to a study of Catalan on my own has been helpful; but more helpful has been my turning to poetry of controlled grief: Gilgamesh's anguish over the death of Enkidu; Catullus's visit to his brother's grave; Dante's adoration of the Beatrice taken from his life; Wordsworth's discovery of celestialism in his tranquil recollections of loss; Shelley's *Adonais*; Gray's *Elegy Written in a Country Churchyard*; Tennyson's *In Memoriam*; Auden's poem about the death of Yeats (*Earth, receive an honored guest . . .*).

Post-Romantic poetry does very little for the heart; it challenges the intellect. Regular meter and rhyme are music; the atonality of suggestively taut lingo-jingles stimulates the mind—musical, perhaps, but only in the manner of serial music. Thinking of my loss of Grayber, I needed restoratives, like Wordsworth's . . . *and never lifted up a single stone,* or . . . *With rocks and stones and trees.* Lines like Mina Loy's *Odious oasis / in furrowed phosphorous // the eye-white sky-light/ white-light district/ of lunar lusts* are entertainingly taut and clever to the point of pretentiousness, but they call attention to their composer and do nothing to compose the sensibility of the reader, at least that of this reader.

Nicholas Baker's *The Anthologist* ostensibly defends the music of rhyme and four-stress meter against the fractionalism of free verse, Futurism, and Modernism; but his fictional defender is an erratic chowderhead named Paul Chowder, who writes poetry in free verse. He is a converse of Marianne Moore's *imaginary gardens with real toads in them*; Chowder is an imaginary toad in the real garden of successful modern poets (Whitman, Lanier, Robinson, Berryman, Oliver, Roethke, Wright, Fenton, and many, many others). The vapidity of Chowder's own poetry makes suspect his critical acumen. Two injuries to his left index finger and one injury to one of his thumbs symbolize the crippled metrician in need of dactyliatry. Flashes of poetic flare appear in his prose: *I ran three forward-falling steps,* and *He found the water that nobody knew was there.* Ultimately, though, in his ineffectuality, he is a loser because he doesn't get to the heart of what Wordsworth calls *the still sad music of humanity.* Baker's genius lies in his reminding us of the loss of this music in our monochromatic and obfuscatory modem poetry.

Walter Pater is right: *All art constantly aspires towards the condition of music.* All graceful living, too, constantly aspires to the condition of the dance. Pope's line keeps echoing: . . .

those move easiest who have learned to dance. Baker takes the musical term, *fermata* (prolongation, as of a note of music) and writes a novel, so entitled, about a loser who prolongs notes of time, stops time so that he can undress women. He portrays another loser in *Checkpoint* (another anti-contrapuntal stoppage): a guy, deaf to the tones of history, makes futile plans to assassinate Fratboy. Losers live atonal lives within their daydreams of lechery and power. Winners dance and sing and play guitars and Yamaha pianos within the spherical ratio of the Golden Section, constantly achieving .618 in second nature and by creative indifference. Winners have no need of praise; losers try self-referentially to manufacture praise within the *baseless fabric* of deleterious daydreams. Grayber, like Baker (a winner who sings sweet songs for luckless losers), was a winner who made me feel unlike a loser: *a little touch of* Grayber *in* life's *night.*

Perhaps it has been George [Has it been you, George?] who sent in my direction Blackie, Shannon, Guinotte, Novy, Kris, Sharny, Anne, and Grayber. Only Kris and Blackie remain: in my present. Kris, with whom I shall get by, and Blackie, who dignifies my loss by naming it. Four brought the light and four the light has brought. Eight to the bar: a Boogie beat. It is the beat that I have heard but did not play. Professor Landis taught me how to listen to perfection's beat; and Jordy, Hedwig, and Schwarz-Bleiler attuned me to serial discord, the dark matter of music. And so, for FDR, Truman, Eisenhower, and Kennedy, there is Nixon, Reagan, and Fratboy—the Heideggerian perfection of Four in dyadic opposition to Logic's imperfect Triad. [George, you are Carrie, weren't you?]

102

A member of our Sociology department had written a best-selling novel. Overcoming my envy, I bought a copy, read it, and sent it to him by campus mail with a request for an autograph and with a glowingly complimentary critique. He invited me to lunch, returned my copy, in which he had written an inscription expressing his gratitude, and let me know that no other faculty member had honored him in this way. My gesture resulted in his becoming exceptionally well-disposed toward me. He sent me inscribed copies of each of his subsequent novels, even after he had left the university to become a Writer in Residence at a prestigious Ivy League institution. Two of his sixteen novels won national awards. Now, with the publication of his seventeenth novel, he has returned to this university for a short lecture series: four lectures, one per week, on *Factional Fiction and Fictive Fact*. After the first of his lectures, I thanked him for my copy of his latest novel, complimented him on his chiastic series-title, and, by way of small talk, mentioned this enterprise of my novel in progress. To my surprise, he seemed sincerely interested and, more surprising, asked if he might read what I had written. When I brought a copy of my work to his suite at the University Lodge, he was entertaining guests informally—hors d'oeuvres, music, cocktails. He welcomed me very cordially, carried my packet to a writing-desk, and guided me through a few minutes of pleasant small talk before

I excused myself and he turned to two arriving guests. After his concluding lecture, and before he left campus, he returned my sheaf of the above 101 segments along with the following letter: *Given the nature of what you have written, I dare to assume that you will include this note in your text. Accordingly, I'm putting it all into italics, so that you need if you so choose, only to cut and paste it in. Your friend, Blackie, is right: you've compiled a memoir and have quite some task ahead of you if you really wish to give it the shape and substance of a novel. Why not work separately with various of your episodes—Shannon, the war experience, Anne, Braham (I was distressed to read about the sensational crime and, I admit, tempted, on my own, to fashion a novel based on Gray's career), not to mention the elusive Klug, whom I suspect you have already fictionalized in good part? You do well in maintaining your point of view as the narrative device, but I think you lose perhaps more than you gain by sacrificing the use of quotation marks to the limitations of a first-person exposition. Your high-school teacher was right, you know, about literary license. Moreover, the characters, all seen strictly from your vantage, attain therefrom to only limited depth; and, as your friend advises, their names really must be fictionalized even though the historical events need not, and, perhaps, must not, be disguised.*

Recollection, of course, is fiction; and recorded fact is a corrective to recollection. As I've been claiming in my lectures here, an effective combination of recollection and fact requires exceptional skill. Hugo, de Beauvoir, Pasternak, Mailer, Pynchon, and a few others achieve this by having actual events shape the actions of fully invented (and convincingly developed) characters. Your lack of such skill is evident in your presentation of real events as a backdrop to real people whose characters and motives are known in degrees of depth only by you.

RAIN AND DARKNESS

If you're writing this simply as a means of understanding yourself (of ascending to your self, as you say Heidegger has it), fine. If you contemplate wide readership and sales, I can only discourage you. Best-selling, or critically successful, novels, or both, are produced by literary engineering. My novels follow a formula—fixed in plot and characterization, variable in style and execution, and susceptible of multiple interpretations—that is grounded in constancy of practice, like that of a musician, and constancy of daily work. Your narrative is serious enough in purpose, images, and motifs; but, without a compelling drive and a rigid core, it warrants an appraisal as dilettantism.

Your writing shows promise; and, if you can break away from the biographical corral and subject yourself to a strict work schedule, practicing, practicing, practicing the fullness of inventive fiction, utilizing the transformation, as opposed to the shackles, of the fictive shifts of recollection, you will succeed. Your appreciation of Heidegger can serve to assure you that it's never too late.

Thank you for entrusting your work to me. And thank you for your friendship.

The criticism is fair; the advice is as firm as my determination not to heed it. Presenting one's recollections (admittedly fiction, whether by definition or not) as a novel must be legitimate, if not commercially profitable. The problematic arises when one incites Oprah Winfrey's indignation by presenting fictional excesses as integers of memoirs. Nonetheless, the fictions by means of which one insulates one's self against the collapse of one's identity is as much a part of the truth of one's self as birth and death certificates and the varying reactions of various people to the self that is presented to them.

After reading the successful novelist's critique, I put it and the typescript into an old amazon.com book-delivery box and onto a high closet shelf for close to a month, knowing that I would return to it, as now I have, but wondering why I would go on with the thing. It occurred to me that only a winner could effectively and convincingly produce the story of a loser. For a loser to set down her or his own story is to aggravate or compound the phenomenon of loss.

There is no market for loss. Losing, however, is to quitting as quitting is to not trying.

How is it that I have *fictionalized* Jordy Klug? What is *elusive* about him? Perhaps it is that part of his being to which I cannot help but feel attracted, despite my otherwise total abhorrence of him. My sense is that he is *intrusive*. Somewhere above delta zero, in the variables of our existences, our parabolas intersect to define the point of female divinity. But he is quite possibly a murderer; and he called Kris a *Polack cunt*. Still, I, quite possibly, have repressed worse obscenity in my expressed dislike of Schwarz-Bleiler, who, even in absenting herself from her divinity, remains superior to me.

Pindar makes the point that losers have recourse to nothing but the licking of their wounds. Loss leaves no space for moral victories or satisfaction in having contended well. If it were otherwise, if in defeat the agony could be lessened to any degree, the meaning of victory would be darkly qualified.

There must be losers, then, if winning is to be a reality. The damned must exist to glorify the Elect. *Ananké*, the Greek concept of Necessity, is grounded in loss. *Nemesis* visits the loser who presumes to have won; presumption is *hubris*. It is incumbent upon the loser constantly to try to

RAIN AND DARKNESS

win without ever entertaining the expectation of doing so. The author of the *Iliad* is a winner who draws, in Hector, the classic portrait of the loser. It is the loser as hero; heroism, as such, exists in proportion to one's distance from victory. The hero, as loser, is superior only in inferiority. This is the integrity of the damned, an exemplar of which is Milton's Satan. These are the pedestrian thoughts of a schoolteacher sitting in the darkness of retirement while winners enjoy the sleep they've earned.

The thing to do, then, is to round the little story off and get it to Andy on a CD, to be read, destroyed, or somehow printed after I have ceased to exist. He's into text-production. Maybe he could translate it into Italian—*Pioggia e buio*—or change all the names, or fill in the middle, the prime that was passed in stable mundaneness. Or he might want simply to keep it as a weary testament of his Old Man, whose interest in others was limited to their interest in himself, the events of whose life are transmuted into recollections and the recollections are expressed in words, which are, by nature, fictions. Weary or bleary, the word *testament* itself is etymologically shrouded in the foggy concepts of *testes, three,* and *witness.*

Eeriness follows my decision: Andy sends an e-mail, *Can't make it for Thanksgiving, as I'd planned. Have to wait out Jordy's being set up with a Pacemaker. See you for the Christmas holidays. Definitely.*

Kris and I had been eagerly anticipating Andy's Thanksgiving visit; Klug had intruded again.

Nancy and Rosie, coincidentally, made plans for Thanksgiving that were to take them away from Blackie—Nancy with two of her oldest friends (dating back to high school), and Rosie with her sons. Blackie, in his new Cadillac XLR, drove down to spend the holiday with Kris and me. He was delighted with his new convertible roadster, although it was not top-down weather, and he was in a good frame of mind. He arrived two days before Thanksgiving and planned to stay through the weekend. Kris fitted up a guest bedroom for him, with her favorite framed photograph of Vera on the night-stand.

We had our usual easy arguments about politics. To my *appalling Palin* and *slack-brained McCain* he countered with *abominable Obama* and *unabidable Biden*. He noted how closely Kris, in her younger days, resembled Palin. *Possibly*; I agreed: *the dark hair, the firm cheek-lines*. Kris now, of course, was white-haired and a bit puffy in cheeks and neck.

After I'd shown him the novelist's appraisal of my work in progress, Blackie shook his head and said, *Well, it's good that you showed it to him; but you wanted praise again, Ped, and you got commercial advice, which is good, but the guy obviously can't see what you're trying to do*. He smiled at my quizzical frown, sipped his Hudson's Bay Scotch, and said that my recognition of my passivity and my putting that recognition into the form of a novel amounted to passive resistance, that passivity, including the need for praise, is for losers and that passive resistance, including my attempt to praise others for their unilateral conferring of benefits upon me, amounts, not to winning, but to ethical compensation. *You're not denying your passivity, or making excuses for it, or trying to get above it; you're attending to it and expressing your gratitude to those of us who have accommodated it because, in some way or other, we genuinely care for you.*

—Whether or not that's the case, that's very high praise, Blackie.

Maybe so.

RAIN and DARKNESS

The big Recession has not been calamitous for Blackie. Ever attached to *The Wall Street Journal*, he nonetheless heeded the columns of Paul Krugman in *The New York Times*. He avoided hedge funds, derivatives, and the dreamy greed that nurtured Ponzi schemes like Bernie Madoff's. He had transferred his various savings and checking accounts to a few banks in the Midwest that refrained from subjecting their investors and depositors to the risks entailed by the cash-flow provision of sub-prime mortgages.

My few investments, entered into on Blackie's advice, had dipped but remained stable and productive of modest but steady dividends. Blackie refused to denounce Reagan-initiated deregulation or Fratboy's tax-cuts-for-the-wealthiest; these were sound business principles in vital capitalism, he said. He blamed the Madoffs and the profit-gluttonous gamblers who ignored the business ethics upon which true capitalist principles were based.

Blackie gave Kris a ride in his XLR. They drove to the Piggly Wiggly and bought three bags of groceries, for which Kris refused to let Blackie pay and which fit well into the trunk of the roadster, while the top was up. They also bought Blue Label Scotch, Port wine, and Grey Goose vodka, for which Kris did not object to Blackie's paying.

After putting away the groceries, we set out salty snacks and sipped chilled vodka (straight up, with twists) and reminisced about the old movies. Kris concentrated on the leading ladies and leading men (Mary Astor, Tyrone Power, Barbara Stanwyck, Fred MacMurray, Robert Mitchum, Lizbeth Scott, Marlene Dietrich). Blackie and I recalled supporting actors, the reliables: Clarence Kolb, Dorothy Peterson, Harry Davenport, Beulah Bondi, John Litel, Jack Lambert, Moroni Olsen, Thelma Ritter. Those are just a few of the names; a catalogue here would be tediously long. We agreed, Blackie only tentatively, that true classic Hollywood was the film noir, beginning with Orson Welles's *Citizen Kane*, including Orson Welles's *The Lady From Shanghai*, and concluding with Orson Welles's *Touch of Evil*.

Thanksgiving Day was cold, with soft rain under a depressingly grey sky. Fully dried hickory logs produced an aromatic and cheering fire in the old fireplace that Kris and I had had cleaned and restored a few years earlier. Kris had prepared a huge Butterball turkey, for which Blackie had made a spicy pork stuffing. There were light, creamy mashed potatoes, over which we poured rich turkey gravy, and a large bowl of exceptionally tartly-sweet cranberries from Wisconsin's crop, which this year had been almost magically abundant. The dessert that awaited consisted of a pumpkin pie, a pumpkin cream pie, and a mince pie—all from Baker's Square.

Kris said *Grace*, giving thanks for the divinely wrought consciousness that formed our perceptions of our blue planet, its black earth, and green growth, of lives lived and being lived, of moments of happiness that could be known only in inevitable passages through valleys of shadow toward chasms of darkness. She expressed thanks for sunshine, rain, and seasons of snow, for faith that defined life, whether or not one actually experienced this defining factor of life, and for guardian angels.

Blackie poured the full-bodied, dark red wine and offered a toast *To the Twentieth Century, America's century, which it was our good luck to have known—the century of Lindbergh, the Greatest Generation, the Salk vaccine, the Moon landing, and Ronald Reagan.*

Kris added, *of Women's Rights, Civil Rights, and Gay Rights.*

RAIN AND DARKNESS

And I added, *of Einstein, Heidegger, FDR, the Marshall Plan, Elvis Presley, and the Word Processor.*

Our meal was one of those long moments of happiness for which Kris had given thanks. There was quite enough food left over to carry us through the remainder of Blackie's visit. We stored it in plastic containers and Saran Wrap. We cleared the table and rinsed the dishes and utensils and stacked them in the dishwasher. Then we relaxed further with Drambuie and, raising our cordials toward the crackling hickory fire, toasted Grayber. We talked about Grayber and Jordy Klug. When I mentioned Jordy's immediate quest for the now imprisoned killers, Blackie said that it had to have been either Andy's idea or the prospect of a large FBI reward. No, I said, Jordy, not Andy, made the decisions for their actions; and the media carried no information about reward money, which it would certainly have done had there been any, not to mention the expeditious success of the FBI's pursuit and capture. Blackie concluded that whatever goodness Jordy may have had in him would have been the result of Andy's influence.

The rain let up by evening but returned in heaviness on Friday and then turned to snow during Friday night. The sky cleared on Saturday, as we lunched on turkey sandwiches and cranberries poured over stuffing. On Sunday morning, a cold rain washed away the inch-and-a-half of snow and the sun shone from a fully blue sky. Blackie went to church with Kris, while I read the Sunday papers and listened to some Beethoven sonatas. Early Monday morning, Blackie backed the roadster out of the double garage and loaded his suitcases into the trunk. The three of us stood in the cold sunlight. Blackie gave Kris a hug and kissed her on the cheek. *'Bye, Kris.* Then he turned to me and said, *So long, Ped.* We shook hands, and I said, *See ya, Old Timer.* Kris and I watched Blackie drive down the street in the bright sunlight that would be at his back for the rest of the morning. Then we went into the house, which was warmed now by our new high-efficiency furnace.

103

During the second week in December, the mild winter disappeared into a thunderstorm blizzard followed by three days of heavily falling snow. Kris prepared the Christmas cards, adding letters to each of them—some lengthy, others brief; I returned to my note-gathering and drafting of chapters for my never-to-be-finished project of a book on Gallus. We hired people now to do the housecleaning, the driveway plowing, and the sidewalk shoveling. Darkness came quickly with the falling snow, and Kris and I shared evening sandwiches and Blue Moon ale by the fireside, as young David Copperfield, his frail mother, and Clara Peggotty had *dined together by the fireside*, in contrast to an earlier dining, that of David and his mother with the insufferable Edward Murdstone, David's *firm* stepfather: *We dined alone, we three together*—the three were together, but each was alone. During our Thanksgiving dinner, I had recalled this passage and had revised it to suit our situation: we are dining together, we three alone—making the three of us one, apart from the rest of the world, the situation that Dickens invites his reader to compare with that of David, his mother, and Murdstone, each in the others' presence, but each completely apart from the others. It was *David Copperfield*, I think, that nudged me, in high school, toward a critical appreciation of literature—and then *Moby Dick* and Kenneth Roberts's *Northwest Passage* and Steinbeck's *Of Mice and Men*.

My first nudging occurred much earlier, though. In the fifth grade, our teacher, Miss Ruthven, had us read Eugene Fields's *Little Boy Blue*, in which poem the little toy dog becomes covered with dust and the little toy soldier red with rust. The concluding two lines are, *What has become of our Little Boy Blue / Since he kissed them and put them there*[?]. Miss Ruthven put the question to the class. Like most of the others in class, I saw only the surface of the words: the boy was gone, the toys were left abandoned for years. After a lengthy silence and then puzzled murmurs, there was a response from the back of the classroom: Jim Marshall said, *Maybe he died*. We all laughed; but Miss Ruthven, delighted, said that that was exactly what had happened. It was then that I learned to read with attention to what was in the text but was not explicitly stated.

This lesson had prepared me to read what Dickens was saying implicitly by means of syntax, rhythm, and word choice, and to catch, for example, the import of David Copperfield's schoolmate Straddles's being *drugged with black draughts and blue pills*. (But David's *verbatim* retention of masses of complex dialogue still unsettles me, literary license notwithstanding.)

Gone was Grayber, my Jim Marshall for Farrés's *Edward Hopper*. Grayber had explained the poet's assumption of the artist's perspective and had clarified the aspects of color in the fifty poems. Without Grayber's continued explication, my disappointments in the poetry recurred. Lawrence Venuti's prize-winning translation is almost impeccably reflective of the original; but, as such, it tends to sustain my reservations. Hopper's calculated passages of blue attest to the ethereal ideal that invades and escapes the integrity of the mundane, like the rich blue shirt against the earthy colors of the deep-green coat and tie and the rich-brown felt hat in *Self-Portrait*, or the ineffably blue cast of *Summertime*.

Farrés is right about the gradation of colors in Hopper's *Railroad Sunset*; but *El tros cobert de blau* (The blue-covered strip) is not blue but green; or, at most, it is the beginning of the transition from green to blue in the visible spectrum. The numerous prints of this 1929 oil painting vary from patent green to the tentative turquoise that appears to be the poet's choice. The high-sky blue is toned down, or muted, to a pale lavender in some prints; but its blue purity should be retained—in freedom from the earth-turned-black-by-the-loss-of-sunlight. Farrés calls the *blau* Ulyssean (*com Ulisses*) and likens it to eyes of turquoise (*com uns ulls turquesa*). *Ulyssean* (preferably *Odyssean*) comports with Hopperesque blue: versatile (polytropic), oceanic, favored by Athena (consciousness) and the female force (Circe, Calypso, Penelope). Farrés's antithesis to Ulyssean blue (*negre com un mal averany*: evil-omened black) is right for Hopper, whose black frequently looms ominously amidst verdure. With equal frequency it stands in contrast to his perfective blue: *Corner Saloon; Soir Bleu; Skyline, Near Washington Square; Drug Store; South Truro Church; Hotel Room; Cape Cod Evening* (in which the verdure has become blue against the encroaching night); *Gas; Hotel Lobby; August in the City; Summer Evening* (against the night, the pale porch-light is blue); *Four Lane Road*; and the remarkable *Second Story Sunlight*.

Grayber had driven Kris, Andy, and me to Chicago some years before to visit the Hopper exhibition. *Nighthawks*, a possession of the Museum of Art, I had already seen, but here was a host of canvases from Whitney and elsewhere; and, surreptitiously, I touched my right index finger to *Early*

Sunday Morning [with your approval, George; remember?], as an act of aesthetic reverence.

My regret now is that I did not study the variations in blue, green, and black; I shall have to do so, perhaps on a visit to the Whitney, if I am properly to investigate Farrés's Hopper poems.

My inchoate investigation is not promising. *Nighthawks* offers the red dress of the red-haired lady, the white uniform of the attendant, and the blue shirt of the blue-suited man: a night banner amidst night-green, black, rust-red, and yellow-light. Farrés's ekphrasis describes the scene and provides a conversation between the blue-suited man and the red-dressed woman. He has the man ask the attendant for *una altra ronda* (another *round* [of coffee]). He does not mention or include the man with his back turned to the viewer. The poet ought not to have neglected the perfective FOUR. Jeremiah Moss, in an archeological quest for the location of the *Nighthawks* diner, has concluded that it *never existed except as collage inside Hopper's imagination*. Like, I would add, Da Vinci's *Mona Lisa*. That's the nature of art and fiction. Moss's comment is much more valuable than Farrés's attempt to express a painting as a poem.

And so it was that Andy came home in mid-December, wearing a dark green overcoat over a black suit, with a French-blue shirt and powder-blue tie. He wore no black homburg over his thick, dark hair (with its sinuous strands of grey); had he done so, he would have looked like a Mafioso, in the style of Al Pacino. His black shoes were wet from snow and slush. He wiped his feet on the bristled doormat, stepped inside, set down two large black suitcases, and embraced his mother. He said he was home to stay. Jordy, having no further need of him, had arranged, through two academicians in Naples, for Andy's appointment as an adjunct instructor in Italian at the university here. Andy had actually taken an advanced degree in political science at the *Federico II* in Naples. He was to begin here in the spring semester, carrying a section of Beginning Italian, a course in Italian Literature in Translation, and, given sufficient enrollment, a seminar in Twentieth-Century Italian novels. He would be the third full-time member of the Italian program faculty, one of whom was to begin a sabbatical in the spring. My son was to be, in effect, my colleague.

Andy moved into the bedroom that Blackie had used. A framed photograph of Gretchen succeeded the photograph of Vera that Kris had placed on the night-stand for Blackie. Andy began immediately to help with the housework and to relieve Kris and me of tasks that had become increasingly difficult for us. He bought a huge Norway Pine tree for Christmas—we had been using the same small plastic tree for the last few years—and trimmed it with large ornaments (including four Elvis Presley ornaments) and gold and silver tinsel.

The pine scent of the tree was an aromatic tonic. Andy kept its green metal-tank base filled with water.

Unhesitatingly, he answered my many questions about his travels and his association with Jordy Klug. The little case that had been given to me by Mischiato enclosed, as Jordy had explained to Andy, a *Kellerschlüssel* (cellar key) that provided the only access to a subterranean room in a Heidelberg *Herrenhaus* (mansion), where a trove of ancient papyrus rolls and tabulae (literature, lists of names and places, hieroglyphics, and cartographic directions) was stored by the *Gallusische Stiftung* (Gallus Foundation). The key that I had carried and had mailed from home was a reserve key, against the loss of the other key, held by an elderly Scaltro, who had distanced himself from the Nazis by retreating to Sestola on Monte Cimone in the Apennines, where he lived, as a bookbinder, with a cousin.

Andy said that Jordy was a dour and unhappy genius, invested with the traditions of the foundation that derived from Gallus's mystic and military feminism; *and he was disappointed in you, Dad, because you were neither brilliant nor active and, later, because you married a Polish woman and not a German or Italian woman.* As events tuned out, Jordy had seen brilliance in Andy and had offered himself as his mentor. Andy, being neither flattered nor diffident, had accepted the offer and had never regretted it. Gradually, as Andy summarized, *Jordy concluded that through Grandma, whom he worshiped, you and he had an antithetical conjunction: he was active, you were passive. He came to see, I think, how right Mom was for you.*

Andy was not at all as surprised by my questions as I was by his responses. When I asked him why he and Jordy readily took up the pursuit of Grayber's killers, he quoted Jordy: *Kinds of inverse bitches, like Cytheris and Clodia, those two: we'd better go after them.* Andy's reaction had been that the chase was a natural, gallant, and necessary act.

Jordy's heart ailment caused Andy some worry, but Jordy had assured him that, *in his conjunction with you, Dad,* he need not worry. Andy could not explain further. After Andy's show of concern near summer's end, Jordy had said, *It's time for us to separate, Kid. You're the* vero alleato. *You've been a perfect complement. Now, alone, I'm going to take my heart to Heidelberg.* When Andy asked him if they'd maybe get together again, Jordy said, *No way. I'll set you up with a job near your Old Man, and you take care of him.*

RAIN AND DARKNESS

Andy's return to Kris and me was greatly beneficial to us. His easy ways and many talents, including his composition of *sonnetti* about Sharny, warms Kris's heart and makes me proud. He is setting up plans to add a large workroom and a home theater to the house. It is April now; and Andy is a very popular teacher.

On this Tuesday in mid-April, a few days before Easter Sunday, after Andy's departure for classes, Kris and I are having a late breakfast at our table in the kitchen. On Kris's side of the table there is a catalogue of Early American furniture; on my side is the current *Nation*. At low volume, our CD player, on its small shelf, repeats the old Dick Haymes rendering of *I'll Get By*. The April morning is bright; and through the small windows above our table stream two shafts of sunlight.

Made in the USA
Lexington, KY
22 December 2011